1,000,000 Books

are available to read at

Forgotten Books

www.ForgottenBooks.com

Read online
Download PDF
Purchase in print

ISBN 978-1-332-99842-5
PIBN 10448132

This book is a reproduction of an important historical work. Forgotten Books uses state-of-the-art technology to digitally reconstruct the work, preserving the original format whilst repairing imperfections present in the aged copy. In rare cases, an imperfection in the original, such as a blemish or missing page, may be replicated in our edition. We do, however, repair the vast majority of imperfections successfully; any imperfections that remain are intentionally left to preserve the state of such historical works.

Forgotten Books is a registered trademark of FB &c Ltd.
Copyright © 2018 FB &c Ltd.
FB &c Ltd, Dalton House, 60 Windsor Avenue, London, SW19 2RR.
Company number 08720141. Registered in England and Wales.

For support please visit www.forgottenbooks.com

1 MONTH OF FREE READING

at

www.ForgottenBooks.com

By purchasing this book you are eligible for one month membership to ForgottenBooks.com, giving you unlimited access to our entire collection of over 1,000,000 titles via our web site and mobile apps.

To claim your free month visit: www.forgottenbooks.com/free448132

* Offer is valid for 45 days from date of purchase. Terms and conditions apply.

English
Français
Deutsche
Italiano
Español
Português

www.forgottenbooks.com

Mythology Photography **Fiction** Fishing Christianity **Art** Cooking Essays Buddhism Freemasonry Medicine **Biology** Music **Ancient Egypt** Evolution Carpentry Physics Dance Geology **Mathematics** Fitness Shakespeare **Folklore** Yoga Marketing **Confidence** Immortality Biographies Poetry **Psychology** Witchcraft Electronics Chemistry History **Law** Accounting **Philosophy** Anthropology Alchemy Drama Quantum Mechanics Atheism Sexual Health **Ancient History Entrepreneurship** Languages Sport Paleontology Needlework Islam **Metaphysics** Investment Archaeology Parenting Statistics Criminology **Motivational**

The Text
of the
Book of Aneirin

Reproduced & Edited
by
J. Gwenogvryn Evans
Hon. M.A., & Hon. D. Litt. (Oxon.)
Hon. D. Litt. (Wales).

Keis a vetrich, ac a ellich guna.

Pwllheli:
Issued to Subscribers only.
M.DCCCC.viij.

All Rights Reserved.

Frontispiece.

Preface.

Bann gwir ban ẟiscleir, bannach ban leveir—Tal.

HUGH LUPUS, THE FAT EARL OF CHESTER, & Hugh the Proud, earl of Shrewsbury, led a joint expedition against Griffyẟ ap Kynan in the summer of 1098. They overran the north-eastern part of Anglesey, ravaging the land, and pressing 'ninety villeins' into their service. They returned 'for rest' to the Castle of Aber Lleinog, and "out of vainglory" Hugh the Proud gave a feast. The revelry went on through the night, but at peep of day a band of sea-rovers, borne by the flowing tide was seen to emerge out of the morning mist, and to be bearing down on the Rhyn coast. Hugh the Proud & his retinue, armed and a-horse, rushed to the shore and advanced into the waters. A fierce battle ensued, first in the shallows and then on the great Strand of Aber Lleinog. Hugh the Proud and most of his men fell; Hugh the Fat and the remnants fled across the Menei; and Mon was saved for the Kymry by the hardihood of Magnus, King of Norway, who captained the sea-rovers. This was the Battle of the Strand, the *Cat traeth* commemorated in our text.[a] Great events sire great songs, and this event was great in its consequences. It restored to Gwyneẟ its glorious line of warrior princes, and practically put an end to Saxon encroachments across the Clwyd. Nothing, then, could be more natural than that Magnus should loom large in our earliest poetry which refers to him as the

[a]. Detailed references are given in the Introduction and Notes for the above statements.

' terrible smiter,'[b] who crushed the expedition of the earls, protected Mon, and befriended Griffyð ap Cynan. And yet strange to say, his very name has been corrupted, and as Munc, *or* Mwng[c] is unknown in the land he delivered. And it was this very ignorance of his disguise that gave birth to the talk about 'sixth century Welsh literature,' and still fosters the farrago which this colossal folly propagates. The very authority quoted in its support is its death-warrant, as we shall immediately see. The wide-eyed attention of the reader is invited to the Facsimile[d] from Harleian MS. 3859. There are four unrelated paragraphs, and the first letter in every paragraph is wanting. Scribes were wont to leave a space for a large coloured initial with every *change of subject*, and to indicate in the margin[e] by a minute letter the one omitted. These minute index letters served to guide the rubricator, whose work it was to fill the blanks. But the Fascimile exhibits neither a rubric nor a marginal index letter, as we can verify by examination.

Let us note further that every paragraph begins with a man's name, followed by words which enable us to identify the four persons named.

i. (I)da filius Eobba tenuit regiones . . . . Umbri
ii. (M)unc du tigirn . . . dimicabat contra gentem Anglorum
iii. (M)ailcunus magnus rex apud Brittones regnabat
iv. (A)dda filius Ida regnavit annis octo

Here the scribe and rubricator have left us to guess the letter missing in every instance.[f] If then we are dealing

b. See B.B.C., 93·1·6, 108·5 : Aneirin 4·6=42.
c. For the varying orthography of this name see *Index*. Note that *u* in M*u*nc has the sound of u in b*u*ll, & like Norman ' lon*c* ' from longus the *c* has the sound of *g*. M*u*nc was pronounced M*w*ng.
d. We have to thank the Cymmrodorion Society and the intercession of Sir Vincent Evans for the loan of the plate of this Facsimile.
e. See the margins of the Facsimile of the Book of Aneirin.
f. The T in 'Tunc' is a *guess* pure & simple. There is no T in the MS.

duodecī· ⁊ unxit dingua ſ·ſ·di guurthbeneich·

une dutigirn· in illo tempore forté dēmicabat contra gentē anglorū· Tunc talhaearn· cataguen in poēmate claruit· ⁊ neirin· ⁊ talieſſin· ⁊ bluchbard· ⁊ cian qui uocat̄ guench guaut· ſimul uno tempore in poēmate brittannico claruer·

ailcunuſ magnuſ rex ap brittoneſ regnabat· id͞ in regione guenedote quia atauū illi· id͞ cunedag· cū filiis ſuis· quorū numer̄ octō erat· uenerat priuſ de parte ſiniſtrali· id͞ de regione que uocat̄ manau guotodin· centū quadraginta ſex anniſ antequā mailcun regnaret· ⁊ ſcottos cū ingentiſſima clade expulerunt ab iſtis regionibuſ· ⁊ nuſquā reuerſi ſunt iterū ad habitandū·

ādda filius ida regnauit anniſ octo·
æthric filius ādda regnauit quattuor anniſ· þeonrich filius ida regnauit ſeptem anniſ· friodolguald regnauit ſex anniſ· in cuius tempore regnū cantorum mittente gregorio baptiſmū ſuſcep· huſſa regnauit anniſ ſeptē· Contra illos quattuor reges urbgen ⁊ riderchhen ⁊ guallanc ⁊ morcant dimicauerunt· þeodric contra illum urbgen cū filiis dimicabant fortiter· In illo aut̄ tempore ali quando hostes nunc cives uincebant· ⁊ ipſe concluſit eos tribus diebus ⁊ tribus noctibus in inſula metcaud· ⁊ dū erat in expeditione iuguladʒ· morcanto deſtinante p inuidia· quia in ipſo p omnibus regibus uirtuſ maxima erat in inſtauratione belli· Eadfered fleſaurs regnauit duodecim annis.

with an unfamiliar word, especially with a proper name unknown to us, and do not understand the context we are more liable to go wrong than right. This has been the case with the second paragraph, which follows in full.

(M)unc[i] du tigirn in illo[k] tempore fortiter dimicabat[l] contra gentem Anglorum.[m] Tunc Talhaern tat aguen in poemate claruit. & Neirin. & Taliessin. & bluchbard,[n] & Cian[o] qui vocatur guenith guaut. Simul uno[r] in tempore poemate Brittannico claruerunt.

Mwng, the Black King, in his[k] time kept bravely struggling[l] with the Anglian race.[m] Talhaearn, Father of the Muse, was in those days renowned in poetry, & Neirin, & Taliesin, & Llwchvarð,[n] & Cinan[o] who is called the Flower of song. They shone together at one[r] time in Britannic poetry.

Seemingly no editor of the printed texts has ever heard of

i. Note that in the same MS. (§62 of the Nennian *Additamenta*) the scribe, who wrote M*u*nc, app. wrote also (§57) Saxones **a**mbronum for umbronum = the Northumbrians. The scribe who writes **a** for **u** is capable of writing **u** for **a**, and likely to do so. If Munc is not the same person as Magnus, there have been two leaders who played identical parts in the same places on the same occasions against the same adversaries, and both were drowned in 1103. See nn. *c.*, *u.*

k. According to Lewis & Short *Ille, a, ud* is used pleonastically '*referring back to the subject already in the same sentence,*' as here. The fact that classical writers used 'illo' in its pleonastic sense raises a presumption in favour of later writers doing so. See note *u.*

l. Note the use of the imperfect. The struggle lasted five years.

m. Magnus fought against the earl of Chester & the earl of Shrewsbury; he slew the latter, & kept a firm hand on the former, 19·4 = 66.

n. Note that in the facsimile the b*l* of **b**luchbard have been elongated upward by another hand suggesting *ll*; the h is also slightly touched as if by mistake, and the second b approximates b. See *Introduction*, p. *xxxi., xliii.*   *o.* Cian : Cian = Cinan (see Index).

r. The bards were contemporaries, though Taliesin was younger. Munc's death and Taliesin's birth were not far apart.

a 2

Munc; and no commentator has ever had an inkling of what the correct reading should be.[s] '(T)unc' they know, and (T)unc they print. But who has seen fresh matter introduced by Tunc, or two consecutive sentences begin with Tunc . . . . Tunc . . ?

The earliest reference to Magnus is in the Book of Aneirin, 19·12, where he appears as Manc *i.e.* Mang, and all the facts of history point to Manc being the correct reading. This is confirmed by the epithet *du tigirn*, which means Black King,[t] niger rex. Norsemen are called Black Heathens, *gentiles nigri*[t] in the Annales Cambrie. Magnus of Norway was the King of the Black Heathens who fought at the Battle of the Strand in 1098.

The second paragraph, written probably at Margam Abbey,[u] gives a precise summary of the deductions from the internal evidence as presented in the Introduction. On turning afresh to the Harley Facsimile with the blinds up & an open mind the meaning of *du tigirn* became transparent, & Munc followed in one of those flashes of 'insight,' which 'surprises' and rewards the earnest worker. Thus external evidence, confirmed by the internal evidence of

s. Owen Pughe, Silvan Evans, & Skene transliterate *Mug maur treuyt* into *Mwg mawr drevyδ* & translate, ' the great burner of towns ' ; ' the great smoke of towns ' ; or ' the smoke of great towns.' (*Four Ancient Books of Wales*, Vol. I., 319 ; Vol. II., 349). *I* pointed out in the B.B.C. *Index* that Mwng was " a mighty smiter," & in the Taliesin Notes that he was *K*ing Magnus of Norway. *Cp.* Pen. Report, 724.

t. Like Edward the Black Prince, the Norse King & his forces were called ' black ' because of the colour of their armour. See *Index* s.v. *gwrym* ; Intro., *xlii.*, n. 35.

u. Important MSS. were written at Margam Abbey. Our oldest MS. of *Historia Brittonum* was written about the end of the first quarter of the twelfth century, the *Additamenta* between 1125 & 1130, and *Historia Regum Britannie* was completed in 1134. Geoffrey of Monmouth *certainly knew the Nennian MS. Had he a hand in its* final form ? As regards the *Additional matter I* believe that he in-

the text, makes the reading ' *M*unc ' a certainty. And mark well that Talhaearn, & Aneirin, & Taliesin, & Llwchvarð and (Griffyð ap) Cinan were the contemporaries of Munc. What then becomes of the " sixth century Welsh literature " alleged to have been written by these bards, who flourished around 1100 and after ? The MS. has been misread & the false reading has thriven for so long a time that the minds of men have become fossilized on the subject. And however difficult it may be to discover facts in times remote from our own, it is far more difficult to convince such minds that the old is not always true. There seem to be no kind of spectacles that will help to adjust our vision to the unaccustomed on the rutty highways of Tradition
' That wears out Truth's best stories into Tales.'
But what has paragraph .*II*. to do with Tradition ? Nothing ! for its record synchronizes with the writing. All doubt and debate have arisen from misreading and misunderstanding the MS., which states that our Bards lived in the time of Magnus *du deyrn* (the Black King) of Norway, d. 1103. The search for Truth is like the search for gold—its bedding must be sifted & the unprofitable matter all washed away.

Rise, said the Lark to his son, Rise high with me to the blue.
Father, ' the higher we soar the smaller shall we become ' !
Aye, ' to those who cannot fly.' The future lies with the true.

spired, if he did not compile it. *The sandwiching of the Munc paragraph, with its* ' in illo tempore,' *between Ida and Mailcunus is very characteristic of the Geoffrey method, which was to father the actions of one age upon the actors of another.* It seems clear that the Manc of Aneirin was changed to M*u*nc for the purpose of identifying him with *Munghu*, the pet name of Kentigern, who was invited by Maelgwn's father to his dominion (c. 560–573). The time fits exactly the place of paragraph *ii.* *H*ere is a straw for Tradition to clutch at. The facts however do not fit,—M*a*nc was a ' black king,' M*u*nc was a bishop— M*a*nc fought the Angles, M*u*nc ran away from them. The change of *a* to *u* is a classic example of *suggestio falsi*, and of the

Here I would like to pause in order to ask students to examine the **Variant Versions** (pp. 101–6), & **List of Scribal Errors** (pp. 107–120) before they proceed to the fuller discussion of the date and contents of 'Aneirin' in the Introduction. In this way the reader will have a certain knowledge in common with the writer, a thing necessary for mutual understanding of the subjects discussed.

I regret my inability to complete the work in uniform papers. The best Japanese Vellum I could not procure at any price, and the cost of even the second grade would leave no margin to pay printer's bill from such support as I receive. The toned paper had been specially manufactured for the Welsh Texts, but the Mills could not procure the right materials for making a fresh supply.

The Manuscript original of this work at one time formed part of the Hengwrt(-Peniarth) collection. How it left that Library is not known. Mr Theophilus Jones (*d.* 1812), the historian of Breconshire, received it from a " Mr. Thomas Bacon who bought it from a person at Aberdâr." It passed next to Carnhuanawc from whose Library it went to Sir Thomas Phillipps, Bart., in 1861. From Middle Hill it passed by purchase to the Cardiff Free Library, where it now forms No. 1 of its Collection of Welsh MSS. Finally it is my pleasant duty to thank the authorities of the Cardiff Free Library, for their ready permission to Autotype and reproduce the text of the MS., and their then Librarian for facilitating my work.

way Geoffrey transformed the facts of history into fiction. History was cultivated at Margam Abbey, the early home of the work of William of Malmesbury=Brit. Mus. Royal MS. 13 D. ii.

J. Gwenogvryn Evans.

Tremvan, June, 1922.

Introduction.

Kyvarvuant ar herw, 37·13.

MISTAKES ARE HARDY EVERgreens. It is a mistake to say that this work was written in the sixth century, and it is a mistake to father the authorship on Aneirin, which is a questionable name.[1] Our manuscript is not one manuscript, but two distinct collections of verse sewn together. Pages 1 and 25 have the rubbed, soiled appearance of outermost leaves which have served as 'covers' to unbound 'books,' whereas pages 24 and 38 are as unsoiled as the other inside pages. This fact bears witness that both parts have lost their respective final gathering, or gatherings. 'Book' should therefore be Books. Both appear to have been copied around 1265, apparently by the same hand. Leastwise I can detect no greater difference in the writing than there is between a heavy and a light impression of the pages of a printed book, especially where the spacing varies. From internal evidence, and the bias of the scribe our two books must have been compiled at the Abbey of Basingwerk,[2] which was founded in 1131 by Ranulf II., earl of

[1] See pages *xxxviii.*, and *xlii*.

[2] Elsewhere *I* have mistakenly named Strata Marcella, being then ignorant of the internal evidence of the text & of the dialect of Basingwerk district.

xi.

Chester, (Lloyd, 458). In order to blur the memory of Catraeth, with its crushing defeat of the house of his patron, the scribe persistently tampers with the text. He turns the vanquished into victors, or omits anything that reflects upon Lupus and the Lupusians. This is the case with Book I., (pp. 1-24) which is the later compilation. While at work on Book II., the scribe evidently had 'second thoughts,' and set to work to revise the text for the later transcript, in which he paraphrases, inserts, omits, or perverts at will.[3] He transcribes nothing twice alike. To bring this home to the reader the cantos in duplicate have been reprinted together in a way that shows their variance at a glance. He who examines these, and observes their differences[*] will gain some insight into the difficulties of editing and interpreting a text which disregards its original. Student and layman should realize once for all that scribes not only fell into ordinary pitfalls, and made involuntary mistakes, but that they also deliberately changed a text as the fancy took them. Fidelity to the archetype is a new birth. In the long ago a 'book' was not a thing to be given to the public, nor to be read, but the private stock in trade of the professional storyteller, and reciter. The Greeks called writing *grammata*,[4] 'scratches,' which no one could read except the grammatist. In this way, if the contents fell under the eyes of a professional rival they were safe. The owner bequeathed his MS. to a son or favourite disciple, who had been taught to read it. With every generation new circumstances would arise, which would necessitate editing the matter to suit the new patrons. Thus some passages

[3] This is no new thing. cp. 'If the old poet went with the conqueror . . . there has come after him who takes all his facts and turns them the other way.' Prof. Murray's *Ancient Greek Literatrre*, p. 42.

[*] see pp. 101-6.

would be omitted others modified, and new matter added till, in the course of time, the result might have little or nothing in common with the original ' book.' Prof. Murray[4] instances *Callisthenes' Life of Alexander* as a case in point ; Meusel states that every MS. of the *Nibelungenlied* represents a different recension, and Gaston Paris has shown the rise and marvellous growth of the *Chanson de Roland*. Indeed we need not go out of Wales for an illustration. Lewis Glyn Cothi[5] has left an autograph MS. where the ends of lines in many poems are mere blanks, so that he alone could recite those poems. In the case of Davyδ ap Gwilim there are so many versions of certain poems that we could form two independent texts with hardly a word in common. In short most scribes combined the offices of copyist and joint authorship. The 'Aneirin' scribe was a blue blood of this class. He was more, he was a 'grammatist.' How otherwise can we account for the stuttering repetitions, the tangling of the words of two or three lines, the transpositions, and the backward spellings.[28] For example :

Nac emmel di . . . a therwyn, (terfyn torret tec teithiawl) (for) Teithiawl ter dorres dervyn. 29.3. cp. 29.10, 14.16. (wy . . . . . . gon) : gonwy 33.19 ; (rud) : dur 17.17, 35.18 ; (get) : teg 24.9 ; (dauc) : raud 34.3 ; (eilth) : leith 34.21 ; pell : lled, 34.13 ; (awc aer) : aerawt 5.13 ; (od gur) : goror 30.15 ; (wog)-ant : (govv)-=govyant 21.14 ; hoew(gir) : hoew (ri) -g 7.9 ; uo-(dog)-yon : ua(r)(god)yon 26.22 ; (ut) bu (lee) : bu(tu)ele= buδu(cre) 36.14 ; [brei-](thyell) : lleyth, 4.16, etc., etc.

It must therefore be manifest that the editing of an old text is not so simple after all. In MS. work one has need of circumspection, and minute observation. Eyesight is important, but insight is more so, and insight is the child of long experience and historical knowledge of the times and

4. See Prof. Murray's *The Rise of the Greek Epic*, p. 119.
5 See Peniarth MS. 70 in National Library of Wales.

circumstances under which a poem was produced.[6] Moreover, we must apply the test of metre, consonance[7] and rhyme. The Laws of cynghaneδ[7] will enlighten, guide and control us at every step. These laws must be deduced for each author from lines which conform to a *recurring practice in his own works*,[6] and not from rules drawn up centuries later from the later practices of later bards. It would appear that no one has observed the rules which regulate the original nine-syllable metre in our text. In the first section of a line there are five syllables, having the second and fifth tied by cynghaneδ.[7] In the second section of four syllables, any syllable (barring the end rhyme) may be tied to a third preceding syllable in the first section. The scheme appears to be as follows :—

a.

Mab-	*an*	i	Gyn-	*an*	ed-	ry-	van-	nawc
o	s*ig*	cyn-	dev-	*ig*	y	rhyd	mi	gav
Gwyr	De*ivr*	a	Bryn-	*eich*	a	δy-	chi-	awr
a	*chwe-*	dy	el-	*wch*	ta-	wel-	**wch**	vu

b.

ar-	*war*	o	garch-	*ar*	a	**gwarth**	ym	dug
o	*gyv-*	le	ang-	*hov*	o	**ang-**	har	dud
Han-	*did*	y	gwel-	*id*	llaw-	**er**	yn	lleid
Cyd	*del*	Wyn-	eδ	*bel*	Go·	**gleδ**	i	rann

c.

Gwyr	*aeth*	**yng-**	had	*traeth*	**y**	gan	y	dyδ
Cyn-	*on*	**mein**	lary	*vron*	**Cein-**	nyon	wled-	ig
Twrv	*tan*	**a**	thar-	*an*	**a**	rhy-	verth-	i
Rhac	bl*in*	**rann**	gorδ-	*in*	**gan**	y	wawr-	δyδ

6 Modern critics are constantly forgetting this. Leastwise *I* have not found modern examples which conform with the practice of the bards of the ' Book of Aneirin.'

7 Cynghaneδ=consonance, whether of vowels or consonants, or both. Cynghaneδ had suggested the burial place of HeS. before *I* learnt it from Ordericus Vitalis. See 5·16=48, 37·1=62.

xiv.

A line may be in triplets tying the third to the sixth syllable, and the fifth to the eighth.

d.

Bleiδ	cae-	*awg*	|	cyn-	hor-	*awg*	|	y·	mar-	an
Go-	doδ-	*an*	|	gor-	**vyn-**	n*an*	|	δy-	**blyg-**	id
Da	i	V*on*	|	doeth	**ad-**	*on*	|	aeth	**ad-**	wen
Gwr-	ol-	*eδ*	|	yng-	**O-**	gl*eδ*	|	a	**o-**	rug

If any of the digraphs *ch, ff, ph, ll,* or *th* occurs in one section there must be an answering digraph in the other section, but the two need not necessarily be the same digraph.

L*la*δei, erlidei ar ni de*ch*yn.
hyd llw*ch*-δor y Por*ff*or bererin.
Sei*th* mwy or L*l*oegrwys a lygrassant.
Cant *ll*ewes a bor*th*es eu gor*ff*wys.

Wherever the nine-syllable lines do not conform with one or other of the above schemes the meaning halts, or is at variance with context and history. Restoration of cynghaneδ[7] as a rule restores the sense, and generally the Chronicles confirm the emendation. That is the reason why an amended text has been attempted, & is now offered as a contribution to the better understanding of this work.

When our text was transcribed the glamour of the Geoffrey cult had influenced and tainted all literature. The perversion of originals had been raised into a fine art. Fortunately for us the test of cynghaneδ, as set forth above, enables us to purge our text of scribal corruptions, as well as to recapture the original sense to a surprising extent. For example 'Godoδin' & 'Aneirin' are metrically impossible, and have been confounded by the scribe himself[8]! We cannot, therefore, do better than examine the geographical names embedded in the text, in order to localize the chief event, and to identify the leading actors and their allies.

8 At 14·6 & 23·14. See p. *xxii.*, infra.

Now most of the places mentioned lie west and south of the Dee, while the chief action is confined to Blaen Gwyneδ, *i.e.* the Rhyn, or promontory of Penmon. Gweryd[9] is the upper reach of the Dee Estuary, and on its left bank lie Aeron & Tud Llwch, Eurgeint, Keint, Llwyn Llwyvenyδ, and Einglyawn, with Trwyn Esyd at the Dee mouth. Aled, Conwy, Llugwy, Derwenyδ and Rhyvoniog are in Denbighshire. Mordrei, Carreg Cynhadvan, Caer Gyngrwn, also Rhyn are in Penmon. Arvon is the southern part of Carnarvonshire, Artro is in Merioneth, Gwyδneu is in north and Bryn Hydwn in south Cardiganshire. Goδeu is the country of the earl of Shrewsbury 32·16, & Moryal has the same letters as Maylor. On the east bank of the Dee we have a part of Eiδyn between Aldford, & ? Farndon; and to the north Elvet, Deivr & Bryneich; also Gogleδ. Finally we have Catraeth & Godoδin. Let us examine the meanings of these *cruces criticorum*.

'This is the Godoδin' is the rubric title at the head of page 1. Again at 28·8·16 we read, pob awdyl or Godoδin, every ode of the Godoδin, & Odleu y Godoδin oll, all the odes of the Godoδin. From this usage it is clear that the rubricator treated Godoδin as a poem. The text confirms this by references to rehearsing the Godoδin.* Then there are 17 references to Godoδin as a place-name, three references to it as a person, and four others of uncertain meaning.† Had all the passages been, like the rubrics, in prose, we should have been left to guess the meaning of Godoδin in them. Not so in verse. With few exceptions the Godoδin lines are metrically a syllable too long, and in the exceptions[10] as well as in most of the other instances the cynghaneδ is

9 Gweryd = ? *outflow*, ' Forth.' cp. *gweryd*-u i varwolaeth, dying of diabetes. *see* Tal. n. 18·6 & correct Gwe-*lyδ*, -*ryδ* to Gweryd.
* adrawδ godoδin, 1·14, 7·4, 17·18, 35·19, 37·5·10
† See *Index*. 10 See 14·2, 33·15, 17·5, 38·8, 19·14.

xvi.

wrong. Therefore Godoðin is nowhere right. That fact is worth remembering. For what then does it stand? On pages 2–3 we have as recurrent first lines 'Gwyr a aeth odoðin' & 'Gwyr a aeth gatraeth' *i.e.* 'men went to Godoðin,'' & 'men went to Catraeth.' At 1·14 we read of Godoðin being 'on the sand of Mordrei'; and at 4·15 of Catraeth being 'at Mordrei.' Here the two words are synonymous, both being on the sand of Mordrei.[11]

What then does Catraeth signify? Let Sir John Rhys answer. " Catraeth means the Battle Strand. But it has often been supposed to stand for Cataracton-e, -i, of the Antonine Itinerary, and surmised to be Catterick in Yorkshire." Sir John adds that it cannot be so derived, (Arthurian Legend, 240). That 'catraeth' stands for cat traeth witness the following use of 'cynhen' as a synonym of 'cât.' A phrit er prynu brei*thyell* catraeth 9·15,* which cynghaneð corrects into A phr*it* erby*nit* lleith gynhen traeth, *Costly was fought the deadly conflict of the Strand*, 34. Similarly at 8·1=6 'gynhen gatraeth' is for '(o) gynhen traeth'; In other words 'cât traeth' and 'cynhen traeth,' are exchangeable terms, therefore 'catraeth' is no more a place-name than cynhen traeth. (Ys Mwng) a ystwng a oreu gynhen 18·8=94. *Magnus will bring him low who waged the conflict (of the Strand)*. We shall see the force of this later on. In the meanwhile let us return to Godoðin, older guo*t*-odin. In manuscripts *r* and *t* are often confounded, and for this reason go*r*-ðin may possibly have suggested go*t*(o)ðin because in seventeen instances metre, cynghaneð and context restore gorðin to the text. In two places it stands for 'godoðyn,'[10] or godoðan,' and in two more for 'ðoðyn,' but nowhere for Godoðin, which has been

---

11 Mordei is a case of haplology for Mord(r)ei=*the Great strand* of Aber Lleinog. Mordei is usually translated '*mansions*' or 'sea houses,' but without explaining their use or location.

xvii.

assumed to represent the Votadini who occupied the northeast coast, ' south of the Forth.'[12] Fortunately the scribe left a crucial passage unaltered. Griffyδ ap Kynan sings, Neud wyv Vynawg blin, Ni δialav orδin 12·9=78, *I am a weary prince, I will not avenge the gorδin*, i.e. the great push of 1098, which caused him to flee from the Rhyn into exile.[13]

12 See *Celtic Britain* by Sir John Rhys & *British Placenames* by Edm. Maclure. In response to my queries Dr. Henry Bradley of the *Oxford English Dictionary* writes :— " Votadini has no documentary authority. The largest number of MSS. read Ὠταδινοί, others have Ὠταδηνοί; but Müller, the editor of the Didot edition of Ptolemy prints Ὠταλινοί which is the reading of half a dozen MSS. The quantity of the *i* before *v* is uncertain as Old Celtic seems to have had both -īnas, & -īnos. To make Gotodin a normal descendant of Votadini we should have to suppose the *a* long . . . *If* you are to be proved wrong about Godoδin your adversaries will have to find better weapons than a doubtful reading of Ptolemy . . . *If* it is *known* that Manau Guotodin was a genuine geographical name. *then* it is a reasonable though not a certain inference that the correct reading is Ὠταδινοί."

I aver that ' Mana*u* Guotodin ' is not a genuine geographical name. It makes its first appearance in the Additional Matter in *H*arl. MS. 3859, fol. 188*b*, l. 12 etc. (See Facsimile). (M)ailcunus Magn*u*s rex ap*u*d Brittones regnabat, [*id est in regione Guenedote quia attavus illius, id est Cunedag, cum filiis suis, quorum numerus octa erat, venerat prius de parte sinistrali, id est de regione que vocatur Manu Guotodin, centum quadraginta sex annis antequam Mailcun regnaret*] et Scottos cum ingentissima clade expulerunt ab istis regionibus etc." Three later MSS. repeat 'Manu,' corrected some time into Manu̅=Manau. That this should be Mañan is reasonably certain, because the *I*sle of Man appears in our text as Mannan, Manhon, Mannon, (*see I*ndex). These forms in Welsh are older than Harl. MS. 3859. The Welsh Mana*w* has no better pedigree than scribal bungles, Professorial knights notwithstanding. There is no Manaw in B.B.C., & rhyme condemns the only instance in Taliesin 67·14 " Tonn Iwerδon, A thonn Vann*on*, A th*onn* Ogleδ." Manaw appears in the Bruts, translated into Welsh after 1196. The italics and [ ] are mine, for it is clear that the statements they enclose are (like *in illo tempore*) the invention of the scribe with no basis in fact. Cunedag's eight (octa corrected into octa°) sons are not named here, but at the end of the

Castell Aber Leinawc.

This passage gives the *coup de grace* to Godoðin, which is a scribal intrusion in our text. Both it and Catterick-Catraeth are the foundlings of fraud and false etymology. Catterick is a Yorkshire inland town, while catraeth was fought on the *Great shore*, the Mordrei of Gwyneð 4·15=72, where knights perished in its foaming shallows 29·15=46. If anyone is still haunted by doubts let him hearken to *Elidyr Sais*. Rhodri, the son of Owein Gwyneð, and his brother David destroyed their half brother, Howel, at Pentraeth in 1170. In 1175 Rhodri wrested Anglesey etc. from David. His nephews drove Rhodri out of Anglesey in 1190, but he again seized it in 1193. Twice, if not thrice, was Rhodri thus ' *able to take by force the lands of Catraeth* '

Gallas dreis ar direð catraeth (M. 242·1).

There can therefore be no doubt that *The lands of Catraeth* lie within the girdle of the Anglesey shores.

   A wado hyn aed a hi   As well this telling fact deny
   a gwaded ir haul godi :   as say the sun mounts not the sky.

Note further that our text definitely states that " *the thrusting was done at the Foreland of Gwyneð.*" i.e. Penmon :

em blaen Gwyneð gwanet, 6·12=32.

The name of Elved still survives on the south-west border of Yorkshire. The boundaries of Deira and Bernicia seem to be those of Northumbria. The ideas of the early Welsh bards were vague on the subject. For example :—

   Lleudir y(w) Deivrdir amgylch Dyvrdwy. P. 84·14
   ' *An open land is the land of Deira about the river Dee.*

   Bryneich a dreisyr dros giawð Offa. P. 44·18

Llewelyn ap Griffyð and his forces '*ravaged Bernicia across Offa's dyke,*' i.e. on the left bank of the Dee. Neither Deira nor Bernicia is known to the Annales Cambrie & Brut Genealogies .ix. are named, & later still .xii. I Of the eleven MSS. used by Mommsen & Zimmer *Harl.* 3859 alone has the passages about Cunedag & Manau Guotodin.   13 See 3·8=70.

y Tywyssogion, nor to Meilir & Gwalchmei. Cynhganeδ rejects the only instance of it in Taliesin, but the Black Book of Carmarthen has one example where, as in Kynδel and the poets who wrote after 1200, Bryneich occurs as a synonym of the first earldom of Chester, or of some portion of it.

Now it is matter of primary importance for the Welsh student of our earliest literature to learn & lodge well in his memory that Hugh Lupus made incursions into Gwyneδ, —that he held land in twenty counties,[14]—that the Earldom of Chester in his time stretched so far north as to include Northumberland, once known as Deira & Bernicia. He should also bear in mind that the early Sees were, as a rule, conterminous with the territories to which they pertained. Nor must he forget that there was no See of Carlisle before 1132,—that this & the See of Ripon were largely "carved out of the See of Chester."[14] The Welsh bards were right when they spoke of Hugh's followers as men of Deira and Bernicia. It is not the bards but our dogmatic ignorance which is at fault. *Without the guidance of History and Historical Geography the student of language and literature is no better than a tinkling cymbal.*

With regard to Gogleδ the verdict of our text is clear & final.

  Bleiδ caeawg cynhorawg y·maran . . . 1·22=4.
  cyd dêl Wyneδ (bêl), *Gogleδ i rann.* 2·3=4.
 Noble Lupus is now leading in the struggle . . Though he comes to Gwyneδ's (war), Gogleδ is his part.

Hugh Lupus, earl of Chester, was at Castell Aber Llëinog in the Gorδin of 1098, and his own bard, Talhaearn, tells us that Gogleδ was the earl's province. Again Griffyδ ap Kynan after his deliverance from the Chester prison, sings,

[14] See Omerod's *History* of Cheshire. "The early bishoprics as a rule coincided with the territories to which they were attached. No kingdom of which we have any record disappeared without leaving a trace of itself in the form of a diocese or group of dioceses." see *The origin of the English Nation* by Prof. *H.* M. Chadwick, pp. 5, 10.

Gwroleδ yng·Ogleδ a orug,
llary vronn, hael adon, i vab alltud.   12·14=52.

'*In Gogleδ an act of bravery was rendered by a gentle-breasted generous lord to an exile's son.*' Nothing could be more explicit than these passages which Llewelyn Varδ confirms.
Ri ruδbar . . . Ryn δy-orδin, Bryneich rann . . . P. 147·11. *The ruddy-speared King (Magnus) . . . pounds the Rhyn, a part of Bernicia . . .* Hugh Lupus, lord of Bernicia, had been lord of the Rhyn, and had built the castle of Aber Lleinog so as to have a base for his operations in Anglesey.

When the Palatine quitted Mon, his one way home was through Keint into " Eiδyn, *the country at his front door,*" Bleiδ êl Eiδyn gor racδor 9·12=44.[15] According to the Domesday survey Roger, earl of Shrewsbury, held Yâl, Edernion, Cynlleith, Nanheudwy,* and portions at least of Moryal,† such as Eyton & Sutton. Yâl and Moryal, wholly or in part, represent Eiδyn ; & the Cluton[16] country across the Dee above Aldford is known as Clytno Eiδyn. The gentle lord Cynon (15·3=84) is the *mab Clytno* of 15·8. Cynon figures also in Englynion y Beδeu as 'mab klytno iδin,' where cynghaneδ corrects Clyt*no* to Clyt*on*. Note that 'Beδ Cyn*on* yn R̈e*on* ryt,' teaches us to read also Beδ Cyn*on* mab Clyt*on* Eiδyn, B.B.C., 64·1-5. Observe a simi-

---

15 See also 14·4, 'i ragran cynhorvan (y Gogleδ), 65.

*See Lloyd's reference to *Historical Atlas*, p. 389, n. 106.

† I use Moryal (=Great Yâl) for the two Maylors, for M*aylo*r seems to be nothing but a mis-spelling of Mor*yal*.

16 Clutone is a hamlet between Broxton and Farndon on the banks of the Clut brook which rises in the Malpas country, and empties into the Dee immediately below Ryt R̈eon (*Vadum Region*-is *trans Devam*, near Eaton) which leads to that part of Cheshire that lies on the left of the Dee. Note that rivers did not always mark boundaries in our early history and see Chadwick. Note also that there was a Cl*o*tone in the parish of Tarvin, and an *Iddin*shall near.

b

lar metathesis in our text at 13·4=54 where rag*no* is rag*on* at 23.15. We know that ' ragon ' is right, apart from cynghaneδ, which endorses the emendation. Note further that Cynon is the bard's name for Owein, the gwledig of the men of Ceint, from the hour he became generalissimo of the Saxon forces at Aber Lleinog in 1098. Now the two Edwins, earl and freeman, had held great portions of the country on both sides of the lower Dee, and their common name seems to be preserved in Clyton Eiδyn & Treiδyn. Adjoining these was Aeron bordering on the brook of that name (now called after Pulford) and stretching perhaps to the Alun. When Hugh succeeded his father he is styled *u*δ *Ei*δ*yn*,[17] lord of Eiδyn, of Aeron, and of the Dee Estuary (see Index). Cynon was a ' war dog ' and a leader, *kynran*, from Aeron, 6·1·21. His father had held the Hope lands. Thus we see that Hugh & Cynon vel Owein were neighbours, and our text speaks of them as bosom friends 1·7, allies and border knights— gold bedight ones of Eiδyn 5·18–20. The Survey states that these lands were nearly ' all waste,' and ' wastes ' have no fixed boundaries, but our text & 'Domesday' indicate generally the areas of the Aeron and Eiδyn districts.

17 Cp. or Eiδyn 29·12=44 ; Eiδyn barth 33·5=16 ; *see* Index, & Bk. of Tal., p. *xix*. For other occurrences of Cynon & Klytno see *a.* LL'N VARD. P. 147·30–11 Clut gamlan, *K*ynran o hil cynrein, mal Clytno Eiδyn prif gyfrin prein . . . Kywrennin. *b.* W.B. MAB. 223·14, 224·3, & 469·34. *c.* RHISSERDYN even rhymes ' gwyngor Beuno ' with ' rhyvig Clydno ' . . . Hawδ i Glut del *ff*awdwyr gwlatoeδ Wllffin (i.e. the soldiers of the countries of the descendants of (Hugh) Lupus . . . cuδ priδlawr gwawr gwerin, bendevic Clut, i aros dic clo daeerin . . . atweδ Etwin . . . eil naf Eiδyn . . . Clytno Eiδyn glot arδwy drin . . . Kynnwryf Bryneich, Kynon hoewvreich. R.B. *Poetry* 94·13, 91·27·36·41, 94·12·28. Rhisserdyn is nominally singing to Sir *H*owel ap Gr., but the quotations above refer to Cynon the fosterling of the lord of Eiδyn, eil nav Eiδyn. *d.* Treiglawd cawd cyffro, trwyr vronn honn heno, o vot klot Clytno dan do dayar, POETRY, 53·4. Just as the Genealogist confuses Clinog with Cluton, so the late bards have confused Cluton with Cevn Clynog. *see* n. 33 infra.

Still further south is Redeg, which the Asaphian Deanery of Marchia traces for us.[18] It was conterminous with the hundred of Mer-sete, which included the *duos fines* of Cynlleith and Edernion. That these three together represent the original Redeg is capable of demonstration. Firstly, Oswestry, the centre of Mer-sete, is now the centre of the hundred of Trev-red. Secondly, Kynδel 'the great bard' sings of the Court of Eva, daughter of Madog ap Meredyδ, as the '*hearth of Redeg*' which cherishes the minstrels who visit it, P. 168·31. In other words Eva's father ruled that division of Powys which included Cynlleith and Edernion, and which earlier formed part of Redeg. In 1116 Owein ap Cadwgan and Llywarch of Arwystli ' combined forces *on the border of Redeg* (21·11=86), before setting out to Deheubarth at the behest of King Henry. Now Owein was at that time lord of Powysian territory bordering on Mersete, (Ll. 422). Again on the north of Redeg is the extreme limit of Cheshire, *tervyn Caer lleon* (*Myv.* 153^a·57), while to the south lies Radnorshire within a ride of it, a ride performed 'between night and day' by Howel ap Owein Gwyneδ, (*Myv.* 198). Thus the geographical position of Redeg is revealed to us by Kynδel, a native of a neighbouring district. As to the nomenclature, *Mer*-sete means '*border settlers*,' and if Trev-*red*[19] means a *March settlement*, the two terms are practically synonymous. Rêd, Redeg (of which Reged is a metathesis) means 'March,' 'Border-land.'

18 See Book of Taliesin, INTRODUCTION, pp. *xii–xiv*. *cp.* n. 14.

19 Oswestry, which was the centre of Mersete, is in Can*trev* Trev-red, which might possibly be for Can*trev* Rêd, the *March* or *Border* hundred. The meaning of 'trev-red' is not established, but *cp.* parth-red, gwarth-red, gweith-red, gwahan-red, gwrth-red, brith-red. *Treb* in Irish, Welsh, Breton, means *house, residence, territory.* cp. Treb Guidauc BK. OF LL. DAV, *xlv.*, & Tref Ret=*villa* Ret, 272. (Hir main Guidauc is on the mountain boundary of Cellan in Cardiganshire. See Lewis *Topographical Dictionary. s.v. K*ellan).

As March after March appeared Redeg lost its original meaning of Marchia, and became a general term to denote any March. In 1098 the earls of Chester and Shrewsbury led a joint retinue of 'the men of Redeg' (cenvein Redegein 20·3, 23·7=28) to the Rhyn of Anglesey, where they had built a castle above Aber Lleinog. On the shore there Hugh the Proud fell, and the 'Rhyn settlement' ceased to be a 'shelter to Redeg' 30·9=68. The earl's body is sent to Redeg, 37·1=62, on the way for burial at Shrewsbury Abbey. We have now arrived at the following five conclusions:—

   i. Godoðin is a scribal fraud for Gorðin, *a push*.

   ii. Catraeth was fought before Aber Llëinog.

   iii. In 1098 Deira and Bernicia formed part of the Earldom of Chester, for which *Gogleð* was an alias.

   iv. Roughly speaking Yale and Maylor with Cluton Edwin east of the Dee represent Eiðyn.

   v. Redeg meant originally the country round Oswestry with Cynlleith & Edernion: later any Borderland between Kymry and her invaders.

Having established the above conclusions by the joint testimony of bards and historians it will be quixotic to cross the Tweed in search of any fact in connection with our text. The coast country from the Lupusian Palatinate to Aber Gwyngregyn, thence across the Heleð (Lavan Sands) and by Ferry to Penmon will better repay our exploration. Aeron is the country which was once held by Edwin the Freeman (n. 37), on the Pulford brook and the Alun. Tud Llwch (*i.e.* the country of the Laches, Eyes, and Saltneys) lies within the bend of the left bank of the Dee. The name of the Ceint country survives in Eur-Geint (Northop), Kil-Cein, and Hal-Kin,[20] *i.e.* the Moor of Ceint. North-west of the

---

20 In the *Valor* we read 'Rectoria de Halkeyn.' In final dis-syllables *ei, ey* are reduced to *e* or *i* (vel *y*) as Ow*e*in to Ow*e*n, or Owin

hundred of Coleshill[21] lies Eingylyawn with Rhuδlan at its head; and Trwyn Esyd is the Point at the mouth of the Dee, the *Set*-eia Aestuaria of the ancient Geographers.

The other place names are too well known to particularize except Carreg Cynhadvan, that picturesque and arresting object, just above the high water line, near the base of the cliff mound & the edge of the pool at Aber Lleinog in Penmon, (see Frontispiece). Caer Gyngrwn is the Round Castle * with the wall-rampart on the rising ground above the Ford.

Having exorcised the changeling godoδin, restored gorδin, equated Gogleδ with the earldom of Hugh Lupus, and located cat traeth on Mordrei Gwyneδ, we will now proceed to sift the text for evidence that will identify the chief actors. First comes the Bard who has suffered so much from the Gorδin that he is 'too weary to avenge' it 12·9=78. He was the son of an exile 12·14, and had lived in exile 31·21=52. He is the scion of high-lineaged Cynan of the Round Hill Fort 31·22, 3·9=52, 70. Cynan ap Iago had an only son, Griffyδ, born of an Irish princess. Griffyδ's grandfather, Iago, was King of Gwyneδ in the true line of descent. Iago was assassinated in 1039, when his son Cynan was a minor. Cynan sought safety in Ireland, where he attained to manhood, married 1053 (Lloyd 379), had an only son Griffyδ, and died. When the second usurper of the power of Gwyneδ was slain in 1075, Griffyδ, who was now of age, hastened to the mouth of the Menei to claim his grandfather's throne. He was welcomed by the men of Mon. Already Kynwric of Powys was oppressing Lleyn, whereupon Griffyδ sailed to Rhuδlan to solicit help of Robert, the lieutenant of Hugh Lupus. Returning with 60 men Griffyδ united his forces,

---

B.B.C., 15·6; Owyn An. 8·22=88, Llund*ei*n to Llund*e*n, cad*eir* to cad*er*, ced*eir*n to ced*yr*n, Cil C*ei*n to Kilken, Halk*ei*n to *H*alkin.

21 Coleshill hundred represents the old Keint area.   * *See* Map.

which destroyed Kynwric, and proceeded to the Artro river[22] in Merioneth to meet his chief enemy, Trahaearn of Arwystli whom he decisively repulsed. " When I hastened (to Mon against its arrogant seizure) my name in my country was well known. Sprung out of Gwyneδ, the scion of Cynan of high lineage I had lived in exile. I led a spare corps of the Palatine's lieutenant. In the crush of the Artro country, no stroke was sharper than the dart of my shooting," 31·20=52.

In the fall of 1075 the Welsh revolted against Griffyδ because of their dislike of his Irish entourage, and his foreign accent, 26·12=80. He became an exile once more. In 1081 he crossed with his supporters from Ireland to St. David's, joined forces with Rhys ap Tewdwr, and slew the usurper Trahaearn in the battle of Mynyδ Carn[23] in Pembrokeshire.

Gwan(eis), ymhyrδ(eis ymHenvro)
Y nerth ni δifferth serth Artro, 13·2*=52.
'*I thrusted and dispersed in Penvro the power that 'failed to defend steep Artro.*' On his way northward Griffyδ was trapped not far from Bala, and cast into prison by Hugh

[22] Artro flows out of the Cwm Bychan lake at the foot of the Roman steps. It runs through woody romantic glens, some of them very steep & narrow, till it emerges at Llanbedr, & thence its course to the sea is as prosaic as ditch water. After the defeat and death of Cynwrig at Clynog Griffyδ ap Kynan marched with his men against Trahaearn who advanced, via Drws Ardudwy and the valley of the Col, to the river Artro where he was met & defeated in or near the great ravine, (glyn cyving). After traversing the country repeatedly it appears to me that Griffyδ took the ' old Road ' over the uplands above Harlech, & emerged on the Artro a little above the Glyn Cyving.

[23] According to a communciation* from Sir Evan D. Jones, Bart., M.P., the actual site of the battle of Mynyδ Carn was the plateau of Glyngath (? Clun Gath) between Mynyδ Llan Llawer and Mynyδ Melyn, some 20 miles north east of St. David's. The place names of the district are reminiscent of battle, and of Irish occupancy; also of Trahaearn. An earlier form of Llan Llaw-er was Llan Llaw-harne,

See his Presidential address since printed in the ARCH. CAMB., 1923.

Lupus at Chester. ' Bent was my knee in the abode underground. An iron chain encircled my ankles twain,' 12·10=78. After the lapse of years he was rescued. " Brave the act in Gogleδ rendered by a hero . . . to the son of an exile. Gently he bore me from an underground prison, from the precincts of oblivion, from an odious country," 12·14·16=52. Griffyδ had been a dozen years, or more, in prison before his re-emergence in 1094 as a leader of a victorious force against the Castle of Aber Lleinog in Penmon. There is a grim Old Testament naturalness about this first act of the ex-prisoner being directed against the power of his former gaoler, and a poetical justice in the capture of a castle built by his enemy. But the end was not yet. " Being mindful of the razing of his castles and the killing of his knights Hugh, earl of Chester, collected a fleet and a large host. Another Hugh, the earl of Shrewsbury joined him with his men so that they might come together as one to avenge the losses Griffyδ ap Kynan had caused them. Thereupon they, with their men, sailed aboard their fleet to the dominion of Griffyδ,

which is an abbreviated form of L*lan Llawr* Tra-*haearn*, i.e. the church of Trahaearn's domain. *Harn* is dialect for 'haearn,' and Llaw-*er* an Anglicism for Llawr. Meilyr associates Trahaearn with Nanhyver.

Am (nav) pryderav yn vawr,	*For my prince I am very anxious,*
arglwyδ yn llawr Nanhyver.	*a lord in the land of Nanhyver.*
Casnar δaw dros vor etwaeth,	*Over the sea a chief will come again*
pobl anhywaeth (i) niver,—	*with a number of wild men—*
Gwyδyl a Dievyl duon	*Irish and Black Devils,*
Ysgogogion δynion lledffer.	*a wandering rather sturdy race.*
Cad a vyδ y·Mynyδ Carn	*A battle there will be on Mynyδ Carn*
a Thrahaearn a laδer . . .	*and Trahaearn will be slain.*

" Llyw & llyw niver "=Casnar=Gr. ap Kynan, who had crossed the sea once before in 1075, when his Norse auxiliaries drove Trahaearn from the Artro (*Intro. xxvi*). The 'pobl anhywaeth' are *not* the people of Nanhyver, but the mercenaries from across the sea who settled in ' llawr Trahaearn.' Meilir wrote :

'*Ry*δoδynt dros vor etwaeth, Pobl anhywaeth, Nanhyver.'

xxvii.

led by Owein ap Edwin and Uchtryd his brother," with " Hugh earl of Shrewsbury as their chief." (Bu. 142, B. 272).

The expedition moves off led by three border Knights, gold bedight ones of Eiðyn 5·17=16. "They encamped over against the island of Anglesey whither the Britons had retired, having invited a fleet from the Irish sea to defend them," Bruts, 272-3. Hugh earl of Shrewsbury overwhelms the open lands, the country of the shallow waters, the Heleð champaigne and turned the men of Ireland, with arms in their hands (34·6*=54), against Griffyð and his friends. When the nobles of Eiðyn penetrate Mon, its notable people resorted to wild places 33·5=16, because the invaders were slaying the inhabitants 5·17=16, entering churches and committing sacrilege 2·16=68. 'Fearing treachery' (B. 273) I (Griffyð) swiftly quitted the Rhyn before the struggle began 3·7=70. For the conflict Hugh enhosts many races 33·7=16. Having molested the adjoining country 1·16=4, nine score villeins, who had fled from the clearings (33·7=16) into concealment were removed (to the Rhyn) 27·6=96, where a feast was given at the court of the Burg. Hugh had brought with him pipes of sparkling wine for the use of his Saxons 23·16=54. It was his wont to be ever gay at the head of his host pouring out mead (1·10=2) into hirlas horns (25·19=22) on his expeditions 33·21=12. His retinue would gather round the store of liquor vivaciously drinking together (33·10=10), even prolonging their revelry into the night by rush-light 4·21=12. One morning at peep of day violent shouting breaks out beyond the castle, causing those awake to rush for their shining armour 28·18=44. A division of the men of the fort marshalled its stalwarts 13·5=54. Hugh quitted the banquet for the tumult of the joust 16·5=20. A-horse (3·51=78, and clad in mail (2.5=4) he hurries to the water meets (ebyr 1·17=4) to stem the attack upon the country 25·17=22, because he would defend Gwyneð as an owner cultivating his own 11·11=38. Mess-mates, captains and men, leaping together rush to the shore (9·3=34, 31.7=30, 36·7=60). As the haven is approached Hugh turns livid (32·12=56), and his crowd is struck dumb by the sight of the ships 25·18=22. Athwart the wide seas Magnus had sailed, his design above detection (4·4=42), in as much as he had arrived unannounced 22·22=8. Ni bu cyvarch rhac ystre, there was no palaver before entering the list 36·13=60. Hugh was foolhardy in his haste at dawn, (7·12=6); he blundered in his strategy—no shelter was taken 1·19, 6·15=4·18. Heavy drinking had bred a reckless spirit 6·14. Advancing headlong beyond the water line (35·4·7=38) he eagerly rushed his retainers against the Norse 34·9=54. He rode at their head (6.8=32), the flashing spears of Goðeu make light his path, 18·19=36.

Standing on the deck of his foremost ship (19·12, 33·3), Magnus fastened on the bearing and proud look of the leader, when he appeared at the entry 13·21=68. As the war shout was being raised (38·17=18), Magnus aimed at (1·17=4) checking and punishing the pride of the loud-shouting war lord (13·21=68), and deliberately shot a gleaming dart (1·17=4) which penetrated Hugh's temple just below the brow line of the helmet, 11·3=20. As Hugh turned a summersault into the abyss (18·6=94), a tragic wave leapt between us (25·15=24), and his riderless charger plunged among the noble torque-wearers, 11·4=20. The bolt from the King's hand was terrible, it consigned a loved one to ruin, and destroyed the manhood of a superior race 8·5=8. Hugh's retinue was daunted . . . at sea the lances could not be held, 29·9=44. Moreover in the assaults the horses stumbled in the sand holes 29·19=46. Pushing his ships

xxix.

forward against the attacks (35·6=38), both the incitement to bravery and the loud shouting of King Magnus is heard (38·19=18), as he swiftly smites such as advanced beyond the water line, 35·7=38. His Norsemen give no quarter (1·12=4), and the Lloegrian leaders perish in the foaming shallows (29·15=46), weighed down by their armour 6·19=84, 18·11=94. Then there was tumult between the Ford and the shore bank (7·11=6), which became a very babel, so great the hubbub and the carnage, 9·22=34. The pressure was ruthless, nor spear nor shield gave protection 1·19=4. Those defending the Rhyn were cut down (30·16=10), and their war steeds, with harness all gory, stampeded from the crimsoned strand, 19·11=66. The steel was plied on the border of the alder swamp (37·22=82), the stockade was broken down (37·20=82), and on the rising ground the battle raged 7·11=6. The Round Fort of the Rhyn was breached (10·17=20, 4·6=42, 26·3=24, 35·12=38), the garrison speared (37·18=82), and the Swans of Dee (Owein & Uchtryd) were surrounded 7·15=6, 6·2=16. Owein reversed his shield and threw down his arms, 33·18=10. He was spared 10·6=36. By the prerogative of his overlords (26·2=24), he sat in the seat of the Lupusian (with plenary powers) over Môn, for nothing he did was subject to revision, 10·12=36. When Hugh the Proud was shot down in the shallows " his dear friend Owein " (1·7=2) who had been second in command 'naturally rose to be head' (18·8=94), with the *nom de guerre* of Cynon *i.e.* Generalissimo, but he did not carry on the war, 18·15=36.

That in brief is the story of Catraeth told, mosaic fashion, in selected phrases of the bards, who celebrated it in song. Judging by internal evidence, two of the four bards participated in the Gorðin, namely, Talhaearn the bard of Hugh the Fat, and Llwchvarð,[n] successively the bard of Hugh the Proud, and of Owein ap Edwin, alias Cynon.

We get a glimpse of the ' Noble Lupus ' taking a leading part (1·22=4), to check the violence of those disembarking 2·2=4. But as such of his men as did not quit the Ford fell like rushes (1·13=2), he flies hither & thither, seeking for a way of retreat, because the King chased the Lord of Gogleð, 29·20=46. It is not clear how soon he got away. Apparently certain of his followers left early, 33·15=10.
>Friends melt away from the coast of the Rhyn,
>In ships like swans they sail away.
>At high tide they carried away the peasants,
>the charming women of the Fort, & their mead.

Talhaearn adds that his ' friend though in real disgrace will not budge from Gwyneð unless he shall bear away the dragon 7·1=6 whose dead body was not recovered till low ebb, nor buried till the 17th day after catraeth (Ord. Vitalis, Bk. x., cap. VI.) Then the Palatine boards his flotilla, and we go to Elved (34·2=12), because Gogleð was his country ; he had only come to Gwyneð to fight, 2·3=4. Griffyð ap Kynan states that there was complaint of Hugh's hardness of heart ; that he was perverse and odious when fighting, that he would thrust again the severely wounded (36·19=62), so that he was well-named ' Lupus.'[24] Talhaearn frequently strikes a personal note. The Norse swooped down upon us. From the feast (our men) rushed to the Ford, hence my soul is sad. In the shallows I lost utterly my loved friends 33·11=10, 16·1=14. Nothing sadder can come to us. Of the mixed races as fostered friends that we went, only the villeins escaped 23·1=8. From the thrusting of the strange force I was saved 1·20=4. Talhaearn calls Lupus, my friend 7·1=6, my fat friend 8·2=8, very fat lord 29·20=46, the thick-set one 11.5=20, 19·22=68 ; the stouter lord 26·22=23·5=8. He also

---

[24] Prof. Lloyd is mistaken when he writes, " There is no ancient authority for the epithet Lupus." *See Index s.v. Bleið.

xxxi.

makes numerous references to Hugh the Proud, and though there had been enmity between them 1·5=2, he will praise him ; but he calls the sons of Edwin false common fellows, 4·18=12, because they deserted Lupus to join the Welsh.

Let us next hear Llwchvarð,[n] perhaps our most reliable historian of Catraeth. The poet was a member of the expedition, he drank mead and wine at Mordrei Gwyneð (6·4=32) he fought on the Battle-strand, he was wounded, captured and ransomed, 28·4=30. Moreover he remained with the garrison at Castell Aber Lleinog after the flight of Hugh Lupus. Llwchvarð, therefore, has first hand knowledge of all that went on. When Hugh, earl of Shrewsbury, fell at the Ford Owein ap Edwin succeeded to the command, 18·8=94 & Llwchvarð became his loyal bard. After the Gorðin Magnus left suddenly (20·6=28), 'but within a short year' he returned to Môn and befriended the exile Griffyð ap Kynan. There had been a revolt against the pro-Lupusian rule. As far as I could see the trouble arose from repressive acts of oppression 25·5=26. Influenced by Magnus 13·19=68, Owein & the garrison went over to the Kymric side, all the more readily, perhaps, as Griffyð was already married to Owein's daughter.[25] Magnus, formerly denounced as the enemy and hateful lord (5·20=16), under altered circumstances, becomes the bard's hero of heroes. I love the victorious King who benefits minstrels 20·10=28. In order to understand the Gorðin, Llwchvarð should be read as a whole. With a view to bringing out clearly the parts played respectively by *i.*, Hugh the Proud, *ii.*, Magnus, & *iii.*, Owein ap Edwin I shall group afresh[26] Llwchvarð's references to the three.

25 Bucheð Griffyð ap *K*ynan (edited by Arthur Jones), p. 138.
26 This involves certain unavoidable repetitions, but these will help to familiarise the evidence.   *n.* see Preface.

1. First comes Hugh, earl of Shrewsbury. The expedition moves off ... the border knights of Eiδyn ... three allied friends (Hugh, Owein & Uchtryd) came to Penmon 5·17=16. The country was over-run by the restless Lloegrians 7·6=30. The men of Redeg harassed the men of Mon (20·3=28), whose notable people resorted to wild places, 33·5=16. Hugh the Knight Errant was very active 6.5=32. He enhosts many races 33·7=16. He pressed forward the veterans of the Rhyn 29·18=46. Nine score captives were brought from open places (33·7=16) to the Rhyn. He commandeered the caparisoned steeds (of Griffyδ ap Kynan) 33·8=16. (The lord of Eiδyn gave a feast) 5·9=48. In the time of the great festivity we drank ensnaring golden mead ere we rushed at dawn (18·20=28) to the shore. Hugh lifts his targe, and brandishes his spear 25·9=22. He wore bright mail 9·18=34. He leads his supporters resolutely to battle 33·8=16. He fights beyond the water-line. His ashen spear defends Gwyneδ like an owner cultivating his own 35·4, 11·11=38. He breaks his spear in the element (29·1=44); at sea lances could not be held (29·10=44), & shields were embarrassing in the waters. In the shallows the darts gleam as they advance, and flashing spears make light the path of Goδeu 18·18=36. Ere the knights were slain in the foaming surf the unpleasant happened 29·15=46. Because of the mead (Hugh's) valour was tempted to headlong ruin 10·18=20. The shooting of the King's arrow wounds Cyvrenhin 10·17=20; his forehead was lacerated 38·16=18. In front of the motley host the King wounds the loud-shouting war-lord near the brow line of his helmet, 11·2=20. With the raising of the war-shout Hugh fell in the fore-front 38·16=18. Of sunshine Morien robbed this wonderful man, the first in Gweryd, and joint head, 11·12=38. He, the bulwark of the expedition was slain (10·8=36) at the Ford when it was rushed at green dawn, 10·15=18. Lord of the Ford he was bowed down by an ugly arrow beyond the marsh 11·9=38. Chief of Eiδyn, Greatire, falls in the conflict of the strand 24·17=40. Bradwen perished, he did not escape 11·19=40. The shout of the Frank, impetuous leader, ceases, 35·5=38. He who embarrassed the Rhyn was cut down in battle, at dawn he was felled 6·7=32. They abandon the steel-mailed chief 9·7=34. Without deliverance he remained in the sea, bedfellow of worms of horrible habit 29·1=44. He who wished for the expedition did not return home. He rolls at the Ferry bottom beneath deepish breakers, beyond the marsh. He called for burial ere he was under cover of the sanctuary, 5·15=48. Neither flood nor shield gave shelter to him who was a casualty 17·6=28. A low ebb benefits Mynyδawg, lord of Eiδyn (35·10=38), who went armed (2·5=4), was felled before the Rhyn (35·11=38), and in the marsh abides 29·1=44. His retinue attended him in the day of stress 9·4=34. Completely were drowned the host of Bradwen 11·14=40. Desperate was the passage before the Rhyn. Such as went were precipitately drowned 5·8=48. Though Lloegria's host was fine, punishment all along was endured, 18·22=28. There was grief for the men of the Battle Strand whose cherishing is mine 26·4=26. At dawn the assembled men are cut to pieces, lost in the deep is Bernicia's ally pierced by the Norse 20·4=28. The hero that is still is sung 38·21 =18. Praise is the due of the faultless colleague, (*cyvreint*) 17·6=28. A friend was the Lupusian captain, I would love him to live, the bulwark of hardihood, the Champion Bull! I grieve for his fall, I'll cherish his grave, 25·13=24.

II. Next comes Magnus, King of Norway. One morning there appears one who presses forward to the Ferry side 31·7=30. Athwart the wide sea Magnus had come suddenly, his design above detection 4·4=42. Unpremeditated was his voyage, he had not concerned himself about a large flotilla 29·4=44. His descent was very fine 31·8=30. When he arrived at the Ford he made a rush, 31·7=30. Darts were showered at the edge of the shallows 7·7=32. (The Bull of Battle did not budge 37·16=82). In his ship he pushed his way against the attack 35·6=38. In front of the motley host the King bruised the shouting war lord nigh the browline of the helmet, 11·2=20. Stout the hand that tangled the lot of a terrible Knight 10·7=36. In the stress his round shield was notched 10·9=36. I prophesied that he would die through Morien 24·20=40. Magnus actively defended on all sides, 35·6=38. His unerring darts loudly wail, I heard their dirge 31·9=32. Heard too was the incitement to bravery and the loud shouting of the King (38·19=18), who swiftly smote such as rushed beyond the water line, and fell upon the division of our brave retinues, 35·7=38. He thrusts back the silk caparisoned steeds of the grandees. He hurls about his darts and spears (9·17=34) atween the two lines (*i.e.* he was in advance of his own force). Leading he penetrated through the Lupusians (9·19=34), with sharp axe he slew (6·9=32), he scattered the attacking force (10·8=36), and chases the Lord of Gogleδ, 29·20=46. The avenger of Arvon attacked the men of Eurgeint 34·4=36. (He broke down the stockade. Twixt the hill and the alder swamp he plied the steel, 37·20=82),— the outworks of the fort were utterly broken, 29·11=44. The villeins of Gwyneδ asked for protection of Gwenn Vanhon . . . who limps; they pray that he may check the fighting of the lords, that he, the Bull of Battle, may ravage the tyrants, so that before his death there shall be an end of aggression 19·1=28. I had seen the Norse coming to the Rhyn in quest of good fortune 20·2=28. (And now) they display their streamers beyond where the enemies sail 20·6=28. The helpless crowd cheer him who is in haste to go to his court (in Man) 20·8=28. The brave men of Mon, whose sufferings the brilliant archer avenged (29·6=44) deplore the withdrawal of the King, for in Mon he slew the Saxons, 4.7=42. The King who loves the ways of his foster brothers hastens to a beautiful Isle, sailing away from the Rhyn. His war-waging effected much general good, 27·15=42. He gave the Ferry to the regent of the Rhyn country (*i.e.* Owein ap Edwin) and a meed of fair fortune to (me), Ceint's minstrel, 9·20=34. The friend of Mon and Man bears great glory 11·7=20. I love the victorious King 20·10=28. His story his Ceint admirer will sing 4·8=42.

III. Finally comes Owein ap Edwin, alias Cynon. Three Knights of Eiδyn . . . came to Penmon, 5·17=16. (Hugh) the leader (fell at the ford, while) 'Uchtryd' and Cynon, captains from Aeron fought angrily in the round castle 5·22=16. The avenger of Arvon attacked the men of Eurgeint, the stout resistance of Cynon tested the power of the Picts 34·4=36. Against the lord of Cyv-lwch Magnus made a breach in the rampart. For the sake of the natives the ultimate action was drawn 26·3·1=24. Cynon, the bulwark of Ceint became the leader of the Rhyn, 29·22=44. He was established ruler by the prerogative of the overlords, 26·2=24. As Generalissimo he does not carry on the war 18·15=36. He collects the arms and marshals the broken ranks, a mere crowd,—He thunders against drunkenness, he thunders against slackness, and against degeneracy. I am an eye-witness that wantonness sways the men of Gweryd 25·1=24. Cynon put up a stockade and a cunning rampart 29·13=46. The damaged Hall was made fair again by the loved lord of Ceint. The country folk loved him 10·11, 18·15=36. I will praise Cynon

xxxvi.

26·2=24. (To sing his praise is due . . . Ere his death (1105) he returned to Aeron. . . . Of those that came to the Rhyn, scarcely was there bred in fair Aeron a better than Cynon 38·1-8=82).

I know of nothing in our text about the war of 1098 contradictory of the Chronicles. And if readers familiar with the history of the expedition of the Lords Marcher to Anglesey remain unconvinced by the foregoing string of extracts, and still hold that the 'Book of Aneirin' could have been written before 1098, I fear that no argument and no fact can be of service to such. Still the champions of Tradition will remember that Griffyð ap Kynan is reputed to have promulgated a Statute for the regulation of Welsh metres. Peniarth MS. 77 etc. present us with copies thereof. I will not discuss its authenticity. The interesting part to us is that a statute of some kind might have been enacted, for Griffyð ap Kynan is one of the four authors of the 'Book of Aneirin,' which contains the oldest poetry (barring some dozen lines) in the Welsh language. He has after the fashion of the twelfth century 'signed' some of his poems, and is frequently autobiographic. He is 'the offspring of an exiled Knight, an only son to Cynan of high lineage,' eisyllut alltut marchauc, vn maban e Ginan edryvannauc, 31·22=52. Men went to Catraeth from an interrupted feast. Fruitful *the conflict that I did not promote* . . . By force I lost what I had made secure (in 1094). While Gwyneð was being over-run *I quitted Mon*. Brave Magnus does not want the Rhynn. He gives it to the *father-in-law of the son of Cynan* of Conical Hill 3·3=70. (The lords marcher) coveted the country that will lift me up 30·8=68. The Norse supported me with their arm against the army and attack of Bernicia, 12·21=52. Their dispossessed land (Magnus) delivered to me 16·19=74. When the Knight

xxxvii.

of Ceint departed (Magnus) assigned to me the country of high-famed Mordrei, 32·20=76.

Let us hark back a few years. It will be remembered that after the Gorðin of 1098, Oweln ap Edwin, lord of Ceint, became castellan of the Round Fort of Aber Lleinog. After a short year Griffyð returned from Ireland. Magnus perceived his strait and took his part, 13·19=68. Owein deserted the Saxon to espouse the Kymric side. He had already given his daughter in marriage to Griffyð, who sings, 12·7=82,

"Though a hundred men were in my hall
  the lord of Ceint should have the chief seat.
  Cares (without number) are my familiars,
  (About the conflict of the Strand) will I sing.
I am a weary prince, I will not avenge the Gorðin.
Ridicule did not disgrace me when down-trodden by the
Bent was my knee in the abode underground,   ['earl.'
An iron chain encircled both my ankles.

    *   *   *   *   *   *   *   *

Around the mead-horns, in the fort near the sea,
slanderous things were sung of me, and I (in exile).
Taliesin, who chatters about Cyvrenhin, knows it.
I sang of the Gorðin ere next day's dawn,"
  i.e. when the facts were fresh.   12·9–12=78.

Now, the author of the above lines could be no other than Griffyð ap Kynan. The only stumbling block is the imperfect couplet, 'mi ... na vi aneirin,' because of the double assumption that 'aneirin is one word, and a proper name. When cynghaneð and metre are set right our 'Book' lends no support to the personal idea. 'Aneirin' occurs only twice in the text, and at 14·6 it is demonstrably pure fiction.

    anysgarat vu y nat ac aneirin, 14·6.=
    nu neut ysgaraf nat a godoðin, 23·14.

The original of these two mis-copied lines probably ran,
    (Galar), anysgar a nat gorðin,
  Sorrow is inseparable from the uproar of war.

xxxviii.

We are then reduced to the solitary instance where the context shows that it should be bisected into 'aneir in.' The *in* is a natural slip for *im*, because the adjoining rhymes all end in -*in*. Aneir, which means 'evil speaking, slandering, ridiculing,' derives point here from the flight (3·7=70) of Griffyδ from Anglesey before the advent of the earls, whose minstrels around the mead cups would be more than human did they not jeer and jibe at the runaway Griffyδ. The '& Neirin' of the Additional Matter is therefore based on a misreading of the MS., which was composed after 1098. Take another confirmatory illustration from the Old Welsh Genealogies in the same MS., which shews their factitiousness, as well as their lateness. The ixth genealogy[27] begins
uallauc map Laenauc map Masgiuc clop.
Gwallawg son of Llaenawg, son of Masgiuc the Halt.
It will help us if we identify Gwallawg and Masgiuc the Halt. On page 97 of the Black Book of Carmarthen we read that Gwallawg is the lord (*arglwyδ*), the captain (*pen llu*), and the prince (*unben*) of Aber Lleinog. This Gwallawg, *the one missing*, ' was pierced in the eye by an arrow ' (*gwyδ ardynnwys i lygat*). The Chronicles record that in 1098 Hugh, earl of Shrewsbury, was lost in the shallows at Aber Lleinog, being shot in the eye by Magnus Bareleg, King of Norway. Now the B.B.C. makes it certain that Gwallawg is no other than HeS., and *Masg*iuc clop no other than *Magnus Bareleg*. The Icelandic for ' bare ' is *berr*, which bard and genealogist confounded with *berr glun*, the Welsh for ' short leg,' hence the *byr* (*gam*), the *short* (*step*) of 19·1=28. A man with a short leg takes alternately a short and a long step, and therefore *halts*, hence the *cloff* of the Genealogist. We have seen that the Aneirin scribe practised mystification,

27 See *Genealogies from Harleian* MS. 3859 edited by *Egerton* Phillimore in *Y Cymmrodor*, Vol., ix., p. 173.

c

and wrote certain syllables and words backwards![28] We
have another instance here in *map . . . iuc* which read
backwards gives cuipa*m* : cuīpa*ut*=cwympawð, *he ʼfelled*.
Note the changes, and double scribal error over *m*.

uallauc <i>m</i>ap Laenauc[29] <i>m</i>ap   Masg-iuc clop=
Wallawg <i>in</i> ap Laenawg <i>tu</i>ap-īuc Mags   cloph=
Yn aber Lleinog cuimpauð Magn(u)s Gloff Wallawg

Note further that for 'map L.' the B.B.C. has "ab' L."
i.e. Ab*er* Lleinog in the first instance, but afterwards " ab "
(without a contraction mark), which leaves the lines a syllable short. It also has '*mab* Lleyn*n*ac' for *Aber* Llëyna*uc*
at 100·4, where the following lines clinch our argument :—

Ny buum lle llas gwallauc   Ni buum lle llas Gwallawg,
mab[30] goholheth teithiauc   Blaen Lloegr wehelyth deithawg,
A<i>t</i>twod[31] lloegir <i>mab</i> lleynnac   a<i>r</i> dŵod[31] <i>Aber</i> Lleinawg

Here again we see that the fate of HeS. was identical with
that of ' *Gwallawg, the leader of the expeditionary Lloegrians
who was slain on the sands of Aber Lleinog,*' where the Gordin,
alias catraeth was fought as we have shown. The B.B.C.
is positively indecent in being so explicit on this point. It
leaves the champions of Catterick-Catraeth stranded, aye
engulphed (dyvn-wall),[32] in the quicksands of tradition and

---

28 On the last page of the Berne Gospels a scribe of the end of the
ninth century has " two acrostichs in honour of *K*ing Alfred . . .
the final words of the second poem have been *written backwards (atel
for leta, sirelaf for faleris murer for rerum*) or their *syllables transposed (taltane for talenta*)." See Prof. Lindsay's *Early Welsh Script*,
pp. 10–11 ; & a further illustrative note on p. 174.

29 cp. Lăen-awc with Dın-llaen, & Llăin with Lleyn & Llëyn-awc.

30 *Mab* if read backwards=ba*m* : ba*in* : b(l)ain=blaen. *cp.* 5·1–6.

31 a*t*-twod : a*r* tŵod, tywod, *on the sands*. *cp.* Strat tui= Tywi

32 Aphenn dyvynwal *a breych* brein ae cnoyn 20.5 (*metriaclly long*).
  a pheñ dyuynwal *vrych* brein ae knoyn 23.9 (*no cynghaneð*).
*H*ere we have an instructive example of the scribe's method of corrupting the text, & his inability to copy anything twice alike. *Breych*:

bad philology. Moreover, it should now be plain to all that the ixth genealogy[27] has no value as such, being demonstrably a perversion of a historic incident in the Gorðin of 1098. That the ninth genealogy should be so clearly manufactured throws suspicion on the trustworthiness of others.[33]

In the Introduction to the Book of Taliesin I promised to return to the Additamenta in Harleian MS. 3859.[34] In that Introduction I slavishly followed the reading of my predecessors, who began paragraph .II. with ' *T*unc Dutigirn ' so that it became a corollary to paragraph .I., which I knew from the internal evidence of the Taliesin text to be mistaken, to be hopelessly out of date. ' (T)unc ' therefore puzzled me, & Dutigirn I could not trace in any Welsh text. Having now further tested and weighed the internal evidence of our text I find not a scrap of evidence in favour of " sixth century " authorship. On the contrary every item & particular confirm my Taliesin thesis, in short prove that I was wiser than I knew. On turning afresh[34] to paragraph .*II*., it became clear to me that *du-tigirn* is not a

Brē- = Bre*n*ych (cp. 2·8), but *vrych* means ' brock, freckled, ? Pict.' Now ' dyvyn-wa*l* ' is at 18·11* dyvyn-wa*ll*, *lost in the deep*, where the dead HeS. remained till the tide had ebbed. Therefore the ' crows', had no chance ' to peck at his head '; a phenn . . . brein ae cnoyn is a paraphrase of an original something like this :—

    Dyvn-wall (drych   car) Brennych, rhein wenyn (*see notes*)
    Lost in the deep is the form of Bernicia's ally, pierced by darts.
So ends the career of ' Dyvnwal.' After surviving seven centuries we see that he is of such stuff as dreams are made of. Goodbye Dyvnwal ! Sleep thee well, and if for ever, then for ever a long farewell.

33 For example the vIIIth genealogy has ' Clinog eitin ' = C*l*inoc Eiðin, a scribal error for Clu*t*ōe = Clutone Eiðin. *Cp.* Clytno idin : cluton-e idin = Cluton Eiðin B.B.C., 64·2. The *Cl*inog is a repetition of *Cl*inoch in the previous genealogy. It would appear that Kevyn Clutno : Cluno*t* (W.B. Mab., 98·14) is an error for Cevn Cluno*c* = Clynog. " Kevyn Clutno " must be near Clynog as the context proves.

34 See *F*acsimile page, and the Preface, pp. *vii–viii.*

c 2

proper name, but means simply *niger rex*, and like ' magnus rex ' in paragraph .III., it must qualify a man's name. And who was the Black King of the *nigri gentiles*,[35] the Norsemen but (M)unc *du dëyrn* who died in 1103? No one had recognized this Munc before it fell to my lot to identify him with King Magnus of Norway in a note on *du gyweithyδ* in Taliesin. Magnus and his men wore black mail—*Gwisgassant eu gwrm duδed*, they donned their dun covering[h] . . . gory the dusky youths 17·14·22=38, 94. Note that our text is all about the struggles of Magnus with the Anglian race—struggles which the Chronicles confirm in detail, thus establishing the reading of *M*unc & his identity past equivocation, or reasonable doubt.[i] Like a bad dream 'Tunc' departs, abandoning its dupes to an unpleasant awakening.

Now the poets ' Talhaearn, [& Neirin], & Taliesin & Llwchvarδ & Cinan ' did live in the time of Munc for they tell us the story of Magnus in Mon. Three of them are named in our text. Had our MSS. been complete, it is practically certain that the names of all the authors would be found in their respective verse. This was the general custom of the twelfth century.[36] But the sixth century fiction could not

35 The *I*rish distinguish between the Norwegians *Finn geinti* (White gentiles) and the Danes *Dubh geinti* (black gentiles) *geinti* being a loan word from the *L*atin.—(Quiggin). In Welsh *Gint* is used without an adjective as in our text (see *I*ndex), in B.B.C., 48·1 & 55·11, but *llu du*, and in the plural form Gynon 1·11, 72·20 in Book of Taliesin which has *du gyweithyδ* at 17·18. An. Camb. has *gentiles* mostly but *gentiles nigri* Aº. 853, the *Kenedloeδ duon* of Brut y Tywyssogion.

N.B. *H*ugh the Proud wore *llurygeu claer* bright mail, 9·18=34 & his men *calch claer*, shining armour 28·18=44. See also 5·1, 17·1.

36 *cp.* Mi Veilir Brydyδ, *Myvyrian*, 142b·7. Gwalchmei im gelwir gelyn Saeson, *Ib.* 143a·22, 147a·17. Ath gyfarwyre barδ bre breuδor, Cynδelw cynhelw yno cynnor *Ib.* 150b·54, 152a·33. So Chrétien de Troyes in his prologue to *Perceval*, and Wolfram von Eschenbach in his epilogue to *Parzival*. *h, i, n.* See Preface notes.

survive without the suppression of the authors' names. It is not surprising therefore that no existing canto names Talhaearn, whom Taliesin mentions (21·16=20). Talhaearn sings the praises of Hugh Lupus, whose bard he was.

Neirin is a shadow without a twelfth century witness to his existence. The scribe of the Additional Matter clips his name, & the scribe of our text confounds him with godoðin. He makes a *fifth* bard, but we find only the cantos of four. It is clear to me that ' aneirin ' is simply a misreading of *aneir im*, (see p. *xxxviii*). But if assumed to be a genuine name, then it is the pseudonym of Griffyð ap Cynan.

Cian is for Cīan *i.e.* Cinan whose only son was Griffyð, King of Gwyneð, the sometime prisoner of Hugh Lupus. The scribe of the Harleian MS., however, blunders into making Cinan a bard, instead of his son Griffyð, whose father-in-law (chwegrwn 3·9=70) was Owein ap Edwin.[25]

Again Llwchvarð[36] was the minstrel of Hugh, earl of Shrewsbury. Cynghaneð suggests that his name survives :—

Minheu (varð Llycheu) geint waedffreu wawd (6·22=30). Whether this emendation be right or wrong, it is certain that our text is corrupt. The line has no verb in the MS., while both cynghaneð & metre are at fault. Elsewhere he styles himself *Ceint gerðawr* (9·21, 4·8), because after the fall of HeS. he became the bard of his successor in the command, to wit Owein, lord of Ceint, the Tut Cyv-Lwch (26·3=20), that is to say the district bordering on Tut Llwch which lies within the Chester bend of the Dee. The name of Owein's father we know was Edwin, and Prof. Lloyd has pointed out that a freeman of that name was settled in Coleshill in 1089. The ruins of the old castle of Bryn Edwin, near Northop, seem to have been this ancient freeman's home.[37]

[37] In the Domesday Survey we read that this Edwin *holds* or *had held* the townships of Cholmondley, both Edges, Hamton, Larkton.

xliii.

And last comes Taliesin, the junior of Talhaearn, Llwch-varδ, and Griffyδ ap Cynan. Our text preserves his name and some of his poems. Griffyδ ap Cynan had an old bard's contempt for the youthful Taliesin whom he accuses of "chattering about the Cyvrenhin," Griffyδ's early enemy (12·13=78). It was natural for Taliesin to praise the quondam prince of his native district, namely, Hugh the Proud, lord of Eiδyn and Aeron; it was also natural for Griffyδ to resent Taliesin's coloured hearsay narrative of catraeth. There was besides racial feeling as implied by Taliesin's use of 'Brython bards.' When he had 'the temerity to enter a bardic contest' he protests, "I do not deserve being cursed" (B.B.C., 102·11·13). In the Book of Taliesin he sings,

'I was sifted in every faculty by the Brython bards' 7·13=7,
& though 'but a slender twig, inexperienced in craft 7·16=7.
I am the bard of the Hall; I am the winner of the chair:
The bards are greatly incensed, loud their anethemas 8·17=8.

* * * * * *

Having surveyed the historical and geographical evidence, we will end with a note on palaeography. A generation ago it was pointed out[38] that the Demetian scribes proved susceptible to the influence of French models. This may be further exemplified by the orthography of the B.B.C., origin-

Bickerton, & Duckington in Malpas parish, of Golborne David in Handley, of Pulton & Eccleston on the left bank of the Dee, of Hope in Exestan, of Aston in Hawarden, & of 'Castretone' (? near Flint). Also 'Robertus de Roelant *tenet Coleselt et Eduinus de eo.* qui et tenuit *ut liber homo*? We are not told the extent of Coleshill but its hundred contains the three parishes of Ceint, viz., Eur-geint, Cil-ceint, & Hal-Ceint as well as of Flint, Holywell, and Whitford. Owein figures in our text as the *Gwledig of the men of Ceint*; the *Mabon* of the *Clut country*—the Clut rises in Malpas parish; and from *Aeron* there came no braver son. Thus we see that the Welsh text and the Domesday Survey are in agreement.

38 *See* Pal. Note in the B.B.C. (1888) & Bradshaw's *C. Papers* (1889).

ally written, for the most part, in Hiberno-Saxon script, as proved by certain recurring mistakes. In Welsh **c** has always had the sound of **k**, but in French **c** had the sound of **s** before the vowels **e** & **i**, hence the reason why **k**, before **e**, **i** and (its biform) **y**, was introduced into our orthography by Franco-Welsh scribes in a Deheubarth district abounding with Norman settlers. According to Prof. Morgan Watkin[39] *ke* & *ki* (for *que* & *qui*) are first found in a MS. of 1160; he therefore argues quite properly that the B.B.C. must be later than that year. Again in French **c** before the Latin **a** was written **ch** with " the sound of the fricative prepalatal

[39] See *French Literary Influence on Mediæval Wales* in Y CYMMRODOR pp. 146-222 (1920), and pp. 1-94, (1921). In these two articles Prof. Morgan Watkin has contributed stimulating suggestions with some original application. But inaccuracy, discursiveness, and chanticleering go far to mar the meritorious kernel of the contributions. We are told on p. 73 that " Dr. Evans ascribes the writing of the first part (of the B.B.C.) roughly speaking to the last 20 years of the first half of the twelfth century." 'Dr. Evans' does no such thing, but "limits the age of the B.B.C. by 1148 and the reign of John." (See *Pal. Note*, p. *xiii*., 1888). He limits the date still further to the "reigns of *Henry II* & his sons." (INTRO. REMARKS p. *viii*., 1906). *The* " 20 *years of the first half of the* 12*th century* " are, therefore, sheer fiction. An indeterminate reference to a reign is more applicable to its close than its beginning, because some time must elapse before a reign can have any characteristic. *Henry II*. died in 1189. In the opening pages of the B.B.C. we have an echo of the *Vita Merlini*, dedicated to Robert, Bp. of Lincoln, supposed to be R. Chesney, 1148-1167. *I* have suggested elsewhere that Taliesin died circa 1175, and the dialogue between Myrδin & Taliesin must have been composed *after* the latter's death. That brings us to circa 1180. This limits the writing to 1180-1217, which cover the years suggested by the paleographers whom Prof. W. jeers at. He himself suggests " about 1170 " (p. 162). Later (p. 75) he " submits that the very end of the third or very beginning of the fourth quarter of the twelfth century is the approximate date." How then comes it that events of the reign of John are related in the B.B.C. ? There is something wrong with Prof. Watkin's patent. Let me invite him to give us *an accurate, concise statement of verified facts*

surd s," as chat, chose, chanter[40]. As **ch** is a voiceless spirant in Welsh, it could not represent the sound **k**, hence the B.B.C. uses sometimes **c** and sometimes **k**[43] before a, but **c** (with nine exceptions) before o & u.

If we now turn to the 'Book of Aneirin' we find quite other influences at work. Griffyð ap Kynan was born, bred, and educated in Ireland. When he crossed to Gwyneð to claim his ancestral throne there were Irishmen in his train. They did not amalgamate with the Anglo-Norman invaders, but rather helped to drive them away. Irish, like Welsh, has no k, and the older orthography, surviving more or less on pages 34-38 of our text, has not a single instance of **k**, which is sparingly used in the rest of the MS. Sparing too is the use of **t=ð** which Prof. Morgan Watkin has shown to be borrowed from the French.[42] Then forms like *krym* 29·1

up to the year 1230. P.S.—I am accused of withholding the opinions of *Hardy, Madden & Macray*. Now those opinions are written on loose sheets which were not forwarded with the MS. when *I* had it. *I* had no knowledge of them at the time. Insinuations of this kind should not be made without good reason.

40 See *Précis Historique de Phonétique Française* par Prof. E. Bourciez, pp. 145, 153.

41 Prof. Watkin writes "In the B.B.C. the sign **k** alternates with **c** before the vowel symbols **a, o, u,** (p. 74). Random statements of this kind are unpardonable where the facts are easily accessible ; they are as stated above, the exceptions being celi 36·12, ceisso 66·5, cev 90·13, cic 100·3, cynull 53·17, cystlun 64·13, cynial 96·6, *K*uynan 3·3, kuynhiw 100·15. Again "**k** is sporadically encountered in the An. Cambriae," p. 172. This pure fiction is apparently contradicted on p. 191, & leaves one bewildered & suspicious of other statements.

42 The earliest instance Prof. Watkin has found of t =ð is in the word "Eglusnewi*t* in Carmarthen Cartulary No. 33, redacted between 1129 and 1131," p. 190. The instances in the Genealogies from Harleian MS. 3859 are, perhaps, two or three years earlier. See Y CYMMRODOR, Vol. IX., Himey*t* & Margetiu*t* (p. 171), Clinog Ei*t*in (p. 173), Elize*t* (p. 181), Guodo*t*in (p. 182). Eglusnewi*t* & these examples

(Ir. crum, cruim) for *pryv* (worm), and *ri-g* 7·9, for *ri* (King) are confirmatory of the dominant Irish influence. This is also seen in the occasional interchangeableness of the **ch** and **g** as *ch*warðaſ : gwarthaſ, chue*ch* : chwe*g*, *g*uero : *ch*werw, *g*uanauc : *ch*wanawc, Clino*ch* : Clino*g*.[33] We see it again in the Irish tendency[43] to reduce **c** to **g** as in bein*g* 12·8, yueing 2.16, kyvran*g* 31·2, dan*g* 31·3, with which contrast kyvran*c*, tan*c*, tran*c*, ieuan*gc*, tran*gc*, dieī*gc* in the B.B.C., which however has dia*g* for dian*gc*. The digraph **gc** is old in Welsh. Tanc is written *tagc* in a ninth century marginal in the Book of St. Chad, which has also *cibrac*=cyvranc. I offer no explanation of **c** for radical **g** in *C*int for *G*int= gentiles, nor in Mun*c* 16·14, Man*c* 19·2, Welsh forms of *Magn*-us, which appears as Mwng at 11·17, and as Mug & Mungc in B.B.C. Old French shows similar dual spellings (but with the same pronunciation) in *borc* and *bourg*, *lonc* and *long* for the Latin burg-us & long-us.[40]

The length of the first limb of ɲ varies in MSS. When it is short it is liable to be misread n, and vice versa, hence the recurrent confusion between ɲ & n, as well as between ſ & r, and for the same reason. This confusion in our text proves that its originals were written in Hiberno-Saxon characters. ɲ=r, & ſ=s. See Facsimiles in B. Ll. Dâv.

We are all familiar with correspondents who omit to dot their **i**s & cross their **t**s. Of that ilk were scribes who dropped n after a vowel, but omitted a horizontal stroke over it, as

provide an unexpected confirmation of the date *I* assigned to *H*arley MS. 3859, viz. 'after 1125,' (Tal., p. *viii*.). On historical grounds *I* limit the writing of fol. 188b. between 1125 & 1130; the officials of the MSS. department at the Brit. Mus. do not dissent from this date.

43 *I* have to thank the Rev. Charles Plummer for explaining to me certain points in old *I*rish orthography. Final c has been reduced to g in Welsh. *H*owever, under the accent a*c*, rha*c*, dys*c*, cws*c*, dys*c*u, but disgyblion, etc. is the better way.

xlvii.

Mūc : Muc=Munc, tac : tāc=tanc, Clan : Cīan=Cinaṅ, Breych : Brēych=Brenych. In the *List of Scribal Errors* it will be seen what letters are generally mistaken for one another. But it is essential never to forget that things which are equal to the same thing *may be* equal to one another in paleography. For instance c, r, t, are frequently confounded; and we have seen that k took the place of c, so k may appear occasionally as a misread r *or* t. Unless the student can visualize the original script, and the varying possible mistakes in repeated transcriptions, the paleographic restorations look very like jugglery to all but the initiated.[44] n, r, s, cannot very well be mistaken, any one for the other, but if the original script was in Hiberno-Saxon characters n is often confounded with ɲ, and as n & u are a sort of indistinguishable twins in most writing we find ɲ may be misread u which in turn may be misread rr, ii, ir, it, ri, ti, characters utterly unlike ɲ. A friendly critic looking over my shoulder has warned me that these references to the transformations of c, m, n, ɲ & u introduce an air of unreality into the subject. Let me then refer the reader to the S*cri*bal Errors under the above letters, where he will find illustrations with chapter and verse for every statement. Truth is always stranger than fiction to the ignorant, but we can have no progress without shocking the " forty millions " and most of their leaders, who fancy that good sight is everything. Good sight is certainly wanted for bad MSS. Insight is wanted for all MSS.,—it is knowledge, experience, and the faculty behind the eyes that count.

[44] Unfortunately there is but one connected with the University of Wales who is experienced in Welsh paleography in the sense of having ordered knowledge of MSS. extending over a long period of time ; knowledge based on scientific observation of the gradual but continuous change which has taken place in the handwriting of every age and school. Ability to read an old MS. & to extend contractions is only an elementary first step in the science of writing

The table of Scribal Errors is not exhaustive. I had the misfortune to lose the first and fuller list when completed. Few can have any idea of the amount of labour involved in replacing it. But a new compilation had to be done to reveal the personal equation of the scribe, and without attentive study of the Scribal Errors no student will ever get at the historical core of the Aneirin text.

The cost of printing has compelled me to condense the Notes within the narrowest limits. But if the student will first scrutinize the list of Scribal Errors my brevity should not embarrass him. There is no escape from the labour of learning the alphabet. I despair only of those who have a nodding acquaintance with MSS. They think they know all there is to know, and are more eager to dogmatize than to learn; the arrogance of ignorance blinds them to all light and leading.

The Index is not on ordinary lines. It is much fuller. It includes beside proper names, Adjectives and Epithets that denote persons, both in alphabetical order, and ranged under the names to which they refer. For instance Bradwen (*i.e.* bradw wen, *broken hero*,) & Bar-vawr, *Great-ire*, have a double entry, alphabetical, and under Hugh, earl of Shrewsbury. By collecting the many aliases of a man under his proper name, it helps us to understand the references and the history involved. Before reading the text I would urge every student to refer to the Index, and read through the entries under Hu, Hu Vras, Magnus, Owein ap Edwin *vel* Cynon, and (Griffyð ap) Cynan. These have so many epithets that any one not thoroughly versed in the history of the English expedition against Anglesey in 1098, cannot get a firm grip of the subject matter. Many common nouns have also been placed in the Index, for various reasons.

J. G. E.

INDEX TO FIRST LINES.

Aches guolouy glasvleid	32·12=58
Aer dywys rydywys ryvel	18·15=36
Am drynni drylaw drylenn	11.9.15, 24·11=38, 40
Am ginyav dry lav drylen	24·16=40
Anawr gynhoruan	5·7 =48
Angor deor daen	32·2-11=56
Angor dewr daen	16·6 =56
Ardwynef adef eidun gwalat	33·4 =26
Ardyledawc canu. see Erdyled	
Ardyledawc canu kyman caffat & ovri	16·12·16=58, 74
Ardyledawc canu claer orchyrdon	17·1·10=82
Arwr y dwy ysgwyd	7·10=6
Aryf angkynnull	25·1, 7·6=24, 30
Bedin ordyvnat en agerw	19·4 =66
Blaen echeching gaer	5·1 =72
Bu gwir mal y meud e gatlew	8·2 =8
Kaeawc kynhorawc aruawc eg gawr	2·5 =4
Kaeawc kynhorawc bleid e maran	1·22=4
Kaeawc kynnivyat kywlat	1·16=4
Kayawc kynhorawc men ydelhei	1·10=2
Cam e adaw heb gof camb ehelaeth	7·18=6
Carasswn disgynnu yg catraeth	20·11=82
Kein guodeo e celyo	31·12=76
Keint amnat amdina dy gell	18·20=26
Keredic caradwy e glot	8·12=84
Keredic caradwy gynran	8·15=88
Ket bei cann wr en vn ty	12·7 =82

INDEX TO FIRST LINES

Kyuaruu ac ac ero	37·13=82
Kywyrein ketwyr kywrennin	14·7–22=64
Da y doeth adonwy atwen	13·19, 30·12=68
delwat dieirydaf y erry	30·6 =68
Diannot e glot e glutvan	21·19=88
Dienhyt y bob llawr llanwet	22·1, 23·21=90
Dim guoiu edui o adam	34·16=76
Disgynsit en trwm yg kesseuin	10·16·20=20
Disgynsit en trwm rac alauoed	11·1, 35·21=20, 80
Disgynnwys en affwys dra phenn	18·6 =94
Doleu deu ebyr am gaer	28·18=44
Dyfforthes cat veirch a chat seirch	19·11=66
Dyfforthes meiwyr molut nyuet	17·13, 35·12=38
Dywal yg cat kyniwng yg keni	31·2 =96
Erdyledam canu i cinon	38·1, 17·1 =82
Erdiledaf canu ciman cafam	16·12, 38·9 =74
Erdiledaf canu ciman ciguereint	38·21, 17·6 =28
Er kryn e alon	13·10=58
Ef guant tra trigant echassaf	37·18=82
Eur ar mur caer crisguitat. *see* Gwr &c.	
Ev gwrthodes tres tra gwyar	21·1=58
Eveis y win a med e mord(r)ei	6·4=32, 6·13=18
Geu ath diwedus tut leo	32·22=76
Gnaut i ar fisiolin amdiffin	35·6 =38
Gododin gomynaf dy blegyt	14·2, 23·10=64
Gorchan kynvelyn	27·13=42
Goroled gogled gwr ae goruc	12·14=52
Gosgord gododin e ar ravn rin	33·15=10
Gosgord mynydauc pan gryssyassant	33·10=10
Gredyf gwr oed gwas	1·1 =2
Gweleis y dull o benn tir adoyn	20·2, 23·6=28
Guelet e lauanaur en liwet	36·16=62

li.

BOOK OF ANEIRIN

Gwyr a aeth gatraeth buant enwawc	..	6·17=30
Gwr a aeth gatraeth gan dyd ..	..	4·2 =72
Gwr a aeth gatraeth gan wawr ..	...	4·10=72
Gur ar mur caer crisguitat	34·11, 11·20=62	
Gwyr a aeth gatraeth gan dyd ..	3·19, 4·2=70, 72	
Gwyr a acth gatraeth gan wawr	3·10·14, 4·10=70, 72	
Gwyr a aeth gatraeth veduaeth ..	..	3·3 =70
Gwyr a acth gatraeth oed fraeth eu llu,	..	2·21=70
Gwyr a aeth gatraeth yg cat yg gawr	..	9·16=34
Gwyr a aeth ododin chwerthin ...	..	2·13·18=68
Gwyr a gryssyassant buant gytneit	..	9·3 =34
Gwyr a gryssyassant buant gytvaeth	..	9·10=34
Guir gormant aethant cennin	..	36·3 =80
Hv bydei yg kywyrein pressent ..	..	16·3 =20
Hui treuit clair cinteiluuat .	..	37·2 =62
Issac anuonawc o barth deheu ..	..	8·8 =84
Llafnaur let rud ..	..	37·7 =100
Llech leut*ir* ...	..	13·4, 23·15, 34·6=54
lletvegin is tawel kyn dyuot e dyd	..	8·12=88
Llithyessit adar	..	38·15=18
Mat vudic ysgavynwyn ...	..	20·6 =28
Moch aruireit i more ...	..	36·12=60
Moch aruireith i meitit ...	..	36·7 =60
Moch dwyreawc y more	..	17·20=94
Moch dwyreawc y meitin ..	..	18·1 =94
Mynawc gododin traeth e annor ..	..	19·14=66
Neum dodyw angkyvwng ..	..	22·22=8
Neut eryueis y ued ar yg kerdet	..	33·21=12
Ni forthint ueiri molut muet ...	35·12 (17·3)=28	
Ny mat wanpwyt ysgwyt	..	13·15=20
Ny phell gwyd aval o avall ...	..	26·8 =80
Ny wnaethpwyt neuad mor anvonawc	..	10·5 =36

lii.

INDEX TO FIRST LINES

Ny wnaethpwyt neuad mor orchynan	..	9·21 =34
Ny wnaethpwyt neuad mor dianaf	..	15·2 =84
Ny wnaethpwyt neuad mor diessic	..	10·11=36
Nyt ef borthi gwarth gorsed senyllt	..	12·19=52
Nyt wyf vynawc blin	..	12·9 =78
O gollet moryet ny bu aessawr ..	..	19·19=68
O vreith-yell gatraeth pan adrodir	..	4·16=12
O winveith a medweith	15·9 15·19=12, 14	
Pan dei y cyuarchant	..	34·4=36
pan doethon deon o dineiðin parth	..	33·5 =16
Pan gryssyei garadawc y gat ..	..	8·20=88
Pan gyrchei yg kywlat ..	..	31·18=52
Pan vuost di kynnivyn	..	12·3 =72
Pan ym dyvyd lliaws pryder ..	..	21·10=86
Pei mi brytwn ..	..	26·18=96
Peis dinogat y vreith vreith ..	..	22·12=90
Porthloed vedin ..	..	21·6 =60
Pwys blaen rydre ..	..	31·7 =30
raclym y waewawr ..	..	10·13=18
Scwyt dan wodef	..	32·16=74
Teithi etmygant	..	5·17=16
trachywed vawr ..	..	7·6=30, 32
Tra merin iodeo trileo yg caat ..	..	35·4 =38
Truan yw gennyf vy gwedy lludet	..	20·16=76
Try cant eurdorch(auc) a gryssyassant	..	30·16·20=10
trywyr a thrivgeint a thrychant ..	..	27·22=30
Uyg car yng wirwar nyn gogyffrawt	..	7·1 =6

liii.

TABLE OF CONTENTS.

	Page
Preface	*v.*
Introduction	*xi.*

    i. Scribal transpositions and spelling backwards *xiii., xl.*, metre *xiv.*, Geography of the text *xvi., xxiv–v.*, Catraeth & Godoδin *xvii–xviii.*, Gogleδ = first earldom of Chester = from Clwyd to Cheviot Hills *xx.*, Eiδyn, Clyton Eiδyn *xxi.*, Aeron *xxii.*, Redeg *xxiii.*, Ceint *xxiv.*, Mordrei *xvi–xix.*

    ii. Griffyδ ap Cynan claims his ancestral throne *xxv.*, Border expedition of 1098 against Gr. ap C., *xxvii.*, HeS., *xxxiii.*, Magnus *xxxiv.*, Owein ap Edwin alias Cynon *xxxvi.*, Statute of Gr. ap Cynan *xxxvii.*, Gwallauc map Laenauc = HeS., *xxxix.*

    iii. Additamenta in Harl. MS. 3859, *vi., xli.*, Talhaearn, Neirin, Taliesin, Llwchvarδ, Cian, *xlii.*,

    iv. Paleography .. .. .. *xliv*

Index to first lines	*l.*

PART II.

Foreword	*lix.*
Amended Text and Translation	1–100

    i. Talhaearn; ii. Llwchvarδ, 15; iii. Gr. ap Cynan, 51; iv. Taliesin, 93.

Variant Versions	101–106
List of Scribal Errors ..	107
Paleographical and other Notes ..	121
Corrections ..	174
General Index	175
List of subscribers ..	193

Frontispiece, Map of Mordrei, & Facsimile.

THE gap in the Cliffs at Aber Llëinawc is some 180 yards wide. At its northern end is Carreg Cynhadvan which stands 34 yards landward of the high-water line on the very edge of the Pool : above it is the Mound where the cliff ends. The Pool is now divided into two. The rubbish shot into the southern half has obscured the original outline. Apparently there was a channel, behind the shingle bank, stretching towards the brook.

The small map shows Aber Lleinog Castle and Mordrei Gwyneδ where catraeth was fought. The xxxxxxx-chain marks the line of palisading which ran from the Cliff Mound to beyond the Castle. There are traces of a footway cut into the sloping ground behind the palisading, in front of which there was a perpendicular drop (of varying height) with a ditch at the base, which seemingly served the Pool with water from the morass higher up. The ground north of the palisading rises all the way from the Pool to the Castle, which is a round, high Mound of earth, surmounted by a stone rampart (one of the earliest) of great thickness. A deep ditch surrounds the Castle base.

The Facsimile from Harl. MS. 3859 gives the first page of the Additamentum, or *Additional Matter*, which follows the Saxon Genealogies, but is wholly unconnected with them as well as with the Welsh Genealogies. Note carefully that Nennius has nothing to do with any one of the three.

₊ *I* have to thank Mr. David Owen of the L.J.C. & M. Bank at Pwllheli for motoring me to Aber Lleinog and assisting me to photograph the *F*rontispiece in a strong wind. Dr. Richard Owen, now of Bangor, also took me to " Rhyd y Merδyn." Murδyn=' a ruin,' and Murδin=a walled fort. The passage across the Menei is repeatedly called *Rhyd* in Aneirin. It would be interesting to find evidence that this Rhyd was known as Rhyd y Murδin.

a gwẏnn a gwrẏat. o gatraeth o gẏmẏnat. o vrẏnn hẏdwn 1
kẏnn caffat. gwedẏ med gloew ar anghat nẏ welef vrun edat.
Gwẏr a grẏffyaffant buant gẏtneit. hoedẏl vẏrrẏon med-
won uch med hidleit. gofgord vẏnẏdawc enwawc en reit. 4
gwerth eu gwled o ved vu eu heneit. caradawc amadawc
pẏll ac ẏeuan.· gwgawn a gwiawn. gwẏnn a chẏnvan. pe- 6
redur arueu dur.· gwawrdur ac aedan. achubẏat eng gawr
ẏfgwẏdawr angkẏman. a chet lledeffẏnt wẏ lladaffan.· neb
ẏ eu tẏmhẏr nẏt atcorfan. ▰▰▰▰▰▰▰ ▰▰▰▰▰ ▰▰▰▰▰▰▰▰◯
Gwẏr a grẏffyaffant buant gẏtvaeth. blwẏdẏn od uch 10
med mawr eu haruaeth. mor dru eu hadrawd wẏ. angawr
hiraeth. gwenwẏn eu hadlam nẏt mab mam ae maeth. mor
hir eu hetlit ac eu hetgẏllaeth en ol gwẏr pebẏr temẏr 13
gwinvaeth. gwlẏget gododin en erbẏn fraeth. ancwẏn mẏnẏdawc enwawc e gwnaeth. a phrit er prẏnu breithẏell
Gwẏr a aeth gatraeth ẏg cat ẏg gawr . Cgatraeth. 16
nerth meirch a gwrẏmfeirch ac ẏfgwẏdawr. peleidẏr ar
gẏchwẏn a llẏm waeawawr. a llurugeu claer achledẏuawr.
ragorei tẏllei trwẏ vẏdinawr. kwẏ͟bẏm pẏmwnt rac ẏ la- 19
        dei
vnawr. ruuawn hir ef rodei eur e allawr. a chet a choel-
Nẏ wnaethpwẏt neuad   Cvein kein ẏ gerdawr. 21
mor orchẏnnan. mor vawr mor oruawr ẏ gẏvlavan.

B   9

dyrllydut medut moryen tan. ny thraethei na wnelei kenon
kelein. vn feirchyawc faphwyawc fon edlydan. feinnyeffit e
gledyf em penn garthan. noc ac efgyc carrec vyr vawr y chy-
hadvan. ny mwy gyfgogit wit uab peithan. ☰☰ ☰☰☰☰⊃

N y wnaethpwyt neuad mor anvonawc ony bei voryen 5
eil caradawc. ny diengif en trwm elwrw mynawc. dywal
dywalach no mab ferawc. fer y law faglei fowyf varchawc.
glew diaf dinaf e lu ovnawc. rac bedin ododin bu gwafgara-
wc. y gylchwy dan y gymwy bu adeuawc. yn dyd gwyth bu
yftwyth neu bwyth atveillyawc. dyrllydei vedgyrn eillt my-

N y wnaethpwyt neuad mor dieffic no   .☾nydawc.
chynon lary vronn geinnyon wledic. nyt ef eiftedei en tal 12
lleithic. e neb a wanei nyt atwenit. raclym e waewawr⸝
calch drei tyllei vydinawr. racvuan y veirch⸝ rac rygiawr⸝
en dyd gwyth atwyth oed elavnawr. pan gryffyei gynon 15

D ifgynfit en trwm yg keffe-   .. ☾ gan wyrd wawr.
vin. ef diodef gormef ef dodef fin. ergyr gwayw rieu ryvel
chwerthin. hut effyt y wrhyt e lwry elfin. eithinyn uoleit 18
mur greit tarw trin. ☰☰☰   ☰☰☰   ☰☰☰☰☰⊃

D ifgynfit en trwm yg keffeuin. gwerth med yg kynted
a gwirawt win heyeffyt y lavnawr rwg dwy vydin. ar- 21
derchawc varchawc rac gododin. eithinyn uoleit mur greit
.☾ tarw trin.

10   B. A.

Difgynfit en trwm rac alauoed wyrein. wyre llu llaef 1
yfgwydawr. yfgwyt vriw rac biw beli bloedvawr. nar
od uch gwyar fin feftinyawr. an deliit kynllwyt y ar gynghorawr. gorwyd gwareuf rith rin ych eurdorchawr. 4
twrch goruc amot e mlaen yftre yftrywyawr. teiling
deith gwrthyat gawr. an gelwit e nef bit athledhawr.
e myt ef krennit e gat waewawr. catvannan er a clut clot 7
vawr. ny chynhennit na bei llu idaw llawr.

Am drynni drylaw drylenn. am lwyf amdiffwyf dywarchen. am gwydaw gwallt e ar benn. y am wyr eryr gw-
ydyen. gwyduc neuf amuc ae wayw ardullyat diwyllyat 11
e berchen. amuc moryen gwenwawt mirdyn. a chyvrannv
penn prif eg weryt. ac an nerth ac am hen. trywyr yr bod
bun bratwen. deudec gwenabwy vab gwenn.

Am drynni drylaw drylenn. gweinydyawr yfgwydawr 15
yg gweithyen. en aryal cledyual am benn. en lloegyr dry-
chyon rac trychant unben. a dalwy mwng bleid heb prenn.
ene law. gnawt gwychnawt eny lenn. o gyurang gw- 18
yth ac afgen. trenghif ny dienghif bratwen.

Eur ar vur caer kryfgrwydyat aer cret ty na thaer
aer vlodyat. vn axa ae leiffyar ar gatwyt adar brwy- 21
dryar. fyll o virein neuf adrawd a vo mwy o damweinny-

B. A.   11

eit llwẏ od amluch lliuanat. neuſ adrawd auo mwẏ en awr
blẏgeint na bei kẏnhawal kẏnheilweing.

Pan vuoſt di kẏnnivẏn clot en amwẏn tẏwẏſſen.gordi⸗
rot ohaedot en gelwit redẏrch gwẏr not. oed dor diachor di⸗
achor din drei oed mẏnut wrth olut ae kẏrchei. oed dinaſ
e vedin ae cretei.nẏ elwit gwinwit men na bei.

Ket bei cann wr en vn tẏ atwen ovalon kenẏ. penn !
gwẏr tal being a delẏ.

Nẏt wẏſ vẏnawc blin nẏ dialaſ vẏ ordin. nẏ chwardaſ ẏ
chwerthin a dan-droet ronin. ẏſtẏnnawc vẏg glin en tẏ deẏ⸗
erẏn. cadwẏn heẏernin am ben vẏn deulin o ved o vuelin.
o gatraeth werin. mi na vi aneirin.ẏſ gwẏr talẏeſſin ovec
kẏwrenhin.neu cheing eododin kẏnn gwawr dẏd dilin.

Goroled gogled gwr ae goruc. llarẏ vronn haeladon nẏ eſ⸗
ſẏllut. nẏt emda daear nẏt emduc mam⸗ mor eirẏan gadarn
haearn gaduc. onerth e kledẏſ claer e hamuc. o garchar an⸗
war daear em duc. o gẏvle angheu o anghar dut keneu y
vab llẏwarch dihauarch drut.

Nẏt eſ borthi gwarth gorſed ſenẏllt. ae leſtri llawn med⸗
godolei gledẏſ e gared. godolei lemein e rẏuel. dẏffor^{th}ſei
lẏnwẏſſawr oe vreẏch⸗ rac bedin ododin a breennẏch.gna⸗
wt ene neuad vẏthmeirch gwẏar a gwrẏmſeirch. keing⸗

B. A.

Lẏell hirẏell oe law. ac en elẏd brẏſſẏaw. gwen ac ẏmhẏrd⁄
wen hẏrdbeit. diſſerch a ſerch artro gwẏr nẏt oedẏn drẏch
draet ſo. heilẏn achubẏat pob bro. 〰 〰 〰 3

Ꝉlech leutu tut leudvre gododin ẏſtre. ẏſtre ragno ar
ẏ anghat. angat gẏnghor e leuuer cat. cangen gaerw⁄
ẏſ keui dullẏwẏſ. tẏmoz dẏmheſtẏl. tẏmeſtẏl dẏmor. e 6
beri reſtẏr rac riallu. o dindẏwẏt ẏn dẏvu wẏt ẏn dẏwo⁄
vu. dwẏſ ẏd wodẏn llẏm ẏt wenẏn. llwẏr genẏn llu. ẏſ⁄
gwẏt rugẏn rac tarw trin ẏ dal vriw vu. 〰〰〰

Er krẏn e alon ar-aſ erẏ brwẏdrin trin tra chuar. 10
kwr e vankeirw am gwr e vanncarw. bẏſſed brẏch bri⁄
want barr. am bwẏll am diſteir am diſtar. am bwẏll am
rodic am rẏchward. ẏſ bo ẏſ brẏſ treullẏawt rẏſ en riwdrec.
nẏ hu wẏ nẏ gaffo e negeſ. nẏt anghwẏ a wanwẏ odiweſ.

Nẏ mat wanpwẏt ẏſgwẏt ar gẏnwal carnwẏt. nẏ 15
mat dodeſ ẏ vordwẏt ar vreichir men—llwẏt. gell e ba⁄
ladẏr gell gellach e obell. ẏ mae dẏ wr ene gell en cnoi ang⁄
hell bwch bud oe law idaw poet ẏmbell. 〰 〰

Da ẏ doeth adonwẏ atwen. ẏm adawſſut wenn heli
bratwen. gwnelut. lladut. lloſgut. no morẏen nẏ waeth 20
wnelut. nẏ delẏeiſt nac eithaſ na chẏnhor. ẏſgwn drem
dibennor. nẏ weleiſt emorchwẏd mawr marchogẏon

B. A.

wẏ lledin nẏ rodin nawd nawd ẏ faeffon. ᵶᵶᵶ   ᵶᵶᵶᵶ⁊

Gododin gomẏnaf dẏ blegẏt. tẏnoeu dra thrumein drum
effẏth. gwaf chwant ẏ arẏant heb emwẏt. o guffẏl mab dw⸗
ẏwei dẏ wrhẏt. nẏt oed gẏnghor wann. wael ẏ rac tan 4
veithin. o lẏchwr ẏ lẏchwr luch bin. luchdor ẏ borfoꝛ berẏ⸗
erin. llad gwawf. gwan mawf mur trin anẏfgarat aͅcͅ vu

Kẏwẏrein ketwẏr kẏwrennin   ..Œ ẏ nat ac aneirin.
e gatraeth gwerin fraeth fẏfgẏolin. gwerth med ẏg kẏn⸗ 8
ted a gwirawt win. heẏeffit e lavnawr rwng dwẏ ve⸗
din. arderchauc varchawc rac gododin eithinẏn voleit
mur greit tarw trin.   ᵶᵶᵶᵶ   ᵶᵶᵶᵶ   ᵶᵶᵶᵶ⁊

Kẏwẏrein ketwẏr kẏwrenhin. gwlat atvel gochlẏ⸗   12
wer eu dilin. ᵶᵶᵶᵶ ᵶᵶᵶ ᵶᵶ . dẏgoglawd tonn bevẏr
berẏerin. men ẏd ẏnt eilẏaffaf elein. o brei vrẏch nẏ we⸗
lẏch weẏelin. nẏ chemẏd nͅẏͅ haed ud agordin. nẏ phẏrth
mevẏl morẏal eu dilin. llavẏn durawt barawt e waetlin.

Kẏwẏrein ketwẏr kẏwrenhin. gwlat atvel gochlẏ⸗   17
wer eu dilin. ef lladawd a chẏmawn allain a charne⸗
dawr tra gogẏhwc gwẏr trin. ᵶᵶᵶᵶ   ᵶᵶᵶᵶ⁊

Kẏwẏrein ketwẏr kẏuaruuant. ẏ gẏt en vn vrẏt ẏt   20
gẏrchaffant. bẏrr eu hoedẏl. hir eu hoet ar eu carant.
feith gẏmeint o loegrwẏf aladaffant. o gẏvrẏffed gwra⸗

ged gwẏth a wnaethant. llawer mam ae deigẏr ar ẏ ha⸝ 1
Ỻ ẏ wnaethpwẏt neuad mor dianaf lew⸝ . . Ꜩ mrant.
mor hael baran llew llwẏbẏr vwẏhaf. a chẏnon larẏ
vronn adon deccaf. dinaſ ẏ diaſ ar llet eithaf. dor angor
bedin bud eilẏaſſaf. or ſawl a weleiſ ac a welaf ẏ mẏt⸝ 5
en emdwẏn arẏf grẏt gwrẏt gwrẏaf. ef lladei oſwẏd
a llavẏn llẏmaf. mal brwẏn ẏt gwẏdẏnt rac ẏ adaf.
mab klẏtno clot hir canaf ẏtẏ or⸝ clot heb or heb eithaf.
Owinveith a medweith dẏgodolẏn. gwnlleith mam hwr⸝ 9
reith eidol enẏal. ermẏgei rac vre rac bronn budugre bre⸝
ein dwẏre wẏbẏr ẏſgẏnnẏal. kẏnrein en kwẏdaw val
glaſ heit arnaw⸝ heb gilẏaw gẏhaual. ſẏnnwẏr ẏſtwẏr
ẏſtemel⸝ ẏ ar weillẏon gwebẏl ac ardemẏl gledẏual. bla⸝
en ancwẏn anhun hediw an dihun⸝ mam reidun rw⸝ 14
Owinveith a medweith ẏd aethant. .Ꜩ ẏf trẏdar.
e genhẏn llurugogẏon nẏſ gwn lleith lletkẏnt. kẏn llwẏ⸝
ded eu lleaſ dẏdaruu. rac catraeth oed fraeth eu llu. o
oſgoɹd vẏnẏdawc vawr dru. o drẏchant namen vn 18
Owinveith a medveith ẏt grẏſſẏ⸝ .Ꜩ gwr nẏ dẏuu.
aſſant. gwẏr en reit moleit eneit dichwant. gloew dull
ẏ am drull ẏt gẏtvaethant. gwin a med amall a amuc⸝ 21
ſant. o oſgord vẏnẏdawc an dwẏf atveillẏawc⸝ arw⸝

B. A. 15

ŷſ a golleiſ om gwir garant. o drŷchan riallu ŷt grŷſſyaſ⸗
ſant gatraeth⸗ tru namen vn gwr nŷt atcorſant.

Hv bŷdei ŷg kŷwŷrein preſſent mal pel ar ŷ e hu bŷdei.
ene uei atre. hut amuc ododin o win amed en dieding ŷng
ŷſtrŷng ŷſtre. ac adan gatvannan cochre veirch marchawc 5

Angor dewr daen ſarph ſeri raen.   ℭ godrud emore.
ſengi wrŷmgaen emlaen bedin. arth arwŷnawl druſſy⸗
at dreiſſyawr ſengi waewawr en dŷd cadŷawr. ŷg cla⸗
wd gwernin. eil nedic nar⸗ neuſ duc drwŷ var. gwled ŷ 9
adar o drŷdar drin. kŷwir ŷth elwir oth enwir weith⸗
ret⸗ ractaſ rwŷuŷadur mur catuilet merin a madŷein

Ardŷledawc canu kŷman caffat.   ℭ mat ŷth anet.
ketwŷr am gatraeth a wnaeth brithret. brithwŷ a wŷ⸗ 13
ar ſathar ſanget. Sengi wit gwned bual am dal med.
a chalaned kŷuirŷnged. nŷt adrawd kibno wede kŷffro cat⸗

Ardŷledawc canu kŷ⸗ ..   ℭ ket bei kŷmun keui daŷret.
man ovri. twrŷſ tan atharan arŷuerthi. gwrhŷt ar⸗ 17
derchawc varchawc mŷſgi. ruduedel rŷuel a eiduni. gwr
gwned divudŷawc dimŷngŷei ŷ gat. or meint gwlat ŷd
ŷ klŷwi. ae ŷſgwŷt ŷſgwŷt ar ŷ ŷſgwŷd. hut arolli waŷw
mal gwin gloew o wŷdŷr leſtri. arŷant amŷued eur dy⸗ 21
lŷi. gwinvaeth oed waetnerth vab llŷwri.

GRedyf gwr oed Hwn gw e gododin. aneirin ae cant.
gwaſ gwrhẏt am diaſ. meirch mwth mẏngvraſ.
a dan vordwẏt megẏrwaſ. ẏſgwẏt ẏſgauẏn lledan 3
ar bedrein mein vuan. kledẏuawr glaſ glan ethẏ eur
aphan. nẏ bi ef a vi caſ e rof a thi. Gwell gwneif a thi
ar wawt dẏ uoli. kẏnt ẏ waet elawr nogẏt ẏ neithẏa⸗
wr. kẏnt ẏ vwẏt ẏ vrein noc ẏ argẏurein. ku kẏueillt 7
ewein. kwl ẏ uot a dan vrein. marth ẏm po vro llad
vn mab marro.

Kaẏawc kẏnhorawc men ẏdelhei. diffun ẏ mlaen 10
bun med a dalhei. twll tal ẏ rodawr ene klẏwei awr. nẏ
rodei nawd meint dilẏnei. nẏ chilẏei o gamhawn enẏ
verei waet mal brwẏn gomẏnei gwẏr nẏt echei. nẏſ 13
adrawd gododin ar llawr mordei. rac pebẏll madawc
pan atcoꝛẏei namen vn gwr ogant enẏ delhei.

Kaeawc kẏnnivẏat kẏwlat e rwẏt. ruthẏr erẏr en 16
ebẏr pan llithẏwẏt. e amot a vu not a gatwẏt. gwell
a wnaeth e aruaeth nẏ gilẏwẏt. rac bedin ododin ode⸗
chwẏt. hẏder gẏmhell ar vreithel vanawẏt. nẏ nodi 19
nac ẏſgeth nac ẏſgwẏt. nẏ ellir anet rẏ vaethpwẏt. rac
ergẏt catvannan catwẏt.

Kaeawc kẏnhorawc bleid e maran. gwevrawr go⸗ 22

A

diwawr torchawr am rann. bu gwevrawr gwerthva- 1
wr gwerth gwin vann. ef gwrthodeſ gwrẏſ gwẏar diſ-
grein. ket dẏffei wẏned a gogled e rann. o guſſẏl mab ẏſ-
gẏrran ẏſgwẏdawr angkẏuan.

Kaeawc kẏnhorawc aruawc eg gawr kẏn no diw e 5
gwr gwrd eg gwẏawr. kẏnran en racwan rac bẏdinawr
kwẏdei pẏm pẏmwnt rac ẏ lafnawr. o wẏr deivẏr a
brennẏch dẏchiawr. vgein cant eu diuant en un awr. 8
kẏnt ẏ gic e vleid nogẏt e neithẏawr. kẏnt e vud e vran
nogẏt e allawr. kẏn noe argẏurein e waet e lawr.
gwerth med eg kẏnted gan lliwedawr. hẏueid hir et- 11
mẏgir tra vo kerdawr.

Gwẏr a aeth ododin chwerthin ognaw. chwerw 13
en trin a llain en emdullẏaw. bẏrr vlẏned en hed ẏd
ẏnt endaw. mab botgat gwnaeth gwẏnnẏeith gwre-
ith e law. ket elwẏnt e lanneu e benẏdẏaw. a hen a ẏe-
ueing a hẏdẏr allaw. dadẏl diheu angheu ẏ eu treidaw.

Gwẏr a aeth ododin chwerthin wanar. difgẏnnẏ- 18
eit em bedin trin diachar. wẏ lledi a llavnawr heb vawr drẏdar colovẏn glẏw reithuẏw rodi arwar.

Gwẏr a aeth gatraeth oed fraeth eu llu. glafved eu 21
hancwẏn a gwenwẏn vu. trẏ chant trwẏ beirẏant en

2   B. A.

cattau. a gwedẏ elwch tawelwch vu. ket elwẏnt e lanneu
e benẏdu. dadẏl dieu agheu ẏ eu treidu. 2

Gwẏr a aeth gatraeth veduaeth uedwn. fẏrẏf frwẏth⁄
lawn oed cam naſ kẏmhwẏllwn. e am lavnawr coch goʒ⁄
vawr gwrmwn. dwẏſ dengẏn ed emledẏn aergwn. ar 5
deulu brenneẏch beẏch barnaſſwn. dilẏw dẏn en vẏw nẏſ
adawſſwn. kẏueillt a golleiſ diffleiſ oedwn. rugẏl en em⁄
wrthrẏn rẏnn riadwn. nẏ mennwſ gwrawl gwadawl
chwegrwn. maban ẏ gian o vaen gwẏnngwn.

Gwẏr a aeth gatraeth gan wawr trauodẏnt eu hed 10
eu hovnawr. milcant a thrẏchant a emdaflawr. gwẏar⁄
llẏt gwẏnnodẏnt waewawr. ef goʒſaf ẏng gwrẏaf. eg⁄
gwrẏawr. rac goſgord mẏnẏdawc mwẏnvawr.

Gwẏr a aeth gatraeth gan wawr dẏgẏmẏrrwſ eu ho⁄ 14
et eu hanẏanawr. med evẏnt melẏn melẏſ maglawr. blw⁄
ẏdẏn bu llewẏn llawer kerdawr. coch eu cledẏuawr na
phurawr eu llain. gwẏngalch a phedrẏollt bennawr rac 17
goſgoʒd mẏnẏdawc mwẏnvawr.

Gwẏr a aeth gatraeth gan dẏd. neuſ goʒeu o gaden ge⁄
wilid. wẏ gwnaethant en geugant gelorwẏd. a llavnavr
llawn annawd em bedẏd. goʒeu ẏw hwnn kẏn kẏſtlwn 21
kerennẏd. enneint creu ac angeu oe hennẏd. rac bedin

B. A.

ododin pan vudẏd neuſ goɀeu deu bwẏllẏat neirthẏat gwẏchẏd.
Ġwr a aeth gatraeth gan dẏd. ne llewef ef vedgwẏn vei
noethẏd. bu truan gẏuatcan gẏvluẏd. e negeſ ef oɀ dɀach‑
wreſ drenghidẏd. nẏ chrẏſſẏwſ gatraeth mawr moɀ ehe‑
laeth e aruaeth uch arwẏt. nẏ bu moɀ gẏffoɀ o eidẏn ẏſ‑
goɀ a eſgarei oſwẏd tutvwlch hir ech e dir ae dreuẏd.
ef lladei faeſſon feithuet dẏd. perheit ẏ wrhẏt en wrvẏd
ae govein gan e gein gẏweithẏd. pan dẏvu dutvwlch dut
nerthẏd. oed gwaetlan gwẏaluan vab kilẏd.
Ġwr a aeth gatraeth gan wawr. wẏneb udẏn ẏſgoɀ‑
va ẏſgwẏdawr. crei kẏrchẏnt kẏnnullẏnt reiawr en gẏn‑
nan mal taran twrẏſ aeſſawr. gwr goɀvẏnt. gwr et‑
vẏnt. gwr llawr. ef rwygei. a chethrei. a chethrawr. od
uch lled lladei a llavnawr. en gẏſtud heẏrn dur arben‑
nawr. emordei ẏſtẏngei adẏledawr. rac erthgi erthẏ‑
Ovreithẏell gatraeth pan . Ɛchei vẏdinawr.
adr°dir. maon dẏchiorant eu hoet bu hir. edẏrn die‑
dẏrn amẏgẏn dir. a meibẏon godebawc gwerin en‑
wir. dẏforthẏnt lẏnwẏſſawr gelorawr hir. bu tru a
dẏnghetven anghen gẏwir. a dẏngwt ẏ dutvwlch a
chẏvwlch hir. ket ẏvem ved gloẏw wrth leu babir
ket vei da e vlaſ ẏ gaſ bu hir.

B. A.

$\mathcal{B}$laen echeching gaer glaer ewgei. gwŷr gweirŷd
gwanar ae dilŷnei. blaen ar e bludue dẏgollouit vual
ene vwŷnvawr vordei. blaen gwirawt vragawt. ef dẏ⸝
bẏdei. blaen eur a phorphor kein aſ mẏgei. blaen edẏſtra⸝
wr paſc ae gwaredei. gwrthleſ ac euo brẏt ae derllẏdei. bla⸝
en erwẏre gawr buduawr drei. arth en llwrw bŷth hw⸝

$\mathcal{H}$nawr gẏnhoruan huan arwẏ⸝ .. $\mathcal{C}$yr e techei. ⸺
ran. gwledic gwd gẏſgein nef enẏſ brẏdein. garw rẏt rac
rẏnn⸝ aeſ e lwrw budẏn. bual oed arwẏnn eg kẏnted ei⸝
dẏn. erihẏd rẏodreſ. e ved medwawt ẏuei win gwirawt.
oed eruit uedel⸝ ẏuei win gouel. a erueid en arued⸝ aer gen⸝
nin vedel. Aer adan glaer. kenẏn kenit aer. Aer ſeirchẏa⸝
wc aer edenawc. nẏt oed dirẏſ ẏ ẏſgwẏt gan waẏwa⸝
wr plẏmnwẏt. kwẏdẏn gẏuoedẏon⸝ eg cat blẏmnwẏt.
dieſſic e diaſ⸝ divevẏl aſ talaſ. hudit ewẏllẏaſ. kẏn bu cla⸝
wr glaſ bed gwruelling vreiſc. ⸺

$\mathcal{G}$eithi etmẏgant tri llwrẏ nouant. pẏmwnt a phẏm⸝
cant. trẏchwn a thrẏchant. tri ſi chatvarchawc⸝ eidẏn eu
ruchawc. tri llu llurugawc⸝ tri eur deẏrn dorchawc. tri
marchawc dẏwal⸝ tri chat gẏhaual. tri chẏſneit kẏſnar⸝
chwerw fẏſgẏnt eſgar. tri en drin en drwm. llew lledẏnt
blwm⸝ eur e gat gẏngrwn. tri theẏrn maon⸝ a dẏvu o

B. A.

vrython. kynri a chenon. kynrein o aeron. gogẏuerchi ẏn′
hon deivẏr diuerogẏon. a dẏvu o vrython wr well no
chynon farff feri alon.

Eveif ẏ win amed e mordei. mawr meint e vehẏr ẏg′
kẏuaruot gwẏr. bwẏt e erẏr erẏfmẏgei. pan grẏffẏei gẏdẏ′
wal kẏfdwẏreei. awr gan wẏrd wawr kẏui dodei. aeffawr
dellt ambellt a adawei. pareu rẏnn rwẏgẏat dẏgẏmẏnei.
e gat blaen bragat briwei mab fẏvno:′ fẏwẏedẏd ae gwẏ′
dẏei. a werthwf e eneit er wẏneb grẏbwẏllẏeit:′ a llavẏn
lliveit lladei. lledeffit ac athrwẏf ac affrei:′ er amot aruot
aruaethei. ermẏgei galaned o wẏr gwẏchẏr gwned em
blaen gwẏned gwanei.

Eveifẏ win amed e mordei can ẏueif difgẏnneif rann
fin. fawt ut nẏt didrachẏwed colwed drut. pan difgẏnnei
bawb ti difgẏnnvt. ẏf deupo gwaeanat gwerth na phechut.
preffent adrawd oed vreichẏawr drut.

Gwẏr a aeth gatraeth buant enwawc. gwin amed o
eur vu eu gwirawt. blwẏdẏn en erbẏn urdẏn deuawt.
trẏwẏr a thri ugeint a thrẏchant eur dorchawc. or fawl
ẏt grẏffẏaffant uch gormant wirawt nẏ diengif namẏn
tri o wrhẏdri foffawt. deu gatki aeron a chenon daẏra′
wt a minheu om gwaetfreu gwerth vẏ gwennwawt.

Uẏg car ẏng wirwar nẏn gogẏffrawt oneb onẏ bei o
gwẏn dragon ducawt . nẏ didolit ẏng kẏnted o ved gwi´
rawt. ef gwnaei ar beithing peithẏng aruodẏawc. ef dif´
grein eg cat difgrein en aelawt . neuf adrawd gododin gwe´
dẏ foffawt pan vei no llivẏeu llẏmach nebawt.
Arẏf angkẏnnull agkẏman dull agkẏfgoget. trachẏ´
wed vawr treigleffẏd llawr lloegrwẏf giwet. heeffit eif
ẏg kẏnnor eif ẏg cat nereu . goruc wẏr lludw a gwraged
gwẏdw kẏnnoe angheu . greit uab hoewgir ac ẏfberi ẏ
Arwr ẏ dwẏ ẏfgwẏd adan e dalvrith . Cberi creu.
ac eil tith orwẏdan. bu trẏdar en aerure bu tan. bu e´
hut e waewawr bu huan:´ bu bwẏt brein bu bud e vran.
a chẏn edewit en rẏdon gan wlith erẏr tith tirẏon .
ac o du gwafgar gwanec tu bronn. beird bẏt barnant
wẏr o gallon. diebẏrth e gerth e gẏnghẏr:´ diua oed e gẏn´
rein gan wẏr. a chẏnn e olo a dan eleirch vre:´ẏtoed wrẏt
ene arch. gorgolchef e greu ẏ feirch budvan vab bleid´
Oam e adaw heb gof camb ehela´ .. Cvan dihavarch.
eth. nẏt adawei adwẏ ẏr adwrẏaeth . nẏt edewif e´
lẏf lef kerdorẏon prẏdein diw calan ẏonawr ene ar´
uaeth. nẏt erdit e dir kevei diffeith:´ dra chaf aniaf dre´
ic ehelaeth. dragon ẏg gwẏar gwedẏ gwinvaeth gwe´

nabwẏ vab gwenn./ gẏnhen gatraeth. ▰▰▰▰▰▰▰▰▰▰▰▰▰)

Bu gwir mal ẏ meud e gatlew. nẏ deliiſmeirch neb marchlew heeſſit waẏwawr ẏ glẏw. ẏ ar llemenic llwẏbẏr dew. kenẏ 3 vaket am vẏrn am borth./ dẏwal ẏ gledẏual emborth. heeſſẏt onn o bedrẏollt ẏ law./ẏ ar veinnẏell vẏgedorth. ẏt rannei rẏgu e rẏwin./ẏt ladei a llauẏn vreith o eithin. val pan vel 6 medel ar vreithin e gwnaei varchlew waetlin. ▰▰▰▰▰▰▰)

Iſſac anuonawc o barth deheu. tebic mor lliant ẏ deuodeu. o wẏled a llarẏed a chein ẏuet med./ men ẏth glawd e offer e 9 bwẏth madeu. nẏ bu hẏll dihẏll na heu dihen. ſeinnẏeſſẏt e gledẏſ ẏm‾penn mamen. mur greit oed moleit ef mab gwẏdneu.

Keredic caradwẏ e glot. achubei gwarchatwei not. lletvegin iſ tawel kẏn dẏuot e dẏd gowẏchẏd ẏ wẏbot. ẏſ denpo car kẏrd kẏvnot ẏ wlat nef adeſ atnabot. ▰▰▰▰▰▰▰▰▰▰▰▰▰▰▰▰▰)

Keredic caradwẏ gẏnran. keimẏat ẏg cat gouaran. ẏſgw./ 15 ẏt eur crwẏdẏr cadlan./ gwaewawr uſwẏd agkẏuan. kle./ dẏual dẏwal diwan. mal gwr catwei wẏaluan. kẏnn kẏſ./ dud daear kẏnn affan o daffar diffẏnnei e vann. ẏſ denpo 18 kẏnnwẏſ ẏg kẏman. can drindawt en vndawt gẏuan.

Pan grẏſſẏei garadawc ẏ gat./ mal baed coet trẏchwn trẏchẏat. tarw bedin en trin gomẏnẏat./ ef llithẏei wẏd./ 21 gwn oe anghat. ẏſ vẏn tẏſt ewein vab eulat. agwrẏen.

8   B. A.

                                             a gwẏn

Ardyledawc canu claer orchyrdon. a gwedẏ dẏrreith dẏlleinw auon. dimconeſ lovlen benn eryron· llwẏt./ ef gorev vwẏt ẏ ẏſgẏlvẏon. or a aeth gatraeth o eur dorchogẏon. ar negeſ mẏnẏdawc mẏnawc maon. nẏ doeth en diwarth o ƀ 4 barth vrẏthon. ododin wr bell well no chẏnon.

Ardyledawc canu keman kẏwreint. llawen llogell bẏt bu didichwant. hu mẏnnei eng kẏlch bẏt./ eidol anant. ẏr eur a meirch mawr./ a med medweint. namen ene delei o vẏt 8 hoffeint. kẏndilic aeron wẏr enouant.

Ardyledawc canu claer orchẏrdon. ar negeſ mẏnẏdawc mẏnawc maon. a merch eudaf hir dreiſ gwananhon. oed 11 porfor gwiſgẏadur dir amdrẏchẏon.

Dẏfforthes meiwẏr molut nẏuet. baran tan terẏd ban gẏnneuet. duw mawrth gwiſgẏaſſant eu gwrẏm dudet. 14 diw merchẏr perideint eu calch doet. divẏeu bu diheu eu diuoet. diw gwener calaned amdẏget. diw ſadwrn bu divwrn eu kẏt weithret. diw ſul eu llavneu rud amdẏget. diw llun hẏt benn clun gwaetlun gwelet. neuſ adrawd godo 18 din gwedẏ lludet. rac pebẏll madawc pan atcorẏet namen

Moch dwẏreawc ẏ more. Vn gwr o gant ene delhet. 20 kẏnnif aber. rac ẏſtre bu bwlch bu twlch tande. mal twrch ẏ tẏwẏſſeiſt vre. bu golut mẏnut bu lle. bu gwẏar gweilch
            gwrẏmde.

C   17

Moch dwyreawc y meitin. o gynnu aber rac fin. o dywyf
yn tywyf yn dylin. rac cant ef gwant gesseuin. oed garw.
y gwnaewch chwi waetlin. mal yuet med drwy chwer⁄
thin. oed llew y lladewch chwi dynin. cledyual dywal
fyfgyolin. oed mor diachor yt ladei efgar ✓ gwrhaual en
Difgynnwyf en affwyf dra phenn. ny deliit .. ᚃ y bei.
kywyt kywrennin benn. difgiawr breint vu e lad ar gāg⁄
en. kynnedyf y ewein efgynnv ar yftre yftwng kyn go⁄
rot goreu gangen. dilud dyleyn cathleu dilen. llywy lly⁄
vroded rwych ac afgen. anglaf affwydeu lovlen. dyfforthef
ae law luric wehyn. dymgwallaw gwledic dal ✓ oe brid
brennyal. eidol adoer crei grannawr gwynn. dyfgiawr
pan vei ✓ bun barn benn. perchen meirch a gwrymfeirch
ac yfgwydawr yaen. gyuoet o gyuergyr efgyn difgyn.
Aer dywyf ry dywyf ryvel. gwlat gordgarei gwrd⁄
uedel. Gwrdweryt gwaet am irved ✓ feirchyawr am y rud
yt ued. feingyat am feirch feirch feingyat. ardelw lleith
dygiawr lludet. peleidyr en eif en dechreu cat. hynt
am oleu bu godeu beleidryal.
Keint amnat amdina dy gell. ac yftauell yt uydei.
dyrllydei med melyf ✓ maglawr gwryf. Aergynglyf gan
wawr. ket lwyf lloegrwyf lliwedawr. ry benyt ar hyt

ỷd attawr. eillt wỳned klỳwer e arderched. gwananhon 1
bỷt ved. ſavwỳ cadavwỳ gwỳned. tarw bedin treiſ trin:⁄
teỷrned. kỳn kỳweſc daear kỳn goꝛwed:⁄ bỷt oꝛfun godo⁄
Bedin ordỳvnat en agerw. mỳnawc llu⁄ .. ℭdin bed. 4
ỷdawc llaw chwerw. bu doeth achoeth a ſỳberw. nỳt oed
ef wrth gỳued gochwerw. mudỳn geinnỳon ar ỷ helw.
nỳt oed ar lleſ bro pobdelw. an gelwir mor a chỳnnwr.
ỳmplỳmnwỳt ỳn trỳvrwỳt peleidỳr. peleidỳr gogỳmwỳt 8
goglỳſſur heỳrn lliveit llawr en aſſed. ſỳchỳn ỷg gorun en
trỳdar:⁄ gwr frwỳthlawn flamdur rac eſgar.
Dỳffoꝛtheſ cat veirch a chat ſeirch greulet ar gatraeth 11
cochre mac blaenwỳd bedin dinuſ aergi gwỷth gwarth⁄
vre. an gelwir nỳ ſaw glaer fwỳre. echadaſ heidỳn haearnde.
Mỳnawc gododin traeth e annor. mỳnawc am rann 14
kwỳnhỳatoꝛ. rac eidỳn arỳal flam nỳt atcoꝛ. ef dodeſ e diliˢ
ỷg kỳnhoꝛ. ef dodeſ rac trin tewdoꝛ. en arỳal ar dỳwal diſ⁄
gỳnnwỳſ. can lleweſ poꝛtheſ mawrbwỳſ. o oſgoꝛd vỳnỳd⁄
awc nỳ diangwỳſ namen vn arỳf amdiffrỳſ amdiffwỳſ. 18
Ogollet morỳet nỳ bu aeſſawr dỳffoꝛthỳn traeth ỷ en⁄
nỳn llawr. rỳ duc oe lovlen glaſ lavnawr. peleidỳr pwỳſ
preiglỳn benn periglawr. ỷ ar oꝛwỳd erchlaſ penn wedawr
trindỳgwỳd trwch trach ỷ lavnawr. pan oꝛvỳd oe gat:⁄ 22

nẏ bu foawr. an dẏrllẏſ molet med melẏſ maglawr.

Gweleiſ ẏ dull o benn tir adoẏn.aberth am goelkerth 2
a diſgẏnnẏn. gweleiſ oed kenevin ar dreſ redegein.a gwẏr
nwẏthẏon rẏ golleſſẏn. gweleiſ gwẏr dullẏawr gan awr 4
adevẏn aphenn dẏvẏnwal abreẏch brein ae cnoẏn.

Mat vudic ẏſgavẏnwẏn aſgwrn aduaon.ae laſſawc tebe⸗
dawc tra moʒdwẏ alon. gwrawl amdẏvrwẏſ goʒuawr ẏ lu.
gwrẏt vronn gwrvan gwanan arnaw. ẏ gẏnnedẏſ. diſgẏn⸗
nu rac naw riallu. ẏg gwẏd gwaed a gwlat. agoʒdiẏnaw:⸌
caraſ vẏ vudic lleithic a vu anaw.kẏndilic aeron kenhan lew.

Caraſſwn diſgẏnnu ẏg catraeth geſſevin. gwert med ẏg 11
kẏnted a gwirawt win.caraſſwn neu chablwẏſ ar llain.kẏn
bu eleaſ oelaſ uffin. caraſſwn eil clot dẏffoʒtheſ gwaetlin. eſ
dodeſ e gledẏſ ẏg goethin. neuſ adrawd gwrhẏt rac gododẏn
na bei mab keidẏaw clot vn gwr trin.

Gruan ẏw gennẏſvẏ gwedẏ lludet.godeſ gloeſ angheu 16
trwẏ angkẏffret. ac eil trwm truan gennẏſ vẏ gwelet.dẏ⸗
gwẏdaw an gwẏr nẏ penn o draet. ac ucheneit hir ac ei⸗
lẏwet:⸌ en ol gwẏr pebẏr temẏr tudwet. Ruvawn a gw⸗
gawn gwiawn a gwẏget. gwẏr gorſaſ gwrẏaſ gwrd 20
ẏg calet. ẏſ deupo eu heneit wẏ wedẏ trinet. kẏnnwẏſ
ẏg wlat nef adeſ avneuet.

B. A.

Ef gwrthodeſ treſ tra gwẏar llẏnn. ef lladei val dewr   1
dull nẏt echẏn. tavloẏw ac ẏſgeth tavlet wẏdrin. a med rac
teẏrned tavlei vedin. menit ẏ gẏnghoʒ men na lleveri lliawſ
ac vei anwawſ nẏt edewẏt. rac ruthẏr bwẏllẏadeu achledẏva⸝
wr lliveit handit gwelir llavar lleir. ⁂   ⁂ 5
Poʒthloed vedin poʒthloed lain. a llu racwed en ragẏr⸝
wed en dẏd gwned ẏg kẏvrẏſſed. buant gwẏchawc gwede
meddawt a med ẏuet. nẏ bu waret an gorwẏlam enẏd frw⸝
ẏthlam. pan adroder toʒret ergẏr o veirch a gwẏr tẏngẏr
Pan ẏm dẏvẏd lliawſ prẏder prẏderaf fun. .. Etẏnget. 10
fun en ardec arẏal redec ar hẏnt wẏlaw. ku kẏſtudẏwn. ku
caraſſwn kelleic faw. ac argoedwẏſ gwae goʒdẏvnwẏſ ẏ em⸝
dullẏaw. ef dadodeſ ar lluẏd pwẏſ ar lleſ rieu. ar dilẏvẏn go⸝
et ar diliw hoet ẏr kẏvedeu. kẏvedwogant ef an dẏduc ar
dan adloẏw ac ar groen gwẏnn. goſgroẏw gereint rac de⸝ 15
heu gawr a dodet. lluch gwẏnn gwẏnn dwll ar ẏſgwẏt
ẏ oʒ. ẏſpar llarẏ ẏ oʒ. molut mẏnut moʒ. gogwneif heiſſẏllut
gwgẏnei gereint hael mẏnawc oedut. ⁂
Diannot e glot e glutvan. diachoʒ angoʒ ẏg kẏman.
diechẏr erẏr gwẏr govaran. trin odef eidef oed eirẏan. rago⸝ 20
rei veirch racvuan. en trin lletvegin gwin obann. kẏn glaſ⸝
ved a glaſſu eu rann. bu gwr gwled od uch med mẏgẏr o
                                                                                      bann.

B. A.   21

Dienhẏt ẏ bob llawr llanwet e hual amhaual afneuet. 1
twll tal e rodawr caſ ohir gwẏthawc rẏwonẏawc diffrei⸗
dẏeit. eil gweith gelwideint amalet. ẏg cat veirch afeirch
greulet. bedin agkẏſgoget ẏt vẏd cat voꝛẏon⸗ cochro llann
ban rẏ godhet. trwm en trin a llavẏn ẏt lladei garw⸗ rẏbud
o gat dẏdẏgei. cann calan a darmerthei ef gwenit a dan
vab ervei. ef gwenit a dan dwrch trahawc. vn riein a mo⸗
rwẏn a mẏnawc. a phan oed mab teẏrn teithiawc ẏng⸗ 8
gwẏndẏt gwaedglẏt gwaredawc. kẏn golo gwerẏt ar
rud llarẏ⸗ hael etvẏnt digẏthrud. o glot a chet echiawc⸗
neut bed garthwẏſ hir o dir rẏwonẏawc.
Peis dinogat e vreith vreith. o grwẏn balaot ban wre⸗ 12
ith. chwit chwit chwidogeith. gochanwn gochenẏn w⸗
ẏthgeith. pan elei dẏ dat tẏ e helẏa⸗ llath ar ẏ ẏſgwẏd llo⸗
rẏ enẏ law. ef gelwi gwn gogẏhwc. giff gaff. dhalẏ dha⸗
lẏ dhwc dhwc. ef lledi bẏſc ẏng corwc. mal ban llad.
llew llẏwẏwc. pan elei dẏ dat tẏ e vẏnẏd. dẏdẏgei ef 17
penn ẏwrch penn gwẏthwch penn hẏd. penn grugẏar
vreith o venẏd. penn pẏſc o raẏadẏr derwennẏd⸗ or ſa⸗
wl ẏt gẏrhaedei dẏ dat tẏ ae gicwein o wẏthwch alle⸗
wẏn a llwẏuein. nẏt anghei oll nẏ uei oꝛadein.
Neum dodẏw angkẏvwng o angkẏuarch nẏm daw 21

nẏm dẏvẏd a uo trẏmach. nẏ magwẏt ẏn neuad a vei
lewach noc ef ꞏ/ nac ẏng cat a vei waſtadach. ac ar rẏt
benclwẏt pennawt oed e veirch ꞏ/ pellẏnnic e glot pe ͛
llwſ e galch. a chẏn golo gweir hir a dan dẏ warch ꞏ/
dẏrllẏdei vedgẏrn vn mab feruarch. ♦♦♦♦   ♦♦♦♦♦

Ⓖveleẏſ ẏ dull o bentir a doẏn aberthach coel kerth a
emdẏgẏn. Gueleẏſ ẏ deu oc eu tre re rẏ gwẏdẏn. o eir
nwẏthon rẏ godeſſẏn. Gueleẏſ ẏ wẏr tẏlluavr gan
wavr a doẏn a phēn dẏuẏnwal vrẏch bꞏein ae knoẏn.

Ⓖododin gomẏnnaf oth blegẏt . ẏg gwẏd cant en
arẏal en emwẏt . a guarchan mab dwẏwei da wrhẏt
poet gno en vn tẏno treiſſẏt . er pan want mawſ
mvr trin . er pan aeth daear ar aneirin. nu neut
ẏſgaraſ nat a gododin.

Ⓛlech llefdir arẏſ gardith tith ragon tec ware rac go ͛
dodin ẏſtre anhon. rẏ duc diwẏll o win bebẏll ar lleſ
tẏmẏr tẏmoꞏ tẏmeſtẏl. tra merin lleſtẏr. tra merin
llu. llu meithlẏon. kein gadꞏawt rwẏd rac riallu o
dindẏwẏt en dẏuuwẏt ẏn dẏouu. ẏſgwẏt rugẏn
rac doleu trin tal vriw vu.

Ⓓihenẏd ẏ bop llaur llanwet ẏ haual amhal afneuet
twll tal ẏ rodavc caſ ohir gwẏchauc rẏwẏnẏauc dif ͛

B. A.   23

fret . eil with gwelẏdeint amalet ẏ gat veirch ae feirch 1
greulet bit en anẏſgoget bit get uoʒon gwẏchẏrolẏon
pan rẏ godet. trwm en trin allain ẏt ladei gwaro rẏbud
o gat dẏdẏgei gantꞏ' can ẏg calan darmerthei. ef gve
nit a dan vab uruei. ef gwenit a dan dwrch traha⸝ 5
wc. vn riein a moʒwẏn a menavc a chan oed mab
bʒenhin teithiauc. ud gwẏndẏt gwaet kilẏd gwa⸝
redauc . kẏn golo gwerẏt ar grud hael etvẏnt do⸝
eth dẏgẏrchet ẏ get ae glot ae echiauc uot bed goʒ⸝
thẏn hir o oʒthir rẏwẏnauc. 10

Am dʒẏnni drẏlav dʒẏlen am lwẏſ am diffwẏſ dẏ⸝
warchen trihue baruaut dreiſ dili plec hen atguuc
emoʒem ae gulau hem hancai ureuer urag denn
at gwẏr a gwẏdẏl a phrẏdein at gu kelein rein
rud guen deheuec gwenauwẏ mab gwen . 15

Am ginẏav drẏlav dʒẏlen trẏm dwẏſ tradiffwẏſ dẏ⸝
warchen kemp e lumen. ar wr baruaut aſgell vreith
edrẏch eidẏn a bʒeithell goʒuchẏd ẏ lav loflen argẏnt
a gwẏdẏl a phrẏden. a chẏnẏho mwng bleid heb
prēn enẏ lav gnavt gwẏchlaut ene lenṅ︀. prẏtwẏſ 20
nẏ bei marw moʒ em deheuec guenabwẏ. mab gwēn.

Arỿt angkỿnnull ang⸌ ℰman e dechreu gorchan
kỿman dull⸌ twrỿf en agwed. e rac tutvwlch
meuwed. e rac mawrwed. e rac matỿed. pan
yftỿern gwern e am gamgỿrn. e am gamgled. e uoli
ri⸌ alluawr peithliw racwed. ỿd i gwelef⸌ ar hual tref
tardei galled. Dỿgochwiawr a chlot a phor⸌ apheith
a pher. A ruduorua ac ỿmozva. ac eivỿonỿd a gwỿnhei
dỿd kein edrỿffed. Trỿbedawt rawt rac ỿ devawt⸌ eil
dal roffed. Tarỿaneu bann am dal hen bann bv e⸌
drỿffed. Bleid e vỿwỿt oed bleidỿat rỿt enỿ dewred.
Pubell peleidỿr pevỿr prỿt neidỿr⸌ o lwch nadred.
welỿd ỿd wỿt gwelỿdon rwỿt riein gared. Carut vre⸌
idvỿw carwn dỿ vỿw⸌ vur heỿwred. Camhwrawc
darw kwỿnaf dỿ varw⸌ carut dỿhed. Baran moz ỿg
kỿnhorỿf gwỿr⸌ ỿ am gatpwll. ỿmwan bran ỿg kỿ⸌
nwỿt. Tardei donn gỿvrỿngon gowỿdawc bỿt. Ef
gwrthodef ar llwrw peuef⸌ ar llef pedỿt petwar lli
wet. Petwar milet miledawr bỿt. aeffawr ỿn nellt
a llavỿn eg wallt eif obedroz. Gwr gwỿllỿaf o gỿrn
glaf med meitin. Gwr teithiawr o blith porfoz⸌ pozth
loed bedin. Breeỿch tutvwlch baranref doft⸌ benn
gwaed gwin. ỿr med a chwrỿf ỿd aethan twrỿf

D

drof eu hawfin. Gwẏalvan weith er cadw kẏvreith bu kẏ⸗
vẏewin. kẏnan kenon teithvẏw o von ar vreint goꝛllin.
tutvwlch kẏvwlch a oꝛeu vwlch arvann caereu. gan vẏ⸗
nẏdawc bu atveillẏawc eu gwirodeu. Blwẏdẏn hiraeth
er gwẏr gatraeth am maeth ẏſmeu. eu lávneu dur eu
med en bur eu haualeu. Ħrẏſ angkẏnnvll angkẏman
dull twrẏſ neuſ kigleu. Ac ebellẏ e terbẏna.   Ƿeithẏon
ẏ phell gwẏd aval o a⸗   e dechreu gwarchan adebon.
vall./ ny chẏnnẏd dẏual a dẏvall. nẏ bẏd ehovẏn
noeth en yſgall./ pawb pan rẏ dẏngir ẏt ball. A ga⸗
rwn ẏ ef carei anreithgar. nẏ byd marw dwẏweith./
nẏt amſud ẏ vud e areith. nẏ cheri gẏfoſni gẏvẏeith. e
miſ emwẏthwaſ amwẏn. am ſwrn am gorn kuhelẏn.
en adeſ tangdeſ collit. adeſ led buoſt lew en dẏd mit.
Rudvẏt keiſſẏeſſẏt keiſſẏadon./ mein uchel medel e alon.
dẏven ar warchan adebon.   Ebellẏ e terbẏna goꝛ⸗
chan adebon. Ema weithẏon e dechreu goꝛchan kẏn⸗
ei mi brẏtwn pei mi ganwn./ tardei   belẏn.
warchan goꝛchegin. Gweilging toꝛch trẏchdrw⸗
ẏt "trychethin "trychinfwrch. kẏrcheſſit en avon kẏnn
noe geinnẏon. tẏllei garn gaffon./ rac carneu riwrhon.
rẏveluodogẏon. eſgẏrn vẏrr vẏrrvach varchogẏon.

tẏllei ẏlvach gwrẏt govurthẏach. rẏt gwẏnn rac eing⁄
ẏl ẏawn llad.ẏawn vriwẏn vriwẏal⸝rac canhwẏnawl   2
cann.lluc ẏr duc dẏvel difgẏnnẏal a lel⸝ẏ bob dewr
dẏ fel. trwẏ hoel trwẏ hemin⸝ trwẏ   gibellawr a gemin.
ac eur ar dhrein a galar dwvẏn dẏvẏd⸝ẏ wẏnnaffed   5
velẏn. e greu oe gẏlchẏn⸝ keledic ewẏn. med mẏgẏr melẏn.
Ꝫil creu oe gẏlchẏn⸝rac cadeu kẏnvelẏn. Kẏnvelẏn gaf⁄
nar ẏfgwn brẏffwn bar. Goboꝛthẏat adar ar denin dw⁄
ẏar. Dẏrreith grad voꝛẏon ⸝ adan voꝛdwẏt haelon. kẏ⁄ 9
vret kerd wẏllẏon⸝ar welling   dirẏon. teẏrn tut anaw
ẏf men e gwẏnaw ⸝ enẏ vwẏf ẏ dẏd taw. Gomẏnẏat
gelẏn ⸝ ehangfeit ervẏn. Gochawn kẏrd keinmẏn ⸝ ẏw
gwarchan kẏnvelẏn. Goꝛchan kẏnvelẏn kẏlchwẏ wẏ⁄ 13
lat⸝ etvẏn gwr gwned gwẏned e wlat . dẏchiannawr
dewr dẏchianat. eidẏn gaer gleiffẏon glaer kẏverthrẏn⁄
neit.kein dẏ en rud enẏf gwerth ruduolawt ved meirch
eithinẏn neut ẏnt blennẏd. Gwarchan kẏnvelẏn ar   17
ododin neuf goꝛuc o dẏn dogẏn gẏmhwẏlleit . e waẏw
drwn oꝛeureit am rodef poet ẏr llef ẏw eneit. Et mẏ⁄
gir e vab tec vann⸝ wrth rif ac wrth rann wẏr   cat⁄
van colovẏn greit. pan vẏrẏwẏt arveu trof benn cat 21
vleidẏeu buan deu en dẏd reit . trẏ wẏr a thrivgeint

B. A.   27

a thrychant ẏ vreithẏell gatraeth ẏd aethant. or ſawl
ẏt grẏſſẏaſſant uch med meneſtri./ namen tri nẏt at⸝
coꝛſant. Kẏnon a chadreith. a chatlew o gatnant. a min⸝
heu om creu dẏchioꝛant. Mab coel kerth vẏg werth ẏ
a wnaethant./ o eur pur a dur ac arẏant. evnẏvet nẏt
nodet e cawſſant./ gwarchan kẏrd kẏnvelẏn kẏvnovant.

Eman e tervyna gwarchan kynvelyn. Canu vn canuawc a dal pob awdyl oꝛ gododin herwyd breint yng kerd amryſſon. Tri chanu a thriugeint athrychant a dal pob vn oꝛ gwarchaneu. Sef achawſ yw am goffau ene goꝛchaneu riuedi e gwyꝛ a aethant e gatraeth. Noc a dele gwr mynet y emlad heb arveu./ ny dele bard mynet e amryſſon heb e gerd honn. Eman weithyon e dechreu gwarchan maelderw. Talyeſſin ae cant ac a rodeſ breint idaw. kemeint ac e odleu e gododin oll ae dri gwarchan yng kerd amryſſon.

Doleu deu ebẏr am gaer. ẏm duhun am galch
am glaer. gwibde adoer adwẏaer. clodrẏd ke⸝
iſſidẏd kẏſgut. brithwe arwe arwrut. ruthẏr anoꝛ⸝
thwe a uebir. adwẏ a dodet nẏ debit. odeſ ẏnẏaſ
dof ẏ wrẏt. dẏgwgei en arẏf en eſgut. hu tei en⸝

28   B. A

wlŷd elwit. gwr a ret pan dŷchelwit. kŷwelŷ krŷm
dẏ krŷmdwẏn. kẏueiliw nac eiliw etvrwẏn nac em⁄
mel dẏ dẏwal a therwẏn. Tervẏn toȝret tec teithẏ⁄ 3
awl nẏt aruedauc e uolawt. diffrẏderaſ ẏ vraſca⁄
wt. Molawt rin rẏmidhin rẏmenon. dẏſſẏllei trech
tra manon. Diſgleirẏawr ac archawr tal achon ar 6
rud dhreic fud pharaon. kẏueillẏaur en awel ada⁄
wavn. Trengſẏd a gwẏdei neb ae eneu ẏ ar oȝthur
teith teth a thedẏt. Menit e oſgoȝd mavr mur on⁄ 9
wẏd ar voȝ nẏ dheli. na chẏngwẏd gil na chẏngoȝ
goȝdibleu eneit talachoȝ nẏt mwẏ rẏ uudẏt ẏ eſ⁄
goȝ. eſgoȝ eidin rac doȝ. kenan kein mur e ragoȝ. 12
goſſodeſ ef gledẏf ar glawd meiwẏr. budic e ren
enẏ annavd wledic. ẏ gẏnnwithic kẏnlaſ kẏnwe⁄
iſ dwuẏn dẏvẏnveiſ. kẏchuech nẏ chwẏd kẏchwe⁄ 15
rw kẏchvenẏcheſ kẏchwenẏchwẏ enlli weleſ. alen⁄
wiſ miran mir edleſ. ar ẏſtre gan voȝe godemleſ.
hu tei idware ẏngoȝvẏnt gwẏr goȝuẏnnaf rẏ 18
annet. en llwrw rwẏdheu rẏ gollet. collwẏd. med⁄
wẏd menwẏt. gogled run ren rẏ dẏnnit. goȝthew
am dẏchuel dẏchuelit. goȝwẏd mwẏ galwant no 21
melwit. am rwẏd am rẏ ẏſtoflit. Ẏſtofflit llib llain.

B. A.   29

blin blaen blen blenwyd. trybedavt y wledic e
rwng drem dremrud dremryt ny welet y odeu
dhogyn ryd. ny welet y odeu dhogyn fyd moz ere⁄
dic dar digeryd. kentaf digonir can welw kyn⁄. 4
nwythic lleithic llwyrdelw kyn y olo gouudelw
taf gwr mavr y wael maelderw. delwat dieiry⁄
daf y erry par ar delw rwyfc rwyf bre rymun 7
gwlat rymun rymdyre. yfgavl dhifgynnyawd
wlawd gymre nac yfgawt y redec ry gre. godiwe⁄
ud godiwef gwlat vre. ny odiweud o vevyl ve⁄
int gwre.

Da dyuot adonwy adonwy am adauffut. awnelei
vratwen gwnelut lladut llofgut ny chetweift nac
eithaf na chynnoz yfgwn tref dy beuwel. ny weleif
oz moz bwyr moz marchauc avei waeth no od gur.
Gry can eurdozch a gryffyaffant en amwyn bze⁄ 16
ithell bu edzywant ket ry lade hwy wy ladaf⁄
fant a hyt ozfen byt etmyc vydant. ac oz fawl a
aytham ogyt garant. tru namen vn gur nyt 19
Grycant eurdozchauc gwnedgar Cenglyffant.
guacnauc trychan trahaavc kyuun kyuarvavc
trychan meirch godrud a gryffywf ganthud try 22

30   B. A.

chwn a thrychant tru nyt at corfant.

Dywal yg cat kyniwng yg keni. yg kyvrang nyt
oed dang af gwnehei yn dyd gwyth nyt ef weith 3
gocheli. baran baed oed bleidic mab eli. erveffit gwin
gwydyr leftri llavn. ac en dyd camavn camp a wneei.
y ar aruul cann kyn oe dreghi. calaned cochwed 6
Pwyf blaen rydre ferei y gadeu dryll Cae deui.
kedyr cat kein cryfgwydyat. bryt am gozlew 8
diechwith lam y orwylam nat ry gigleu. ef gwneei
gwyr llydw a gwraged gwydw kyn oe agheu. breint mab bleidgi rac yfberi y beri greu. 11
Kein guodeo e celyo ery vyhyr ohanav ar a fyf-
gut af eiryangut. pan efgynnei baub ti difgynnvt
ceuei gwin gwaet meirw meint a wanut. teir 14
blyned a phedeir tutet en vavr yt naer afgym
myrr hut ath uodi gwaf nym gwerth na the-
chut preffent kyuadraud oed breichyaul glut. 17
Pan gyrchei yg kywlat e glot oed anvonavc ef
dilydei win gwr eur dorchauc ef rodei gloyw dull
glan y gwychiauc. ardwyei can wr arwr my- 20
nauc. anvonavc eiffyllut alltut marchauc vn
maban e gian o dra bannauc ny fathravt

B. A. 31

gododin ar glavr foffaut. pan vei no llif llymach   1
Angoʒ deoʒ dain farff faffwẏ graen   **C**nebaut.
anẏfgoget vaen. blaen bedin arall arlwẏ treif tra
chẏnnivẏn. rwẏ gobʒwẏ goʒdwẏ lain. enwir ẏt   4
elwir oth gẏwir weithret. rectoʒ rwẏfẏadur.
mvr pob———kẏuẏeith. tutvwlch treiffic aer
Angoʒ deoʒ dain farph faffwẏ   **C**caer o dileith.
grain. blaen bedin enwir ẏt elwir oth gẏwir   8
gverit. kewir. ẏt[h] elwir oth gẏwir weithret.
rectoʒ rwẏvẏadur mur pob kiwet. merẏn mab
madẏeith mat ẏth anet.   11
Achef guolouẏ glafvleid duuẏr diaf dilin. angoʒ deoʒ
dain anẏfgocvaen em blaen bedin letrud lenir a
meirch a gwẏr rac gododin re cw gẏuarch kywuẏ-
rein bard kemre tot tarth rac garth merin.   15
Scwẏt dan wodef. nẏ ẏftẏngei rac neb wẏneb cared erẏthuaccei dirẏeit oeirch meirch ẏg kẏndoʒ aur
gwrẏavr hein gwaewaur kelin. creudei. pan wa-   18
net ẏg kẏueillt [ef] gwanei ereill nẏt oed amevẏl ẏt
a dẏccei. dẏuit en cadw rẏt kein afmẏccei pan dẏ
duc kẏhuran clotuan moʒdei.   21
Geu   ath diweduf tut leo na deliif meirch

neb march lew kenẏ vaccet am bẏrth ampoʒth oed
cadarn e gledẏual ẏnẏoʒth ur rwẏ ẏſgeinnẏei ẏ onn
o bedʒẏ holl llavɉ ẏ ar vein erch mẏgedoʒth.　　　3

𐌀rdwẏnef adef eidun gwalat. gwae ni rac galar
ac avar gwaſtat. pan doethan deon o dineidin parth
deetholwẏl　　　pob doeth wlat. ẏg kẏwrẏſſed　6
a lloegẏr lluẏd　amhat. nav ugeint am bob vn am
beithẏnat. ar demẏl meirch a ſeirch a ſeric dillat ar⁄
dwẏei waet nerth ·e gerth oʒ gat.　　　　　　　　9

Oofgoʒd mẏnẏdauc pan grẏſſẏaſſant. gloew dull
e am drull ẏt gẏnuaethant. o ancwẏn mẏnẏdauc
handit triſtlavn vẏ mrẏt ⁒ rwẏ e rẏ golleiſ ẏ om
gwir garant o drẏchan eurdoʒchauc a grẏſſẏwſ　13
gatraeth tru namen vn gur nẏt anghaſſant.

Gofgoʒd gododin e ar ravn rin. meirch eiliv eleirch
a ſeirch gwehin. ac ẏg kẏnnoʒ llu lliwet diſgin　16
en amwẏn called amed eidin. o guſſẏl mẏnẏda⁄
uc troſſaſſei ẏſgwẏdaur. kwẏdaſſei lafnavr ar
grannaur gwin. wẏ ceri gon gwẏlaeſ diſgin.　19
nẏ phoʒthaſſan warth wẏr nẏ thechẏn.

Neut erẏueiſ ẏ ued ar ẏg kerdet gwinuaeth rac
catraeth ẏn vn gwaret pan ladhei ae lavnawr　22

E　　　　　　　　　　　　　　　　　　　33

ynyſgoget yn dayr nyt oed wael men yt welet 1
nyt oed hyll ydellyll en emwaret.atwythic ſcyn⸝
dauc madauc eluet.

Pan dei y cyuarchant nyt oed hoedyl dianc dialgur
aruon cyrchei eur ceinyo arurchyat urython bʒowyſ
meirch cynon. Lleech leud   ud tut leu⸝
ure gododin ſtre ſtre ancat ancat cyngoʒ cyngoʒ 7
temeſtyl trameryn leſtyr trameryn lu heidilyaun
In ıneidlyaun let lin lu o dindywyt en dyowu ſcu⸝
yt grugyn iractaryſ trun tal briv bu. 10
Eur ar mur caer criſguitat dair caret na hair
air mlodyat un ſ ſaxa ſeciſiar argouuduit adar
bʒo uual pelloid mirein nyſ adraud a uo byv odam
gueinieit lui odam lun luch liuanat nyſ adraud 14
a uo biu in dit pleimieit na bei cinaual cinelueit.
Dim guoiu eduı o adam neınim un huc an
guoloet guoreu ſdlinet em ladaut lu maur 17
iguert i adraut ladaut map nuithon o eur
doʒchogyon cant o deyrnet hit pan grimbu⸝
iller bu guell prit pan aeth canwyr y gatraeth
oid eilth gur guinuaeth callon ehelaeth oed gur 21
luit eınım oed luric teınım oid girth oed cuall.

ar geuin e gauall ný wifguif ımil ımil luit he 1
inim i guaiu ae ýfcuit nae gledýf nae gýllell
no neim ab nuithon gur a uei well. 3
Ꝥra merin iodeo tri leo ýg caat tri guaid frant
fraiduſ leo bubon a guoȝeu bar deo.
Ᵹnaut i ar fifiolin amdiffin gododin im blain 6
trin terhid rei gnaut illuru alan buan bithei
gnaut rac teulu deoȝ em difcinhei gnaut
mab goliftan cen nei bei guledic itat indeuit 9
a lauarei gnaut ar lef minidauc fcuitaur trei
guaurud rac ut eidin uruei. 11
Ni foȝthint neiri molut muet rac trin riallu
trin oȝthoȝet tebihic tan terýd drui cinneuet.
diu maurth guifgaffant eu cein duhet diu 14
merchýr bu guero eu cit unet diuýeu cenna⸍
deu amodet diu guener calanet a ciuriuet diu
fadurn bu didurnn eu cit gueithret diu ful 17
laueneu rud a at ranhet. diu llun hýt beñ
clun guaet lun guelet nýf adraud gododin
guedý lludet hir rac pebýll madauc pan atcoȝhet.
Difgýnfit in trum in alauoed dwýrem cinte⸍ 21
bic e celeo erit migam guannannon guirth

B. A.

med gurẏt muihiam ac guich fodiauc guichauc
inham eithinin uoleit map bodu at am.

Ӡuir goʒmant aethant cennin gwinweith   3
a medweith oedẏn o ancwẏn mẏnẏdauc anthuim
cim mruinauc o goll gur gunet rin mal taran
nem tarhei fcuẏtaur rac rẏnnaud eithinin.   6

Ḋoch aruireith ımeitit pan crf cinerein imidin
o douif ın towẏf ınilin rac cant em gwant ce⸗
feuin oed moʒ guanauc idinin mal iuet med   9
neu win oed moʒ diachar ẏt wanei efgar uıd
alt guanar gurthẏn.   11

Ḋoch aruireit imoʒe icinim apherẏm rac ſtre
bu ciuarch gueir guiat ıgcin oʒ oʒ cat ciueillt
ar garat ınit gene buguo lut minut bu   14
lee bu guanar gueilging gurẏm de.

Ӡuelet e lauanaur en liwet in ciuamuin gal
galet rac godurẏf ẏ aeffaur godechet techin   17
rac eidin vre uiruiet meint a gaffeilau nẏt
atcoʒẏei ohanau cuir oed arnaᵛ ac canet cindẏ⸗
nnẏauc calc drei pan griniec grıniei nit at   21
wanei ri guanei ri guanet oed menẏch guedẏ
cwẏn i efcar i cimluin oed guenuin hic caraitet

B. A.

a chin iolo atan tit guet daiar dirlifhei etar 1
ıued ıuet. Huitreuit clair cinteiluu at claer
claer cleu na clair air uener fehic am fut feic 3
fic fac adleo gogẏuurd gogẏmrat edili edili
Lui puillẏat nẏſ adraud gododin in dit pleigheit
na bei cinhaual citeluat.   6
Vlafnaur let rudlaun cıuachlud guron guo⁄
rut ẏ maran laun gur leidẏat laguen udat
ſtadal vleidiat bleid ciman luar th teulu la⁄ 9
ur ın ladu cinoidalu ni bu guan enuir ith
elwir od guur guereit rectoꝛ liui dur mur
pob kẏuẏeith tutuwlch treiſſic hair caer   12
Kẏuaruu ac ac erodu leidiat lu ℭ godileit.
hero nẏ bu ac cihoit ac i hero nı bu hero
cıued guec guero gniſſint gueuılon ar   15
e helo nit oed ar leſ bꝛo bot ero ni ciliuſ
taro trin let un ero trauſ ẏ achauſ liuirdelo.
Ef guant tratrigant echaſſaf ef ladhei   18
auet ac eithaf oid gu̇iu e mlaen llu llara⁄
haf godolei o heit meirch e gaẏaf gochoꝛe
bꝛein du ar uur caer cenı bei ef arthur rug 21
cıuın uerthi ig difur ig kẏnnoꝛ guernoꝛ
                                               ℭguaurdur

B. A.   37

Erdyledam canu icinon cigueren ın guanth 1
ac cin bu diuant dileit aeron riuefit i loflen
ar pen erirhon luit en anuit guozen buit
i fglıuon ar lef minidauc marchauc maon 4
em dodef itu ar guaiu galon ar gatraeth oed
fraeth eur dozchogyon wy guenint lledint
feıuogion oed ech eu temyr treif canaon 7
oed odit ımıt o barth urython gododin obell
Erdiledaf canu ciman cafa 𝈢 guell no chenon.
m cetwir am gatraeth ri guanaid brit ret 10
britgue ad guiar fathar fanget fegit guid
gunet dial am dal med o galanet cuıei rig
Let nif adraud cipno guedi kyffro cat ceuei
cımun idau cini daeret. 14
Llithyeffit adar a da am edifmicaf edeuu
niat eithunat aruhicat ef guifguf aur ig
cınnoz gaur ig cin uaran edeiuinieit ballauc
tal gellauc cat tridid engiriaul erlinaut 18
gaur arth arwynaul ar guıgiat guoz vlodi
at riallu eriglunat hir lu ceni bu gipno mab
Erdiledaf canu ciman ci 𝈢 guen gat. 21
guereint llawen llogell bit budit did dr

Foreword.

I read much with ease in Latin, and was bold enough to believe I understood the authors because I missed nothing of the literal sense. Indeed I was very indignant when I heard that Grotius had insolently declared " he did not read Terence as boys do." Happy narrow-mindedness of youth !—nay of men in general that they can ... fancy they know all there is to know, and inquire after neither the true nor the false ... elderly professors deliver on the whole only fixed views, and, in details much that time and research have already condemned as useless and false. Goethe's Autobiography, Bk. vi.

WELSH POETRY is governed by stricter rules of assonance and rhyme than English poetry. When we find the laws of cynghaneδ violated, we know that the text is corrupt. The various irregularities of our source have been examined, exposed, and detailed in the Notes. The rules of the prevailing nine-syllable metre have been deduced from recurring examples in our MS. Those rules have guided the restoration of the text, and every emendation has been subjected to paleographical analysis, while the subject matter has been tested throughout by the historical records of contemporary Chroniclers. The amended text is, therefore, offered with some confidence as an approximation to the original. Verbally correct in every instance it cannot be. Only a monster could produce a perfect work. There are more ways than one of saying the same thing, and the emendation may carry the right sense without always reproducing the *ipsissima verba* of the authors. The majority of the alterations have been worked out almost mechanically by the science of paleography just as one works out mathematical equations. Except in paraphrases, paleography can test the changes, and where it approves we are on ground reasonably safe. This could be demonstrated

BOOK OF ANEIRIN

orally with the help of a blackboard, but lack of type showing the gradations of change make it impractical in the printed page beyond what has been done in the Notes, where the reader must look for the why and wherefore of every emendation. The printed page shows few changes because many italics and brackets would distract attention from the sense, and offend the eye.

As regards the Translation let me call the attention of all that it represents my amended version of the text. To quote the MS. reading where it is corrupt, and contrast it with the English version is misleading & dishonest. The ways of translating are many, and vary from the schoolboy's soul-less Dictionary and Grammar method to that of Fitzgerald's Omar Khayyam. My version of the Gorðin of Mordrei Gwyneð has gone through six phases. First I made a strictly literal word for word rendering of the MS. text, a rendering such as should win full marks from the most pedantic philologist. This made strange, not to say bewildering reading. It was full of mystery, and might have originated in the primal chaos when 'intemperate men turned into leeks,' (Gwir gormant aethant cennin, 36·3 = 80). The effort, however, served to open my eyes to the personal equation of the scribe as manifested in the duplicate versions, variations, inconsistencies, and contradictions in the repeated accounts of the same historical event. It also helped to connect 'Noble Lupus,' 'Hugh' the Proud, & Munc with Mordrei Gwyneð, the site of catraeth. I read up the Chronicles, visited Aber Lleinog time and again, mounted its "large squat stone at high water line" (10·3), and followed the trench from the foreshore pool to the round castle on the rising ground some 350 yards inland. I observed the cynghaneð of the lines that yielded clear sense, and were consistent with the records. I set to work afresh, reducing the limp of many a line where cynghaneð, metre, & sense were faulty. And so I went on clearing up

FOREWORD

the story of the subject matter, regrouping the cantos according to the internal evidence of authorship, and the sequence of events, amending and retranslating the whole, a third, fourth and fifth time. At last I felt that I had grasped the meaning of most of the poetry in all its details of statement and allusion. Then I set about the present translation which aims at producing in the *English* reader the same effect as had been produced in me by a prolonged study of the original. Having realized that there were at least four bards who sang to contending chiefs, their respective bias explained the many inconsistencies. I did my best to enter sympathetically into the feeling of each bard in turn, and to render his exact sense in the most idiomatic English at my command. I imagined Talhaearn, and Llwchvarδ, and (Griffyδ ap) Cynan, and Taliesin living to-day, and singing in English for Englishmen. Every man who uses two languages habitually year in year out, knows perfectly well that he must phrase the same material differently in the two languages, if he wishes to be understood. And if the speaker is a master of the two idioms, neither can be said to be a translation of the other. The structure of Welsh is so different from English that a literal translation of the one is often unintelligible in the other. Where a literal rendering made sound English I practised literalism faithfully, but wherever it darkened the sense I deliberately set it aside, even to the extent of occasionally interpreting the text, and I make no apology. For the scholar I have provided a collotype Facsimile and a reproduction in type so ruthlessly literal that even pedant and pedagogue can find no fault. No serious student need then be led astray by my editorial work and translation. Let him go to the source. If however he sink in a morass he may occasionally be grateful for an extended hand, and for the ballast thrown in to provide a foothold. Mine has been pioneer work, and if it bears traces of its origin, it is some-

BOOK OF ANEIRIN

thing to have waded through the morass, and sketched in outline actors, time and place. No sane man will again pursue sixth century ghosts, for there can be no doubt about Griffith ap Cynan being one of the poets. He sings definitely in the first person as the ' scion of high lineaged Cynan ' ; he sings of his exile, of his foreign accent, of his coming to Mon, of his reception, of his seeking and obtaining men from Robert of Rhuðlan, of the slaying of Cynwric at Clynog, of the repulse of Trahaearn on the Artro, & of his death later on Mynyð Carn in Penvro, of his own ' imprisonment underground ' by Hugh Lupus, of his rescue and the wresting of Castell Aber Lleinog from his ex-gaoler in 1094, of his flight to Ireland before the advent of the earls into Mon in 1098, of the friendship of Mang enabling him to return to the Rhyn in 1099, of his " father-in-law," Owein ap Edwin, commandant of the Rhyn Castle, and of the death of Mang in 1103. Now Griffyð ap Cynan's M*a*ng vel M*u*ng is Magnus, ' The Black King,' (the Du tigirn of Harl. MS. 3859), in whose time flourished Talhaearn and Llwchvarð, and Griffyð ap Cynan. By 1130 when The Additional paragraph was written the youthful Taliesin had shot into prominence, and as he sang to Catraeth his name is included in the list of bards. In 1130 the facts were known ; Griffyð and Taliesin were alive. It is therefore idle to talk grandiloquently about our sixth century Literature. It was Robert Vaughan who first labelled Aneirin & Taliesin ' Cynveirð.' Dr. Owen Pughe extended the list in the ' Myvyrian,' and popularised the use of Cynveirð and Go-gynveirð. This terminology should be left to his echoes, " whose fixed views . . . . research has already condemned as false." The time is coming when enlightened Welshmen will be as much ashamed of the sixth, or ninth century tradition, as we are of those who, a century ago, babbled of Welsh being the ' Language of Paradise.'

Y Gorddin

y Mordrei Gwynedd:

AMENDED TEXT & TRANSLATION.

Now the time is come to ask the strangers who they are . . . Strangers, who are ye? Whence sail ye over the wet ways? on some trading enterprise, or at adventure do ye rove, even as sea-robbers, over the brine, for they wander at hazard of their own lives bringing bale to alien men—ODYSSEY III.

THE GREAT STRAND PUSH

of 1098 at

ABER LLEINOG IN PENMON

attributed to

TALHAEARN

Father of the Muse.

THE FIRST PART OF

'TALHAEARN' LAMENTS

GREÐV gwr oeð ir gwas,
　　gorhydr am ðias;
1　Oeð march mwth myngvras
2　　dan vorðwyd mygrwas,
　　Aes yscavn ledan
4　　ar gledr Mein-vüan,
　　Cleðyv mawr glas-lan,
　　Ethy eur affan.
5　Ni bi, ev a vu
　　　gas y·rov a Hu;
　　Ys gwell y gwneiv,
6　　ar wawd y moliv;
　　Gynt yð aed lawr
　　　nogyd i neithawr;
7　Gynt yn vwyd i rein　　　　15
　　　nog yn argyvrein.
　　Cu gyveill Owein!
8　　cwl i vod dan vein.　　　18
　　Marthwyd ym·Henmon
9　　vu vad yn Aeron.

10　Caeawg Vynyðawg men yð eihei,　21
　　rhac bun oeð ðillyn með ðywallei.
11　Seithid, tal-dyllid yn awr glywei.
12　Y Gynt ni noðynt meint ðilynei,　24
　　(ar ystre sawl ware wy) verei.
13　Mal brwyn yd gwyðyn Rhyd ni giliei.
14　Or ðin, ar gorðin ar lawr Mordrei,　27
　　neb byth rhac pebyll Rhedeg ðelhei.

THE BOOK OF ANEIRIN

THE FALL OF HUGH, e. S.

   THE knight had the spirit of a hero, 1
     He was over-eager for the tumult;
Long-maned was the swift steed,
   which the majestic knight rode;
Light was the broad shield
   on the shoulder of Slender-swift;
Large his purple-glancing sword,
   and wondrous his spurs of gold.
There was, there shall not be
   enmity between Hugh and me;
I shall make amends,
   I will celebrate him in song;
He was sooner gone to the ground
   than to a wedding-feast.
Lances fed upon him   15
   before his funeral rites.
Loved friend of Owein! 't is
   a sin he should be entombed.
He, who was smitten in Penmon,
   had been a blessing in Aeron.   20

   The noble Myny5awg wherever he went was gay,   21
  At the head of his host, he poured out mead.
As he heard the war-shout he was shot, & temple-   23
  pierced. The Norse gave no quarter to his followers,
  but thrusted all who jousted in the arena.
Those who did not quit the Ford fell like rushes.
From the fort, and the push on Mordrei strand,
  none ever came before the tent of Rhedeg.   28

TALHAEARN SINGS

Caeawg cynnivawd cywlad orwyd,
   (pan llynghes yn aches edrychwyd).
1 Rhuthr Eryr yn ebyr ban lethwyd,
17   i arvod a vu nod a gavwyd.
18 Neu·r wnaeth wall arvaeth, ni argelwyd,
   rhac midin gwyr Llychlyn llu drychwyd,
19 Hydr gymhell ar draethell ry·wnaethpwyd,
   Ni ðifferth nac ysceth nac yscwyd.
20 Adver ni aller neb a gollwyd,
   Rhac erwan cor advan ym cadwyd.

BLEIÐ caeawg cynhorawg y·maran,   11
   Gwevrawr gorwychvawr torchawg am rann.
2 Ev ystwyis wrys gwyr ðiscynnan ;
3 Cyd del Wyneð bel, Gogleð i rann.
   O gussyl mad Eryr yscyrran,   15
4 Hyd lawr yscwydawr ys anghyvan.

Arvawg Mynyðawg ðy·vyð yng·awr,   17
   Cyn no diw, yng·wyrðliw, ev gwyðawr.
6 Cyv·lan, yn rhacwan rhac ðywanawr,
7   cwyðwyd ym·hlymnwyd lu ymlaðvawr.   20
   Gwyr Deivr a Brynneich a ðychïawr,
8 Ubein cant yn·ivant yn un awr,
9 Cynt yn lleid yð eithid no neithawr,
   a chynt beynt yn vwyd rhein no llywawr.   24
10 Cyn prein argyvrein wy ðygrein lawr,
11 Gweith með yng·hynteð trang lliwedawr.
12 Hyder edmyger tra vo cerðawr,
   (Caeawg Vynyðawg) hir (vyð glodvawr).   28

OF BATTLE STRAND

The noble one, having molested the near country, 1
 was resting (when a fleet in the offing was espied).
Crushed the Eagle, as he rushes into the water meets,
 His overthrow was an object that was gained. 4
He blundered in his strategy, no shelter was taken,
Before the Norse ships his host was cut down.
Ruthless pressure on the sand-bank was applied,
  Nor spear nor shield gave protection.
  Not one of the lost can be restored,
From the thrusting of the strange force I was saved.

NOBLE Lupus is now leading in the struggle,
 Very magnificent amber beads encircle his brow, 12
He checked the violence of those disembarking,
Though he comes to Gwyneð's war, Gogleð is his part.
By the counsel of their good prince they fiercely fight,
Along the ground their shields lie shivered.

Clad in mail Mynyðawg comes into the battle, 17
 Ere day, in the green-hued dawn, he is felled.
Along the bank, thrusting against chance comers,
 the fiercely fighting host, struggling, fell. 20
The men of Deira & Bernicia are downcast,
Within an hour one hundred lie moaning in their ruin.
Sooner into the mud they went than to a wedding feast,
And they were sooner food for lances than rulers. 24
They crawl on the ground ere the feast of the funeral rites,
Because of mead at the court the host perisheth.
Courage will be admired while a minstrel lives,
 and noble Mynyðawg will long be famous. 28

TALHAEARN DESCRIBES

VYNG·HAR, yng·orwarth, niw gogyffrawd,   1
    onid o Wyndyd dragon ðygawd.
7 Pei di·dolid ni o wŷd gwirawd
3   gwnäem ar Voryen boen arvodawg.
   Hu grein o vael rein yn ael drawd,
5 Pan iach nid llymach cleðyv nebawd.

    Ꮐarw rhyd! rhy·vriwid Hu dan i daleith,
11   Gynt oe leith orwyðan,
    Bu trydar (rhwng Rhyd a glann),
    Yn aer·vre bu go·varan.
12   Bu ehud wawr, bu vuan,
    Bu vwyd rhein, bu ruð i rann ;
 A chyn edir yn rhychdon yngolithr
    Eryr ruthrei dirion,
14 Ac o dywasc gwaneg dwnn vronn
   Beirð a varnant wyr o gallon.   16
   Dïen yrth yn gerth i gynghyr,
15   Divawyd i gynrein gan vyr.
 A chyn golöyn ðeu alarch Gweryd,
    oeð wrhyd yn i arch,   20
16   Gorolches i greu i varch,
   Cuð man Bleiðian di·havarch.

    Ꮯam vu adaw Hu yn ehelaeth drei,
    am na bei adwraeth ;   24
20   Ceris i lys lês cerðoriaeth,
    .Prydan ðiw Calan i arvaeth.
21 Y tir nid erðir yd vyð di·vaeth
   dra chas anialwch, tranc ehelaeth.   28
22 (Gwaeth Mon heb) ðragon wedy gwinvaeth,
8 Madw gwenn, celein wen, o gynhen traeth.

THE BATTLE OF THE STRAND

My Friend, in great disgrace, will not budge,   1
    unless from Gwyneð he shall bear the dragon.
Were we weaned from the lure of the drink
    we could inflict on Morien a timely punishment.   4
Hugh, after the iron dart enters his brow, lies grovel-
    ling, When alive no man's sword was sharper.

Fatal the Ford, Hugh was wounded below his coronet,
    Because of his death (the Norse) are conquering,   8
    There was tumult twixt ford and bank,
        and on the hill the battle raged.
    Hugh was foolhardy in his haste at dawn,
He was food for lances, his cheek was crimsoned ;
And though the Eagle, that attacked the district, is left
        gently swaying in a furrow of the sea,   14
    and the wave pounds upon his breast,
    the bards will decide who are men of spirit.
    Violent death certainly ends his counsels,   17
    His leaders were devoured by the seas.
And ere they surrounded the two Swans of Gweryd
    Bravery was in its coffin,   20
    His blood drenched his steed,
    Hidden the (resting) place of the Lupusian bold.

'Twas wrong to leave Hugh on the spacious strand
    for there had been no cowardice ;   24
    His court loved to promote minstrelsy,
    On New Year's day they will praise his prepar-
        ations. Land untilled becomes unproductive,
    a disagreeable wilderness, a growing waste.   28
Worse, Mon is without a dragon after the banqueting,
Inert the hero, a white corse, after the strife of the strand.

MAGNUS ARRIVES

⁸ Gwir, mal y með vyng·har Tew,
2   ni ðelïis neb marchawg glew.
3 Tevlid gwaewawr gan y glyw
    y·ar lemenig lwybr ðoðyw.
4 Cyn ni vacced am vyrn borth,
    dywal gleðyval yniorth.
5 Heyessid onn bedryollt,
    o law Mein bu erch y bollt.
6 Yd rannei gu i rewin,
    Yd laðei ŵraeth gorllin.
7 Val pan ðel lliv ar vreithin
    y gwnäei Marthlew waedlin.

Compare with the

³² Geu, ath ðywedws uð Tew,
22   na ðelïis neb marchawg glew.
33 Cyn ni vacced am byrth porth,   15
2   Cadarn cleðyval yniorth.
3   Rhwyv y ar veinc a vliv erch vollt,
2   ac yscein onn bedryollt.   18

Deu·r ðoeth cyvwng o ang·hyvarch
    ðiscyn, Ni ðaw i·n vyð trymach,
23 Ni vagawð neuað vei lewach,   21
2   nac yng·hâd a vei wastadach.
Yn Rhyd y byryid oeð y·ar varch (gweðig),
3   Pellynnig pwys i galch,   24
4   Cyn golohid a dan dywarch,
    Derllyðer cyrn tëyrn ffyrvach.

UNANNOUNCED

'Tis true, as my Fat friend saith,
   No one caught the brave knight.
Spears were hurled by the prince
Who on a wandering course had come.
Ere support was organised about the burn
   fierce was the sword-play opposing.
Showered were the ashen quarrels,
From Magnus's hand terrible was the bolt.
It consigned the loved to ruin, and
   destroyed the manhood of a superior race.
As when a flood comes with showery weather,
   so the brave Smiter caused blood to flow.   12

preceding canto.

Falsely the Fat lord told thee that
   no one caught the brave knight.
Ere support was organised about the haven
   mighty was the sword-play opposing.   16
The King from the rowers' bench shoots the
   fell bolt, and scatters ashen quarrels.

The trouble arose from arriving unannounced,
     Nothing sadder can come to us,   20
   No hall fostered a braver one,
     nor was there a steadier in battle.
At the Ford was thrown the rider of a fine horse,
   His armour weighs down this wanderer,   24
Ere he was covered beneath the sod, emptied
are the horns of the Tyrant of great girth.

SOME ARE CUT DOWN

TRYCHAWG eurdorchawg a gyrchassant,   1
   Wy amwyn y Rhyn yn vu drywant.
30 Cyd nad ry·laδad, wy laδassant,
18   a hyd δiweδ byd mygeδ vyδant.
   Or amhad aetham o vaeth garant
19   namyn y dengyn nid enghyssant.

Trychawg trahäawg, dragon arvawg,   7
20 Trychawg eurdorchawg gwleδgar gwancawg,
22 Trychawg meirch truδawg ganthuδ gryssiant,
   Ar sawl athrychawr ni δychwelant.   10

33 **G**wyr arvawg Mynyδawg ban vyδant
10 y·am drull, gloew y dull yd gydvaethant.
   Or ancwyn yn asswyn crysassant,
12 Handid trist vy·mryd, (rhac) y rhyd (ant),   14
   Y·meis rhwy golleis om hoff garant,
14 Namyn y dengyn nid enghyssant.

15 **C**arant odoδant y·ar δy·lann Rhyn.
   Yng·wyδveirch eil eleirch yδ elhyn.   18
16 Yng·orlliv dymhor lliwed δugyn,
   a mwyn wrageδ twyn a meδ eiδyn.
18   O gussyl pennawr   21
     drosassei aesawr,
     gwyδassei lavnawr,
19   ar gronn gaer Rhyn,
    Cein (wys esgynnwys)   25
    i Gonwy hwylwys ;
20   Gwarth neb ni phorthwys,
    gweith na thechyn.   28

WHILE OTHERS DEPART

Cut down the nobles that rushed to the attack,
  They defend the Rhyn till there was a breach.
As long as they remained unslain they slew,   3
  and to the world's end they will be honoured.
Of the mixed races, as fostered friends, that
  we went, only the villeins escaped.

Cut down was the haughty armed dragon,   7
Cut down were the nobles, greedy lovers of feasts,
Cut down the spurred horses that gallopped with
  them, And such as are cut down will not return.

Mynyðog's armed men when they gather around
  the store of liquor, vivaciously drink together.   12
From the feast they rushed elated (advancing
  to the Ford), hence my soul is sad.
In the shallows I lost too many of my friends—
  the villeins alone escaped.   16

Friends melt away from the Rhyn coast,
In ships like swans they sail away. At the time
  of high tide they carried away the peasants, the
  charming women of the fort, and their mead.
      By the counsel of the Commandant,   21
      who had reversed his shield,
      and thrown down his arms
      at the round fort of the Rhyn,   24
      The fine folk embarked
      and sailed to Conwy:
      They were without reproach,
      for they had never flinched.   28

FEASTING BEFORE BATTLE

GWRAETH weis catraeth, bann adroðir,
  Mäon (ðeuyn Von) eu hoed vyð hir,
4 Oeðyn ði·eðyrn amygyn dir,
18   (rhac pleid Edwin) veib, gwerin enwir,
  ðy·phorthyn wys (Llych)lyn olochir,
20 Ys tru dynghed vu angheu gerir.
  Með yvem yn llawen wrth babir,
22 Cyd vei da vlas crei, i gas vyð hir.

33 Yng·wleð yvem veð ar yn cerðed, Gwin-
22   vaeth rhac catraeth in vu warthred.
  Ban laðawr vu yscawl niw yscoged,
34 Yn aer nid oeð wael men y daered.
1 Neud oeð hyll i gyllyll ban golled,
2 Mynawg escyn rawd, (awn yn) Elved.

    15   O win a međweith
        di·doled Cynlleith,
    10 Mawr hyrðieith Roger yn Ial.

      Ermyged ware
        rhac bronn Buðugre,
    11 Rhein vyriei yr wybr escar.

      Cynrein yn cwyðaw
    12   val glas heid arnaw,
    Heb giliaw yn gyhaval.

      Ffynn ffwyr yng·hyvyl
    13   y·ar weillion gweryl,
    Ae arðelwy gleðyval.

    14   Blaen ancwyn a·n hun,
        Heðiw a·n di·hun,
    15 Mawr eiðunwn rwyv trydar.

WAS OUR UNDOING

THE hardihood of Catraeth knights will be trumpeted
 The grief of the vavasours who came to Mon will last
They, who were without a prince, defended their land [long.
 against the party of the sons of Edwin, the false fellows,
 who supported the Norsemen that were welcomed ;   5
A sad fate had befallen, the death of one that is loved :
We (oft) drank mead merrily together by rush-light,
Though good the taste when fresh, long the revulsion.

At a feast we drank mead on our expedition,   9
Wine feasting ere the battle of the Strand was our undoing.
When he who had been active was slain he was not removed,
In battle he was not futile when thrown to the ground.
 Ugly were his blades when he was lost,
 The Palatine boards his flotilla, we go to Elved.   14

 By feasting on mead and wine
  Cynlleith was sequestered,
 Great the thrusting of Roger in Yale.

 His jousting was admired   18
  in front of Buðugre,
 The darts he hurled shut out the sky.

 His captains fall upon it
  like a virgin swarm of bees,   22
 Bee-like they do not retire.

 His attack prospers within reach
  of the darts of the cross-bow,   25
 Whoso challenges him he smites with the sword.

 At first the feast soothes us to sleep,
  but to-day it rouses us awake,   28
 We long greatly for control of the clamour.

END OF TALHAEARN

15 O wleð gwin a með yð aethom yn llu,
16   genhym llurygogion,
Nis gwyr Gynlleith wynnieith Mon,
Y Gynt (ðisgynnynt arnom).

17 Gan las y dyð llas a ðyvu gatraeth,
     ban oeð ffraeth y maeth·lu,
18 Gosgorð Mynyðawg, ys mawr dru!
O gant namyn un ni ðyvu.

19 O winweith a meðweith yd veðwant,
Ðyð rheid ev ni cheid neb di·chwant,
21 Y·am drull, gloew y dull, yd gynnullant,
Rhac beð gwin a með niw amucsant.
22   Goscorð Vynyðawg
          gwyð yn adveilawg,
Rhwyð weis a golleis om hoff garant.

From wine and meadfeast we went in a crowd,
        wearing our coats of mail,   17
    Cynlleith wots not of the havoc of Mon,
        The Norse swooped down upon us.
At grey dawn were slain those who came to Catraeth
        when the well-fed host was merry,
    Of the retinue of Mynyðawg, great is the pity,   22
        but one returned out of a hundred.

By feasting on mead and wine they got drunk,
On the day of stress none was found abstemious,
Around the liquor they beamingly assemble,   26
Wine and mead did not save them from the grave.
        The retinue of Mynyðawg
            crumbles away,   29
Fine fellows I lost from among my loved friends.

Y Gorddin

y Mordrei Gwynedd:

AMENDED TEXT & TRANSLATION.

Now the time is come to ask the strangers who they are . . . Strangers, who are ye? Whence sail ye over the wet ways? on some trading enterprise, or at adventure do ye rove, even as sea-robbers, over the brine, for they wander at hazard of their own lives bringing bale to alien men—ODYSSEY III.

THE GREAT STRAND PUSH

of 1098 at

ABER LLEINOG IN PENMON

attributed to

LLWCHVARDD

the bard of

i. *Hugh, earl of Shrewsbury*

ii. *Cynon, alias Owein ap Edwin*

THE SECOND PART OF

THE EXPEDITION

𝔊EITHIEID a vudant,
Trylwyr yd voriant,
5 Penmon ban ðoethant,
18 Trychyn athrigant,
Tri ffin gadvarchawg,
Eiðyn eurwychawg,
19 Tri llu llurygawg,
Tri thëyrn torchawg,
Tri marchawg dywal,
  gyvneid rhac casnar.
Tri char cyhaval
21 chwerw ffyscynt escar.
Tri yn·hrın yn drwn
  (un a las gan Vwng)
22 Deu dëyrn väon
  ðyvu i Benmon— 16
6 Uchtryd ac Owein,
1 cynrein y Ceinnyon,
5 Wy leðyn yn vlwng
21 yn y Gaer Gyngrwn, 20
6 Deivr ðifferogion
1 gyv·nerthid yn hon,
2 Ni ðaeth o Aeron
  wr well no Chynon 24

Ban Mon dreið dëon Eiðyn ystrad,
33 Odiaethol wys aeth ðiffwys y wlad.
6 Yng·hywryseð Hu lüeð amhad, 27
Naw ugein ceith ðug o beithynad.
8 Arðel veirch serig-seirch devig gwlad,
Ardwy ae nerthwy yn gerth ir gad. 30

THE BOOK OF ANEIRIN.

SAILS TO PENMON

THE expedition moves off,
  They sail to the last man,
When they came to Penmon
  they slew the inhabitants.
Three border knights of battle—
  the gold bedight ones of Eiδyn,
Three mailed hosts,
Three torque-wearing princes,
Three fierce knights rise together,
  against a hateful lord.
Three allied friends rushed
  desperately on the foe,
Steadfast the three in action—
  (One was slain by Magnus),
Two princes of the vavasours   15
  came to Penmon—
Uchtryd and Owein,
  captains of the men of Ceint.
They slew angrily
  in the circular castle—   20
Deira's defenders
  were fortified in this.
There came not from Aeron
  a better man than Cynon.   24

When the nobles of Eiδyndale penetrate Mon,
  The notable people resorted to wild places.
In the incursion Hugh enhosts many races,   27
Nine score captives he brought from the clearings.
He seizes the native prince's silk caparisoned steeds,
And leads his own supporters resolutely to battle. 30

LLWCHVARDD DRINKS

10   Rhaclym i waewawr,
14   calchdrei i aesawr,
      Rhyssei liwedawr
      rhac buan varchawr.
15 Adwythig ðyð gwyth oeð i lavnawr,
    Yn Rhyd ban gryssid gan wyrð y wawr.

6   Yveis win a með
13   y·Mordrei Gwyneð.
14 Gan weis yd yveis rann lywian dud,
    A thra chyveð wnaeth goleð wŷn drud ;
15 Cryssem ban (Vorien) ðiscyn yn Rhyd,
    Caffad gwae anvad gweith na thechid. 12

    38 Illithiessid dâr,
    15   a da onn bâr
        oðis mignad ;
    16 O ðy·vyriad,   16
       yn ethrinad,
        tal a rwygad.
      Hu gwyðws lawr,
    17   yng·hynnor gawr,   20
       yng·hynvaran.
      Dewin balawg,
    18 Tad llad cellawg,
       (a ðarogan)   24
      Dri dyð ingawl,
    19 Gawr arwynawl
    18   yð erlynan.
    19 Annog gwychrad,   28
      A gorvloðiad
    20   Rhi erglywad.
      Hir o gibno
       cyn bu dan do,
    21   madw wenn ganad.   33

AT MORDREI GWYNEDD

Sharp pointed his spears,
 Enamelled his shields,
He flustered the people,
 at the head of his swift knights.
Destructive on the day of wrath were his blades at
the Ford, when it was rushed at the green dawn.

I drank wine and mead
 at Gwyneδ's great strand.
With knights I drank of the store of the country's
ruler, & heavy drinking bred a reckless spirit;
We rushed when Morien was arriving at the Ford,
There was terrible woe, because no shelter was taken. 12

Bolts of oak and of
 good ash were shot,
  below the swamp;
By the hurling, in the 16
 fighting, a forehead
  was lacerated.
Hugh fell down, at the
 raising of the war shout, 20
  in the forefront.
A bald-headed divine,
A blessed hermit father,
 vaticinates that 24
For three awful days
 the terrible fighting
  will be pursued.
The incitement to bravery 28
 and the loud shouting
  of the King was heard.
'Twas long after the feast ere
 the hero was under cover,
He that is still was praised. 33

THE BOLT OF KING MAGNUS

10 **Y**S tryn y discyn yng·hysevin,
17 Ergyr Rhi yscyr vriw Gyvrenhin.
20 Gweith meδ yng·hynteδ a chyveδ gwin,
18 hudid i wrhyd i lwrw rewin.   4
21 Tavlawr Mwng lavnawr rhwng dwy vyδin,
17 Gormes δīosces, ev dorres δin.

11 Điscynnyn trwn gyrchyn Alarchawr,
 1 Wy δylein lu cynrein escynawl.
 2 Rhac biw y rhi vriw Veli vloeδvawr
 3 y·min gwyal-ffin penffestinawl.
   Cyn llwyd dillyngwyd y·ar gynghorawr,
 4 I amws a ruthrws eurdorchawr.
   Gorug Trwch ovud, cyrch ystre gawr,
 6 Cam teiling ys deil yn ystrywiawl.
   Elwid i wynvyd   i vri ledawr,
 7 Yn Rhyd y crymid y gan waewawr.   16
   Car Mon a Mannan a glud glod vawr,
 8 Cynhennid na byδid lüyδ lawr.
10 Y rhawg argyrchawd yn erch orδin   19
22   eδyw, moleid yw mygreid Darw Trin.

   16 **Ƕ**u yng·hywyrein vyδei,
    3 Mal bela yδ ymlaδei
    4   yn y deuei adre.
       Hu rhac gallu Mwng orδin,   24
       Ev δy·adei veδ a gwin
    5   er ystrin ar ystre.
       Dan Gâr Vannan oeδ coch·re
    6   veirch marchawg druδed vore,   28
       (ban gyrchawδ vid δwyre).

   13 **Ɖ**i mad wanpwyd yscwyd,
   15   ar gynwan y cornwyd.
   16 Ni mad δodes vorδwyd
       ar gevn Meinvuan llwyd.   33

20

STRIKES DOWN HUGH THE PROUD

FIERCE the descent from the first, The
   shooting of the King's arrow wounds Cyvrenhin.
Because of mead at the court and wine-bibbing
   his valour was tempted to headlong ruin.
Magnus hurled his darts atween the two armies,
He threw off the invasion & breached the fort.
They that landed fell heavily upon the (Dee) Swans.
They slay a host of the retreating chiefs. In front of
   the motley herd the King wounds the loud-shouting
   war-lord near the brow-line made by his helmet.
Before dusk he was released from the councils,
His charger plunged among the noble torque-wearers.
Hugh the Fat made trouble ; he goes to the arena
   and cunningly checks an enveloping movement.
Spread is the praise of one called to Paradise,
At the Ford he was bowed down by the spears.
The friend of Mon and Man bears great glory,
It was destined that none should muster the land.
Shortly the one assailed in the terrible gorðin left,
Praiseworthy is the majestic Bull of Battle.

  In whatever expedition Hugh might be,
    he would fight like a brock
      until he should turn home.
    Hugh pushes against the force of Magnus,
    He had quitted mead and wine
      for the tumult of the joust.
    Under the Friend of Man were the steeds
      of the knight thrust in the morning,
        (when he rushed upon the ship just come).

  His shield was not pierced for his good,
    At the first onset he was gored.
    Nor was it for his good that he
      bestrode his grey Slender-swift.

THE DOWNFALL OF

13 Tyrr i baladr yn ðellt,
17 ae avlach gyll obell.
 Y mae dewr yn i gell,
 yn cnoi graeanell.
18 Boed in vuð, boed o law,
 ac iðaw boed yn well.

25 Gwr ðywallas,
19 yng·hyrn hirlas,
 veð y·mei-ðin;
20 Gwr teithïol,
 o barth Porffor,
 borth lüeð din.
21 Bryneich dud bost,
 o varan tost,
 berei waedlin.
22 Er með ar cwrw 16
 yð aethan lwrw
 dros yr hal-ffin.
 9 Tarian ev bann,
 ae bar herian, 20
 bu gywrysseð.
10 Blawð i vywyd,
 Oeð leiðiad Rhyd
 yn i ðewreð. 24
11 Rhuðell beleidr
 bevran bryd neidr
 o luch nadreð.
17 Ev wrthodes 28
 ar·llwrw peues,
 arves beðyd.
18 Parwar lliwed
 ban y gweled
 midawr yn rhyd. 33

HUGH THE PROUD

He shivers his lance,
  and loses his seat.
The brave one is in his cell
  biting the fine sand.   4
May we have blessings out of hand,
  And may he fare better.

The hero poured mead
  into hirlas horns
    at the field fort;
A perfect hero
  from the Pulford part
    supports the garrison.
The pillar of Bernicia,
  from furious rage,
    caused blood to flow.
Because of mead and ale   16
  they went headlong
    beyond the marsh.
He uplifts his targe and
  brandishes his spear—   20
    violence ensued.
Tempestuous his life,
He was cut off at the Ford
  full of bravery.   24
He crimsons javelins,
  which gleam snake-like,
    with the radiance of snakes.
He was stemming the rush   28
  upon the country—
    He armed the infantry.
The crowd was struck dumb
  when the ships were seen
    at the Ford.   33

CYNON SUCCEEDS

25   Aesawr yn nellt,
19   a bliv yd bellt
          eis gobedryd.
Hu varan yng·hyn-fflam gwŷd y·am rac-
15   bwll, Ymwan dwll i gynbryd,   5
     Tarδei gyvryngom donn (δybryd),
     Gorwyδawg (wr gwyδwyd ym)hŷd.
13   Car, gŵreiδ lyw,   8
      Carwn i vyw—
        mur heywreδ.
14   Camhwrawg Darw,
      Cwynav i varw,
        Carav i veδ.
      Dy·gollitor
       a chlod a phor,
         a pharth Gwyneδ.   16
      Ar (Bleiδ) vordwya,
       hyd y·morva
        (y·ar Erch Heleδ).
26   Dug Vynyδawg,   20
 4   vu adveilawg,
        o'r gwin ar meδ.
      Gwyalvan weith,
       er cadw cyvieith,   24
      vu gyviewin.
      Canav Gynon,
      Rheith-lyw ar Von,
        o vreint gor·llin.   28
25   Arv ang·hynnull,
 1   Anghyman δull,
        torv yn agweδ.
      Twrv rhac meδweδ,   32
      Twrv rhac marweδ,
       Twrv rhac madreδ.

TO THE COMMAND

The shields are shivered,
The cross-bow projects
squarish arrows.
Hugh appears in a blaze of passion beyond the
fore-ground pool, jousting pierces his front,   5
A tragic wave leapt between us,
The mounted hero fell into the pit.
My Friend, the manful Captain,
I would love him to live,
the bulwark of hardihood :
A champion bull,
I grieve for his fall,   12
I'll cherish his grave.
Utterly lost are
both tame and lord, &
the Gwyneδ country.   16
And (Lupus) sails away,
as far as the marsh
(above Erch Heleδ.)
He bore away Mynyδ-   20
awg who had fallen
because of wine and mead.
The ultimate action, for
the sake of the natives,   24
was drawn.
I shall praise Cynon, the true
prince over Mon, by the
prerogative of the over-lords.   28
He arms the stragglers,
He marshals the broken ranks,
a mere crowd in appearance.
He thunders against drunkenness,   32
He thunders against slackness,
and against degeneracy.

25

WANTONNESS SWAYS

25 Gweledyð wyv,
12 Gwerydon rhwyv
    Rhïein gareð.

4 Pan ystern gwerin
  am eu cam drin
    ae cam goleð.

5 Hyd y gweleis,
  o'r hual-dreis
    tarðei gareð.

7 Ar Henevyð
  a gwynei ðyð
    cein edrysseð.

8 Trybeðant rawg
  rhac y ðevawd—
    eil dal rosseð.

5 Y teithawl Ri,   16
  Llyw (marini),
    volyn rhacweð.

26 Rhac uð Cyv·lwch,
3 Ev oreu vwlch   20
    ar vann caereu.

6 Er i lavn dur
  er·veðyn byr
    yn hualeu.   24

4 Vlwyðyn, bu aeth
  am wyr catraeth,
    ae maeth ys meu.

33 **A**r dwm eiðunwn aðev a gwlad, 28
4   Rhac galar am escar yn wastad.

18 Ceint nad ; amðivad vyng·hell
20   vyðei iðaw ystavell.   31

THE MEN OF GWERYD

I am an eye witness
  that wantonness sways
    the men of Gweryd.

Wherefore the people are restless   4
  under unjust treatment,
    and an unjust regime.

As far as I could see, trouble
  arose from repressive
    acts of oppression.

And the Elders kept
  lamenting the day
    of sweet plenty.

They stand firm for a time
  against the (new) customs—
    (Cynon) avenges excesses.

Before his face they   16
  praised the roving King,
    Captain of the sea host.

Against the lord of Cyvlwch
  Magnus had made a breach   20
    on the ramparts.

But despite his steel blade,
  they carried lords
    away in fetters.   24

For a year there was sorrow
  for the men of Battle-strand,
    whose cherishing is mine.   27

On the hillock I longed for home and country,
  Because of grief at partings constantly.

I have sung a lament; empty my cell
  that served him as a chamber.   31

ENSNARING MEAD

18 Yvyn veð melyn maglawl yng·wrys
21   cyn aer gryssyn gan wawr,
22   Cyd glwys oeð vrwysc Loegr liwedawr,
    Rybenyd ar hyd ðy·attawr.   4
19 Eillt Gwyneð erchyn noðeð Gwenn Vannon,
1   (mab Hakon), byr (gam) veð,
    Savwy gadavwy wŷneð,
    Tarw Trin, treis dryn dëyrneð.
3   Cyn cywest daer cyn gorweð,
    bid dervyn ar orðineð.

20   **A**dvydig ys cevnyn,
6   Ar hyn, advanon
    eu llassawr debedyn,
7   tra mordwy alon.
    Gwrawl ðy·vrys awr i ly(s iðaw),
8 Gwŷr tru gorwan lu wênan arnaw.   16
    I gynneðv discyn rhac (ðiscyn)nawð
    yng·wyð a orðwy a gorðrynaw.
10 Carav vuðig nav a vuð anaw,—
    Lleithig Cyndevig, cenlliv arnaw.   20

17 **E**rðyled canu cyman Cyvreint,
6   Llanw n(ac aes niw) lloches, bu ðichweint.
7 Hu vynnei y·Mordrei veð ormeint,
    Ae anant (gy)veð(ant) yn veðweint.   24
8 Namyn ban ðelyn o wleð gereint,
    Aeron gyn-ðragon, ys cwynoveint.

20 **Y**s du hîl Benmon dir a ðôyn,
2   Am goelverth wy yn gerth ðisgynnyn.   28
3 Cenvein Rhedegein Rhyd a dreisyn,
    Gwyr Môn, eil Nwython, ry·goethessyn.
4 Drylliawr y·gan wawr wyr gynhullyn,   31
    Dyvnwall drych car Brennych, Gynt wenyn.

LURES TO DISASTER

Eagerly had they drunk ensnaring, golden mead 1
   ere they rushed into the fight at dawn,
Though Lloegria's drunken host was fine,
Punishment all along was endured. 4
Gwyneδ's villeins asked protection of Gwenn Van-
   hon, (Hakon's son,) who limps,
Let the eager lust of war be stayed,
Let the Bull of Battle ravage the tyrants. 8
Ere communion with earth, ere their lying down,
Let there be an end of aggression.

   The distressed turned away;
     Thereupon the new comers 12
     displayed their streamers
     beyond where enemies sail.
The brave one now hastens to his Court,
The wretched, a helpless crowd smile upon him. 16
His plan was to fall upon marauders, & to drive
   them away in the presence of those they molest.
I love the victorious king who benefits minstrels,—
Dead my former prince, the flood covers him. 20

Praise is the due of the faultless Colleague, neither
   flood nor shield gave shelter, he was a casualty.
Hugh would have at Mordrei overmuch mead,
   and the minstrels caroused till they were drunk. 24
But when they leave the banquet they love,
   they bewail the former dragon of Aeron.

Blackmailed were they that came to Penmon, 27
   In quest of good fortune they eagerly landed.
The host of the Borderers had stormed the Ford, &
   harassed Mona's men, fosterlings of Nwython. 30
At dawn the assembled men are cut to pieces, lost in
   the deep (is) Bernicia's ally, pierced by the Norse.

THE DISASTER

    GWYR aeth yng·hatraeth hynt vu enwawg,   1
    Yng·wleð, gwin a með bint eu gwirawd.
6 A·n erbyn nid urðyn y ðevawd,
19 Rhyvyrian athrychan wyr torchawg.
20 O·r sawl gryssyn awr o lyn ormawd—
    o·r Ffreinc ni ðieinc o vri ffossawd,
21 namyn tri, deu gar Rhi, deu gadr vrawd,
    A (Mynawg gwych ffodawg aeth ffoawd).
    Cyn-ðragon gwyr Aeron a ðaerawd,
22 Minheu (varð Llycheu geint) waedffreu wawd.

27·22–28·6 *This canto is a derivative version of* 6·17,
    above.   Metre and cynghaneð present difficulties.

27 Gryn wyr athrychir yn rhych drigant,
28   i vreichell y draethell y daethant.
1 Or sawl gryssyn awr o orlawn lestri,
    namyn tri atcorsant.
3   Cwynan reith a lleith gad y·nant,
    a minheu (varð Llycheu) gymrant.   16
    Vyng·werth, mal ceith, certh yd wnaethant
5   o bur eur, a dur, ac aryant ;
    Niwed, nid noðed, Ffreinc gawsant,
6   Gwarchawt Gynvelyn gwynovant.   20

       7 Gra chyveð mawr,
       6   treiglessid llawr
          gan Loegrwys gleu.

      31 (Vore dwyre)   24
       7   bwys vlaen rhyd·re,
          ffer yng·hadeu.

       8 Dryll gedyrn cad,
          Cein grysgwyðad,   28
          Prydav oreu.

OF CATRAETH

THOSE who went to Catraeth's famous expedi- 1
tion, usually drank wine and mead at feasts.
They who oppose us did not honour the custom,
They fall upon & cut down our nobility. Such of
    the Franks as rushed to battle from excessive
    drinking there escape by the fame of their smiting,
    but three, two friends of the king—two brave
    brothers, & (the noble thick-set Palatine who fled). 8
Buried the former dragon of the Aeronians, & I, Bard
    of the Lagoons, have sung of the shedding of blood.

Having regard to the known history of the circumstances,
the following amended version is offered pending a better.

The brave men, who came to the armlet of the Strand,
    were cut down and rest in the grave. 12
Of such as rushed from overflowing cups at the
    warshout only three returned.
They lament the decisiveness & slaughter of the rav-
    ine, & me, (Bard of the Lagoons), the Norse take. 16
    Of my ransom as a captive they make sure
        in gold, and mail, and silver;
        Injury, not protection the Franks received,
        Of the wardship of Cynvelyn they complain. 20

        During the great festival
            The country had been over-run
            by active Lloegrians.

        Of a morning there appears one, 24
            stout in exploits; he presses
            on to the ferryside.

        He destroys mighty warriors,
        Fine his sudden descent, 28
            I will sing of his doings.

MAGNUS SLEW

31   E·chwith lain
9   δy·or·wylain,
      nad rhy·gigleu.

7   Heyessit eis
8   yng·hynnor veis,
      yng·had vereu.

    Gorug wyr lleδw,
      a gwrageδ gweδw
      cyn oed angheu.

    Greid vu hoew Ri
      gar ysperi,
10   yd beris greu.

6   Yveis win a meδ
4   y·Mordrei Gwyneδ,
    Mawr meint wehyner
5   yn arvod gwyδer.   16
Cyn brwydr Eryr Crwydr ersymudei,
Ban grys traeth i gydvaeth gydgodei.
Yngawr gan wyrδ wawr cymhwy δoded,
Am bellt aesawr dellt ys adawed.   20

7   Bares Rynn rwygiad
      gymined yng·had,
8   Blaen bragad briwed,
      Liw dyδ y cwyδed.   24
9   Werthws i eneid
      er·wyn grybwylleid.
    Mein a llavn lliveid
10   laδei y Bleiδieid ;   28
    Yn affwys abred
      amod arvaethed,
11   Calaneδ laδed
      o wyr gwychr Rhedeg.
    Ymlaen Gwyneδ gwaned.   33

THE LUPUSIANS

    His unerring lances
      very loudly wail—
        I heard their dirge.
    Darts were showered at
      the edge of the shallows
        in the battle of the pikes.
    He made men prostrate,
      and women widowed,
        before their time.
    Ardent was the alert king
      who loves spears,—
        he caused blood to flow.   12

I drank wine & mead
      on Gwyneδ's great strand,
    Lavish was the distribution
      on the first opportunity.   16
Before battle the Knight Errant was very active,
When he rushes to the shore his comrades rose too.
During the war-shout at green dawn there was grief,
About the ground splintered shields were left.   20
    He who embroiled the Rhyn
      was cut down in battle,
    Foremost of the line he was wounded,
      At dawn he was felled.   24
    To him who has sold his life
      very glorious are the references.
    Magnus with his sharp axe
      slew the Lupusians;   28
    In the abyss of time
      their allotted span was fixed.
    There was slaughter of
      the noble men of Rhedeg.
At Gwyneδ's foreland the thrusting was done.   33

THE RUSH TO BATTLE.

Ⓖwyr ffraeth gryssynt draeth, buant gydneid.
9 Byryan hoedl, meδwon, am veδ hidleid.
4 Goscorδawg Mynyδawg yn·yδ rheid,
  (ar gwyr syrth yn llyr gyll) eu heneid.
5 Madawg a Chradawg, Pyll a Ieuan,
  Gwgawn a Gwiawn a gwynvanan.
7 Arveu dur benadur a·r·adan.
  Hyd lawr yscwydawr, ys ang·hyman.
8 Ac hyd y lleδid y llaδassan,
  Gwych wyr iw tymhyr nid ymchwelan. (*cp.* 38·7).

Ⓖwyr ffraeth gryssan draeth, buant gydvaeth, Vlwyδyn y llewyn yn llawn alaeth.
11 Mor dru yw traethu eu tra hiraeth,
  Chwerw nam eu hadlam, nid mad ae maeth,
13 Hir edlid ae herlid ar herw aeth,
  oe tymhyr syrth pybyr wyr gwinvaeth.
14 (Gwrthrin rac) gorδin a erbyn ffraeth,
  Golyged (lleith Redeg) yn edgyllaeth (13).
15 Cwyδawd Mynyδawg yn arvawg aeth,
  A phrid erbynid lleith gynhen traeth.

Ⓖwr δaeth yng·hatraeth, ing gâd yng·awr,
  Gwrth veirch serig seirch wyr gorwychr-
18 Peleidr a ymdeivl ae lym waewawr, [awl,
  A δûg glaer luryg dorvynyglawr.
19 Rhagorei, ev dreiδei drwy Vleiδawr,
  Cwyδei sawl δelei draws i lavnawr.
20 Rhyd vawr hi roδawr i lyw Rhyn lawr,
  A ched δichwein deg i Geint gerδawr.

21 Ⓓeu·r wnaethpwyd or traeth mor orchy-
  Mor vawr y gyvawr ar gyvlavan. [nan,
10 Dy·lydid moryd tra Morien wân,
1 Ynhraeth gwnel i saeth gelein gynran.

THE HUBBUB AND CARNAGE

𝕿he men chattering, leapt up & rushed to the shore, 1
The drunk throw away their life because of sparkling
   mead. His retinue attends Mynyδawg in his day
of stress, Those that fell, in the flood lose their life. 4
   Madog and Cradog, Pyll and John,
   Gwgon and Gwion they all lament.
   They abandon the steel-mailed chief,
     and broken shields lie on the ground.
Until they were slain they kept on slaying,
The gallant ones did not return to their possessions.

𝕸essmates were the merry men who rushed to the shore,
For a year they went on drinking full of lamentation. 12
How sad is the story of their great grief,
Bitter the stigma of their return, unfostered of good,
Long vexation pursues them, who a-roving went.
Out of their country fall the stout wine-bibbing men. 16
He who confronts the merry ones counters the attack,
   and the dead of Rhedeg were viewed in sorrow.
Fallen Mynyδawg who went clad in mail, and
   costly was fought the deadly conflict of the Strand. 20

𝕬 hero came to Catraeth, & with the warshout trouble,
He thrusts back the grandees' silk caparisoned steeds.
He hurls about his darts and sharp spears,
He who wore bright mail was thrown headlong. 24
Magnus led, and penetrated through the Lupusians, &
   such as came across his blades he felled. The great
Ferry was given to the ruler of the Rhyn country,
   and a meed of fair fortune to Keint's minstrel. 28

𝕿he shorebank became a very babel,
So great the hubbub and the carnage.
While Morien is thrusting the channel widens,
Shorewards his arrow makes a corpse of the captain. 32

MORIEN DESTROYS THE

10 Un seirchawg saffwyawg oeð rhwyvan,
2 Seinir i glod îr ymhob midlan.
3 Nid aresgyn Garreg Gynhadvan
   vyth mwy, cyscodwy wys vad porthan,

> 34   Ban ðel dir crymant,
> 4   Nid oeð oed dïanc.
> Dïalwr Arvon
>   gyrchei Eur Geinnion.
> Arwrthiad Cynon
>   brovwys vreich Brithion.

10 (Morien wnaeth ðïen ffraeth) anvonawg,
5 (Cynon ae väon vu w)aredawg.
6 Dïengis yn drymysc y Mynawg
   rhac Arth dywalach noe gar ffwyrawg.
7 Ffer y llaw vaglwys ffawd ffrowys varch-
9 Ynghymwy i gylchwy a vylchawd. [awg,
8 Llyw las vu dinas llu di·ovnawg,
   Rhanc byðin y gorðin wascarawd.
10 Dyð gwyth bu adwyth nêr adveilawg,
   Dywallyn eillt veðgyrn Mynyðawg.

11 Gwnelid din dorrid yn ði·yssig,
   Cynon, mein lary vronn, Ceinnion wledig,
12 nid aeth, eisteð wnaeth ar dal lleithig,
   Ar neb a varned, ni waredid.

> 18   Herlyw ni dywys ryvel,
> 15   Gwlad-gorð ae car ; gwrð vedrer,
> 16   Gorweðid gwaed am irveð,
> Lluryg am·ruð yd arweð.
> 17   Am veirch ae seirch y sonied,
> Ar ðelw lleith escawr lluðed.
> 18   Y·meis peleidr eis yn eit yng·had,
> Goleu hynt Goðeu ym·heleidrad.

EXPEDITIONARY FORCE

This leader was in harness, and bore a lance,
On every field his ever green fame will be trumpeted.
Nevermore will he mount the Cynhadvan Stone,—
May it shelter the good folk of the inlet.

    When (Magnus) lands they bowed their heads,
        There was no time to escape.
        The avenger of Arvon
            attacked the men of Eurgeint.
        The stout resistance of Cynon
            tested the power of the Picts.

Morien destroyed the chattering expeditionary force,
Cynon and his vavasours were spared.   1.
The Palatine escaped in confusion from a Bear
    more fierce than his attacking friend. Stout the
    hand that tangled the lot of the turbulent knight,
In the stress his round shield was notched.   16
The slain leader was the bulwark of the fearless host,
The ' line ' of the attacking army was scattered.
The day of wrath was the ruin of the perishing lord,
The villeins emptied the meadhorns of Mynyδawg.   20

The damaged fort was repaired faultlessly,
Cynon, the gentle breasted lord, Gwledig of the men
    of Ceint did not leave ; he sat at the head of the
    Bench and such as were condemned had no escape. 24

The (young) commander discontinues the war,
The country-folk love him ; hit is the ardent one.
    Blood lies around his green grave,
        Gory all over the mail he bears.   28
    There was talk about his steeds and their harness,
    In the form of death is his weariness thrown off.
In the shallows darts gleamed as they went to battle,
    Flashing spears made light the path of Goδeu.   32

THE CREEK BECOMES

35·4 Yn·hrîn tra merin trylew ing gäant,
Trig gwaeð Ffranc, ffrawdus lyw,
(Ev saethwyd ac aseth loew),
5   gan bor a oreu varn Duw.

6 Gwawr yn ffysciolin amðiffynnci,
Rhac gorðin y·midin terhydrei.
7 Yn llwrw ðaeth am lanw buan brathei,
Rhac vu ðewr deulu ev ðiscynhei.
9 Mablan golystan cyn escynnei,
Ma wledig, endewid ðywedei.
10 Mynyðawg arleshawd isel drei,
Rhac Rhyn uð Eiðyn rhuðwaew vriwei.

12 Dengyn ni phorthyn, din orthorred,
Rhac rhuthr Rhi allu ni luð moreb.
13 Baran tebig tân deryð ar led,—   15
Diw Mawrth wy yn rawth wiscyn duðed,
15 Diw Merchyr vu chwerw, ev tryvered,
Divieu cennadeu a amoded,
16 Diw Gwener carneðer ryveðwed,   19
Diw Sadwrn bu didrwm cyndriged,
18 Diw Sul arveu dur a adranned,
Diw Llun hyd lawr clun, gwarthal weled.
19 Adroðyn am orðin, am luðed,   23
am ffawd Mynyðawg ban ðymchweled.

11 Glyw Rhyd amdrymid drwy asen anlwys,
9   am ðyvrwys dywarchen,   26
10   Dy·gwyðawð dellt ar i benn,
ac am wyr Eryr Gwyðien.
Gwyndyd neu·s amug i onnen arðulliad
11   di·wylliad i berchen,   30
12   A dûg Morien wyndawd mir wenn,
Priv yng·Weryd a chyvran benn.

38

A PLACE OF THE DEAD

Fighting beyond the tide-line the bold meet with distress,
The shout of the Frank, an impetuous leader, ceases ; 2
   (He was shot by a gleaming dart), by a lord
   who executed the judgment of God.
The hero (Magnus) actively defended on all sides, 5
In his ships he pushed his way against attack,
He swiftly smote such as rushed beyond high water line,
He fell upon the division of the brave retinue, 8
The creek was a place of the dead before he left,
Gwledig of the battle-field his word was law,
A low ebb will benefit Mynyδawg, lord of Eiδyn,
   whom a gory spear bruised before the Rhyn. 12

They did not support the villeins, the fort was broken,
Against the rush of the Kings's force the ebb was no
   check. Anger, like fire, spreads rapidly abroad—
Tuesday they eagerly donned their armour, 16
Wednesday was bitter, they were speared,
Thursday ambassadors made terms of peace,
Friday the drunken dead were heaped together,
Saturday the old inhabitants rejoiced, 20
Sunday steel weapons were redistributed,
Monday, along the meadow, men were seen bartering.
After their return they spake of the great push,
   of the exhaustion, and of the doom of Mynyδawg. 24

   The lord of the Ford was bowed down by an ugly
      arrow, beyond the marshland,
     Darts fell upon his head, and
      about the men of Gwyδien's Eagle. 28
His ashen spear defended Gwyneδ like an
     owner cultivating his own,
    Of sunshine Morien robbed this wonderful hero,
      who was first in Gweryd, and joint head. 32

COMPLETELY WERE THE HOST

11 Ni nerth, (ni ðifferth dan lenn yr yssig
13   a·r unig) a·r cam hên,
14   Trylwyr y boðid bun Bradwen,
    Dy·hewyd abwyd am vadw wenn.   4

    Yn dryn yn llawr Rhyn dryllien gweinyðawr
    yscwydawr yng·weithen,
16   Arial cleðyval am benn hên,
    Trychan Loegr ðrychion rhac unben.

    (Yn vlwng) cnivwys Mwng Vleiðig benn o law,
18   Gwnaeth wychrawd y·ni-lenn,
    O gyvranc gwyth bu ascen,
19   Trengis ni ði·enghis Bradwen.

Another version.

24 Yn Rhyd am·drymid drwy asen an·lwys
11   am ðyvrwys dywarchen,
    Hoedl Barvawr, dreisawð dri·phlyg hên,
13   ar·ðwg Morien ae wïalen.   16

    Rhanc með a rheuveð rhawg ðên Ynt arwyr
14   a Gwyðyl i Bryden,
    ar·guð celein y rhein ruðen,
15   Dy·hewyd abwyd am vadw wenn.   20

    Rhyd lawr amgreinawr dan lenn ton tran ðwys
16   tra dyvrwys dywarchen,
    Cwymp arwr Bar·vawr, Eiðyn benn,
    Ni welych i ðrych nae lwyven—   23
18   aseth vreith goruch i lovlen,
    Gwant Ynt a Gwyðyl ymHryden.

    (Yn vlwng) cnivei Mwng Vleiðig benn o law,
20   Gwnaeth wychrawd y·ni-lenn,   28
    Prydwn y bei varw drwy Vorien,
    Dyhewyd abwyd am vadw wenn.   30

OF BRADWEN DROWNED

Under cover he can neither support nor defend the 1
    bruised, the orphan, & the bent old,
Completely were the host of Bradwen drowned,
Eager the worms for the hero that is still.

Stoutly, in the Rhyn country, the liegemen shivered
    the shields in action, Vigorous 6
the sword-play upon the veterans, Lloegria's
representatives they cut down before the prince.

Out of hand Magnus sadly afflicted the Lupusian chief,
    who had acted bravely in the open,
From the encounter of passion there was scathe,
Bradwen perished, he did not escape.

Another version.

At the Ford he was bowed down by an ugly arrow
    beyond the marsh-land,
Greatire's life, who oppressed the thrice-bent old,
Morien takes with his arrow. 16

A passion for mead and booty for some time tempt
    the Norse heroes and Gwyðyl to Pryden,
Hidden the corse which the darts crimsoned,
Eager the worms for the warrior that is still. 20

He is rolled about the Ferry bottom beneath deepish
    breakers beyond the marshland,
The hero Greatire, chief of Eiðyn, falls,
You can see neither his form nor his elm-lance— 24
Striped the shaft above the grasping point,
He had speared Norse & Gwyðyl in Pryden.

Out of hand Magnus sadly afflicted the Lupusian
    chief, who had acted boldly in the open, 28
I prophesied that he would die through Morien,
Eager the worms for the warrior that is still.

ATHWART THE WIDE SEA

  RHI gryssyws gatraeth,
4   traws mor ehelaeth,
5   i arvaeth uch arwyð.
  Ni bu moe gyvor
  yn Eiðyn yscor,
6   Escarei oswyð.
 Tud vylchis, caer dorris erch Drewyð,
7 Y·Mon llað Saeson, llaðei seith nyð.   5
 Perheid i wrhyd, ev orvyð,
8 ae govein gân i Gein edmygyð.
 Ban vu drei Bleið welei, y·meryð,
9 wyar ar wyal i vad Gilyð.

27 **G**orchan o gyrð ceinmyn
12   yw gwarchawd Cynvelyn.
13 Gorchenyn Gynvelyn gylch gwleðiad,
 Edvyn gwyr wneðyn Gwyneð eu gwlad. 16
14 Dewr Mon lawr ðychïawr ðychiliad
 y Rhi gar deithi gy·veithriniad.
16 Dy·vrys gein ynys, gwrth Rhyn voriad,
 Midin yn eithyn neud leith breiniad. 20
18 Gorchenyn Gynvelyn ryveliad,
 Neus gwnaeth oðynaeth ðogn gymhrwyad.
19 Aes dron ae waewffon lliveid   a·n noðes,
  Boed er lles iw eneid,
  20 Edmygid i wrthriv teleid 23
   a wrthrymyn wyrth colovn greid.
   21 Ban vriwynt arveu,
    ar benn cad Vleiðeu,
   22   buont ðewr ðyð rheid. 29

MAGNUS CAME & WENT AGAIN

A KING rushed to Battle strand
athwart the wide sea,
   his design above detection.
There was not his match
in the Eiδyn camp—
   He dispersed the cavalry.   6
The dread Smiter breached the land & broke the fort,
In Mon he slays the Saxons, he slew for seven days.
His hardihood endures, he will prevail,   9
 and his life-story his Ceint admirer will sing.
When there was ebb Lupus saw, in the marsh,
  blood on the temple of his loved Colleague.   12

A paean of fine songs is
  the wardship of Cynvelyn.
They celebrated Cynvelyn the round of the feast,
Men who made Gwyneδ their country departed.   16
The brave men of Mon deplore the withdrawal of
 the King who loves the ways of his foster brothers.
He hastens to a fair Isle, sailing away from Rhyn,
The moment the ships left the festival languished.   20
They celebrated Cynvelyn's war-waging, which
  effected thenceforward much general good.
His strong targe and sharp spear protected us,
   may it be for the good of his soul,   24
Admired were his glorious opposing force that over-
  powered the worth of the attacking column.
    When they broke their weapons, on the
    heads of warring Lupusians, they were
    valourous in the hour of stress.   29

THE CRY OF ALARM

DOLEV dêr ry·dyrr am gaer, 1
Y dy·hun gyrch am galch claer.
28 Gwibδe aδoed aer adwy,
    clodryδ ceisidyδ cys(twy.
20 Gwely as edy yn es)cud
    vrithwy arwe ae wrhyd.
21 Rhuthr anorthwy a vegid,
    Adwy δoded ni debid.
22 Oδevwys ias dôv i vryd,
    Dygwyδ i arv yn escud,
29 Yr elvyδ huδ i onwyδ,
1 Di·wared trig yng·weryδ.
2 Cywely prŷv, dygn ymδwyn,
    Cyveilin nar edryv vrwyn.
3 Nac ymhel di a therwyn,
    Teithiawl têr dorres dervyn. 16
4 Nid arveδawg i vorawd,
    Di·phryderas am vras rawd.
5 Vordwyawδ Ryn vuδhwy Von,
    Dy·lys dreisyn, câr Mannon. 20
    Discleir archawr dâl aethon
7   ar ruδ δreic, mud pharäon.
    Cyveill gawr yna welid,
    Adwân yn·hranc a gwyδid. 24
8 Nêr ae eneu y·ar leithig
9   orthor reith tud a thevig.
    Mênid goscorδ, mawr murnid,
10 Onwyδ ar vor ni δelhid, 28
    [na chynghor, na chil gynghyd].
11 Gorδibleu caer dalchattor,
    Nid mwy rhy·luδit y hescor.
12 Bleiδ êl Eiδyn, gor rhacδor,
    Cynon, Ceint vur, Rhyn ragor. 33

44

AT THE CASTLE

VIOLENT shouting breaks out beyond the fort,　　1
Those awake rush for their shining armour.
Expedition will stay the fight at the breach,
Freely praised will he be who attempts chastise-
He who quits his bed with alacrity　　　　[ment.　　5
　　will have his web shot with bravery.
Irresistible was the attack prepared,
A breach once made will remain.
Crushed the spirit of one who has experienced
　　a shock, and his weapon speedily drops.
The element closes over his shaft,
Without deliverance he remains in the sea,—
　　a bedfellow of worms of horrible habit,
For him, associate of the chief, the folk grieve.
Never strive with the strong,
　　the ardent voyager has broken bounds.
Unpremeditated was his voyage,　　17
He did not concern himself about a large float.
May he who sailed to the Rhyn benefit Mon,
The friend of Man chases away the oppressors.
The brilliant archer avenges the inflictions
　　on the red dragon, the dumb lord.　　22
His war Colleague then was seen, He thrusts
　　afresh the fallen in their death agony.
This lord, by word from the judgment seat,　　25
　　violates the right of country & prince.
The retinue was daunted, mostly destroyed,—
At sea the lances could not be held,　　28
　　[nor council, nor a corner unitedly.]
The outworks of the fort were utterly demolished,
No longer could its deliverance be frustrated.
Lupus goes to Eiδyn, the country at his front door,
Cynon, the bulwark of Ceint, leads the Rhyn.　　33

HUGH LUPUS

29 Gosodes gledr,
13 ar·glawð hyvedr,
    rhac morwyr dig.
    Rhëen buðig,
14 Ni nawð Vleiðig,
    yn adwythig.
    Cyn llas cyn·weis
15 y·ny·wyn veis,
    chwêg ni gwyðes.
16 Herw chwenyches
    ni ðymchweles,
    lli ev lewes.
17 Arwyr ymwan
    lenwis vidlan,
    moreb yd lês.
29 Ar ystre bu vore odorun,   16
18 Hu ðwyre i ware yng·orvyn.
21 Y·ar orwyð yn elvyð y tevlid,
30 Ym·laen (gweis) a blin eis y blivid.
 1 Ev leðid drybeð rhwng meryð Rhyd,   20
 2 Cigleu uð Goðeu ban ðygyvyd—
    Gweli y goðiv a ðwg yn fud,
 4 Mor vâr a dig ðâr ae di·gar byd.
    Cyn yd ðigonid oeð welw gynwythig,   24
 5   Cyn lleithig oeð llwyr welw,
    Cyn i olo oeð goruð ðelw
 6   dal, orvawr, o waell vael ðerw.
29·18 Yn Rhyn gwyr gorwyn ry·annoged,   28
19 Yn rhuthreu, yn rhwylleu rhy·golled,
    A veðwyd cyminwyd yn enwŷd,
20 Cun Gogleð gan riheð a dyrvid.
20 Gorthew bor ymchwil fforð i chwelyd,
22 Am rwyð mwy ev alwy or erlid.   33

46

RUNS AWAY

He put up a stockade,
  a cunning rampart
    against the angry sea-farers.
The victorious King will not
  protect the Lupusian
    in sore distress.
Ere the young leaders were slain
  in the foaming shallows,
    the unpleasant befell.
He who wanted the expedition
  did not return home,
    He gulped sea-water.
The fighting champions
  filled the battle field,
    The ebb will aid them.
On the battle field there was uproar one morning,
Hugh appears, and jousts in rivalry.
He falls from his horse in the water, At the head
  of his knights with grievous arrows he was shot.
He who was slain stays amid the Ford's wrack,
I heard the lord of Shrewsbury when he led off
(But) in silence he bears the wound of the missile—
Unloved are the seething sea and the angry oak dart.
  Ere he was foredone he was singularly pale,
    In death he was very pale,
    Ere his burial his tall big form was red-
    dened by the iron-tipped dart of oak.
The veterans at Rhyn were urged forward,
In the assaults they were lost in the holes.
The drunken were cut down in the great fury,
The lord of Gogleδ was chased by the King.
The Fat lord seeks on all sides a way to return,
  & prays for greater ease from pursuit.

THE ELEGY OF

𝕳r awr gynhorwan
   arwyrein huan.
5 Glyw gwyð o gyff gein,
   Nêr evnys Prydein.
   Garw Rhyd rhac y Rhyn,
      aeth yn llwrw, boðyn.
   Bual oeð arwyn,
      yng·hynteð eiðyn.
10 Y rhïyð (roðes
      wleð o) ry·odres.
   Yng·hyveð meðwawd,
      yvei win wirawd.   12
11 Oe ðerllyð Gwyðel
      yvei yng·over.
   Aer veið ar·veðwer,
      aer gevnyn Wyðel.   16
12 Or aber dan gaer,
      cevnyn gyvid aer.
   Or gwyðveirch aerawd
13   cåd llysc edenawg.   20
   Oeð dyrys yscwyd,
      yn·yvrawr plymnwyd.
14 Cwyðyn gyvoedion,
      yng·had blym Benmon.   24
15 Yssig yn·ïas
      divevl as talas.
   Huð ewyllyssias,
      cyn bu dan glawr clas.   28
   Gorweð brwysc wellig
      (yng·hor Amwythig).   30

HUGH THE PROUD

As the thrusting begins
  the sun is rising.
A prince of fine lineage falls,
  the lord of the foes of Prydein.   1
Desperate the passage before the Rhyn,
Such as went precipitately were
  drowned. The drinking horns were
  foaming at their court.   8
Its lord gave a feast
  from vain-glory.
At the banquet he gets drunk,
He drank wassail wine,   12
  which as it flows the Gwyðel
  drank in a stream.
The drunken venture into battle,
  but the Gwyðel turn their backs.   16
From the Aber below the Fort they,
  who began the fighting, fled.
From the battle-ships were
  received flying darts.   20
Shields were embarrassing
  in the struggle in the waters.
Companions fell in the
  terrible battle of Penmon.   24
The one bruised in the tumult
  utterly paid for it.
He called for burial ere he
  was under the cover of an abbey.   28
The one precipitately lost lies
  in Shrewsbury chancel.   30

Y Gorddin

y Mordrei Gwynedd:

AMENDED TEXT & TRANSLATION.

Now the time is come to ask the strangers who they are . . . Strangers, who are ye? Whence sail ye over the wet ways? on some trading enterprise, or at adventure do ye rove, even as sea-robbers, over the brine, for they wander at hazard of their own lives bringing bale to alien men—ODYSSEY III.

THE GREAT STRAND PUSH

AND OTHER POEMS

BY

GRIFFYDD AP KYNAN

King of Gwynedd

1074–1132.

GRIFFYDD AP CYNAN

<small>B</small>AN grysseis Von rhac treis trahäawg,   1
  vynghlod yn vyngwlad oeð hanvodawg.
<small>31</small> Gwyndyd eisyllyd, bum alltudawg,
<small>22</small> Maban i Gynan edryvanawg.
<small>19</small> (Ceveis,) derllyðeis o drull torchawg,
<small>20</small>   win a með achlân di·wychïawg.
   (Er ymlid gelyn bro Gelynawg)
<small>20</small> Ardwyeis gôr rhwy arwr Mynawg.
<small>22</small> Yn sathrawr Artro lawr neb ffossawd
   vei lymach no·m gavlach ban vlivawd.

<small>12·14</small> Gwroleð yng·Ogleð a orug
   llary vronn, hael adon, i vab alltud.   12
<small>15</small> Daear nid ymða, nid ymðug mam
   eirian mor gadarn, haearn gaðug.
<small>16</small> O vaeth claer arvaeth taer ym achub,
   Arwar o garchar a gwarth y·m dug,   16
<small>17</small> O gyv·le anghov, o anghar dud,
   Kenwrig, vad devig, oeð edmyg drud.

<small>19</small> Nid o warth y portheis orseð,
   llestri 'menestri oeð llawn með.   20
<small>20</small> Go·veðeis vyng·hleð o gareð,
   vy llin a·m lläin o reueð.
<small>21</small> A·m porthwys Llychlynwys oe breich
   rac byðin a gorðin Bryneich.   24
<small>22</small> Oe llað yn neuað bu·m vythveirch,
   a gwawr wyarawl i·w (claer) seirch.
<small>13</small> Cein gyllell ys hiriell i·m llaw,
   ac yn êl yd ry·wnel brysiaw.   28
<small>2</small> Gwaneis, ymhyrðeis ym·Henvro
   y nerth ni ðifferth serth Artro.
<small>3</small> Gwyr (Llychlyn) nid eiðyn draed ffo,
   Ennillyn achubyn y vro.   32

CLAIMS GWYNEDD'S THRONE

WHEN I hastened to Môn against its arrogant
    seizure, my fame was thriving in my coun-
Sprung out of Gwyneδ, the Scion of Cynan   [try.
    of high lineage, I had lived in exile.
I received and dispensed, from a noble's store,
    wine and sparkling mead, free from wax.
For driving away the enemy of Celynog dale,
    I led a spare corps of the Palatine's lieutenant.
In the crush of the Artro country no stroke could
    be sharper than that of my dart when shot.   10

In Gogleδ an act of bravery was rendered by a gen-
    tle-breasted, generous lord, to an exile's son.
There treads not the earth, no fair mother
    bore one so strong, clad in steel.
By dint of clear forethought he eagerly rescued me, 15
Gently he bore me from prison and disgrace, from
    the precincts of oblivion, from an odious country,—
Kenrick, the noble prince, was admirably bold.

Not unworthily did I support the throne,
My cupbearers' vessels were full of mead.   20
I quietly restrained my sword from crime,
    my race, and my lances from activity.
The Norse supported me with their arm
    against the army and attack of Bryneich.   24
By killing them at the castle I secured swift horses,
    whose bright harness had a gory hue.
Fine the glaive that gleams in my hand,
    and where it goes it causes swift flight.   28
I thrusted and overthrew in Pembroke
    the power that did not save steep Artro.
Norse feet never turn back in flight—
They won and occupied the dale.   32

HUGH THE PROUD

A. Lleth leu-direð,
B. Tud lleu-ðyvreð,
C.   Heleð ystrad.
D. Ys try rhagom
E.   wyr Iwerðon,
F.   arv yn anghad.
G. Anvad escor
H.   vu oe cynghor,
I.   yn lleuver cad.
K. Hu ðug bibyll
L.   o win diwyll,
M.   ar lês Saeson.
N. Ter yd ware,
O.   yn rhac ystre,
P.   a gwen Vanhon.
Q. Cangen gaer wys   16
R.   cewri ðulliwys,
S.   tymhestl ðarvu.
T. Tra mor dymhestl,
U. Tra merin lestr   20
V.   dy·lann ðyvu.
W. Hu Eiðynion
X.   ffwyr vaetholion
Y.   rhac Llychlyn lu.   24
Z. O·n dirdynwyd,
α.   ev dy·vyriwyd
β.   a·n dy·orvu.
γ. Cwyð yn grugyn,   28
δ. Rac arvawd tryn,—
ε.   i dal briw vu.
ζ. Llym ðy·wenyn,
η. Dwys yd voðyn,
θ.   Llwyr gevnyn llu.   33

54

RAVAGES MON

He overwhelms the open lands, 1
The country of the shallow waters,
 Arllechweδ's champaigne.
He turns against us
 the men of *I*reland
 all ready armed.
Not for their good was the
 issue of their deliberation,
 in the light of battle.
Hugh brought pipes of
 sparkling wine, for the
 benefit of his Saxons. 12
Ardently he jousts,
 in the fore-front,
 with the hero of Man.
A division of the fort men 16
 marshalled its stalwarts,
 & the tempest burst.
An over-sea tempest,—
A vessel in the offing 20
 drew towards the shore.
Hugh, of the Eiδyn country,
 eagerly rushes his retainers
 against the Norse host. 24
If we had been violently handled,
 overthrown was he who
 had been crushing us.
He falls all of a heap be- 28
 fore the stroke of the strong,
 wounded in the forehead.
Those who fiercely thrusted
 densely sank in the sea,—
 one & all turned and fled. 33

MAGNUS

32 Angor dewr daen,
    Anyscog vaen,
2   Saiv saffwy raen
3   y·mlaen midin.
    Arall arlwy,
4   Treis tra chymwy,
    Yn rhwyð gobrwy
        orðwy läin.
7   Angor dewr daen,
    Anyscog vaen,
    Saiv saffwy raen
8   y·mlaen midin.   12
12 Hu, as gwelwy,
    Aches ðelwy,
    Glas vleið ðyccwy,
        Dïas ðilin.   16
13 Angor dewr daen,
    Anyscog vaen,
    Saiv saffwy raen
        y·mlaen midin.   20
    (Hu ry·seithir,)
    Lledruð lliwir,
14   y·ar varch cwyðir
            y rac gorðin.   24
16 Angeu dewr daen,
6   Saiv seri graen,
    Sengid claer gaen,
        y·mlaen midin.   28
8   Arth arwynawl
        drussia dreisawr,
    Sengid waewawr
9   yng·hlawr gwernin.   32

56

CASTS ANCHOR

The brave one casts anchor,
   a ponderous stone,
He confronts the cruel lance
   at the head of his ships.
The other spreads a feast,
He oppresses distressingly,
Liberally he rewards those
   who thrust with their lances.   8
The brave one casts anchor,
   a ponderous stone,
He confronts the cruel lance
   at the head of his ships.
Hugh, when he sees him,
   approaches the haven—
His visage turns livid,
   The tumult follows.   16
The brave one casts anchor,
   a ponderous stone,
He confronts the cruel lance
   at the head of his ships.   20
Hugh is shot dead,
He is stained rather red,
From his horse he is felled
   as the onset begins.   24
The brave one spreads death,
He confronts the raging furies,
He tramples on their bright
   mail, ahead of his ships.   28
A savage bear
   he wards off the oppressors,
He tramples on their spears
   in the alder swamp.   32

THE HILL SLOPE AND

    32 Rhyn ev gyvarch—
14   cynwyrein barth,
15 Cymmer dorr arth—
    rhag·arth merin.

13 Ergryn alon i arv,
10 Ev ry·vrwydr tra chwarð,
   Côr o Vann gewri
11   am·dwrr vangori;
   Bysseð y Brithion
   vriwant Vargodion.
12 Amrygur amðystyr y discar,
   Yn bwyllig am·orðid am·ry·chwal. 12
   Y vro vrys, ys treul rys yn rhyw dres,
14 Ni hunwy ni gahwy i neges—
   Neb anghwy, a wanwy odawes.   15

37·12 Bylchid caer treisig aer o gylched,   32·6
  10 Yn wir y gelwir ðug Ryn wared— 32·8
32·10 'RECTOR, rhwyv pob or, mur pob ciwed',
16·11 Morien am·Hadien, mad yð aned   32·10

    16 Ysiges nar,   20
    9 Neu·s dug, drwy var,
     Wleð i adar
     o drydar drin.

21 Eu tres gwrthodes tra aches llynn, 24
 1 Llaðei, erlidei ar ni thechyn,
 2 Tavl hoew aseth loew ysceth vrwydrin,
   O veð rhac tyrveð tavled byðin.
 3 Mynner cynghor nêr men leverid,   28
   Y traws vei anwaws nid endewid.
 4 Rhac ffawd bwyellawd a llavn lliveid,
   Handid y gwelid llawer yn lleid.   31

>   (Magnus) salutes the Rhyn—
>   the part rising up in the front,
>   He takes the slope of the hill—
>   the hill above the shore.

>   His weapon terrifies the enemy,
>   He fights with zest laughingly,
>   A corps of the Vann champions
>   throng the palisading;
>   The fingers of the Picts
>   crush the Borderers.

He lays about for the destruction of the enemy,
Deliberately he scatters the buffeted in all ways,
The dale bustles, spending energy in some labour,
None can rest who may not gain his object—
None escapes, those he thrusts become silent.

The tyrant fort is breached by a surrounding assault,
He who delivered the Rhyn will be called
' RECTOR, lord of every land, bulwark of every race,'
Morien son of Beneficence, noble was he born.

>   He destroyed the lord who,
>   through his fury, brought
>   a feast for birds (of prey)
>   by the tumult of battle.

He opposed their labour beyond the haven pool,
He slew, he pursued those who did not hide. Brisk
flinging of gleaming darts pushed back the battle,
Of mead before the tumult the army perished.
The counsel of the King is taken as soon as spoken,
The arrogant, who had been harsh, was unheeded.
Because of the doom of the axe-stroke with its
  sharp blade, mayhap, many will be seen in the mud.

HUGH LIES PRONE

21   Ꝑorth lwyð vyðin,
6   Porth lwyð läin,
      a llu rhacweð.
7   (Hu) vu wythawg,
      wedy meðdawd,
        (o hir gyveð).
8   O veð yved
      ni bu wared,
        (na gorod beð).
6   Ev ragorweð,
      yn·yð gwŷneð,
      yng·hywrysseð.
8   Ae gorwylant
      enyd ffrwysiant ;
      Ban adroðed
9   Torred ergyr   16
      o veirch a gwyr,
      Tyngid tynged.

36   Ⅿoch arwyleint y·mei-ðin
7   ban grys Morien y·midin.   20
8   Ðovid ni dowys ðy·vin,
      Rhac cant ev gwant cysevin.
9   Oeð mor hwanawg i ðiwin,
      mal yn yved með neu win.   24
10   Di·achar gwaned yn·hrin,
      Yscarwyd gwanar gorðin.

12   Ⅿoch arwyleint y·more
7   ban grys cynrein ir gware.   28
12   Yng·hyniv a pheriv rhe
13   ni bu cyvarch rhac ystre.
      Gweis gwyðad yng·hynwyre cad,   31
4   ar adad yn rhyd·re.
      Bu golug Vryn Buðugre
15   i wanar gweilgi wrmðe.   34

ON THE DAY OF WRATH

Support prospers an army,
Support prospers its lances
 (when) confronting a host.
Hugh was furious
 after intoxication
  from long feasting;
After drinking mead
 there was no deliverance,
  nor a mound grave.
He lies prone,
 on the day of wrath,
  in the thick of the fight. 12
They, who greatly lament him,
 fight violently for a while;
When the news was told,
 broken was the onrush 16
  of horses and men;
   their fate was doomed.

They will speedily mourn within the field fort
 when Morien hies in shallow ships. 20
The vanquished one will not rule the coast even,
At first he fought at the head of a hundred.
He was given to act impulsively,
 just as one drinks mead or wine. 24
Unsparing had the spearing been in battle,
Cut off was the leader of the push.

They will speedily mourn in the morning
 when the captains rush to the jousting.
In conflict with the active sovereign, there 29
 was no greeting before entering the list.
The knights, who were felled at the onset of
 battle, were left (at the bottom of) the ford.
  The glory of Victory Hill belonged
   to the lord of the dark sea. 34

COMPLAINT OF THE

36 **G**WELED llavnawr yn lliwed 1
16 yn cyvamwyn gal galed.
Rhac twrv aesawr go·deched,
18 Rhac (g)orðin vre gwyr vriwed, 4
Rhac meint y meðweint gaffed
19   o halawg nid atcored.
20 Y Mynawg (yna weled),
19 Cwyn oeð arnaw oe galed.
20 Oeð gyndyn cas ban drined,
    neu·r adwanei ry·waned.
22 Gwedy cwymp car cymrwyned,
    Oeð gwenwynig, carei ged. 12
37 Cyn golo gâr dan dudwed
1   dyrlyssei ev i Redeg.

2 **H**ynt drewid gan Ynt eilwad,
Claer oeð i daer arweinad. 16
Seithid, suðid Seis dig sad,
4 Ad·lyw go·gyvurð gymrad.
Eðyl ry·ðylwy bwyllad,
(Gwyr Eiðyn a ðinystrad). 20
5 Neu·s adroðyn ðyð plygad
na vei haval Gynt eilwad.

Another version.

34 **G**wr vrys o gaer crysgwyðad,
11 Da carei aerva vloðiad. 24
12 Ar neb un Seis, sisialad,
    a voðwyd, rhwng gwŷg adad.
13: Bro Vual lled oeð virein,
    (or Rhyd ev aeth werydrein). 28
Nis adrawð byw ðamweinad
14   vu i Lwch vun lyvanad.
Neu·s adroðyn ðyð plygad
15   na vei haval Gynt eilwad. 32

62

PALATINE'S HARDNESS

*B*LADES were seen to be stained
   in defending a difficult goal.
From clashing shields refuge was taken,
In front of Fort-hill slope men were crushed.
Because of the quantity of the drink taken
   there was no returning from the marsh.
Then the Palatine was observed,
There was complaint of his hardness of heart.
He was perverse and odious when fighting,
He would thrust again the severely wounded.
He was distressed at the fall of his friend,
   & worried because he hankered after booty.   12
      Before covering one he loves beneath
         the sod he sent him away to Redeg.

*T*he expedition was smitten by the Norse captain,
Brilliant was his steadfast leadership.   16
Shot and sunken was the irate doughty Saxon,
His deputy of much the same rank was taken.
An expedition demands circumspection,
Destroyed were the men of Eiδyn, who were   20
   saying, on the day of their humiliation, there
   could not be the like of the Norse captain.

Another version.

*H*e who rushed from the fort was precipitately
   felled, he did intensely love the tumult of war.   24
And this very Saxon, it was whispered, who
   had been drowned, was left amid the wrack.
The country of the Grosser Lord was pleasant
(From the Ford he went to his champaigne).   28
Those surviving will not tell of the misfortune that
   befell the Lache host, utterly worn. They were
   saying on the day of humiliation that there
   could not be the like of the Norse Captain.   32

THE LLOEGRIANS DEPART

    GODOÐAN, gorvynnan ðy·blygid
       dynòeu tra drumeu Trwyn Esyd.
14 Gwasceryn, di·ervyn heb ermyg
3   o gussyl mad Eryr Dwyv Weryd.
    I ragran, cynhorvan y Gogleð,
5 Wy eithyn, (rhy·lithryn gan liveð,)
    o lychwr i lychwr ar lwch bin,
    hyd lwchðor y Porffor bererin.   8
6 Llað oeð gwaws, rhuthr oeð maws y·mloeð
    trin, Galar, an·yscar a nâd gorðin.

7 Cynrein gywyrein gan Gyvrennin,
    yng·hatraeth gwerin ffraeth ffysgiolin 12
8 Gweith með yng·hynteð a chyveð gwin
9 (yng·awr Hu gwyðawr) rhwng dwy vyðin.

20 Cedwyr mor arwyr gyvarvuant,
    y·gyd yn unvryd yð ymhyrðant.   16
18 Llaðawð, cyminawð Gynt a lläin
    garneðawr tra gygawl o wyr trin.
21 Byrr hoedl, hir yw hoed ir ae carant,
22 Seith mwy or Lloegrwys a lygrassant. 20
    O wryseð eu gwrtheð ys gwyrth wnant :
15·1   Aml vam, i deigr lam, ar i hamrant.

14 Gwlad adver, go·glywer y·Nulyn,
13 Clud tonn Iwerðon bevr bererin.   24
14 Ban äei eilassei i läin,
    mal beyn wrych ni welych wyelin.
15 Nis cydvyð vy haer uð a·m gorðin,   27
    Attal vevl Morial yn or·ði·vlin.
16 Parawd i ðurawd i grei gwaedlin
10 Eðyw, moleid yw mygreid Darw Trin. 30

& GWYNEDD IS RESTORED

THOSE bowed down melt away, & eagerly seek
 the plains beyond the ridges of Esyd Point.
Without honour they dispersed and disarmed
 by the counsel of the Eagle of Dee Estuary.
To the frontier, the threshold of Gogleð,
 they went gliding with the flowing waters, from
 lagoon to lagoon, borne by the tidal bore
 as far as the watergate of the Pulford pilgrim.
Killing was sad, but charging & shouting was a joy,
Sorrow is inseparable from the uproar of war.

The captains set forth with the Cyvrennin,
At catraeth the merry men are impetuous
Because of mead at the court & wine bibbing, as the
 war shout rises Hugh falls atween the two armies.

The warriors met the sea heroes,—Unitedly,
 with one mind they thrust on every side.
The Norse slew, they cut down with lances
 heaps of the warriors, scowling greatly.
Their brief life was long a grief to their friends,
Seven times more Lloegrians rolled in the mud.
By the violence of their resistance they do wonders:
The tear of many a mother leaps to her eyelid.

The restoration of the land is whispered in Dublin;
The Irish sea bears away the splendid Pilgrim.
When going he disposed alternately the lances,
They were like bristles, you could not see the shafts.
My resolute King will not tolerate attacks on me,
He will unweariedly check the mischief of Morial.
His steel blade that was ever ready to shed blood
 has gone, Praised is the majestic Bull of battle.

19 (**M**ang) orðyvnad yn agerw,
4 Mynawg, llywyð a llaw chwerw.
5 Bu ðoeth a choeth a syberw,
 Nid oeð wrth gyveð go·verw.
 Muner Geinnion er Mon elw,
7 Nid oeð ar lês bro bod herw.
 Ae gelwyn ' Morgun Plymnwyd.'
 Yn·hryvrwyd peleidr yrrwyd.
9 A glasur hëyrn lliveid
  cwyðad ir llawr henavieid—
 Syrthyn yng·orun trydar,
10 Ffrwythlawn fflamður rhac escar.

11 **D**y·fföes cadveirch,
  yn greulyd eu seirch,
  o gatraeth goch·re.
12 Mang vlaen wyð-vidin,
  Dinistr a orðin,
  gwyth aerlyw gwarthvre.
13 Gelwir yn ffaw o glaer ffwyre,
  ech·adas heiðyn haearnðe.

14 **M**ynyðawg a orðawd yn arvor,
 Gan Vynawg ae gatrawd cwynhattor.
 Rhac Eiðyn y catgun nid atcor,
16 Ev godis yn ðilis yng·hynnor.
 Yn arial arðywal dy·gwyðwys,
17 Cant llewes a borthes eu gorffwys.
 O drawd Vynyðawg ni ðiangwys
18 arv, namyn amðiffyn amðiffwys.

19 **C**ollad y vorgad, neu·r vu aeth mawr,
 Ni phorthed, ni chadwed traeth na llawr.
21 Gwys dreiglyn beriglyn odrigawr,
 A·r orvyð as edryð werydawr.

66

THE PALATINE POWER

(Magnus) was inured to seething seas,
He controls the Palatine with a severe hand.
He was wise, refined, and dignified,
At a banquet he did not lean to babbling.
He upholds the men of Ceint for Mon's benefit,
Being marauded was not for the country's good.
They called him the ' Great lord of Battle,' 7
(When) at the ferry the javelins were hurled.
With sharp purple-glinting axes
   the veterans were felled to the ground. 10
They fell in the tumultuous surf—Full of
   fruition is a flaming sword against an enemy.

Their war steeds, with harness
   all gory, fled from the 14
   crimsoned Battle-strand.
   Magnus, who was a-head of his ships,
   destroys whom he pursues, and
   chafes the captain of the near hill. 18
His fame will be known for his brilliant onslaught,
He did not spare such as deserved the sword. 20

Mynyðawg was cut down on the seashore ;
By the Palatine and his men he was lamented.
The war-lord will not return before Eiðyn,
He rose with assurance at the start, 24
In fierce activity he fell, and one hundred
   swallowed what brought about their rest.
From Mynyðawg's expedition no arm escaped,
   except the one defending the steep round (fort). 28

Lost was the sea-battle,—loud the lamentation,
The strand was not supported, nor the land held.
The wandering race had menaced the inhabitants,
He who had conquered restores the lands. 32

THE RHYN SETTLEMENT

19 Dûg Morien oe lovlen las lavnawr   1
22 Tryn ðygwyð, Trwch deryð tra chylchawr.
    Ban orffid câr gollid bu ffoawr,
20 O ðilin með melyn y maglawr.

30 Delwad di·arvad vore y rhelyw,
 6   arðelwy rwysc rhwyv Bre,
    Rhymynnyn y wlad rymdwyre,
    Yscawl ðiscyn vlawð gynwyre.
 9 Nid noðed i Redeg Rhyn gre,
    Goðiwesid gormes gwlad Vre,
10 Ni ðeweint o vevl veint ware.

13 Da i Von doeth adon aeth adwen,
19 Edy yn heli vradw gelein wenn.
21 Neu·r ðelyei, ban gynnei yng·hynnor,
    ar ystum brwysc dremyn y pennor.
20 Lluðei a llostei ymffrost Bradwen,   16
    Ni waeth Morien wnaeth porthas ðïen.
22 Neu·r gwyðei orchwyð y marchogion,
14 Rhylaðei, ni laesei y Saeson.
30 Gwnn gel bob gorwel or mor bwy'r mor,
15   ni weleis wr o Seis yng·oror.   21

 2 Gwyr aeth orðin traeth chwerðyn o gnaw,
13   chwerw ynhrin a llaïn yn drylliaw.
14 Yn heð byrr vlyneð yð ynt ynðaw,   24
    Ban bor cad ðiffeith wlad wrth deithaw—
16 Cyrch eu gwynn lanneu i'w anreithaw,
    Dÿen weis a hên dreisid o law.   27

18 Gwyr aeth orðin traeth chwarð yn wamal,
    Discynnieit midin gyrch ði·achar,
19   ledawr ae llavnawr yn llanw trydar,
    Colovn rheith glyw gobeith rotho war. 31

IS NO SHELTER TO RHEDEG

𝕸orien bore in his grasp sharp blades, the Bold   1
   one falls, & the Fat one hies beyond bounds.
When his lost friend was overcome he fled,
The lure of the yellow mead entangled them.

𝐈n the morning were disarmed those that were left,
   who followed the proud Bre ruler.
   They coveted the country that will lift me up,
   Their violent descent is stirring up a rising,
The Rhyn settlement is no shelter to Rhedeg.
The oppression of the Bre land has been checked,
They will not escape the evil of so great a joust.

'𝕿was good for Môn that a King came who sees my   12
   straits.   He leaves a still white corse in the sea.
He fastened on the bearing and proud look of
   the leader, when he appeared at the entry.
He checked and punished Bradwen's pride ;   16
No matter what Morien did he wrought execution.
He brought low the haughtiness of the knights,
He did not set the Saxons free but destroyed them.
I know the refuge of every horizon from sea to sea,   20
   I saw never a Saxon in the land.

𝕸en went to the strand push laughing nervously,
They were bitter in battle rending with their lances.
In peace they continue but a short year,   24
When the wandering war lord ravages the country—
He enters their holy churches, committing sacrilege,
The agile & the old were plundered out of hand.

𝕸en went to the strand push laughing fitfully,   28
Those that disembark attack the hateful ones, who
   lie with their weapons in the tumultuous surf. May
   the pillar of justice, the rudder of hope, give us rest.

MERRY WERE THE MEN

2 GWYR aeth yng·hatraeth oeðyn ffraeth lu,   1
21   Með gwyn eu hancwyn ae gwenwyn vu.
   Cryssiant liveiriant yn trywanu,
3   a chwedy elwch tawelwch vu.
1 Cyrch cleu wynn lanneu oe hanallu,
   Dieu ðaðl angheu yn anghenu.

3 Gwyr aeth yng·hatraeth o veðvaeth dwn,
   Ffrwythlawn y camhawn nas cymhwyllwn.   8
   Am uð lavnawr rhuð garm vawr a gwnn,
5 Dwys ðengyn ymdaeryn vel aergwn.
6 Teulu gwasarn Hu bei barnasswn
      diliw dyn advyw nis adawswn.   12
7 O dreis y colleis a ðiffleiswn,
   Rhugl yn ymerbyn Môn ry·adwn.
   Ni mynn Gwrawl Rynn, gwaðawl hwegrwn
9 Maban i Gynan, o Vryn Cyngrwn.   16

10 Gwyr aeth yng·had traeth y gan wyrð wawr,
   Yn heð gynt travodynt eu hovnawr.
   Milawr athrigawl a ymdavlawr,
12 Creulyd y Gwyndyd ae hynn waewawr.   20
   Yngwriav wy orsav yngorawl,
   Rhac trawd Mynyðawg dyvyð Mwynvawr.

14 Gwyr aeth yng·had traeth y gan wyrð wawr,
   Eu moes gymodes eu cyvnesawr.   24
   Yvyn veð melyn meðal maglawl,
16 Vlwyðyn bu lewin lawer cerðawr.
   Ni chochawr paladrawr na pharawr,
      nac aestalch oeð wengalch, na phennawr.   28

19 Gwyr aeth yng·had traeth y gan y dyð,
   Wy oreu yng·hilieu gewilyð.
   Gorugant yn geugant geleuryð,
21 Llawenawr lliwedawr y·medyð.   32

WHO WENT TO CATRAETH

THE men who went to catraeth were a merry band,
  Fresh mead at their feast was their undoing. 2
They rush into the flooding tide, a-thrusting
  with loud acclamation, then all was still.
The swift retire to the holy churches in their impo- 5
  tence, driven by the fixed idea of death.

Men went to catraeth from an interrupted feast,
Fruitful the conflict that I did not promote. 8
Around the lord's ruddy blades a great shouting rises,
The stolid villeins disputed like dogs of war.
Of Hugh's prostrate retinue, had I been deciding, not
  the shadow of a man reviving would I have spared.
By force I lost what I had made secure, 13
Swiftly, at the moment of the struggle, I quitted Môn.
Brave (M.) wants not the Rhyn, but settles it on the
  father-in-law of the Scion of Cynan, of Conical Hill.

Men went to the strand battle with the green dawn,
In peace formerly they discussed their fears. 18
The garrisoning warriors are scattered,
Gory the men of Gwyneδ and their ashen spears.
Most bravely they make a successful stand, 21
Against the advance of Mynyδawg comes Mwynvawr.

Men went to the strand battle with the green dawn,
Their customs had won their associates. 24
They drank golden mead, soft and ensnaring,
For a year many a minstrel was radiant.
Nor spears nor bolts were crimsoned,
  nor white-enamelled targe, nor helmet. 28

Men went to the battle strand with the day,
  who had done in corners deeds of shame.
They had certainly caused blood to flow,
The soldiers are comforted by baptism. 32

WITH THE GREEN DAWN

3 Cymhorth hwnn cyn cythlwng a chythruð,
22 Eneint cleu rhac angheu oe hennyð.
4 Rhac blin ran gorðin gan y wawrðyð,
1   bwyat vu neirthiad Duw ir gwychyð.

2 Ⓖwr aeth yng·had traeth y gan y dyð,
   Llewei veð gwyn vei (ðengyn) vwythyð.
3 Truan gyvatcan gyvlüyðes,
   ae neges o dra gwres a drang ðyð.

10 Ⓖwr ðaeth i gad traeth y gan wyrð wawr,
   Wyneba yscorva oscorðvawr.
   Trei gyrchyn gynnullyn yn ffullvawr,
12 Yng·hynwan mal taran twrv parawr.
   Gwr gorvynt yn edvynt or·ledawr,
   Ev rwyged a chethred a chethrawr.
14 Oð uch llei Mang laðei a llavnawr,
   Yng·hystuð duc enyð arbennawr,
15 Y·Mordrei gwaredei anðledawr,
   Rhanc erchei, ethrychei a gyrch lawr.

5 Ⓑlaen claer eching gaer llynwyn engei,
1 Gwyr hydrem Gweryd ae dilydei.
   Ar bluðveð glyw llüeð ðywallei
3   yng·hibawr tramorawr y·Mordrei,—
   O·r gwirawd a vragawd rhagorei.
4 Eur drysor blaen Porffor Mein barthei,
   ae bascawl eðystrawr ðinystrei,
   O vryd ev weryd ae derbynei.
6 Blaenawr ðwyre awr ae buð mawr drei,
   ar aeth llwrw yn·hraeth hwerw y techei.

12 (Ⓡhi lu Rhyn or)vu yng·hynniv clod,
   yn amwyn gysyriyn gôr divrod.
4 O haeðad y galwad ' Rhi gorvod,'
   Oeð dor di·achor a châr Mordrei.

MAGNUS CAME TO CATRAETH

'Tis a support ere the great fast and the anguish,   1
    a swift salve before death for their souls.
Against the sad fate of the push at dawn,
    the ' bwyat ' was divine support to the nobility.   4

A hero went to the Battle strand with the day,
He drank fresh mead that was the villeins' dainty.
Full of pity was the talk of the assembled host.
His purpose through impetuosity perished that day.   8

A hero came to Battle strand with the green dawn,
He fronts the castle of the great retinue, which,
    assembling in great haste, rushed to the shore.
At the onset like thunder the clatter of the shafts,   12
The predatory hero while fighting is stretched out,
He had been cut down and pierced by darts.
Above the mud Magnus slew with blades,
    and imprisoned the souls of the chiefs.   16
At Mordrei he delivered the villeins,—He de-
    manded satisfaction and destroyed the invaders.

The brilliant leader of the liberated fort a pool held,
The keen-eyed men of Gweryd searched for him.   20
And the soft mead, (Owein), the war leader poured
    into the cups of the over-sea men at Mordrei.
Among fermented liquors mead excelled.   Magnus
    divided the gold treasure of the Pulford chief,   24
    whose well-conditioned chargers he destroyed.
With a will he delivers such as welcomed him,
The leader who raised the shout a low ebb will aid,
Such as rushed to the shore slunk bitterly away.   28

The King's force won the Rhyn in the famous conflict,
    defending those who dreaded the devastating band.
Deservedly was he styled ' King of Victory,'   31
He was an impregnable bulwark & friend of Mordrei.

MAGNUS WAS COURTEOUS TO THE

12 Oeð mynud wrth alltud ae cyrchei,
5 Oeð wir ðin y werin ae credei.
6 (Tymhor ban escor yr atcorei)
Gwynvydig neb elwid ban elei.

38 Erðyled canu, cyman cahed,
9 Rhi wnaeth am gatraeth anvad vrithred
11   (ar) gedwyr (Rhedeg a Mon ðengyn),—
Brathwys, gwyarwys sathar sengyn.   8
      (Ymlid) wys guneð,
12   Dïal am darveð,
      Gorug galaneð
        cyn bei ynhrigeð.   12
      Nid adwnawd cibno
      wedy cad gyffro.
14   Cynrein gymuned
      awr cyni daered.   16

16 Erðyled canu cyman ovri,
16 Twrv tan a tharan a rhyverthi.
18 Gwychrawg arðerchawg Ri erch vysci
ry·vedei, a rhuðei Eiðyn riv.   20
19 Di·veð or guneð i·m gynygei,
Ynghad gormeil gwlad a ðyglywei.
Yscwyd ar·yscwyd, hydr arossei   waew,
21   mal gwr hoew llesteirei,   24
Með ar·yvyn, ev nid yvei,
22   Nid archwaeth win, ni vaeth lywiei.

32 Goðeu wys a gwyðwys nwy gwystlei,
16 Rhac neb dyn caled gwŷn ry·vaccei,   28
17 Pan diried, seirch eirchieid, ðyrreith drei,
Gynt hëyn eis celyn gweis greuðei.
19 Ban waned, yng·hyvred (Mang) hyrðei,
Ir eillt ev cyveillt, mevl niw dyccei.   32

74

WEAK, & A TERROR TO THE RAVAGER

He was courteous to the exile who approached him, 1
  & a strong refuge to the peasants who trusted him.
(When the time came for his return home),
No one was called happy when he went. 4

A song is due, let it be perfect. Around Battle-strand
  the King threw into terrible confusion warriors
of Rhedeg and villeins of Mon. He gored
  & bled those who trampled on the down-trodden. 8
      He pursues the gens of the earls,
      He avenges the alarms,
      He worked execution
        ere he took rest. 12
      The feast was not renewed
        after the commotion of war.
      The captains were shriven in
        the hour of mortal distress. 16

One needs must sing of faultless renown,
Of the roar of fire, of thunder and tempest—
Of the hardy glorious King of dread tumult, who
  mowed down and crimsoned the Eiδyn number. 20
The dispossessed land of the earls he delivered to me,
In battle he learnt of the oppression of the country.
He brandishes his shield, confident he awaits the spear,
    and like an alert hero checks it, 24
    They drank much mead but the (king) would not,
    nor taste wine, which fosters not a leader.

He felled the men of Goδeu, he would take no hostages,
Against the hard-hearted he nursed his wrath. 28
When wastrels returned at ebb seeking equipment the
  Norse showered holly darts which crimsoned them.
When there was thrusting, on the run (Magnus) hurtled,
To the villeins a friend, he would not harm them. 32

THE ELEGY OF MAGNUS

³² Diwyd cadwas Ryd Ceint was mycrei
²⁰ pan ðyd im rhan dud glodvan Mordrei.

³¹ Ɑun Goðeu yngeleu ry·vyrut,
¹² ar tud a ffyscut as ry·angut.
¹³ Ban escyn y gelyn rac wnelhut, clyw-
    ei wynt gwaed meirw meint a wanut.
¹⁵ (Pym) mlyneð an tüeð vawrygut,
    astut cyminut (cyn ti) voðut.
¹⁶ (Kein) was ni·m gwerthas am na thechut,
    Traethad dy reithad vy mreithawdl glud.

²⁰ Ɒs tru, gwedy lluðiaw rhed gwys Goðeu,
¹⁶   gloes angheu amgyffred,
¹⁷ As trwm gennyv a thru gweled
    gwyðaw gwyr iðaw benn o draed.
    Dygn alaeth ac hiraeth vaged,
¹⁹ Gwyr pybyr oe tymhyr duðed.
    Tra bu, Mang ae lu olyged wriav,
²⁰   Wy orsav yng·haled,
    Y Rhyn ðoðyw im oe trined,
    Gwlad nev vo aðev eu neued.

The elegy of Magnus, killed in a skirmish
³⁴ Yn·ygn waew yð wyv
¹⁶   am ðiva vei·m rhwyv.
    Huð am goloed,
¹⁷ Goreu ystyried.
    Llu mawr ev laðawð
      yng·werth i adrawð—
    Llaðawð eil Nwython,
¹⁹   o eur dorchogion,
    gant o dir Reged
    hyd ban gymhwylled.

WHO FELL IN A SKIRMISH

When the Ceint captain, who sedulously kept the Ford,
  migrated, M. gave me the country of famous Mordrei.
The Lord of Goðeu you overthrew at the creek,
  and the land to which you hied you delivered.
When the enemy retires because of your work, he 5
  smelled the blood of the dead, so greatly you speared.
During (five) years you saved our coast, assiduously
  you cut down ere you perished. The Ceint captain
  did not betray me because you did not withdraw.
The story of your righting things my ode conveys. 10
'Tis sad, after checking the progress of the men of
  Goðeu, to realize the pains of death,
    I am heavy and sad at seeing
    his heroes falling headlong. 14
  Grievous the sorrow and the longing that grew,
    after ardent men buried out of their country.
While they lived (Magnus and his host) were deemed
  most heroic—they were steadfast in hardship, 18
The Rhyn has come to me from their fighting,
Heaven, for which they yearn, be their home.

    at Downpatrick in 1103.
  I am in deep pain
    at the wrecking of my King. 22
  Gloom has enveloped me, for
    the best he was deemed.
  He slew a great host—
    it is worth the telling— 26
  The fosterling of Nwython slew
    one hundred wearers of the gold
    torque from the land of Rheged,
    up to the time of the truce. 30

GRIFFYDD AP CYNAN

34 Bu gor·δrud ban aeth
20   cann wyr i Gatraeth.
   Oeδ leith gwr gwinvaeth,
     dragon y dalaeth.   4
22 Oeδ lywyδ cyn·vin,
   Oeδ lurig teilin,
   Oeδ gerth, oeδ güall,
35   ar gevn i gavall.
1 Ymyl Rhi gyrchwys,
  Llurig ni wiscwys.
  Llaδ lwyd a heiniv,
2 Gwaew ac aseth vliv.   12
3 No Mein, eil Nwython
  (ni weled y·Mon),
  heb gleδ na chyllell
3   neb gwr a vei well.   16

12 Neu·d wyv wledig blin,
9 Ni δïalav orδin.
  Ni·m gwarthes hwerthin
10   a dan droed cunin.   20
  Ystumiawg vyng·lin
    yn·hy deyerin.
11 Cadwyn heyernin
    am ffer vyn·eulin.   24

* * * * *

  Am veδ-vuelin
12   ynghaer traeth-verin,
   (tra) mi (gerδenhin)
    anyn aneir im.   28
  Ys gwyr Taliesin
13   oδeg gyvrennin.
  Neu ceint i orδin
    cyn gwawr dyδ dilin.   32

AND TALIESIN

There was rashness when the hund-
   red men went to the Battle-strand.
Sodden was the wine-fed hero,
   the dragon of the March.
He was ruler of the coast,
He was enveloped in armour,
He was eager, he was foolhardy—
   on the back of his horse.
The King, who wore no armour,
   drew to the shore.
He slew the old and the active,
Spear and dart he hurls.   Than   12
Magnus, Nwython's fosterling,
   there was not seen in Môn,
   without sword or glaive,
      a hero who was better.   16

I am a weary gwledig,
I will not avenge the Gorδin.
Ridicule did not disgrace me
   when down trodden by the earl.   20
Bent was my knee
   in the abode underground.
An iron chain encircled
   my ankles twain.   24

* * * * * * *

Around the mead-horns
   in the fort by the sea,
   while I was in exile the minstrels sang spiteful things of me.
Taliesin, who chatters of the   29
Cyvrennin, knows it.
Now I sang to the Gorδin
   ere next day's dawn.   32

79

THE CONFESSIONS OF

Gorchan aδevon.

26 **G**WALL yscar aval ac avall,
8   Ni chynnyδ rhïyδ o δy·wall,
10 Y doeth ni byδ noeth yn yscall,
   Ban angel ry·dynger yd ball,
12 Ni cherir ovnir anghyvieith,
   Neud amluδ i vuδ i areith.
13 Evnys yn vwythus am·wylltyn
      am swrn (lyn), am gyrn buelyn.
14 Yr aches darves a gollid,
      ar Tew led-vu lew, ergyr vid.
15 Rhuδid, ceisiessid treisiadon,
   Mein uchel, medei i alon.
11 As carwn, nid adei anreith,
      ae gâr ni byδ marw y·niffeith.
      Dyben ar orchan aδevon. 16

35 (**M**wy, o·r treis) encilie(is, ni gel)av,
21 O sîg cyndevig y Ryt mi gav.
36 Gwen Vannon gwyδ veδ(won o wleδ nâv
1   a deil) Weryd eil, wrhyd mwyhav. 20
2 A·r hawg gwych ffodawg aeth ffo yn hav,
   Eδyw y·mordwy madw bor arav.

3 **G**ormant wyr aethant wernyn,
      (yn ôl gwleδ) wîn meδw oeδyn. 24
   Rhac ffawd Mynyδawg rhuthryn,
5   cymrwynawg o δwyn gwar Rhyn.
   Mal taran Gynt ae tarvyn,
   Rhac rhynnawd pawb ry·edyn. 28

GRIFFYDD AP CYNAN

The Pæan of Confessions.

'TIS a mistake to separate an apple from a tree,
A prince will not prosper by neglect,
The wise will not go naked amid thistles,
An angel when denounced will flounder,
Unloved and distrusted is the alien of tongue,
   his speech impedes his interests.
The enemy, voluptuous around buffalo
   horns, were wild for a share of the drink.
He who threw the offing into confusion was lost,
The Fat one, rather bravely, attacks the ship.   11
Crimsoned were the oppressors that were pursued,
The sovereign lord mowed down his enemies.
Him I loved ; he would not allow pillaging,
   nor any friend to perish in the wild.   15

An end of the paean of Confessions.

(From the oppression) I fled (I will hide no more.) By the crushing of the prince-leader I shall have the Ford. The hero of Man fells the drunk from their lord's feast, Predominantly brave, he captures Gweryd's deputy, 20 And shortly the noble thickset one fled in summer! By sea departed this inert, slow prince.

The intemperate men sought the alder swamp.
After the wine-feast they were drunk.   24
From the fate of Mynyðawg they rushed,
   grieving for the taking of the Rhyn country.
     Like thunder the Norse scared them,
     Within a brief hour all were gone.   28

THE SAXONS AND NORSE MEET

37 **Cy**YVARVUANT ar vuð herw,
13   Dy·leidiad (Hu) ae lu meðw.
14   Ni bu ae cyhoeð ar enw,
     Ni bu elw ciwed gwyth hwerw,
     Cnivynt gwehilion avlerw,
16   Nid oeð ar lês bro bod berw,
17 Nis ciliwys Tarw Trin gwys ledw,
   Blivis y traws, anwaws ðelw.   8
20 Go·thor (gledr) bangor, a·r gaer vur (gyr-
21   chei) Cyn y bei (r)ev orthur.
   Rhwng twyn merthig vei ði·vur
23   ae gyv·or gwernol, gwant ður.   12
18 Ev gwant a drigant ech adav,
   Llaðei a welei oe eithav,
19 Oeð gwiw y·mlaen llu, oeð llariaf,
   Goðolei olieid yngaeav.   16

20 **C**arwn (vod ar dwm o) gysevin,
11   gweith með yng·hynteð a chyveð gwin.
12 Neu·r wanwn a chlwyvwn a lläin,
     cyn bu y llas llu o glas y ffin.   20
13 Carwn arglod Mwng orug waedlin,
14   ev saethes aseth yn yscethin.
   Carwn wrhyd trwn dewr vab Edwin,
15   a vei rhac Mordrei wr clodvawr trin.   24

12   **C**yd bei cannwr yn vyn·hy
8   Penn Ceint tal beinc a ðyly,
7   Adwen ovalon (diriv,
         Am gynhen traeth y) ceniv.   28

38 **E**rðyled canu clod i Gynon,
 1 Gynt vereu ni dereu lyw caer gronn.
 4 Marthawd Mynyðawg, llywyð mäon,
 2 Bu leith cyn dyrreith i dir Aeron.   32

82

ON A PLUNDERING EXPEDITION

They had met on a plundering expedition, Hugh 1
   & his drunken host were rolled in the mud,
None would refer to it by name,
Bitter strife did not benefit the community,
The disorderly wastrels gave trouble,
Commotion was not for the country's good,
The Bull of Battle budged not a furrow strip,
He shot the oppressor, an unpitied relic.
He broke down the stockade & made for the castle
    wall ere there was stout resistance,
  Twixt the wasted, defenceless hillock
    and its alder edge, he plied the steel. 12
Out of hand he speared those who tarried,
He slew his best all he saw.
Active at the head of his host, he was most gentle,
He enriched his followers in winter. 16

I should have loved to be on the mound from the first,
   because of mead at the court and wassail wine.
I should have thrusted, wounded with lances,
   ere the host of the Borderers had been slain. 20
I should have loved Magnus's high fame for shedding blood, 'Twas he who shot the dart with force.
I should have loved the fine hardihood of Edwin's brave
   son who, before Mordrei, was a renowned warrior.

  Though a hundred heroes were in my hall 25
    the chief of Ceint deserves the chief seat.
Cares (without number) are my familiars,
(About the conflict of the strand) I shall sing.

  To sing his praise is Cynon's due, the Norse 29
    darts did not hit this chief of the round Castle.
Mynyδawg, leader of the vavasours, was smitten,
He was dead ere he returned to the land of Aeron. 32

IN PRAISE OF CYNON

<small>38</small> Gatraeth aeth or ffraeth eurdorchogion
<small>6</small>   gwyδid, athrigid llurygogion ;
<small>5</small> Divodes eu harles gwaew galon,
<small>3</small>   ae habwy a vu vwyd ysclyvion.
<small>7</small> Herwyr oe tymhyr oeδ treiswyr Mon,
<small>17·12</small> a Phorffor oeδ wych δor amdrychion.
<small>38</small> Odid y megid, yn·hêg Aeron,
<small>9</small>   ir Rhyn a δoδyn well no Chynon.

<small>15</small> E͡dryd neuaδ glyd yn δi·anav,
<small>2</small> (Y gaer gron ae gwron a garav).
<small>3</small> Rhan vael, ev glyw hael o lwyn vwynhav,
   Cynon lary adon y wlad deccav.   <small>12</small>
<small>4</small> Dinas y·nïas ar llid eithav,
   Angor, byδin δor, buδ eilassav.
<small>5</small> Ac y·myt   or welid   ni welav
      δwg arv·gryd   yng·wrhyd   i wriav.   <small>16</small>
<small>7</small> Oswyδ a drewyδ a llavn llymhav,
      mal brwyn yd gwyδyn rhac i adav.
<small>8</small> Mabon gwlad Clyton, clod, hir canav—
      clod hêd bob parthed heb or eithav.   <small>20</small>

<small>8</small> Y͡s tanc anvonant o vro·r Deheu,
<small>8</small> Gwanar yd gynnal y devodeu,
<small>9</small>   o wyl a llarieδ,
      a cherδ a chyveδ.   <small>24</small>
Cyn clawδ drothwy nawδ i bwyth maδeu,
<small>10</small> Di·hyll ni bu hyll na geu diheu.
   Heintid, cwilyδid gwyryδ mameu,
<small>11</small> Mygreid oeδ voleid i vab Gwyδneu.   <small>28</small>
<small>12</small>   Car eiδig nis carei i glod,
      achubei, gwarchatwei i nod.

& THE FESTIVAL OF 1109

Such of the merry nobles as went to Battle-strand
　were struck down, and the mailed ones perished.
The thrusting of the enemy shattered their welfare,
　and their dead bodies fed the birds of prey.
Adventurers from home were the oppressors of Mon,
　and, Pulford was the fine citadel of the slain.
Of those who came to the Rhyn scarcely was there
　bred in fair Aeron a better than Cynon.

The cosy hall was restored faultlessly—
(The round fort and its champion I'll cherish).
He gives boons, a generous prince of noblest lineage
　is Cynon, the gentle lord of the fairest country.　　12
A stronghold in the tumult at its fury, he is our
　stay, the army's bulwark, & patron of minstrels.
Of those seen in life bearing a quiver
I shall not see in hardihood his hardier.　　16
The ravagers he drives away with a very sharp blade,
Like rushes they fall before his hand.　The praise of
　the scion of the land of Clutton long will I sing,—
It will fly afar, to every quarter, without limit.　　20

'Tis 'good will' they send from the Southern part,
　　The chief upholds the customs,
　　　　of festival and largess,
　　　　　　of minstrelsy and banqueting.　　24
Though he undermined thy sheltering threshold do not
　retaliate. The fair was never foul, nor the false true.
Corrupted, shamed are the chastity of mothers,　The
　majestic of aspect was worshipful to Gwyðneu's son.
　　　The fatuous lover cared not for his good　　29
　　name, he seized and clung to his object.

85

OWEIN AP CADOGAN

21 **B**AN ym·ðyvyð
10   llïaws prydyð,
        prydant wenn ffaw.   3
11 Ffun yn or deg,
    ar dal Rhedeg,
        ar hynt hwylaw.
    Cun gystuðiei,
    Cam garassei,
        Colledig ffaw.
    Ac Argoedwys
    gwae ordynnwys
        i ymðulliaw.
13 Ev ðarbodwys
    lüyð Powys
        ar lês Rhïeu.   15
    Ar·ðilyn goed,
14 Ar·ðyluð hoed
        a chyveðeu.   18
    Cyveð, coviant,
    ae dy·ðugant
        dan adlöeu.   21
15 Ar gŵyn Owein
    i oscorð erein
        rhac y Deheu.   24
16 Gawr a ðoded,
    Llwch Gwynn dorred—
        trydoll yscwyd,   27
17 Yspar llary ior,
    Molud mynor
        wneiff eisyllyd.   30
18 Cereint gwynei
    Hael a gwyðei,
        (gwledig) oe dud.   33

86

FALLS AT LLWCH GWYN

WHEN scores of poets shall come
from all parts, they will
sing of the renown of war.
A combined force in a fair country, on the border of Rhedeg,
is on the point of setting out. 6
A lord was grieving for
the wrong he had loved—
lost his good name.
And the men of Argoed
were attracted by his woe
to marshal for battle. 12
He provided
the host of Powys
for the King's benefit. 15
He clings to the woods,
He avoids delay
and carousals. 18
'Twas festivity, they recall,
that brought them
under animosities. 21
At the plaint of Owein
his retinue cry out
against the South. 24
The war shout was raised,
Llwch Gwynn was taken—
perforated is the shield, 27
Speared is the generous lord,
The praise of marble
his kin will carve. 30
Friends lamented the prince
that fell, a regent
out of his country. 33

GRIFFYDD AP RHYS

21 **D**I·ANNOD i glod eglur dann,
19 Di·achor angor yng·hyman.
20 Di·echyr eryr gwyr varan,
 Tryn oδev orδeu, oeδ eirian.
21 Rhagorei veirch mei rhacvuan,
 As meigryn lleδyn yng·Wynn bant.
22 Cyn glas veδ glas (gleδ) vu i rann,
 Bu gor·wleδ uch meδ mygr o bann.   8

AÐWYN Lledvegin cyn dyvod
 i δyδ, go·wychyδ i wybod,
8 Ys deupo car cyrδ gyvnod,
14 Y wlad aδev i adnabod.
15 Hyrwyδ caradwy gynran,
 Ceimad yng·had govaran.
16 A gwaewawr ev grwydr gadlan,
 ae yscwyd yn uswyδ man.   16
17 Cleδyval dywal di·wann,
 Mal gwr cadwei wyalvan.
18 Cyn cystuδ daer, cyn affan,
 o δaffar differth i rann.   20
19 Ys delwy gynnwys nev lân
 drindawd yn undawd gyvan.

20 **B**an gryssei vab Rhys cadr ynghad
 Mal baeδ coed y trychei drychiad.   24
21 Tarw byδin yn·hrin gyminad,
 Ev lithryn gwaewffyn oe anghad.
22 Ys vyn·hyst Owyn glyw y wlad,
9 a Gwrien, a Gwynn a Gwriad—   28
1 Aethant Borth Hoδnant gyminad,
 a Brynn Hydwn, cynn y caffad.
2 Gwedy eu meδwi y tranghad,
 ac ni weles yr un i dad.   32

88

RETURNS FROM IRELAND

STRAIGHTWAY his conspicuous fame spreads, 1
He was a steadfast anchor in council.
An unflinching Eagle, he learns what fury is,
Doughtily he endures buffettings, he was brilliant. 4
He would outstrip the fleetest war steeds,
Him they surprised and slew in the Gwynn hollow.
Ere the green grave, the purplish sword was his lot,
A high feast was held over the glorious mead-cup. 8

GENTLE is the Fosterling till the coming of
his day,—Rather fine his manners,
The time of the lover of minstrelsy will come,
and the country will acknowledge him.
Spirited is the lovable captain,
and a comrade in the rage of battle.
With lances he moves to and fro in the field,
and a shield that is shivered in pieces. 16
Fierce and mighty his sword strokes,
Like a man he kept his post.
Before the grave and its muteness, he de-
fended, from a sense of duty, his division. 20
May he be received into the holy heaven
of the Trinity in perfect union.

When Rhys's heroic son rushed into action,
Like a wild boar he would rend the render. 24
He was the army's bull in the conflict of battle,
The javelins glided from his hand.
My witness is Owein, prince of the land,
And Gwrien, and Gwynn, and Gwriad— 28
They went to the conflict of Porth Hoðnant,
and to Brynn Hydwn, ere they were taken.
After making them drunk they perished—
not a single man saw his father again. 32

THE FOUNDERING OF THE WHITE SHIP

*This canto refers to the loss of the " White Ship"
(Nov. 25, 1119, Yorke Powell), and to the conflicts
(of 1118, Lloyd) between Howel ap Ithel and the*

22	DIHENYÐ lŷr bob dyð lanwed,	23·21	1
1	Hoewal amhaval avneued,		
7	Rhïein mor ðilein, a mynawg,	24·6	
8	ac a oeð dëyrneð teithawg.		
4	Bid in amðiffyn rhac tynged	24·2	
	Mawrion wychrolion ry·golled.		
2	Tyllvawr i rodawr, gwas vrathed,	23·22	
	gwychawg Ruvoniawg a ðiffred.		8
3	Eil Ceint welyðeint am Aled,	24·1	
	a seirch eu cadveirch yn greuled.		
6	Howel vab Ithel a orffei,		5
6	Anant, galan, gant orugei.		
5	Trwm trin, a lläin y llaðei,		
	Garw rybuð o gad ðyðygei.		
7	Gwenid gan Wchtrid trahäawg,		5
9	Cilyð Gwyndyd uð waredawd.	7	16
	Howel, cyn gro ðêl ar i ruð,	8	
10	edvyn, ae cyrchyn ymachluð.		
	I gêd, gwych glodred echïawg,		
11	a thwm yngArthmyn Rhyvoniawg.		20
12	Peis ðivodad oeð vreith-deg,		
	o grwyn (cathod) ban greithed.		
13	Hwibanei ' hŵit ' hwidogeith,		
	Hwibenid ' hŵit, hŵit ' wyth gweith.		24
14	Ban elei Howel i heiliaw,		
	Llath ar i yscwyð llorv yn llaw,		
15	Geilw i gwn, i hely ae dwg,		
	Daly Giff, daly Gaff, daly Dïwg.		28

& THE DEATH OF HOWEL AP ITHEL

sons of Owein ap Edwin on the Banks of the Aled. See Bruts, 303—304. The two events, apparently, followed each other closely in time.

THE tide of tragic death is daily at the flood,   1
   It whirls in eddies just as it listeth.
The sea destroys the princess, & the etheling,
   & the lords that were voyaging (with them).
May there be for us a shelter against the fate
   of the great nobles that were lost.
Riddled with holes is the shield of the speared
   knight, who is defending glorious Rhuvoniog.
The fosterlings of Ceint settle down beyond Aled,   9
   with their harness and war steeds all gory.
Howel the son of Ithel prevailed, on New
   Year's day the minstrels will praise his deeds.   12
Heavy the fighting, with lances he slew,
   (but) bore a bitter warning from battle.
He was speared by the haughty Uchtryd,   15
The colleague of Gwyneð's delivered lord.
Howel, ere gravel covers his cheek, returns
   home, and his attackers disappear.   18
His guerdon, a glorious, echoing fame,
   and a grave at Garthmyn in Rhuvoniog.

Striped and fair was the coat of the dead (Ho.)   21
It was made of (cat)-skins that were sutured.
He would toot " hoo-it " in tooting language,   23
   " hooit, hooit " he would repeat eight times.
When Howel went to provide for a feast,
   lance on shoulder and spear in hand,   26
He calls his dogs and takes them to hunt,
Catch it Giff, catch it Gaff, catch it Dïwg.   28

HOWEL AP ITHEL

22 Ys gwânei bysc yng·Honwy
₁₆   ban lam ffithell yn Llugwy.
₁₇ Ban elei Howel vynyδ
          dy·δygei ev, yr un-dyδ,   4
₁₈   benn-iwrch, benn-avr, benn-hyδ,
          benn-grugiar vreith y gweunyδ,
₁₉   benn-pysc rhaeadr Derwenyδ,
₂₀   a gwythwch Llwyn Llwyvenyδ.
₁₉ Or sawl gyrhaeδ ar gigwein
₂₁   nid eing ni vo or·adein.   10

      He speared fish in Conwy   1
  when the young salmon leap in Llugwy.
When Howel went to the mountain,
    he would bring, in the course of a day, 4
    the finest buck, finest goat, finest hind,
    the finest mottled grouse of the moors,
    the finest fish of Derwenyδ falls,   7
    and a wild sow from Llwyvenyδ Forest.
Of such as he reaches with barbed spear,
    none escapes that is not very swift. 10

Y Gorddin

y Mordrei Gwynedd:

AMENDED TEXT & TRANSLATION.

Now the time is come to ask the strangers who they are . . . Strangers, who are ye? Whence sail ye over the wet ways? on some trading enterprise, or at adventure do ye rove, even as sea-robbers, over the brine, for they wander at hazard of their own lives bringing bale to alien men—ODYSSEY III.

THE GREAT STRAND PUSH

of 1098 at

ABER LLEINOG IN PENMON

attributed to

TALIESIN

TALIESIN SINGS OF THE

    Ⓜoch ẟwyre awr y·more,
        Cynniv Aber rhac ystre.
17 Bu vwlch rhac twlch, bu danẟe,
22 Mal Twrch y tywys weis bre.
    Bu govud myn yd vu lle,
    Bu gwyar ar weilch gwrmẟe.

18   Ⓜoch ẟwyre awr y·meiẟin,
1   Cynniv Aber rhac midin.
2   Dy·vrys, tywys i ẟilin,
    Rhac cant ev gwant cysevin.
3   Oeẟ garw y gwnäei waedlin,
    Mal yd vei lliv ar vreithin.
4   Oeẟ llew, llaẟei yn ẟiwin
      o gleẟyval ffysciolin.
    Oeẟ mor ẟi·achar ys trychei escar,
      gwr haval yn y bei.   16

6 Ⅾiscynnwys yn affwys benn dra phenn,
    neu·r ẟeliid yng·hynwyd y cynben.
    Dysgïawr breint drangawl ar gangen,
8 Ys cynneẟv escyn Ewein yn benn.   20
    Nu, Mwng a ystwng oreu gynhen,
    a rhein y dy·lein cyd bei di·lenn,
10 Lüeẟ lwyroẟev ry·wyth ascen,
    yng·hamlas avlwyẟas i lwyven.   24
      Dy·fforthes aelaw,
      Lluryg wehyn (nawv).
    Dyvnwall rawg lleid ẟal
12   o ebrwyd brennial.   28
    Eiẟol oeẟ oergrei,
    Grannawr gwynnion vei.
12   Ban (Bleiẟ ae gwel drei),
      dy·chïawr (na) bei.   32

BATTLE OF THE STRAND

Hastily he raises the war shout in the morning,
    He fights for the Aber in front of the arena.
There was a breach before the knoll, & conflagration.
Like a boar he leads the warriors of the Hill.
There was trouble whenever there was a chance,
The black-mailed knaves were covered with blood.

Quickly he raises the war shout in the field-fort,
He contests the Aber against the ships.
He rushes, he leads his following,
At the head of a hundred foremost he thrust.
He was brusque, he caused blood to flow,
    as if it were a flood in showery weather.
He was a lion, he slew fiercely
    by rapid sword strokes.
He was so irrepressible, he would cut down the
    foe like a man, wherever he might be.

He plunged into the deep head over heels,
Caught in destruction was the former ruler.
His perishing rights were stripped by the arrow,
By the rule of succession Owein rises to be head.
Now Magnus brings him low who made the strife,
    killing him with darts though himself unmailed.
The wager of war paid the extreme penalty of
    disaster. In the shallows his lance failed.
        He suffered dolour, mail
           prevents him swimming.
        Dyvnwall, awhile the mud
           holds from speedy burial,
        His corse was frigid,
           and pallid were his cheeks.
        When Lupus sees him at the ebb
           he laments that he is no more.

TALIESIN'S PAEAN

18 Rhi brawv berchenawr
13   meirch ac yscwydawr.
14 Gwae ! o oed discyn
    cyvergyr escyn.   4

31 Ys blwng yng·hyvwng Hu gynnivei,
2 yng·hyvranc nid oeð danc gyhoeðei.
  Ðyð lleith y cochweith nis gochelei,
4 Baeð dig oeð Bleiðig, i leid elei.   8
Yng·wleð gwin a með ŷv o lestri llawn,
    ðyð camhawn, wnant gam vri,
6 Y·ar amws, cawr, cynn oe drenghi ,
    calaneð cochweð ae dybi.   12

26 PERYV brydav,
18   Gorchan ganav,
19   a darð wrthrin.
    Gweilging yn fforch,   16
21 Twrch drwyd am dorch,
    trych tra chethin.
27 Gyr rei i gilvach,
1 Go·vurth wyr hydrach.   20
2 Rhac canhwynawl (nêr),
3   cann llwgr ðwg dyvel.
    Disgyn n ial ansel,
    i bob cwrr yð el—   24
4 Drwy heol, drwy gernin,
    drwy gîb llawr gerwin.
5 O oror dreinwyð
    galar dwvn ðyvyð.   28
  Gwynneð as gwelyn
6   a chreu oe gylchyn.
    Celedig ðengyn
    a vygr(ed ir Rhyn.   32

TO THE RAVAGING BOAR

The King tests the owners
of chargers and shields.
Alas ! from the moment of descent
the conflict waxes more & more.

Fiercely, in a strait, Hugh would fight, In an
encounter he would never cry peace. On the day
of slaughter he did not shun ruin ; An angry
Boar was the Lupusian ; into the mud he sank. 8
At feasts he drinks mead & wine from full beakers,
which on the day of battle bring ill fame ;
On his charger before death,
Red carnage overtakes the champion.

I WILL celebrate a lord,
A paean I will sing
that will start reaction. 15
The jousting rod is in place,
The Boar advances for the prize,
and fights very fiercely.
He drives some into hiding, 19
He repels the more daring.
Against the native lord, the
ravager brings a hundred ills.
Unseen he descends into the open, 23
& visits every nook and corner—
By road, by mountain sides,
& the edge of rough ground.
From the border of prickly bush 27
a sound of deep wailing comes.
He was seen foaming white
with blood flowing around him.
The villeins in concealment
were removed (to the Rhyn. 32

THE BOAR

    Ynghynteð meiðin
        gwleð win vu a) með,
   (Bu dwrv gan y dyð,
       galon ban ðyvyð).
26 Twrch gyrch yn Avon,
 21   rhac tarv Rhi wr(th) honn.
    Cyn nawð oe Geinnyon
      rhyll garn i waewffon.
27 Eis grein oe gylchyn
  7   rac badeu gelyn.
    Cynvelyn, gas nâr,
  8   ys gwna briffwn bâr.   12
  1 Rhyd chwyrn rhac Einglyon
  2   vriwyn ardal Vôn.
26 Rhyvel Vargodion,
 22   a bliv ysgyrion,   16
      rhac ffyrvach adon,
      a gwych varchogion.
 27 Dyrreith Tramorion,
  9   ad·vordwy haelon,   20
 10 Cyvred coed gwyllion,
      a'r weilgi dirion.
    Tëyrn tud anaw,
 11   ys meu i gwynaw.   24
    Gorvyniad gelyn,
 12   ehangseid ervyn,
  8 Goborthei adar,
      ae dênyn d'ÿar.   28
37·7 Llavnawr lledruð
      llawr gyvachluð.
    Gwron go·ruð
  8   guð y marian.   32

ENCOUNTERS CYNVELYN

At the court of the burg there was 1
   a feast of wine and) mead.
(There was tumult at dawn
   when the enemies were coming.) 4
The Boar repairs to the Avon,
   against the scare on its bank.
Ere the men of Ceint can aid
   he rives the shaft of his spear.
Darts hem him round
   in front of enemy boats.
Cynvelyn, hateful lord,
   causes the burden of his fury. 12
He rushes the Ford against the Eng-
   les ravaging the borders of Môn.
He makes war on the Borderers,
   and shoots his darts 16
   against the stouter lord,
   and the noble knights.

The oversea force returned,
Our princes sail home. 20
The gloomy woods run paral-
   lel with the sea coasts.
The prince of the land of Song,
'Tis mine to lament him. 24
The envy of the enemy was
   his long hafted weapon,
   which fed the birds (of prey)
   lured on by the tumult. 28
Blood-stained weapons
   cover the ground,
The champion incarnadined
   the gravel covers. 32

LUPUSIANS FLEE

37   Llanw orlediad,
 8   Rhawg enhuðad,
 9   As dal Vleiðiad—
      nid Bleið ciman.
    Llu arth-deulu,
10   Llanw yn lladu,
    Cyn oe daly
      wy ðïangan.

The high spreading tide,
  a temporary covering,
  holds the Lupusian—
    not the real Lupus.
The men of the garrison,
  blessing the flowing tide,
  make their escape
    before they are caught. 8

VARIANT VERSIONS

38·1	Erdyleda*m* canu *i cinon*	*a.*
17·1	Ardyledawc canu *claer orchyrdon*.	*b.*
38·1	cig ueren in guanth	*c.*
	* * * * * *	*d.*
38·2	ac *cın bu diuant dıleıt* aeron	*e.*
17·1	a *gwedy dyrreith dylleinw au*on.	*f.*
38·2	*riuesit i* loflen *ar* pen eirırhon luit	*g.*
17·2	*dimcones* lovlen benn eryron . llwyt.	*h.*
38·3	*en anuıt* guoreu buit i sgliuon	*i.*
17·2	*ef* gorev vwyt y ysgylvyon.	*k.*
38·4	ar *les* minidauc *marchauc* maon	*l.*
17·4	ar *neges* mynydawc *mynawc* maon.	*m.*
38·5	em dodes itu ar guaiu galon	*n.*
17·5	* * * * * * *	*o.*
38·5	ar gatraeth o*ed fraeth* eur dorchogyon	*p.*
17·3	or *a aeth* gatraeth o eur dorchogyon.	*q.*
38·6	wy guenint lledint feiuogion	*r.*
	* * * * * * *	*s.*
38·7	*oed ech eu temyr* treis *canaon*	*t.*
17·11	*a merch eudaf hir* dreis *gwananhon*.	*u.*
38·8	oed * * * * * *	*v.*
17·12	oed porfor gwısgyadur dır amdrychıon.	*w.*
38·8	*odid ımıt* o barth urython	*x.*
17·4	*ny doeth en diwarth* o barth vrython.	*y.*
38·8	gododın *o* bell guell no chenon	*z.*
17·5	ododin *wr* bell well no chynon.	
38·9	Erdileda*f* canu ciman ca*fam*.	A.
16·12	Ardyleda*wc* canu kyman ca*ffat*.	a.
38·10	cetwir am gatraeth *ri guanaid* brıt ret.	B.
16·13	ketwyr am gatraeth *a wnaeth* brithret.	b.
38·11	britgue *ad* guiar sathar sanget.	D.
16·13	brithwy *a* wyar sathar sanget	d.
38·11	segi*t guid* gunet	*dial* am dal med	E.
16·14	Sengi *wıt* gwned	*bual* am dal med.	F.
38·12	*o* galanet	*ciueu rig*|*et*	G.
16·15	*a* chalaned	*kyuırynged*.	H.
38·13	nis adraud cipno	guedi kyffro cat	I.
16·15	ny*t* adrawd kibno	wede kyffro cat.	K.
38·13	*ceuei* cimun *id*	*au* ciui daeret	L.
16·16	*ket bei* kymun	keui dayret	M.

VARIANT VERSIONS

34·6 *Leech* leu*d*ud	A	L*l*ech leu*tu* 13·4
tut leuure	B	tut leu*d*vre
8 gododin *stre*	C	gododin *ystre*.
stre	D	*ystre* ragno
....	E	....
......ancat	F	a*r* y a*n*ghat. 5
ancat *cyngor*	G	angat ......
cyngor	H	......gynghor
....	I	e leuue*r* cat.
....	K	....
....	L	....
....	M	....
....	N	....
....	O	....
....	P	....
....	Q	cangen gaerwys
....	R	keui dullywys. 6
....	S	tymo*r* dymhestyl.
8 .... temestyl	T	tymestyl *dymor*.
trameryn lestyr	U	e be*r*i *r*estyr 7
trameryn lu	V	....
heidilyaun	W	....
9 *lu meidlyaun*	X	....
let lin lu	Y	*rac rial*lu.
o dindy wyt	Z	o dindywyt
....	k	yn dyvu wyt
en dy *ow*u	β	yn dy*w*ovu.
10 scuyt *grugyn*	γ	ysgwyt *r*ugyn 9
i rac *taryf trun*	δ	rac *tarw trin*
tal briv bu	ε	*y* dal vriw vu.
....	ζ	Dwys yd wodyn 8
....	η	llym yt wenyn.
....	θ	llwyr genyn llu.

102

VARIANT VERSIONS

23·15	L*l*ech lle*s*di*r*	A	Lle*th* leudir(e)δ
	....	B	Tud lleu(δy)vre(δ)
16	gododın ..	C	(Heleδ) ystra(d).
15	di*th* ti*th* rag*on*	D	Ystr*y* rhagom
	....	E	(wyr Iwerδon)
	ar*y*s ga*r*	F	arv yn anghad.
	....	G	An*v*ad (es)cor
	....	H	(vu oe) cynghor
	....	I	yn lleuver cad.
16	R*y* du*c* diwyll	K	*H*u δug bibyll
	o win bebyll	L	o win diwyll
	a*r* lles tymy*r*	M	ar les (Saeson).
15	Tec wa*r*e	N	Te*r* (yd) ware
16	.. *r*ac yst*r*e	O	(yn) rhac ystre
	.... anhon	P	(a gwenn V)anhon.
	....	Q	Cangen gaer wys
	....	R	ce(w)ri δullywys
	....	S	tymhestl (δarvu).
17	tymo*r* tymestyl.	T	T*r*a mor dymhestl
	t*r*a me*r*in llestyr.	U	Tra merin lestr
	tra merin llu.	V	(dy·lann δyvu).
18	llu meithlyon.	W	H(u) Eiδy*n*ion
	*k*ein gad*r*awt rwyd	X	(ffwyr) vaetholion
	*r*ac *r*iallu	Y	rhac Llychlyn lu.
19	o dindywyt	Z	On di*r*dynwyd
	en dyuuwyt	k	ev dy·vy*r*ywyd
	yn dyo*u*u.	β	an dy·o*r*vu.
	ysgwyt *r*ugyn	γ	Cwyδ (yn) grugyn
20	rac *d*ole*u* t*r*in	δ	rhac (arvawd) tryn
	tal vriw vu.	ε	i dal briw vu.
	....	ζ	Llym δy·wenyn
	....	η	dwys yd voδyn
	....	θ	Llwyr ge(v)nyn llu.

103

VARIANT VERSIONS

35·12	*Ni* forth*int* uei*ri* molut *m*uet	*a.*
17·13	*Dy*fforth*es* mei*wyr* molut *n*yuet.	*b.*
35·12	rac trin ri allu trin orthoret	*c.*
17·13	* * * * * *	*d.*
35·13	*tebihic* tan teryd *drui* cinneuet.	*e.*
17·13	*baran* tan teryd *ban* gynneuet.	*f.*
35·14	diu maurth guisgassant eu *cein* du*h*et	*g.*
17·14	duw mawrth gwisg' eu *gwrym* dudet.	*h.*
35·15	diu merchyr *bu guero* eu *cit* unet	*i.*
17·15	diw merchyr *perideint* eu *calch* doet.	*k.*
35·15	diuyeu *cennadeu amodet*	*l.*
17·15	divyeu *bu diheu eu diuoet.*	*m.*
35·16	diu guener calanet *a ciuriuet*	*n.*
17·16	diw gwener calaned *amdyget.*	*o.*
35·17	diu sadurn bu di*d*urnn eu cit gueithret	*p.*
17·16	diw sadwrn bu di*v*wrn eu kyt weithret.	*q.*
35·17	diu sul laueneu rud *a at ranhet.*	*r.*
17·17	diw sul *eu* llavneu rud *amdyget.*	
35·18	diu llun hyt beñ clun guaet lun guelet	*t.*
17·18	diw llun hyt benn clun gwaet lun gwelet.	*u.*
35·19	*nys* adraud gododin guedy lludet	*v.*
17·18	*neus* adrawd gododin gwedy lludet.	*w.*
35·20	*hir* rac pebyll madauc pan atcor*h*et.	*x.*
17·19	rac pebyll madawc pan atcoryet	*y.*
35·20	* * * * * * *	
17·20	namen vn gwr o gant ene delhet	*z.*
20·2	Gweleis y dull o benn tir adoyn.	*a.*
23·6	Gveleys y dull o bentir a doyn	*b.*
20·2	aberth *am* goelkerth a *disgynnyn.*	*c.*
23·6	aberth*ach* coel kerth a *emdygyn.*	*d.*
20·3	gweleis *oed kenevin ar dref redegein.*	*e.*
23·7	Gueleys *y deu oc eu tre re ry gwydyn.*	*f.*
20·4	*a gwyr* nwythyon ry gol*l*essyn.	*g.*
23·8	*o eir* nwython ry godessyn.	*h.*
20·4	gweleis gwyr *dullyawr* gan *awr* adevyn	*i.*
23·8	Gueleys y wyr *tylluawr* gan *wavr* a doyn	*k.*
20·5	a phenn dyvynwal *a breych* brein ae c'.	*l.*
23·9	a pheñ dyuynwal *vrych* brein ae knoyn.	*m.*

104

VARIANT VERSIONS

22·1	Dïenhyt y bob llawr llanwet	A.
23·21	Dihenyd y bop llaur llanwet	B.
22·1	e hual amhaual afneuet.	C.
23·21	y haual amhal afneuet	D.
22·2	twll tal e rod*awr* cas ohir	E.
23·22	twll tal y rod*avc* cas ohir	F.
22·2	gwy*th*awc rywonyawc diffre*idyeit*.	G.
23·22	gwy*ch*auc rywynyauc diffre*t*.	H.
22·3	eil *gweith gelwide*int amalet.	I.
24·1	eil *with gwelyde*int amalet	J.
22·3	*yg cat* veirch *a* seirch greulet.	K.
24·1	*y gat* veirch *ae* seirch greulet	L.
22·4	bedin *ag kys*goget *yt vyd cat*	M.
24·2	bit en any*s*goget *bit get*	N.
22·4	vor*yon. coch*ro llann ban ry godhet.	O.
24·2	uor*on gwychyrol*yon pan ry godet.	P.
22·5	trwm en trin a *llavyn* yt *lla*δei	Q.
24·3	trwm en trin a *llain* yt *la*dei	R.
22·5	*garw.* rybud o gat dydygei.	S.
24·3	*gwaro* rybud o gat dydygei *gant*.	T.
22·6	cann calan *a* darmerthei	U.
24·4	can *yg* calan darmerthei.	V.
22·6	ef gwenit a dan vab *e*rvei.	X.
24·5	ef gvenit a dan vab *u*rvei.	Y.
22·7	ef gwenit a dan dwrch trahawc.	Z.
24·5	ef gwenit a dan dwrch trahawc	a.
22·7	vn riein a morwyn a my̆nawc	b.
24·6	vn riein a morwyn a me̊navc	c.
22·8	a *phan* oed mab *teyrn* teithiawc	d.
24·6	a *chan* oed mab *brenhin* teithiauc.	e.
22·9	yn*g*gwyndyt gwaed*glyt* gwaredawc.	f.
24·7	*ud* gwyndyt gwaet *kilyd* gwaredauc.	g.
22·9	kyn golo gweryt ar rud *llary.* hael	h.
24·8	kyn golo gweryt ar grud *hael*	i.
22·10	etvynt *digythrud*.	j.
24·8	etvynt *doeth dygyrchet*	k.
22·10	*o glot a chet* echiawc.	l.
24·9	*y get ae glot ae* echiauc	m.
22·11	*neut* bed garthwys hir o *dir* rywonyawc.	n.
24·10	*uot* bed *gor*thyn hir o *or*thir rywynawc.	o.

105

VARIANT VERSIONS

34·11	Eur ar mur caer crisguitat	A.
11·20	Eur ar vur caer krysgrwydyat	B.
34·11	*dair caret* na *hair* air mlodyat	C.
11·20	*aer cret ty* na *thaer* aer vlodyat.	D.
34·12	un *ſſaxa secisiar*	E.
11·21	vn *axa ae leissyar*	F.
34·12	ar*gouud*uit adar	G.
11·21	ar *gatwyt* adar	H.
34·13	*bro uual pelloid* mirein	I.
11·21	*brwydryar. syll o* virein	K.
	* * * * *	L.
34·13	*nys* adraud a uo *byv* o damgueinieit	M.
11·22	*neus* adrawd a vo *mwy* o damweinnyeit	N.
34·14	lui o*dam lun* luch liuanat	O.
12·1	llwy o*d a*mluch lliuanat.	P.
34·14	*nys* adraud a uo *biu* in *dit pleimieit*	Q.
12·1	*neus* adrawd a uo *mwy* en awr *blygeint*	R.
34·15	na bei cinaual cin*elueit.*	S.
12·2	na bei kynhawal kyn*heilweing.*	T.
37·12	tut uwlch treissic hair caer godileit.	A.
32·6	tutvwlch treissic aer caer o dileith.	B.
	Bylchid caer treisig aer o gylched,	
37·10	enuir ith elwir od guur guereit	C.
32·8	enwir yt elwir oth gywir gverit.	D.
4	enwir yt elwir oth gywir weithret.	E.
9	kewir. yth elwir oth gywir weithret.	F.
16·10	Kywir yth elwir oth enwir weithret.	G.
	Cywir yδ elwir δug in wared	
37·11	rector liuidur mur pob kyuyeith	H.
32·5	rector rwyfyadur.mvr pob kyuyeith.	I.
10	rector rwyvyadur mur pob kiwet.	K.
16·11	ractaf rwyuyadur mur catuilet	L.
	'*Rector, rhwyv pob or, mur pob ciwed,*'	
16·11	merin a madyen mat yth anet.	M.
32·10	meryn mab madyeith mat yth anet.	N.
	Moryen am·Hadyen, mad yd aned.	

106

LIST OF SCRIBAL ERRORS.

a : o, e

3·9 maban (: ? -on) 31·22   o
13·11 vanncarw : vancori
13·15 carnwyt : cornwyt
20·15*mab keid : mordrei
21·2·8 a : o, 23·11, 27·5*
21·11 ar : or 25·5
23·21 haual : ho(e)wal
27·8 adar : o δar
27·22 buant : buont
29·6 tramanon : tramorion
29·12 kenan : Kynon
33·19*grann : gronn
33·19*gwylaes : hwyl-oes = wys
37·19 ac : oe
38·15 am : onn
16·12 caffat : caffet   e
20·8 gwanan : gwenan
21·5 llavar : llawer
31·22 o dra : edre- : edry-
35·22 guannannon : Gwen Vannan
36·22 carai : carei

b : ð, h, k, v, ʚ

2·3 mab : mad, 4·9, 9·12,   ð
  10·4, 11·14, 14·3, 20·15. 27·20
16·14 bual = dial 38·12. cp. 36·15
24·15 mab : mad(w), 24·21, 38·20
28·18 ebyr : ev dyrr
29·22 llib : -lid
31·4 baran : daran
32·16 eb : dē = dyn
34·5* browys : dorwys
36·15 bu : di-, 37·10 di(a)ngan
11·12 beli : heli   h
13·18 ymbell : ymhell
21·17 bu : Hu
34·19 grimbuiller : gymhwyllet
7·17 buδ : kuδ   k
28·21 uebir : vekit
26·16 adebon : aδevon   v
31·22 o dra ban- : edryvannawc
35·22 tebic : tevic, 35·12
17·16 byt : ʚyδ   ʚ

b : δ, l, ꝓ

25·11 Pubell : Ruδell   δ
4·9 vab : yal   l
28·4 mab : mal
7·12 buδ : ꝓuδ
15·13 gwebyl : gweꝓyl
20·15*mab- : moꝓdrei

c : e, g, r, t

13·7 bwch : boet i
32·14 cw : ev
36·19 ac : oe, 37·19,
37·14 ac : ae cyhoeδ
37·3 sehic : seithei
19·2 Mac, Muc 16·4, = Mang   g
31·12 celyo : geleu   [11·17
34·15 cin, 38·1 cig, cint 37·2, cit
  37·6, kynh 12·2, kynt 15·16 =
37·3 cleu : glyw   [Gynt
4·13 chethrei : rhethrei   r
10·3 ac : ar, 36·1, 37·13·14
17·20 -awc : -awr 18·1, 20·6
20·15*mab keid : moꝓdrei
23·15 tec : ter
26·15 keis : treis-
29·2 nac : nar
29·4 cawt : rawd
34·3 dauc (v.b.) : rawd
35·16 ci : ry   35·17 cit : tri = try
4·11 crei : trei
10·3 noc : nyt   t
11·11 Gwȳduc : Gwyndyt
11·14 deheuec : dyhewyt, 24·15·21
13·12 rodic : orδit
17·2 cones : torres = (b)riues 38·2
19·3 kywesc : kywest
20·10 lleithic : lleδit
32·21 duc : dut
35·22 ec el : yt el
36·3 cen-nin (v.b.) : uernin
36·20 griniec : driniet
37·3 c[l]air : taer ·13 āc : -ant
37·22 ciuin uerthi ig : tuyn merthig
38·15 mic : mit

BOOK OF ANEIRIN

c : s, t=δ

2·22	trych- : crysſiant	s
7·10	beri creu : beris creu	
13·13	drec : dres	
14·15	nychemyδ : nys ketuyδ	
19·13	ec -hadas : es lladas	
37·3	seic : Seis	
34·16	huc : hut=huδ	δ
36·1	guic : guit=gwyδ	

ch : ɡ, ll, th

12·9	chwarδaf : gwarthaſ	ɡ
29·15	chuech : chweg	
37·18	echassaf : y gua(e)sav	
25·6	dygochwi[aw]r : -gollwyt	ll
27·13	gochawn : gorllawn	
12·5*	achor : ? a thŵr, a char	th
13·2	differch serch : differth serth	
13·4	Llech : Llêth, 23·15, 34·6	
13·11	brych : brith	
18·10	rwych : rwyth	
19·9	sychyn : syrthyn	
21·7	gwych- : gwyth-awg	
26·19	gorchegin : gwrth[e-cin :] rin	
29·6	achon : aethon	
31·17	breichyaul : breithau(dy)l	
34·5	arurchyat : arwrthiad	

cg : ɡ, ch, th

10·16	muc greit : mygreid	ɡ
32·15	racgarth : rhagarth	
27·1	rycgwynn : ry·chwyrn	
37·15	guec : gwyth	

d : b, ɡ, t=r, δ=v

21·13	dadodes : da(r)bodes	b
29·17	mired : moreb	
32·16	dan : ban	
37·13	du : bu	
31·7	gadeu : gampeu	
12·4	redyrch : rygyrch	ɡ
15·22	dwyf : gwyδ	
18·16	uedel : rygel	
19·15	dodis : godis	
22·7	dan : gan	
25·9	ed- : de=gy-(w)rysseδ	
27·8	dwyar : gwyar	v : ɡ
34·2	dellyll : gyllyll	
37·13	godile[i]t : o gilget=gylchet	
37·21	brein du : bandur=bangor	
7·8	lludw : llutw=llwrw =t : r	
10·1	medut : mot=moryt	
14·15	haed : haet=haer	
16·9	clawd : clawt=clawr	
23·8	god- : got-= gor(m)essyn	
30·10	godiues : got-=gormes	
34·7	god[o]δin : got-=gorδin	
36·2	bod : bot=bor	
38·11	guid : guit=gwyc=gwys	
10·15	[o]eδ=eδ : ev =δ : v	
15·11	δwyre : vwryei	
18·10	-oδeδ : oδev	
29·9	teδyt : tevic	
35·17	diδurnn : divwrn	
2·20	roδi : rothui =δ : th	
12·9	chwarδaf : gwarthaſ	
19·9	assed=asseδ=asseth	
32·15	bard=barδ : barth	
23·8	god-=goδ- : go(e)thessyn	

e : c, i, o

20·13	oe las : o clas
27·3*	[d]ewr : cwrr
34·22	einim : cynfin
4·2	ne : ni
8·6	vel (r.b.)=lev : liv
12·4	re : ri
12·16	em : im, 38·5*
12·17	keneu : keniv
15·4	llet : llit
22·4	bed in : bit im
24·2	bit en : bit im
27·16	ved m- : vidin
29·21	ychuel : ymchwil
32·19	er : ir
32·13	leuir : liwir
38·5	dem- : div-odes
	e prep.=i everywhere.
2·16, 10·15	e law : o law
4·19	gelor***hir : golochir
5·10	e ved : w(l)eδ o
7·11	ei-l fith : oi leith
8·6	eithin : orllin

LIST OF SCRIBAL ERRORS

e : o, u, y

10·3*	gled-yf= -iu : glod in	o
12·17	angheu : anghov	
14·8	e gatraeth : o gatraeth	
16·11	merin : Mori(e)n	
16·18	eiðuni : gorðini	
17·13	meiwyr : morwyr	
21·12	kelleic : kolletic	
21·20	eið-[ef=eu :]orðen	
22·7	ervei : orvei	
25·6	peith : porth	
25·7	eiðyð : orvyð	
27·5	ac eur : a ecur : o oror	
27·10	kerd : koid	
28·22	enw[l]yð : onwyð	
29·17*	godem[el] : godoru(n)	
36·18	eiðin : orðin	
38·15	eðis : oðis	
38·15	eðyv : oðyv	
29·9	teth : tut	u
35·5	deo : Duw	
4·13	ef : yf, 17·2	y
5·11-12	o ueðel : o Wyðel,	
7·2	o ved : o wyd	
9·5	eu : yw	
12·3	tywyssen : -yn	
12·15	emða : ymða	
13·2	gessevin : gys-	
13·4	ystre : ys try	
15·13	temel : cyvyl	
16·15	wede : wedy, 21·7	
17·6	keman : kynran	
18·16	uedel : pygel	
20·19	temyr : tymhyr	
21·3	vedin : vyðin	
21·3	menit : mynnit	
21·10	pryder : prydyð	
21·11	en : yn	
24·15	deheuec : dyhewit	
24·15	gwen : gwŷn	
26·14	adef : adev : adwy	
27·16	enys : ynys	
28·20	brith-we … anorth-we :-wy	
32·14	re : rē=ryn	
35·5	leo : lyw, 37·4 adlyw	
35·22	e rit : y ryt	
36·10	esgar : ysgar	
37·3	cleu : glyw	
38·7	lureg- : lurygogyon	

ei : a

7·16	eleirch : alarch	
7·17	feirch : farch	
7·20	pryd-ein : -au=prydav	
7·21	dreic : drāc=tranc	
8·2	meirch : march 10·14, 23·3	
12·2	eilweing : alweint	
20·13	eil : ar 20·17 eil : af	
20·18	eilywet : arwylet	
23·4	gweir : gwar, 36·13	
25·10	bleið : bla(w)ð	
26·4*	atveill- : ? arwallawc	
27·16·18	-neit : -nat, -eit : -at	
29·11	eneit : caen	
30·6	dieirydaf : diaryfad	
31·13	eiry- : a ry-angut	
31·12*	kein : ? ? kan	
32·14	a meirch : ar uarch	
34·14	damguein-ieit : -iat	
34·15	cin elueit : Gint eilwat	
37·5	ple[i]gheit : plyghat	
cp. 5·7	arwyran : arwyrein	

N.B. -ei,3 sing. Impf. Indicative of verbs, often stands for the Passive forms, -er, or -et

-f : ð, l, m, ſ, u, b

2·7	y lafnawr : ymlaðuawr	ð
15·22	dwyf : gwyð	
16·1	rwyf : rwyð	
6·14	fin : liu=llyw	l
30·6	taf : tal	
14·2	gomyn-af : -am= -ant	m
21·10	pryder-af : -am= -ant	
25·14	kwyn-af : -am : -ant	
21·20	eiðef : orðeu=orðen	n
4·13	ef : yf, 17·2	ſ
5·13	diryf : dyryſ	
12·9	chwarðaf : gwarthaſ	
8·14	nef : neu; ef : (n)eu 9·20	u
20·16	Goðef ; 32·16 woðef : Goðeu	
23·15	llefdir=lleutu 13·4 : lleudir	
5·8	nef : neu=nen	u=n
29·13	gled-yf : -yu=gledyn	

Final -f=v except in

5·8	gyf : gyff	
21·17	gwneif : gwneiff	

BOOK OF ANEIRIN

	f- = ff *except in*	
10·7	*f*aglei : *v*aglei	v
10·17	*f*in : δin	
19·13	-t or*f*un : ter*v*yn	
29·3	*f*uδ : *v*uδ	
3·12	e*f* : *v*e = wy	
26·14	ade*f* : ate*f* = a*r* tew	

	ff = ff *except in*
4·5	gyffor : gy*v*or
16·6	sa*rff* : sai*v*
10·18	e*ff*yt : e*ff*yt
6·10	a*ff*rei : a*b*re*t*
8·9	-d ro*ff*oe : dro*th*wy

	g : c, δ, t, ch	
5·16	*g*las : *c*las	c
12·8	bein*g* : beinc	
11·18	kyuran*g* : kyvranc 31·12	
26·19	gorch[e]-*g*in : gorchcin =	
31·3	dan*g* : tanc [gwrthrin	
2·8	u*g*ein : u*d*ein = ? u*b*ein	δ
5·17	*mygant : ? mu*d*ant	
6·5	my*g*ei : ? mu*d*ei	
10·4	*g*ysgog- : cysgod-, 22·4	
11·10	*g*wallt : *d*ellt	
13·11	am*g*wr : am*d*wrr	
14·3	dy*g*ogl- : dy*g*lud-awδ	
22·12	din*o*gat : diu*o*dat	
24·9	*g*et : *d*ec	
24·12	a*l*guuc : arδwg	
25·4	*g*yrn : *d*ryn : dri*n*	
25·19	e*g* wallt : y*d* bellt	
25·19	*g*wyllyas : *d*ywallas	
28·22	dy-gw*g*ei : dy-gw*e*g i = dy-gw*y*δ i	
34·20	*g*riniec : *d*riniet, 36·20	
38·16	gwi[s]*g*ws : gwyδws	
13·21	ysg*w*n : ys*t*um	t
30·13	llosg- : llos*t*ei	
9·12	gwe*n*w- : chwe*ŗ*w	ch
17·6	lloge*ll* : lloche*ff*	
18·12·18	dy*g*iawr : dy*ch*iawr	
20·6	as*g*wrn : ys *ch*wyrn	
27·1	ry[t] *g*wynn : ry·*ch*wyŗn	
31·20	*g*lan : (a)*ch*lan	
35·15	*g*uero : *ch*werw, 37·15	
36·9	*g*uanauc : *ch*wanawc	
38·19	*g*uigiat : gwy*ch*rat	

	h : b, δ, k, ci, ſi, li, ll, u	
7·12	*h*uan : *b*uan	b
13·19	*h*eli : *b*eli	
26·4	*h*ir : *b*u	
26·6	*h*ualeu : *b*ualeu	
13·19	*h*el : le*d* : ryd	δ
15·9	*h*wr : *d*yr	
34·21	e*h*elaeth : y *d*alaeth	
35·14	du*h*et : du*d*et, 17·14	
14·15	*h*etuyδ : *k*ytvyδ	k
24·13	*h*an : *k*an	
27·4	*h*emin : *k*ernin	
24·19	cyn*h*o : cni*ſi*o	ſi
2·22	try*ch*ant : crys*ſi*ant	ſi
37·20	o*h*eit : o*li*eit	li
24·13	guia[u] *h*em : gwia*l*en	l
19·13	ec-*h*aδa*f* : ys *ll*aδa*ſ*	ll
37·18	ac-*h*aus : angu*a*ws	u
	contrast gueu*ı*l- : gwe*h*ilion 37·15	
34·2	*h*yll : *u*ell = well	
31·12	vy*h*yr : vy*u*- : ve*ŗ*ut	

	i : e, l, r, t
17·9	d*i*lic : d*e*fic
34·22	g*i*rth : g*e*rth
35·9	*ı*n- : endew*i*t
35·22	gu*i*rth : gwerth
	In older orthography we have blain, clair, daiar, dair guaid, guaiu, hair, oi, oid
17·7	mynne*i* : myn e*l*
29·1	kyueil*i* : kyveil*l*
34·4	de*i* : de*l*
37·17	l*i*uir : *ll*wyr
38·12	cin e*i* : cyn e*l*
8·6	o e*i*thin : go*rll*in
14·4	e*i*dy : e*r*yt : eryr, 23·11
20·9	gorδ*i*- : gorδ*r*ynaw
21·20	e*i*δef : o*r*δen
25·6	pe*i*than : po*r*than
26·18	Pe*i* mi : Pe*r*im = Peryv
35·3	ne*i* : ne*r*
35·7	b*i*thei : b*r*(a)thei
36·4	[a]*n*thuim : ŗuth*r*in
36·18	e*i*δin : o*r*δin
38·7	fe*i*uog- : lu*r*ego(g)ion
12·12	*i*v : *y*t
29·2	e*i*liw : e*t*ryv

110

LIST OF SCRIBAL ERRORS

i : u, y

7·13	tith : ruth(rei)	i : u
11·4	rithir : ruthur	
18·11	oe briδ : o ebruiδ	
19·22	trin : trun = trwn	
20·2	tir : tu	
27·37	eithin : euthyn	
24·20	prit : drut ? gloss	
35·5	ffraidus : ffraudus	
37·1	tit : tut	
2·19	lleδi : lleδyn	y
2·20	roδi : rothwy	
3·8	ri : ry, 36·21	
3·20	kewiliδ : kywilyδ	
5·11	gennin : geunyn	
5·13	diryſ : dyryſ	
5·17	tri : try	
8·8·13	Is : ys	
10·4	wit : wyc = wys, 16·14 = 38·11 guid	
12·6	gwinwit : gwyn vyt	
13·12	diſtyr : dystyr	
13·13	riw : ryw	
19·16	trin : tryn, 21·20	
25·5	liw : lyw . . . yd i = hyd y	
26·13	emis : evnys	
27·8	denin : dynyn	
27·17	eithin in : yn eithyn	
29·1	elwit : elvyδ	
31·14	diliw . . . gwin : dyluδ . . . gwynt	
32·22	diw- : dywedws	
34·11	crisguit- : crysgwyδat	
34·15	cin, 37·6 cit, 37·2 cint, cig 38·1 = Gynt	
35·6	fis- : ffys(c)iolin	
36·5	rin : ryn	
37·4	trileo : trylew	

Pages 34–38 have too many instances to quote.

k

29·1	krym : pryv
26·13	kuhelyn : buelyn
29·15	ky- ⇌ cy- : ry·chwenychwys
6·1	kynri : kyttri : yktrit = uchtryd

l : ſ = b, ſ, r

7·5	ſliv- : ſliv- = blivyeu	ſ = b
10·13	lleithic : ſleiδic = bleiδic	
17·9	dilic : defic, 20·10, 35·8	
17·22	golut : goſut	
18·9	diluδ : diſuδ	
29·16	weles : voſes = voδes	
33·3	llavj : ſljv a = a vliv	
34·14	lui . . . lun : ſu i . . ſun,	
36·8	inilin : yn·yſin	⌊35·19
11·9	len : (gor)ſen, 24·11	ſ
16·9	eil : eſi-	
21·9	frwy[th]lam : frwyſiant	
25·8	eil : eiſ, 27·7	
27·3	ālel : anſel	
33·6	wyl : wyſ	
34·20	cal : caſ, 36·20 calc : caſs,	
5·11	govel : gover	r
7·13	wlith : vrith	
8·10	gleδyv : greδyv	
9·14	gwl- : goruget, 20·4	
13·16	gell : cell = tyrr	
14·12	atvel : atver	
16·14	dalmeδ : darveδ, 38·12	
18·21	glys : grys 20·13 eil : ar	
24·20	gwych-laut : -rawt	
25·12	gwelydon : Gwerydon	
27·16	uolawt : voriat. cp. 29·4	
27·17	blenn- : breini(a)d	
29·1*	dych-elwit : tric (yng)weryδ	
29·2	eiliw : etryv	
29·4	uolawd : vorawd	
29·22	mel[w]it : meryδ	
35·16	cal[a]net : carneδ(er)	
36·14*	ut bulee : buδucre	
36·22	cimluin : cymrwyn	
26·15	medel : medei	
34·17	sdlinet : sdinlet = (y)styriet	
8·2	gar lew : gar tew	
23·11	aryal : arvant, see 14·3	

ll : ff, ſſ, u = n = r

10·1	llawr : ffawr = vawr
25·17	arlles : arffes = arves
27·1	tyllei : dyffei
16·20	ar[u]olli : aroſſei
17·6	llogell : llocheff

20.4	rygoll- : rygo(e)*th*essyn	t**ħ**	36.6	nem : ne*v*	m : **ƀ**
24.17	as[g]c*ll* : ase*th*		38.5	emdodes : d*em*- = divodes	
9.20	a*ll*- : a*u*- : a*n*awr	ħ	9.12	*m*am : *n*am	ħ
13.15	gynwa*l* : gynwa*n*		24.11	am- : a*n*lwys	
25.6	ga*ll*- : ga*u*- : ga**ꝓ**e*ð*	**ꝓ**	24.13	ganghe*m* : ganghe*n*	
27.18	gym-hwy*ll*- : **ꝓ**hwyat		24.16	*t*rym : cryn	
34.20	gue*ll* : guo**ꝓ**		11.7	e*m*-yt, 14.3 -*w*yt : e*nn*yt	
			38.15	a*m* : o*nn* ·	
			29.5	midhin : uu*ð*h*u*i	
	m		19.8	gym- : gy**ꝓ**rwyd	
1.9	*m*-arrō : *in* aeron	i*n*			
12.20	le*m*- : le*in* [-ein]		final -*m* = *v*, 35.21–36.2		
14.20	dru*m* : dru*in* = trwyn				
24.13	more*m* : -e*in* = Morien		**n : iꝓ, it, ri, rr, ꝓ**		
29.20	*m*-enwit : *in* e**ꝓ**vid				
29.22	*m*-elwit : *in* elvy*ð*		34.19	dey*r*net : di*r* reget	i*r*
31.9	la*m* .. orwyla*m* :		31.1	trychw*n* : trychwi*t*	i*t*
	la*in* .. orwyla*in*		29.6	tra ma*n*on : tramo*r*ion	r*i*
34.15.16	ci .. di*m* : ī dici*n*		17.2	co*n*es : to*rr*es	r*r*
36.4	i*m* : r*in* = ryn, ? 36.8		1.13	*n*yt : **ꝓ**yt, 36.14	**ꝓ**
16.6	godru*ð* emore : godru*ð*-		4.9	[l]a*n* : a**ꝓ**	
	ei *u*ore	i*u*	9.12	gwe*n*w : chwe**ꝓ**w	
24.17	lu*m*en : lu*iu*en = lwyven		9.20	*ru*-vawn : ri*t* vaw**ꝓ**	
34.16	da*m* : di*ua* = diva		10.1	kēnon : kyn**ꝓ**an	
15.20	*m*oleit : *ni* cheit	*ni*	10.1	tan : t**ꝓ**a	
35.12	*m*olut *m*uet :		11.3	a*n* : a**ꝓ**, 11.6 ; *n*a : a**ꝓ** 13.21.	
	ni lu*ð* mo**ꝓ**eb		11.18	gwych*n*awd : -**ꝓ**awd	
11.7	e*m*yt : e*n* *r*yt	*nr*	12.11	be*n* : ve**ꝓ** : fe**ꝓ**	
35.6	ke*m*an : kyn*r*an		12.16	a*n*war : a**ꝓ**war	
21.8	gorwyla*m* : -a*nt*	*nt*	13.7	di*n*dywyt : di**ꝓ**dynwyt	
21.9	ffrwy[th]*l*am : ffrwy*f*a*nt*		16.18	*n*i : **ꝓ**i(v), : **ꝓ**y 38.1	
33.8	ardemyl : ar*ð*ely*nt*		19.14	a*n*nor : a**ꝓ**uor	
27.4	he*m*in : ke*r*nin	*rn*	25.9	he*n* ba*n*n : he**ꝓ**-[*v* =]yan	
27.4	ge*m*in : ge*ru*in	*ru*	25.21	be*n*n : be**ꝓ**i*t*	
27.11	go*m*- : go*ru*yned		27.1	gwy*nn* : chwy**ꝓ**n. cp. 20.6	
29.17	gode*m*- : godo*ru*(n)		27.14	dychia*nn*[awr] : dychia*u***ꝓ**	
32.·	a*m*arch : a*r u*arch		27.22	deu [e]*n* : dew**ꝓ**	
34.16	*m*un : *ru*im = rhwyv		29.19	a*n*ned : a**ꝓ**ue*ð*	
30.9	gȳ*m*re : gyn*ui*re	*ui*	29.20	*m*-e*n*wyt : *in* e**ꝓ**wyt	
33.8	ardemyl : ar*ð*el[y]*ui*		29.20	dy*n*nit : dy**ꝓ**uit	
15.9	ma*m* : ma*u*r, 15.14	*ur*	29.21	*n*o : o**ꝓ** & ca*n*n : cau**ꝓ**, 31.6	
15.13	*t*emel : c*v*yl	**ƀ**	34.9	lui*n* : fui**ꝓ** = ffwy*r*	
26.13	ē*m*wyth : en *v*wythus		34.16	*n*imu[n] : **ꝓ**uim = rwyv	
26.13	e*m*ys : e*m*nys : e*v*nys		34.17	sd*l*inet : (y)sdi**ꝓ**iet	
26.18*	Peri*m* : Pery*v*		35.5	bo*n* : bo**ꝓ** = po*r*	
27.6	med … *m*elyn : (ag)ue*ð* ..		35.15	ci*t* unet : *tr*yu(e)**ꝓ**et	
31.8	bryta*m* : bryta*v*	[*u*elyn	36.14	ī *n*it : yn **ꝓ**yt	
34.16	ada*m* : ada*u* = ada**ƀ**		36.14	gēne : gy*n*(ui)**ꝓ**e	
34.17	e*m* : e*v*		37.7	lau*n* : law**ꝓ**	
35.22	miga*m* : mi ga*v*		38.3	enanuit : e**ꝓ**(w)anwyt	
			38.15	deu*u*niat : dyvw**ꝓ**iad	

112

LIST OF SCRIBAL ERRORS

n ː r̄=l, b, w, m

30·20	gwn : gwr̄- : gwleδgar r̄=l	
36·19	hanau c- : har̄- : halauc	
36·19	can- : car̄- : caled	
22·17	ven-yδ : veū-=weunyδ	u
24·13	denn : denu	
4·3	noethyδ : voythyδ	u=b
4·7	en : ev, 13·7, 21·6, 23·19	
5·11	cennin : cevnyn	b
16·9	nedic : veδic	
18·9	leyn : leiv	
18·20	amdinat : amδivat	
20·10	kenhan : kenhiv	
22·22	dinogat : divodat	
31·2	kyni-wng : kyvwng	
34·11·16	na : va & nei : vei,	
37·22	kynnor : kyvor [35·3	
4·12	gynnan : gynwan	m
7·1	nyn : niu=niw	
11·4	-n ych : wych	
15·2	ny : wy ; 37·10 ni : wy	
18·4	dynin : dywin 34·9, 36·9	
2·18	wanar : wamal	m
12·12	aneirin : aneir im	
13·4	ragno : ragom	
11·7	krennit : krymit	
11·9	am-drynnid : -drymit	
12·10	ystynn- : ystumiawc	
27·20	wrth-rann [: ramī :] rymyn	
32·4	chynniv : chymuy	

o : a, e

9·1	o..o..o : a..o..a	a
10·1	kēnon : kynr̄an	
12·4	haeδot : haeδat	
12·5	achor : achar	
22·2	ohir : ahet	
34·16	guoiu : gwaiu	
38·12	o gal- : a chalaneδ, 16·15	
1·8	po : pē=pen	e
19·3	-t orfun : tervyn	
29·22	ystoflit : ys tevlit	
30·10	od=do- : deweint	
30·15	no=on : en : eu	
31·22	o dra : edry-vannawc	
32·12	guol*vy : gwelwy	
36·13	oror : orro : oere=wyre	
37·1	iolo : idol : yd el	

o : u, w, y

12·10	ronin : ? cunin	
31·12	guodeo : Guoδeu 35·4	
31·12	celyo : geleu	
37·11	odg=dog : dug	
4·3	voethyδ : vwythyδ	w
7·15	diuaoed : divawyd	
8·9	drothoe : drothwy	
12·14	gor- : gwroleδ	
20·14	goeth : gweδ 21·6 loeδ	
21·15	g[r]oen : gwyn [: lwyδ	
26·19	gorch[e]gin : gwrthrin	
30·3	dhog : δwg	
32·2	deor . dewr	
35·4	tryleo : trylew	
35·5	deo : duw	
35·15	guero : chwerw	
37·4	adleo : adlyw	
37·13-17	ero, hero, guero, helo & delo : w	
3·12	gwynnod : Gwyndyd	y
8·21	gomynad : gyminad	
10·3	noc : nyt	
10·5	anvon- : anwynawc	
17·8	o vyt : y vyt	
19·22	orvyd : yrwyd	
25·19	obedror : obedryt	
27·18	o δwyn : ymδwyn	
36·2	uoleit : wyleiδ	

p : b, d, R

16·3	pela : bela	
36·1	map bodu : mapu bor : madw	
19·21	preiglyn : dreiglyn [bor	
19·21	perig- : (g)odrigawr	
34·13	pell : lled	
25·11	Pubell : Ruδell	

r : c, e

16·17	gwrhyt : gw(y)chyr	
4·14	dur : duc	c
21·20	gwyr : gwyc(h) [29·21	
23·18	rwyδ : cwyδ & run : cun	
1·9	m-arro : in aeron	e
36·16	oror : orro : oere=wyre	
4·5	mor : moe=mwy	
7·10	dal[v]rith : daleith	
16·22	llywri : llywei	
27·10	kerd : koed ar : ae 28·20	

BOOK OF ANEIRIN

r : i, l, r : n, ſ, t

2·11	gwerth : gweith, 6·22, 10 i
16·6	sarff : saif = seiv 32·2 ⌊·20
26·1	kyvreith : kyvieith
27·15	kyverth- : kyveithrynat
35·6	im[blain]trin : imrtin : y·midin
3·22	creu : cleu l
4·17	eδyr[n] : eδyl
11·3	gwyar : gwyal
13·13	ry-chwar[δ] : rychwal
23·7	eir : eil Nwython. cp. 20·4
23·17	restyr = lestyr 34·8
25·20	teithiawr : teithiawl
32·16	cared : caled
36·7·12	aruireīt : arwyleint
37·14	hero : helw
37·22	difur : di(v) ful
6·4	vehyr = -yr : wehyn r : n
9·7	peredur : penadur
19·1	clywer : clywyn
27·19	roδes : noδes
29·2	dykr : dycn
29·7·12	yaur : iawn & mur : Mon
31·16	gymyrrhut : gyminut
33·19	ceri : cein & cuir : cwyn
37·10	laur : laun : lanw ⌊36·19
37·14	herw : henw
4·4	maur : trawr = traws ſ = s
17·1	orch- : orgorδion
22·14	llory : llori : llost
34·11	armur : ar uryr = vrys
36·13	gweir : gwar, 23·4
7·22	gwy[a]r : gwyt t
21·5	lleir : lleit & gwel-ir : it
21·9	adroδer : adroδet
21·14	dyδuc ar : dyδucant
23·4	golo-hir : golohit
25·15	gwyr : gwyt
26·21	careu : catyr = cadr
28·19	aδoer : aδoet
34·12	adar : adat
36·14	[g]arat : atat
8·9	offer : hoff-et = -eδ t = δ
18·16	gorwer- : gorwetyt
21·10	pryder : prydyt
24·13	ver : vet = veδ
37·14	hero : mero : meδw

ſ : f = b, ff, l, th

5·12, 18·17	feirch : feirch f = b
5·20	cyfneit : cyf- = cyvneit
7·17	feirch : farch = varch
21·22	glaf-fu : glas . . . vu
29·17*-lef : lef = lev
5·18	fi : fi = ffin ff
15·13	fyn[wyr yf]twyr : ffynn ffwyr
6·8	fyw : -[ye-] liw dyδ l
7·21	aniaf : anial
26·12	amfud : amluδ
5·9	aef : aeth th

ff : ff, f = b, th

13·2	differch : differth
19·19	aeffawr : aethawr
3·22	kyfllwn : kythlwng
8·8	Iffac : ys tanc
17·22	tywyffeift : tywys feis[t] = veis = weis
37·15	gniff- : gniff- = gniv-ynt

t : c, δ, i, r, th

2·22	trys- : crysant
4·8	dut : duc
4·15	erth : erch
13·12	distar : discar
15·13	temel : cyvyl
22·22	gwyth- : gwychawc
24·16	trym : cryn
25·8	rawt : rawc
29·9	teδyt : tevic
35·4	frant : Franc
36·14	guolut : goluc(h)
36·22	tet : cet, 37·1 tar : car
4·5	arwyt : arwyδ δ
17·6·8	byt, vyt = wyδ
18·1*	meitin : meiδin
22·1	dihenyt : dihenyδ
25·12	wyt : wyδ = wyv
25·12	rwyt : rwyδ = rwyv
29·1	elwit : elvyδ
34·17	laδawt : laδawδ
5·2	dygwoll-it : -et
21·2	tavlet : tavlei
21·21	trin . . . veg : veigrin
34·11	caret : carei
37·19	auet : a w(el)ei

LIST OF SCRIBAL ERRORS

t : r, th

5·20	ca*t* : ca*r*, 11·7		r
7·11	*t*an : (gova)*r*an		
7·13	*t*ith : *r*uth(yr)		
10·1	*t*an : *r*(acw)an		
11·6	bi*t* : b*r*i		
12·3	*t*y- : *r*ywyssyn		
13·22	ga*t* : ga*r* Vannan 16·5		
14·4	rac *t*an : rac*r*an		
19·2	by*t* : by*r*		
21·19	eglu*t* : eglu*r*		
23·3	pennaw*t* : pennaw*r*		
24·12·17	baruau*t* : barvaw*r*		
24·12	a*t*guuc : a*r*dwc		
24·14	a*t*- : a*r*-gwyr. *cp.* 26·4		
25·17	pe*t*- : pa*r*-war		
26·21	*t*yllei : *r*yllei		
32·15	to*t t*arth : to*rr* arth		
31·22	sathr-av*t* : -aw*r*		
32·19	y*t* : y*r* & a*t*am : a*r*av 36·2		
2·10	ae*t* : ae*th*		th
20·11	guer*t* : gwer*th*, 34·18		
34·9	Le*t*lin : *Leth*- : Ly*ch*lyn		
38·2	dilei*t* : dyrei*th*		
38·10·11	bri*t* : bri*th*		

th : δ, ff, ll, ſſ, t

2·13	chwer*th*in : chwerδyn	δ	
14·10	ei*th*in : eδiu = eδyw		
20·14	goe*th* : gweδ		
32·17	ery*th* : eryδ		
35·22	gwir*th* : gwyδ		
36·11	gwr*th*yn : gorδin		
6·10	a*th*rwys : affwys	ff	
8·6	ei*th*in : or*ll*in	ll	
22·5	rygo*dh*et : rygo*ll*et		
29·19	rwyδheu : rwylleu		
21·9	ffrwy*th*lawn : ffrwyssiant	ſſ	
33·3	-*dor*th : bo*ll*t		
14·3	essy*th* : Esy*t*	t	
29·9	te*th* : tu*t*		

u : i, if

10·1	dyrllyd*u*t : dylyd*i*t	i	
16·14	b*u*al = d*i*al 38·12		
28·18*	d*u*hun : d*i*·hun		
37·10	b*u* guan : d*i*(a)ngan		
33·16	ll*u* : ll*if* = ll*iv*		if
	cp. d*i*ſ- : d*u*gyn		

u : ir, it, ri, ti ſſ, ll, ɲ, o

13·4	leu*d*u = llefd*ir* 23·15		ir
	cp. tir : tu 20·2, gri : gu =		
	gym- 34·19 & hir : bu 26·4		
13·7	dyv*u*- : dyv*ir*- : dyv*yr*wyt		
9·15	pryn*u* : pryn*it*		it
9·20	r*u* : r*it* vawɲ		
5·17	no*u*ant : uo*ri*ant		ri
20·4	d*u*ll- : d*ri*ll-yawr		
32·21	dyd*u*c : δyd r*it*		
30·10	goδiw-e*u*d : -e*ti*d		ti
2·20	*u*yw : *ll*yw		ll
5·11	oeδ er*u*it : oe δer*ll*yδ		
29·11	*u*uδit : *ll*uδit		
37·15	gue*u*- : gwehi*l*ion [26·6	l
2·8	e*u* : y*ɲ*, 6·18, 14·13·18,	ɲ
27·2	huit · hint = hy*ɲ*t, 37·6		
37·23	gua*u*r : gwa*ɲ*t		
27·5	ac e*u*r : *a ec*u*r* : *o or*o*r*	o
29·8	orth*u*r : orth*o*r		
30·15	odg*u*r : gor*o*t : gor*o*r		
36·5	g*u*r ... rin : g*uo*r Ryn		
36·11	g*u*rthyn : g*o*rδin		
37·8	g*u*r : g*o*r-		
9·5	v*u*eu : vɲiw		
10·10	ne*u* : neɲ		
11·1	ala*u* : alaɲ		
13·6	ke*u*i : kewɲi		
18·6	*u*edel : ɲygel		
20·21	e*u* hen : e ɲhen = y Rhyn		
27·7	cade*u* : cadyɲ = cadr		
28·18	de*u* : deɲ		
30·5	go*u*ud : goɲuδ		
32·19	ky*u*ei- : kyvɲet		
35·12	mo*u*et . moɲeb		
35·18	[l]a*u*neu : aɲueu		
37·2	*u*edet : ɲedec		
38·5	t*u* : tɲ(es)		
38·7	se*u*i- : seɲ(ch)ogion		
38·16	eith*u*nat : ethɲinat		
5·12	ke*u*it : kyvit		
25·9	e*u* : ev		
28·18	dole*u* : dolev, 23·20		
30·3	oδe*u* : oδiv		
35·1	ge*u*in i ga*u*all :		
	gevyn i gavall		
24·15	a*u*wy : av- : abwy		
25·3	me*u*= : mev- : meδweδ		
29·11	*u*u- : vu- : fu- : luδit		

BOOK OF ANEIRIN

u : w

5·11 uedel : Wyδel   w
5·19 euruych : eurwych
7·14 tū : twn ; keui : kewpi, 13·6
13·10 chuarδ : chwarδ
24·15*deheuec : dyhewyl, 24·21
26·11 dyual : dywal
27·2 llucyr duc : llwgyr δwc
30·12 adau : adawsei
31·12 baub : bawb
31·14 ceuei : c(l)ywei
34·15 biu = byv(l.13) : byw
34·17 guoiu : gwaew
34·18 Nuithon : Nwython
36·10 uid : wyd
24·12 atguuc : arδwg
37·2 eiluuat : eilwad

b : b, δ, ff, f, u, w, p

26·16 dyven : dyben. cp. auwy b
12·13 ovec : oδec   [: abwy δ
19·22 orvyd : orf- = orffid   ff
26·22 vyrrvach : f- = ffyrivach
25·12 vyw : fyw : lyw, 26·2   f
1·8 vro : uro = mō = Mon   u
16·13 Hv : Hu
20·5 devyn : deuyn
31·13 vt : uδ
21·13 dilyv : dilyu = dilyn = u : n
21·12 gor-dyv- : dynnwys
33·15 ravn : raun : rann
8·18 vann : uann : pann = u : p
20·3 kenevin : kynpein
8·6 vreith : ? wraeth   w
10·17 ryv : riw
14·14 vrych : wrych
15·19 win-veith : -weith
17·8 vyt : wyδ
18·9 llyvr : llwyr
21·5 llavar : llawer
21·21 vegin : wehyn
21·22 veδ : weδ
22·19 venyδ : weunyδ
23·9 wavr : wawr
24·11 lav : law(r)
26·11 dyvall : dywall
27·2 vrial : wrial
28·5 enyvet : eniwet
27·6 velyn : welyn

4·9 vab : yal, 6·15 nvt : pyt   b : p
7·17 bleiδvan : bleiδyan
12·3·12 vn : yn, vi : ȳt
18·? escyn-nv : escyn-yn
32·14 cynniv : cymuy

w : o, u, p, b, p

4·7 wrvyδ : orvyδ
5·17 pemwn[t] : penmon
7·13 wlith : olith(r)
9·14 gwl- : golyget, 20·20
13·11·18 kwr : kor, bwch : boet s
16·18 gwr : gor 18·16, 19·10, 30·6
17·5 wr : or, cp. 38·8
21·16 dwll : doll
26·20 fwrch : fforch
13·21 ysgwn : yscun : ystum   u
14·19 gwneδ : cuneδ, 19·2
21·14 di-liw : liu : lul = luδ
21·15 adloyw : adloeu
25·11 lwch : luch
26·13 mwythw[a]s : mwythus
31·8 gorlew : goreu
5·1 ew- : eu- : engei   u : u
17·4 diwarth : diu- : dinarth
25·8 trybeδ-awt : -aut = ant
29·2 kyueil-iw : -iu = -in
26·1 haw- : hau : hap : halffin
34·9 dy·owu = dy·wo-vu 13·7
    : -ow- = ou = opvu   u : p
13·7 dy·vu-wyt : vir-uuyt =
    -vyr-yδyt cp. 34·6 in-
    fra, & atguuc 24·12
7·16 wyr : vyr
12·4 wann : vann
12·12 werin : verin
12·13 cyw- : cyvrenhin. cp. 17·6
13·8 woδyn : voδyn
13·9 wy : vy, 30·11
17·6 cywreint : cyvreint. see 12·13
18·1 wys : uuys : vpys
21·14 diliw : diliv : dyluδ
28·22 wryt : vryt
29·1 elwit : elvyδ
29·2 eiliw : etryv
29·14 wledic : vle(i)δic. see 10·12
29·16 weles : vofes : voδes
34·6 browys : brouuys : brovbys
6·5 bwyte : buuyte : brδyde(r)

LIST OF SCRIBAL ERRORS

3·3-5   -wn : -yn   w : y|
5·18   trychwn : trychyn
10·16   trwm : tryn
15·9   gwnlleith : Gynlleith, 15·16
15·9   hwr : dyr
26·11   dwy=dywwcith : dyvv- : diffeith

y : a, e, i, u, v, w

13·2   drych : drach   a
25·19   gwyll : gwall
34·1   yn- : anysgoget
5·6   hwyr : hwer(w)   e
7·9   gwyδw : gweδw 31·10
8·6   rywin : rewin
12·20   ryuel : reueδ
13·7   yn : en=eu : ev, 23·19
13·17   dy wr : dewr
21·15   adloyw : adloeu
25·12   gwelyd- : gweledyδ
30·19   ayth : aeth
31·10   llydw : lleδw, cp. 78
31·12   celyo : geleu   e : g
31·15   gym : gein
33·7   lluyδ : llueδ
4·2   gwyn : gwin   i
5·18   athryc-hant : athrigant 6·19, 28·1
9·16   yg : ing
10·17   ryv : riw
12·11   deyeryn : deierin
15·20   -gwyr : -gwir
18·4   dynin : diuin, 29·15
18·9   dyleyn : dilein
20·14   godoδyn : gorδin
21·9   tyngyr : tyngir
25·4   gyrn : dirn : trin
26·11   dwyw- : diww- : divv =diffeith
28·5   enyved : eniwed
29·9   teδyt : tevic
29·15   dyvyn : diwyn 18·4
32·20   dyuit : diwyd
34·19   deyrnet : dyr neet= tir ne(g)et
        N.B. ny : ni, nyt : nid, & verbs ending in -yt : -it are too numerous to be enumerated.

3·3   ffyryf : ffuryf   y : u
4·5   ny : nu
5·5   derllyδci : darlluδei
9·14   gwlyget : goruget
19·3·7 by : bu & -cyn : -cun
22·17   llywywc : lluucwy=Llûgwy
30·3   fyd : vud
30·21   kynin : cunin
31·12   eryvyhyr : tryvenut
31·15   oet yt : oeδut
14·3   aryant : arvant, 16·21   v
23·11   aryal : arvant
20·15   yaw clot : clotvaw(r)
26·19   trych : trvch = twrch   w
1·16   -yat : -ayt : -avt= -awt
10·18   lwry : lwrw
21·11   aryal : argal=ardal
29·7   yawr : gawr
30·1   ywavt : gwawr
        cp. ag : ay 29·8

Anticipations.

2·7   [p]ym pymwnt : ym p(l)ym-
3·5*   gwrmwn : garmwn   [nuit
4·17   eδyrn dieδyrn : oeδyn di- ? dëyrn
5·12   Aer adan glaer : al=or A(b)er dan gaer
7·17   buδ van ... bleiδ- : cuδvan
8·10   heu diheu : geu dïeu
10·3   noc ac es-gyc carrec : nyt ares- gyn garrec
11·8   llu iδ[aw] llawr : lluyδ llawr
13·4   ystre, ystre : ystrat, ys try
14·2   trumein drum : trumeu drwyn
14·15   haed ud : haet : haer uδ
15·4   vro[nn] adon
15·8   [or] ... heb or heb : hed heb or eithaf
15·9   o win[veith] a meδweith
15·10   [rac]vre rac : w(a)re rac
15·12* fynn[wyr y] ftwyr y-ftemel
18·1   dywys[yn] tywys : dyvrys, t.
18·17   [seingyat] .. seingyat : soniet
19·8   [gog]ymwyt goglyssur
19·14   Mynawc ... mynawg : Myn(yδ)awc ... M.

BOOK OF ANEIRIN

Anticipations.

21·17 [yor] ... yor
22·22 [ang]kyvwng angkyuarch
24·15 [gwen] ... gwen
25·1 [Ang-] ... angkyman
25·7* uor[u]a ... morva
25.8 Trybeδ-awt rawt : Trybeδ-ant rawc
26·3 tut[vwlch] kyvwlch : tut kyvlwch
26·5 am maeth : ae maeth
26·20 trychethin trych : tra-
26·22 vyrr vyrrvach
27·13 kylch[wy] wylat
27·16 [eirch] eithin
29·6 disgleir[yawr] archawr
29·14 y gynn withic kynlas : yn adwythic k-
29·21 [d]ychuel dychwelid : ymchuil ...
30·2* [drem dremrud] dremryt
30·8 [nyaud] wlawd : vlawδ
30·17 [hwy] wy
30·22 [trychwn] athrych-ant : -aur
31·14 baran baeδ : taran vaeδ
33·4 ar dwyn [ef] adef
34·11 da[ir] hair : da air
36·15 gueilgi[ng] gurymde
37·3* c[l]air ... [claer] claer
37·6 [cin]haual cīt eluat

Repetitions.

2·20 glyw reith[uvw]
3·3 veδuaeth [ue]dwn
5·1 ech[ech]ing : eching
6·2 a dyvu ... [a dyvu]
7·3* beithing [peith]yng
7·8 eis ... eis : (v)eis
7·12 bu bwyt [b]rein bu [b](r)uδ e [v]ran
7·17 -van ... bleiδvan : bleiδyan
12·20 lem : lein[-ein]
13·1* gwen ac ymhyrδwen
13·5* anghat angat : anvat
13·12*am..am..am..am..am
14·2 trum-ein drum : -eu druin
14·1 nawδ [nawδ]   [yl
15·12 ſtwyr yſtemel : ffwyr yn cyv-

Repetitions.

18·7·9 cangen ... cangen : cynhen
19·8 peleidyr [peleidyr]
21·10 pryder pryd[er]af
21·17 molut myn[ut m]or
21·20 oδef eiδef : orδeu
22·15 llory en[y]
25·10 Bleiδ ... [? b]leiδyat, cp. 17·9
26·3 kyvwlch ... vwlch
27·2 yawn llad [yawn]
27·14 dychi-aup[=awr] ... dychianad
29·1 elwit ... dychelwit : elvyδ ... -weryδ
29·5 rin [ry]midhin [ryme]non : Ryn uuδhui uon
29·6 trech tra : car
29·9 tcith tet[h] a theδyt . reith, tut a thevic. cp. 2·20, 26·2
29·12 eſgor eſgor Eiδin : el E., or
29·15 kynweis ... [ky]chuec[h] ny c[h]wyδ [kyc]h[w]erw [ky]chvenyches [kychwen-
29·22 am rwyδ [am ry]   [ychwy]
29·22 yſtoflit. yſtoffl-it
30·1 blin blaen [blen blen]wyδ
30·8 rymun ... [rymun]
30·9 wlawd ... yscawt : ? yscor
30·10 goδiweud ... [oδiweud]
30·12 adonwy [adonwy] see 13·9
32·3·8 blaen bedin : midin
32·21 duc [k]y∗iu : ym=im
33·1 am byrth [am] porth
34·2 seciſiar : sisi(a)ſat
34·13 o damguein- ... [o dam]
34·14 [nys adraud a uo biu] see l.13
35·1 imil [imil]
35·13 trin ... trin : mur
35·13 tebi[hi]c=tevic
36·2 iued [iu]et : i pedec
36·14-15 bu .. [bu]
36·17 godechet [tech]in rac : rac meiδin
36·21 wanei ri [guanei ri]
36·20 griniec [griniei]
37·4 gogyuurd [go]
37·22 uerth ig ... [ig]

LIST OF SCRIBAL ERRORS

Metathesis.

1·16	kynniv-*yat* : *ayt*=avt
2·7	pym*wnt* : p(l)ymn(*vv*)t
4·2	*ne* : *en*=ev
4·9	gwa*et* : gw*eat*=gwyar
7·16	v*re*-yt : v*eryt*=Weryd
7·10	y dwy=yd*ui* : ȳ d|ıi =yn |ıid
10·9	ade*u*- : adu*e*- : adw*y*awc
10·18	*el*fin : *le*fin : revin=rewin
11·4	rith*ri* : ruth*ir*
11·5	tw*rc*h : T*rw*ch
13·4	rag*no* : rag*on*, 25·15
13·7	dy*w*ovu : dy*ou* = dy·o|ıvu
13·13	ro*δ*ic : or*δ*it [23·19
15·4	d*or* : d*ro*=dron
15·8	klyt*no* : Klyt*on*
16·9	ei*l* : e*l*iuedic
18·10	llyvr- : llv*y*ro*δ*ev
21·3	gel*w*id- : g*wel*y*δ*eint, 22·3
22·15	gel*wı* : ge*ıl*w
24·13	ureuer u*ra*g : reuuet *ra*ug
25·3	ma*w*r- : ma*rw*eδ
25·4	g*yr*n : g*ry*n=drin
26·3	cyv*w*lch : Cyv*l*wch
26·11	d*wy* : d*yw*weith=dyvv- : diffeith
26·18	Pei *mi* : Pe*r im*=Peryv
27·4	*ho*el : *he*ol
27·10	welli*ng* : weil*gi*[n]
28·21	oδef *y*nyas : oδef*uy*(s) yas
29·5	dy*ff*y*ll*ei : dy*ll*y*ff*ei
29·11	tala*ch*or : talc*ha*(tt)or
30·2	[dr]emru*δ* : mery*δ*
30·7	*er*ry : *re*ry : rely(*w*)
30·10	o*δiw*eud : *δowei*ud : *δeweint*
30·21	gwac*n*- : gwa*n*cawg
30·21	ky*uu*n : k*uu*yn=cunin
31·17	breich*yau*l : breith a*u*(d)*y*l
31·22	*ny* : *yn*
32·14	ky*wu*yrein : ky*nw*yrein
32·15	kem*re* : cyme*r*
33·6	*de*- : *od*(ia)ethol
33·17	au*rg* : *ga*ur : *gay*r=*gae*r
33·19	ce*ri* : cei*r*=cei|ı=Cein(t)
34·5	aru*rc*hyat : a ruth*ry*at, or arwrthyat
34·12	argouuδuit : a g*or*vuδwyt
34·16	ad*am* : ā di*ua*=am δiva
34·17	sd*l*inct : (y)sd|ıuet
34·21	e*ıl*th : *le*ith
35·22	gu*ırth* : gu(e)r*hıt*=Gweryd
36·20	nȳ-awc=*nym*- : *my*nawc
37·8	lau*n* : lan*w*
37·9	*ft*a : a*f*[t]
37·9	lau|ı : lau*n*=lan*w*

Transpositions.

1·22	K.K. blciδ : Bleiδ k.k.
4·1	vuδyδ : δyvuδ
5·13	awc aer : aerawt
8·9	yth glawδ : clawδ yth
9·21	kein y : y *K*ein(t)
11·4	-us rıth *ri* : rıthı*rus*
11·5	twrch goruc : goruc twrch
11·9	dry la*v* : la*n* ryd
11·13	yr boδ : boδir
13·13	ys brys : brys ys
14·4	dywye*i dy* : *eiyt*=e*ryr* Dwyw
14·4	gynghor wann . . y rac tan : y racran gynhorvan
15·8	or heb : heb or eithav
15·4	vro*n*[n] adon : adon [*u*=]y
15·20	gwyr en : en gwir reit [vro
16·19	gwr gwneδ divu*δ* . . . dimyngei : diveδ or guneδ im dyngei
18·8	Ewein esgyn : esgyn Ewein
18·9	llywy : y llyw
18·14	gyuoet o gyuergyr esgyn disgyn : o g. dısgyn, cyver-
18·21	aergyn : cyn aer [gyr esgyn
20·15	*y*aw clot : clotvaw(r)
21·21	en *ı*rin llet-*veg*-in gwin : e*v veg*trin : v*eig*rin, lletin (yn) gwyn bant
22·3	y(g) catveirch a feirch : y seirch ae catveirch
22·4	get yt (*r.b.*) : tyget=tynget
24·11	dry la*v* : (g)la*n* ryd
26·11	gar nybyδ mawr : (mwy) ni byδ marw (yn)gar(w)
26·20	trychethin trych : trych tra*c*hethin
27·16	*kein dy [e]n ruδ enys : dyurus kein ynys
28·19	adwy aer : aer adwy
29·11	ene*i*t : enat : taen : cae|ı

119

BOOK OF ANEIRIN

Transpositions.

29·13 e buδic ren : reen buδic
29·21 (am ry) gorwyδ mwy gat-
 want no melwit. am rwyδ
 ystoflit: (y·ar) orwyδ in
 elvyδ ystevlit am rwyδ
 mwy (ev) alwy oṅ (er)lid
30·4 can welw : welw gan
30·15 odgur : gor-od= -ot= -oɣ
30·18 etmyc : mycet=mygeδ
31·4 ervessid gwin : er gwib
 (y)vessid
31·19–21, 32·16, & 33·2–3. see nn.
32·1 ffossawt pan vei no llif llymach nebawt : neb ffosawd
 vei lymach nom ... pan
33·19 wy .. gon : Gonwy [ſlifawt
33·19 -aur g- : gaur=gayr=gaer
34·11 na hair : aerua
34·17 em laδaut lu maur : llu
 mawr ev laδawδ
35·11 guauruδ : ruδwa(e)w
36·1 map bod-u : mapu bot :
 madw bor

Read backwards.

4·1 vuδyδ : δyvyδ
5·2 dy-g[o]llou- : guoll=guallit
5·10 ryodres e veδ : w(l)eδ o ryod-
7·9 hoew gir : hoew ri g-, [res
 cp. bleiδgir-ac 31·11
8·6 vel : lev=liv
8·9* -d e offer : droffoe=drothwy
11·3 deliit : dileit
13·11 keirw : kewri
14·16 llavyn durawt barawt e :
 parawt e δurawt lavyn
15·10 eidol : iodel=roger.
16·11 uil-et : liu-et

16·4 [o] win a meδ en δieding :
 ue δyedynt veδ a gwin
17·7 eidol : loδi e : roδi=roi i
17·17 rud : dur, 35·18
18·16 gwrδwe[r]yt : gorweδit
19·6 mudyn : munyd
20·10 dull : llu[d]
21·14 wogant : govv- : govyant
22·2 twll tal : lat=fa(w)r
24·9 get : teg
25·15 gat : rag pwll
26·22 uo-dog- : va(r)-god-yon
26·22 esgyrn vyrr : llyv=
 bliv ysgyr(io)n
28·1 catraeth : ractraeth
28·21 uebir : uerib=vecid
29·2 [ei] liwet : etriv=edryv
29·3 Tervyn torret tec teithyawl :
 teithyawl ter torres tervyn
29·10 na chyngyd gil na chyngor :
 na chyngor na chil gyngyd
29·18 tei idware : dwire i ware
30·6 dieirydaf : diaryfad
30·20 godruδ : druδog
32·12 duuyr : duruy : ducwy
32·16 wyn-eb cared : bē=dyn
 caled (g)wyn
32·16 ystyng- : guysty(l)-ei
33·8 ardemyl : arδelynt
33·17 call- : frac- : vrag- : wrageδ
34·3 dauc : raud
34·13 pell : lled
34·16 ut bu lee : butuele=buδucre
34·20 call- : rrac : trac : dragon
35·3 neim : mein=Magnus
35·12 mo-lut m-uet : ni luδ moṅeb
35·13 teryd- : ethid
35·16 ciu-riuet : ryveδ-uit
36·18 uiru : uriu-et
36·20 nȳauc=nym- : mynawc
37·11 od guur : δog run=δwg Ryn
38·1 cig : gīt=Gint

PALEOGRAPHICAL & OTHER NOTES.

The following contractions are used in the Notes.

( ) = insertion
[ ] = omit
: = for
am. t. = amended text
An. = Book of Aneirin
antcpn. = anticipation
app. = apparently
B. = Bruts   [Carm.
B.B.C. = Black Book of
Buch. = Bucheδ Gr.
   ap Kynan [ance
c. = cynghaneδ, *conson-*
cp. = compare
er. = error
f. = faulty

Gr. = Griffyδ
HeC. = Hugh, earl of Chester
HeS. = Hugh, earl of Shrewsbury
hist. = history, -ical, -ly
l. = long
Ll. = Lloyd's Hist. of Wales
m. = met-re, -rical, -ly
MS. = manuscript
metath. = metathesis
M., Myv. = Myvyrian Archaiology
n. = note

or. = original, -ly
P. = Poetry from R.B
r.b. = read backwards
pal. = paleography
prob. = probably
reptn. = repetition
s. = short
scr. = scribe, -al
sug. = suggest, -s
Tal. = Bk. of Taliesin
trans. = translat-ed, -ion
trs. = transpose, -d
wr. = written
δ = sound of *th* in *this*
ɼ = s   ɼ = r

1.1 Hwn yw y gododin, *this is the gododin.* See INTRO., *xvi.*
Read, y Gorδin, *the push, the onset. Cp.* ni dialav ordin, 12.9.
  b. greδv, *innate endowment, spirit, mettle, instinct.*

2 gwas, *one of fighting age. Cp.* juventus. I have deliberately trans. gwas (= HeS.) by 'knight,' a word used to denote "one of the class of equites, originally the cavalry of the Rom. army."
  b. gwrhyt : gor-hydyr, *over-bold, over-confident.*

3 Ysgwyt (*m.l.*) *a gloss for* aes. See 5.9.

4 pedrein (*m.l.*) *scr. corruption for* cledr, *shoulder.*
  b. mein-vuan. *Cp.* Mein ... llwyt 13.16. Cledyv (m)awr.

5 The use of the second person is manifestly a scr. change. The reptn. of 'athi' in the rhyme, and the change of v*u* to v*i* prove the corruption. *Read,* ni bi, ev a v*u* gas y·rov a [*thi* : h*it* =] H*u*, (Ys) gwell (y) gwneiv [a thi], ar wawd [d]y moli(v).

6 ? a proverbial refrain. *Cp.* 2.9-10.   Kynt [y *w*-aet : y*w* =

7 y [v]rein, *antcpn.* of argy*u*rein.   [y*v* =] yδ aet [e] lawr.

8 Ewein, son of Edwin, of Coleshill was chosen by HeS. to lead the expedition of 1098 to Gwyneδ. B. 272., INTRO., n. 37.
  b. a dan v[r]ein. The scribe's fondness for *brein* is remarkable.
  c. [po : pē =]pen [v*r*o = u*r*ō :] *m*on. *Cp.* ge*m*in : ge*r*uin, 27.4.

121

BOOK OF ANEIRIN

1.9 [llad] vn ma*b m*-arrō : v*u* ma*d in* Aeron, *or* llad v*u* [mab] in Aeron. The scribe is ever trying to disguise the fall of HeS. by fabrications like ' mab marro." *See next note.*

10-15 *N.B. Wherever the text reflects the defeat, or fall of Hugh of Montgomery, earl of Shrewsbury, the scribe is ever apt to paraphrase his original, and to make Hugh victorious. We have in this canto a typical example of this perversion of History. The* cynghane δ *is faulty throughout, a sure evidence of corruption. As my attempted restoration is far more extensive in this canto than usual a literal translation of the scribe's version follows* : " The coroneted one, leading where he went, breathless at the head of the host dealt out mead. He pierces the front of his shield at the very time that he heard the war-shout. He would give no shelter to those he pursued. He would not withdraw from the conflict until he drew blood. Like rushes he cut down men who did not retire. He speaks not of Gododin on the floor of Mordrei before the tent of Madog when he returned,—only one out of a hundred came." *And yet notwithstanding all this praise HeS. was dead at the time.*

 b. kynhorawg, *leading (f.c.)* : Mynyδawg men *y*δ elhei. *See* 2.5.

 c. diffun : di*ll*yn . . . me δ *adalhei* : δyw*a*llei.

11 tw*ll* tal y rodawr. *A round shield,* rodawr, *can have no* tal, wh. *refers here to the temple of HeS. See* 22.2, 23.22. *? read,* (Seith*i*d) tal-dyll*i*d en[e] awr k*l*ywei.

12 *no c., ? read,* (y GYNT) ni no δ YNT meint δ ilyNei.

 b. no c., ? read, (Ar ystre sawl wa*r*e wy) v*e*rei [waet].

13 gomynei : YD gwyδynt (*cp*. 15.7) (*n*yt : *r*yt=) RHYD ni

 b. [nyt echei=ny techei] *a reptn. of* ni giliei. ⌊giliei (.12).

14 nys adraw δ godo δ in. *how could he, being dead ? ? read,* (or δin, **ar**) gor δ in **ar** lawr Mor δ rei, (neb byth) rac peby*ll* (Reg**ed**) δelhei. *c. rejects* madawc.

15 ' namyn un gwr o gant ' *' returned.' This is everywhere a scr. addition, having nowhere a companion line to form the regular couplet. Note also that the number of the expeditionary force was* ONE HUNDRED, *un o gant. All the other numberings of the men of Ei*δ*yn are interpolations. See* 2.22, 6.19, 27.22, 28.9–12,

16 kynniv-[yat : avt=]awt . . . e : orwyt. [30.16 –31.1)

****There is clearly a line missing here as pointed out by sense and an unmated ninth line. See* am t. *The rushing* (rhuth*e*r) *that follows is unintelligible without some cause.*

17 pan lithiwyd (*f.c.*), *lured* : lethwyd, *was pressed down.*

 b. amot *has the sense of* tymp, *allotted time, but ?* aruot, *overthrow.*

 c. a v*u* not a ga*t*wyt (*no c.*) : a gavwyt, *was a mark that was hit.*

MISCELLANEOUS NOTES

1·18 gwell : gwall a wnaeth [e] *metath. for* (neu·r) wnaeth wall arvaeth ni [giliwyd : ?] argelwyd. *The mistake = not seeking shelter, rather than not withdrawing inland.*
    b. (*f.c.*) rac *bed*ın ododin *paraphrase for* rac midin gwyr Llychlyn (llu) d(r)ychwyd. godechu (*is intrans.*) = *to lurk, a flat contradiction to* ' ni gilywyd ' *of l.* 18. *see* Let lin lu, n. 34·8.
19 ar vreithe*ll* (*imposs. construction*) : ar draethell ry·wnaethpwyd, ·20, [vanawyt] . ni noδi (*no c.*) *a gloss for* ni δifferth.
20 ni ellir a*net* (*no c., no sense*) : ? a(d)*u*er (. . . neb a gollwyd).
21 (*m.s., no c.*) ergyt, *gloss on* erwan, c(*or*) atvan[nan], *i.e.* rac erwan cor **ad**van ym **c**adwyt, = *Talhaearn, the bard.*
22 *f.c., Transpose as in am. text.*
2·1 godiwawr (*f.c.*) : go*r*wychvawr to**r**chaw*c.*
    b. [*read*, gwevrawl vu gwerthvawr yngwrthryn Vann. *The amber-beaded one was serviceable in the resistance of the hillock.* scr. expansion, and an odd line. gw[*e*]rth [g]*u*in : gwrth-ρyn].
2 ef gwrthodes (*no c., gloss* :) ef ystwyis wrys [gwy[a]r δisg[r]e-*in* :] gwy*r* δisgynan.
3 (*f.c.*) *read*, kyd del Wyneδ (bel), Gogleδ i rann. *Since* ' *Bleidd Caeawg* ' *is the subject of* ' *dyffei,*' *and came to Gwyne*δ *in* 1098, *it follows that Gogle*δ = *the earldom of Chester, wh. was the* " *rann* " *of Hugh Lupus.*
    b. o gussyl ma*d* (e*r*yr = HeC.) yscy*rr*an, *they fight fiercely* (hyd lawr) **ys**cwydawr (**ys**) anghyvan.
5 [kaeawc kynhorawg, *vain reptn.*] ? *read*, Arvawg (Mynyδawg δyvyδ) yng·awr, cyn no diw, eg[wr] = yng·w(y)rδ(liw) ev gwy(δ)awr.
6 kyn*r*an, *chief* : ? kyu·lan, *along the bank*, or *edge*. Mynyδawg is nowhere styled ' *Kynran.*'
    b. byδinawr : δywanawr, *chance comers.*
7 kwyδ-[ei : e*t* =]wyt [p.— *antcpn.*, ym pym*u*nt : pym*n*wt :] ym p(l)ymnw(y)t (lu) [rac] ȳ la*f*nawr : ymlaδ*u*awr.
    b. o wyr : *g*wyr Deivr a Brynneich a δychïawr = HeC. *Hugh Lupus held land in* **twenty counties** *extending northwards as far as Northumberland goes.* ORMEROD'S *Hist. of Ches.*
8 ugein cant = 2000 (*see* n. 1·15) : *u*dein, *or* ubein cant *en* d.
9 kynt [y gic. or. MS. prob. had ' cit ' = cynt *repln*] e-*v*-leid : *en* l(l)eid, *mud. see* map, and *cp.* e lawr, 1·6. *? read*, kynt yn lleid (yδ eith*i*d) no [gyt e] neithawr.
    b. kynt ē vud e vran nogyt e allawr *m.l., no c., no sense.* *? read*, a chynt (beynt) yn vw(y)d rhein no ll(yw)awr, *cp.* 1·6-7.
10 cyn [noe] (prein) argyvrein [*e-w*-aet e *a gloss for*] wy δygrein) lawr. *The men who fell in the swirling shallows were crawling on the ground.*

123

2·11 gwerth : gweith. *gan* : (tr)*ang, perish.*
 b. an unmated line. m.l., c.f. Hyveiδ, *gloss on* HyδER etmygER tra vo kERδawr (Caeawg Vynyδawg) hir (vyδ glod-awl, -vawr). The scribe omitted last line because it shows that HeS. was dead.
13 (*no c.*) Gwyr [a] aeth [o]δodin :] orδin (traeth) chwerδyn
14 en [em] du- : drilliaw, *rending*. [o gnaw.
15 Mab [botgat : ?] Bargod *son of the March*, or as in am. t. [wnaeth wynnyeith, *no. c., ? a paraphrase for*] δiffeith wlad [gwreith e law : ?] wrth deithiaw. see Bargodion *nn*. 13·12, 26·22 ; & *cp*. Mab Syvno 6·8, mab Gwyδneu 8·11, & ' Bargat Varδ,' *Tal*. 19·14. Note that Tal. was a *Border* bard. See *enlarged note on p*. 174.
16 ket elwynt (*no c.*) : wy EUthyn lanNEU i anreithaw. *See* Gir. Camb. *Itinerary*, caput. vii., Ll. 409. *See p*. 174.
 b. a hen a yeueing *a paraphrase of* ? Dyen weis a hen dreisyn
17 dadyl *etc., an odd line, see* 3·2. [o law [*a hydyr, no c*.]
18 *See* n. 2·13 chwer*th*in wa*nar* : chwarδ yn wama*l*.
19 disgy*nn*ieit [e]m [b]edin = mid*in* [trin :] (gyrch) δi-achar.
 b. wy lledi (*no c.*) : lled(awr) a(e) llavnawr [heb vawr, n. 1·15], (yn llanw) trydar [roδi arwar :] rot*h*o war.
20 *transpose into* colovn rheit*h* [*u*yw = ? *ll*yw] glyw (go·beith)
21 *f.c., read, ?* Gwyr [a] aeth (yng·)hatraet*h* [oeδ ffraeth e*u* : oeδ*en* ff. =] oeδyn ffraet*h* lu.
 b. glas-veδ, *green* (=*fresh*) *mead*. meδ gwyn (4·2) = *white* (*fermenting*) *mead*. *cp*. maiδ glas *and* maiδ gwyn = *boiled whey*, & gwneyd yn goreu glas, *doing our very best* i.e. *when we are fresh*.
22 *t*rychant (*f.c.*) : crys*f*iANt [trwy] (li)veiriANt yn [cattau *gloss on*] trywANu. (? trwy lyriant).
3·1 ke*t el*-wynt e l. : cy*r*ch *c*leu wynn l. [e benydu no. c. :] ? oe hanallu. First they sought sanctuary. [*pervading them*].
2 *c. sug.*, Dïeu δaδl anghey yn (anghenu) [yn eu treiδu (*f.c.*),
3 *see* n. 2·21. [ue- *r*ep*t*n.] dwn, *broken*. [fyryf . . oeδ] (y) cam-
4 *c.f.* e am (och) lavnAwr coch gorvawr garmwn. [(hawn).
5 [eδ emleδyn *gloss on*] ymdAERyn (vel) AERgwn.
6 ar deulu brenneych beych (*no c., a paraphrase* :) Teulu (gwasarn Hu) bei[ch] barnasswn, diliw dyn advyw nys adawswn. [le*i*s-wn.
7 [kyueillt . . . oeδ-. *see* n. 1·15]. C. *sug.*, (o dreis y) colle*i*s a δiff-
 b. rhugl, '*of free motion*' O.P., i.e. *neither forced nor restricted = voluntarily*. Gr. ap *K*ynan, on the Irish mercenaries going over to the two earls, ' left the island of Mon . . . fearing betrayal.' B. 273·3–8. *Read*, Rhugl (c)yn ymwrthryn Mon ryadwn. *note c. In the secondary part, the letters of the cynghaneδ are often reversed. cp.* lewin lawer l. 16. *Rynn* is wanted in l. 8.

MISCELLANEOUS NOTES

3·8 ny my*nn*[ws] Gwrawl R*y*nn, gwaδawl [c]hwegrwn, *Brave (Magnus) will not have the Rhyn, but settles it on the father-in-law of the scion of Cynan of Conical Hill.* ma*b*AN i [Gian=] Gy*b*AN o v*r*yn cyngrwn=Castell Aber Lleinog. N.B.—*The father-in-law, hwegrwn, of Gr. ap Kynan was Ewein ap Edwin* (n. 1·8). *This passage proves the authorship of this part of the text; it proves also that* 'catraeth' *was fought at Aber Lleinog in* 1098.

9 o vaen g[w]yn*n*gwn (*f.c.*) : o v*r*yn gyngnwn=cyngr̩wn, (5·22)

10 (y) gan (wyrδ) wawr. *E*n heδ (gynt) travodynt.

11 mil[c]a*nt* : milau*r* athrig-[ha*nt* : hau*r*=]awl.

12 gwyarllyt (*f.c.*) *gloss on* creulyd (y) Gwyn-[nod :]dyd [yn*t* :] (ae h)ynn waewawr. e*f*=ev : *wy* orsaf, *trs*.

13 eg·gwryawr, *reptn*. : yng·orawl, *effectively*.

   b. rac [gosgorδ *m.l.*, *no c*. :] trawd, *progress*, Mynyddawg (dyvydd) Mwynvawr, *the Much-kind* (Magnus).

14 *no c*. [dy] gym*y*rrws : gymo*tt*es eu [hoet :] moes eu *hanyan*awr *Context and c*. *sug*. eu *moes gymodes eu cyvnesawr i.e. the* amhad *whom HeS. forced to fight on his side. see* n. 33·7·

16 llewin, *radiant, light*. LEwin lawER *is good c. see* n. 3·7, *b*.

   b. cleδy*u*awr : *p*aladyr̩awr=paladrawr, *spears*. *n*a requires a neg. before it. ? (ni) choch(awr) paladrawr na ph*a*rawr.

17 eu lläin (*no c*.) : nac aestalch (oeδ) wengalch na ph[edryollt

18 [rac &c. *reptn*.] of l.13.   b]ennawr.

19 o gadeu (*f. c*.) : *e* gilieu=yng·hilieu gewilyδ.

20 wy wnaethant (*f. c*.) : gorugant yn geugant [gelo*r*wyδ : gelo*w*ryδ=] geleuryδ. [a] llav(e)nawr.

21 llawn anna*w*t : llaw(e)n anna*wr*, *a gloss on* lliwedawr. *cp*. "Teulu Madawc, mad anhawr"=? *good warriors*. B.B.C., 103·4.

   b. Goreu yw : ? cymhorth hwnn cyn kythlwng a chythruδ. *This introduction of baptism and the mass is a foreign note in our text, dating prob. a century later than the or. MS., but earlier than our scribe, for he blurs the meaning of the passage*.

22 enneint c*l*eu (r)ac angheu oe hennyδ.

   b. rac beδin odoδin pan vu δyδ (*c.f.*) ? *read*, rac midin yng·orδin ar doriad dyδ, *against the ships in the attack at dawn; but see am. t.*

4·1 neus goreu Duw bwyllyat ... *m.l., c.f.* ? *read* Bwyat vu neirthiad Duw ir Gwychyδ. *Note that we have* B a p t i s m *for the soldier, and the* P e r i c u l o s a o r a t i o *for the nobles*.

   b. pwyllyat=*deliberation. Perversion could no further go* "Headlong rashness" *characterised HeS. at Battle-strand*.

3 gyvluyδ(es, a)e neges [ef] o[r] **dra** gwres (a) **drang** δyδ. trenghid *from* trengi. *c. sug*., trang *from* trangu.

BOOK OF ANEIRIN

4·4 *Lines 4–9 should app. follow* 6·22.
  b.   ny : ρi = Rhi, *King* (Magnus) . . . *mawr* : tραwc = traws,
5 ni bu moe [gyff- =]gyvor. [athwart.
6 tut vwlch-hir : tud vylch-ir (caer dorris) e(r)ch drewyδ
  [ech e dir ae drevyδ = *out of his land and settlements !*] *Magnus
  like Teukros was a dread* smiter. *See* B.B.C. 93·1·6, & *vii.*, n.g.
7 (Y·Mon lladd) Saeson [ef] lladdei seith[uet] nyδ (17·14–18).
  b. en wrvyδ : eu = ev orvyδ.
8 ae govein gân I Gein [gyweithyδ *no c., for*] edmygyδ.
  b. pan δyvu Dutvwlch duc nerthyδ, *when T. came he brought
  succour. The goal of the son of Kilyδ was a place of blood.
  m., c., sense, Hist., are all at fault. ? read,* Pan [dy] vu [tut– :]
  tρ(e)i (Bleiδ) [vwlch :] wel(e)i [duc] y·mer[th]yδ [oeδ waet :]
  wyar [l]aρ wyal[uan] (i) vad gilyδ.
10 Gwr (*i.e.* Magnus δ)aeth yng·had traeth y·gan (wyrδ) wawr
  b.   (*f.c.*) wyneb(a) [uδyn] ysgorva [yscwyd- *no c.,* :] osgorδ-
11 trei gyrchynt gynnullynt [reinawr *no c.*] : (yn ffull)vawr.
12 eng(h)ynuan mal taran twrv [aes *no c.* :] parawr.
  b. gwr . . . gwr . . . gwr (*scr. stutter*) : g.g. yn edvynt or·l(ed)awr
14 lled : llet : llei, *mud,* (Mwng) loδei.
  b. eng(h)ystuδ [h]eryn dur *metath. for,* duc eny[r : t =]δ.
  (see Tal. 16·12). arbennawr, *the grand seigneurs.*
15 ystyngei aδledawr. *no c., scr. perversion. Magnus delivered,*
  gwaredei anδledawr, *or* amhad.
  b. rac erthgi. *scr. trem of contempt for Magnus* = ' arth ' *elsewhere. Read,* Ranc, erchei erth(r)ychei [vyδinawr *no c.*]. *A
  paraphrase for* ? a gyrch lawr.
4·16–22. *This canto offers many difficulties. But the meaning
becomes clear when we remember that Owein and Uchtryd, with
their men, deserted the Franco-Saxons to befriend the Venedotians.
It was, therefore, natural for the bard of Hugh Lupus to denounce the 'Keintians' as false common fellows' 'gwerin enwir.'*
16 (*no c.*) O *is a mistake for* G *as at* 33·10, *cp.* 33·15. vreith-*yell
is a questionable word*; *here it* = Gvreith veri : Gwraeth weis
17 dychïorant, *no c.,* : ? (δeuyn Von) eu hoet v. h. [catraeth.
  b. [eδyrn antcpn. :] oeδyn δieδyrn a. d.
18 a meibyon Godebawg, *The sons of Edwin occupied the district of Coelion* (22.3, 24.1) *named after* ' Coel Godebawg.'
  ? read, (Rac pleid Edwin) veib, gwerin enwir. *See* nn. 4·16–22.
19 lyn-wys-[awr] : wys (Llych)lyn gelor[awr] hir : golochir.
  b. (ys) tru dynghet[ven] vu angheu cywir = HeS. ' cywir ' *is
  antithetic to* ' enwir,' *but* ? gyw- = geu : geρir.

126

MISCELLANEOUS NOTES

4·20 tynghetven . . . [a dyngwt y dutvwlch a chyvwlch hir *interpolated*] *a line without a mate, or c., wh. sug.*, a dyngwyd i drechwyd o Gyvlwch dir,=*the Laches. That would be true history.*
21 ket yvem veδ gloyw, *a paraphrase for* meδ yvem (yn llawen) wrth [leu] babir. *cp. mod.* ' gweitho wrth ganwll ' =
22 ket vei da [e] vlas (crei) i gas vu hir. ⌊wrth oleu c·
5.1 [ech] ech-ing, *out of distress, delivered. trs. into* Blaen claer eching gaer llynwyn [ew : eu =] engei. *cp.* P. 171·2. claer *describes the shining mail of the Saxons in contradistinction to the Norse*
  b. Gwyr (hydrem) Gwe[i]ryd [gwanar] ae dilydei. ⌊gwrm.
2 *trs.* ar [e] bluδveδ [blaen *gloss for*] glyw (llüeδ) dy g[o]*ll*ouit : dyguoll*it* : dywall*ei.*
3 vual *en* e vwynvawr : *em*üalawr (*m.l.*) y Mwynvawr *a paraphrase* : yng·hibawr tramorawr y·Mordrei.
3 [blaen *reptn.*] (Or) gwirawt a vragawt ev [dybyδei blaen *a gloss* :] ragorei.
4 eur a phorphor ke*in* as mygei (*no c.*), *gold and fine purple he admired, for* Eur (drysor) ku*n* Porffor as (parthei).
  b. blaen eδystrawr pasc ae gwaredei (*no c.*) *the fastest of his fat steeds delivered him* = HeS., *already dead ! ? read,* ae basc(awl) eδystrawr (δinystrei). ⌈(weryd) ae derbynei.
5 [Gwrthlef ac] eu o bryt ae der*ll*ydei *context sug.*, o vryd ev
6 Blaen-[er : or =]awr (δ)wyre awr [buδvawr, *no c., a gloss* :] a weler drei . arth : ar (ae)th llwrw yn(hraeth) [byth *a gloss on* hwyr :] hwer(w) y techei.
7 A*p* awr gynhor-w*â*n ; h. a. *trs. into* arwyrein huan.
8 gwledic : ? glyw (= HeS.) gw(y)δ o gyf*f* gein.
  b. ne[f : *v = u* :] *p* = ner e(v)nys Brydein = Gwyneδ here.
9 aes : ae*th.* [*cp.* pys- : py*th*ewnos, ws- : w*th*nos]. b*u*- : boδyn.
10 y rhïyδ (roδes wleδ o) ry·odres . e(nghy)veδ. HeS.
11 oeδ-er*u*it = oe δer*ll*yδ. (G)uyδel . . . [w]in = yn.
  b. a er- : aer ueiδ [*en* :] a*p*·ueδ(*wer*), aer ge*u*nyn = gevnyn.
12 Aer : (or) A(b)er [a] dan g[l]aer, ke(v)nyn gyvid aer.
  b. *aer f*eirch-[y]*awc, trs. into* (or gwyδ-)*f*eirch *aer-awt.*
13 (c)ae*t* (llysc) edenawc. note -*c* ends word before ae*t*.
  b. [nyt : ne*u*t] oeδ dyry*f* yscwyd (yn·yvr)awr p. ' gan waywawr ' turns *spears* into *spearmen. A long light shield could not be*
14 yng·hat blym[nwyt *reptn.* ;] (Benmon). [*handled in the waters.*
15 [di]yssig yn·ïas . . . huδ[it] ewylly(ss)ias cyn bu (dan) glawr clas, *under the roof of the Abbey.*
16 [beδ gwr :] gor6eδ [uelli[n]g vreisc :] breisc wellig (yng·hôr A*m*wythig). gwellig *is a biform of* gwallawc, *cp.* Tal. 18·25 and Pughe *s.v.* gwallygiaw. *HeS. was buried at Shrewsbury.*
ORD. VITALIS, bk. x., cap. vii.

BOOK OF ANEIRIN

5·17 Teithi et- *for* Teitheit *expeditionary force. Note the wrong divisions of syllables here and* l. 11 *above*—oed er- : oe der-, a cr-ueid : aer veiδ, and -awc aer : -awt caer (l. 13).
  b. myɡant : ? myg(r)ant, *or* mudant try lw(y)r y(t) uqrant.
  c. pymwnt a phym cant. *The* TEITHIEIT *numbered* 100 *so that* ' pymwnt ' ' & 500 ' *cannot be original. Context and Hist. sug.* Pēnmon[t a] *pan* (δoethant). *cp.* nn. 1·8, 5·14.
18 trychyn athric[h]ant. Tri [ſi :] *ff*in gatvarchawc Eiδyn euru(y)chawc. *These three border knights of Eiδyn, three allied friends* (·20) *were HeS., the generalissimo with Owein & Uchtryd*
19 tri [eur] thëyrn torchawc. [*as guides.* B., 272-273.
20 tri [cha*t* :] cha*r* cyhaval [tri chy*ſ*- :] gy*ſ*neit rac [kyſ :] casnar =Magnus, 27·7. *This line should follow* ' dywal.' *Llwchvar*δ *originally was the bard of HeS. He was therefore pro Franco-Saxon, and anti Norse-Welsh at the outset. But after the death of HeS. he was the bard of Ewein alias* Cynon, *and became pro Norse-Welsh.*
21 tri yn·hrin yn drwn. [llew :] (un a las yn·wvn) *should be followed by* [tri :] de*u* dëyrn váon (·22), *K*ynri a Chynon. n. 6·1.
22 (wy) leδynt [blwm :] yn vlwng e*u*[r] : e*n* e ga(e)*r* gyngrwn= Castell Aber Lleinawc.
  b. a δyvu o vrython. *This line is repeated at* 6·2, *wh. points to scribal corruption. See am. t.*
6·1 kynri. *? metathesis for* yk*tt*ri : yctrit=Uchtrit *who is certainly meant.* Cynon *is the nom de guerre of* Owein. *These two were* Kynrcin y Ceinnyon *rather than of Aeron, but see Intro., xliii.,* n. 37, & 10·12. *c. sug. as in am. t. see* 38·8
  b. [go] gyuerchi : cyvner*th*(id) yn honn, Deivr δi*ff*erogion, *or* niuerogion. *cp.* Tal. 3·4 & dievyl duon M. 142·7. *See Intro., n.* 23.
2 a dyvu o vrython. (*m.l.*) *sense sug.,* ni δoeth o Aeron wr well no Chynon. Sarff *ff*er yn galon, '*the stout serpent of our enemies' is a spiteful scribal addition, because* Cynon *alias* Owein *went over to the Welsh.*
4 Y·Mord(r)ei (Gwyneδ). *We are distinctly told infra* (*l.* 12) *that cat traeth took place* " em blaen Gwyneδ " *i.e. on the shore of the foreland of* Gwyneδ=*promontory of Mon.*
  b. e vehyr=? wehyner y[g kyu] arvot gwy(δe)r, *or* ii. mawr meint y gwehyn yngwleδ gwyr (Eiδyn).
In ll. 5-12 *oratio obliqua has been changed by scr. into oratio recta.*
5 (Cyn) b(r)wyde(r) Eryr (Crwydr) er-[ys :]symudei.
  b. *paraphrase for* pan grys[syei] (traeth e) gyd[ywal :] vae(th) [kyfδwyreei *gloss on*] kydgodei. *cp.* cyvneit 5·20.
6 (yng) awr g. w. w. [kyui : kȳui =]kymwy δodet. *trs. into* am bellt aesawr dellt (es) adawet.

MISCELLANEOUS NOTES

6·7 Bar[eu = ev = ef] = ef Rynn rwygiat [dy]gyminet yng·had.

8 briwet [mab Syvno, *son of Coombe Syvno*]. " On the confines of Montgomery and Denbigh there is a place called Bwlch Cwm Syvno ; and in the same locality, rising out of this pass, and standing between Moel Ferna and Cadeir Ferwyn is a hill called *Moel Sywedy*δ." T. STEPHENS, Y *Gododin*, p. 187. *The words* ' Mab Syvno ' (*as proved by c. & m.*) *are interpolated. Roger of Montgomery was lord of Cwm Syvno, and father of HeS., the b.* ſyw[ye] : *l*iw dyδ [a] e cwyδ[y]e*t*. ["bruised one." *cp.* 8·11.

9 [a] . . . erwyn[eb] g. (Mang) a llavn lliveit laδei (y) [lleδessit :] lleιδieit *the slayers*, or bleiδieit *the Lupusians, synonymous here. The bard would hardly call his own people lleiδieid, but might distinguish the* Ceinnyon *from the* Bleiδieit.

10 ac a*th*rwys ac a*ff*rei = (yn) a*ff*wys abre*t*. *See* Tal. 4.23.

b. [er] amot [aruot] arvaethet. [er] mygei : ? maget. (*cp.* 5·4·17, 6·5) ? *read*, calaneδ (laδet) o wyr gwychr (Redec). Gw(y)neδ *is a scr. perversion* (n., 1·15)—*it occurs in next line*.

13 can . . *di*[sgyn]*n*eis : *u*eis =]weis *id* yveis rann [ſin ſaw-t ut :] *l*iuvan *t*ut = lyw*y*an dut, [nyt di = *affirmative, hence read*] a thra chyveδ (wnaeth) gol[w]eδ (wŷn) drut.

14 [pan δisgynnei bawb ti, *scr. nonsense* :] (cryssem ban Morien. δisgyn[*nυt*=] (en) nyt, *or ii*. c. ban welem vid δel yn rhyd.

15 [ys deupo *gloss on*] caffad gwae [āu- :] anvad gweith na *t*hech*i*t [pressent . . . drut]. *See* 31·17.

17–22 *This canto must be a paraphrase of the or. text, for the c. is faulty throughout. cp*. 27·22–28·6.

17 buant, *no c.* : (hynt) vu enwawc. (yng·wleδ), gwin a meδ [o eur vu :] bint eu gwirawd.

18 blwydyn yn erbyn, *for a year on end*, ? *for* b*r*wyd(r)yn in erbyn, *a paraphrase for* a·n erbyn (nid) *u*rδyn δevawd.

19 trȳ wyr = try*n* wyr, *brave men*, (*no c.*) *Read backwards* = rywyr*t* = ry·vyri(an) *they cast down utterly. cp*. n. 28·9 [a thri ugeint] athrychant, *e*[u]r : *or* (gwych) t.

20 Or sawl [yt] gryssȳ-[ass-]an*t* = gryssyn a*ur* = awr o (lyn) ormaut. [uch gormant wirawt *is app. a paraphrase without c.*]. *b*. ? *read*, (Or Ffreinc) ni δieinc[is] o w*r*[hydr]i = *v*ri ffossawd.

21 namyn tri [deu ga*t*ci *used twice* :] deu ga*r r*i, deu ga*t*i*r* [w[i]raw*t* =] vrawt a (Mynawg gwych ffodawg aeth ffoawd) *i.e. Owein, Uchtryd, and HeC. were the three leaders who survived* *b*. Cen(δrag)on (7·2) (gwyr) Aeron a δaerawd = HeS. [*Cad traeth*.

K
129

BOOK OF ANEIRIN

6·22 a minheu om gwaetffreu [gweith :] (geint) [wenwawd, *war-song, no. c.*] *ae*thwawd, *And I, bleeding, sing his dirge.* [*cp.* 28·4 *where the bard appears to be a captive*]. *Context sug. as in am. t. Note that the bards of the xiith cy. embedded their names in their songs, as the* ' *scion of Kynan* ' *does at* 3·9. *see Intro.* xlii., n. 36.

7·1 Vyng·har (HeC.) yngorwar(th) [ny*u*=] niw gogyffrawd. (The *ff* requires an answering digraph). ? vynghar yngwir*v*ar niw *y*sga*r*awd, *or* yngwirwarth niw di*r*gyffrawd.

b. *o neb* ony bei, *paraphrase for* Onid o Wyn(dyd) dragon (HeS.)

2 n*y* di. *metath. for* (Pei) didolid n*i* [yngkynteδ] o wŷd g.

3 ? *a paraphrase, see am. t.* Peithing *a gloss for* Moryen.

b. ef=Pcithing, *wh. is perverted hist.* Read, Hu [δis]grein [eg cat, *perversion* ; disg- *reptn.*] (o vael) rein yn ael (d)rawd.

4 [neus adrawδ etc.] *scr. expansion. How could the dead* ' *tell* ' ?

5 Pan vei n*i* (?) *b*liviei ll. n. (*f. c.*) ? pan (iach) n**id** llymach bidog) nebawd, *or* nid llymach cleddy*v* nebawd.

6 [Aryf ... goget]. *See* 25·1.

7·7–9 & 31·6–11. Tra chyveδ mawr ... [giwet, *tautological with*

8 ynghynnor (v)eis ... ll*u*dw : lleδw, *prostrate.* !gwys :] gleu.

9 kynn oe(t) a. Greit [uab :] vu hoew [gi*r* ac=*r*ig ac :] ri ga*r* ysberi y(d) beri(s) greu. rig *might be Irish gen. of* ri=King.

10 [Arw r y d :] (G)arw ryd (5·8) *wy* : *uy*=ny [*y*ʃcwyt :] *f*ywyt [*or fy*rwyd] (Hu) [a] dan e dal[*v*]eith (Gynt) [ac e*i*-l-*t*ith :] oe leith orwyδan. *If* ' Arwr '=Hu, *it reverses Hist. & what follows makes nonsense.*

11 bu trydar (rhwng Rhyd a glann) ... bu (gova)*r*an.

12 Bu ehut [e wae] wawr, bu *b*uan, bu bwyt [b]rein bu b(r)uδ (: ? ruδ) e[v] rann.   [*r*uth(rei) dirion.

13 a chyn ed[ew]i*r* yn ry(ch)don [gan w-lith :] yng·olith(r) eryr

14 ac o d*y*·wasc [ar]gwanec [tū=] twn vronn beirδ [byt].

15 dïe=dïen [b]yrth ... diua *oe*d=diva*wy*d.

16 *wy*r=*vy*r, seas. [*e* olo :] golöyn [a d*a*n eleirch]: de*u* alarch [*v*re : *v*er=]Wer-yt=*The two swans of the* (*Dee*) *estuary*= Owein & Uchtryt. *Note that* " golo a dan (dyw)arch " *is an old phrase for burial, but* golo *means also* ' to surround.' *The brothers were in the Castle of A. Ll.*

17 *f*eirch : *f*arch (*note c.*). buδ : kuδ man [vab] Bleiδyan.

18 cam (vu) [e] adaw (Hu) [heb gof=*expansion*] [camb, *reptn.*] (yn) ehelaeth (drei) =Mordrei.

19 nyt adawei adwy yr *paraphrase* : (am na bei) adwraeth.

b. nyt edewis *paraphrase for* Ceris i lys les cerδoria*e*th.

20 prydei*n* : prydan δiw calan [yonawr en] e arvaeth.

MISCELLANEOUS NOTES

7·21 *trs. into* y tir nid erδir [*ke* : *ec*=et *vet*=] yd vyδ di*ff*eith gloss *on* divaeth (*note c.*) dra chas ania*l*(wch).
  22 dreic : drāc=tranc *death, waste.* dreic *sug.,* 'dreis' (Corn. & Bret.)=(W.) dris, '*brambles*' *but there is no c.*
  b. dragon [yn gwyar (*no c.,*)] *see* am. t.

8·1 Gwen, *f.,* [abwy *m.* gloss :] celein, [va*b* :] ma*d*(w) gwenn (o) gynhen [ga]traeth. *trs. into* Madw gwe**nn**, celein we**n**, o gynhe**n** traeth. *This* cynhen traeth *proves* catraeth=cat traeth, *for* cynhen *and* cat *are synonyms.*
  8·2–7, & 32·22–33·3. *Cp. the two* VERSIONS.
  2 [Bu] *Gwir* mal y [meud e ga*t*-lew=meδ-*u* e ga*r* tew=] meδ [u*ē*=] vyng·ha*r* tew. (*cp.* 7·1 Uyg car). 32·22=*Geu* ath δywedws tut lew. *If* ca*t* lew=ca*r* tew *then* tut lew=[t]uδ tew ; *but if* tut *is or., then* cat=g(wl)at. Gat *may*=go*r*-tew=Gorthew (29·20)=Hugh *the Fat, who is meant here. N.B. It is true,* gwir, *to say that* HeS. *was not caught, because he fell, and was lost under water* ; *it is also false,* geu, *because he did not escape.*
  b. Ni δeliis [meirch] neb march(awg g)lew=HeS.
  3 [heessit *recurs at end of line* 4] *gloss* : ? tevlid waewawr (gan) y glyw... (δo)δyw. Kyn ni vaccet am vyrn [am] borth.
  4 dywal [y] g. e*m*[b]orth : y*n*iorth, *opposing. see* 33·2.
  5 onn [o] b. [y :] o law [y ar] Mein [ny=*uy*=] bu. [e*ll* :] e(r)ch [vygedorth, *gloss on*] y bollt (33.3). *It was Magnus* (Mein)*'s bolt that killed HeS. according to the chronicles.*
  6 [ry] gu i rewin, yt laδ(ei) [a llauyn *interpolation*] wraeth [o *ei*thin :] go*r*llin, val pan [*vel* [me]del *metath. for*] δel lev=liv ar vreithin... va*r*thlew (*cp.* trewyδ).
  8 I*f*-*f*ac : is *t*āc=ys tanc anvon[*auc* :]ant o [barth, *no c., gloss on*] vro Deheu (=Penvro).
  b. tebic mor liant, *like the flowing tide,* a paraphrase. tebic : Tevic, *lord,*=Gwanar (**yd** gynnal) **y d**evodeu. *cp.* cyntebic, n.
  9 o ŵyl[ed] a llaryeδ a che[*in* :]*r*δ (a ch)yveδ.   [35·21.
  b. [men *reptn.* :] cyn [yth] clawδ [e offer *read backwards* =ro*ff*oe=] (d)rothwy (nawδ) i b**wyth** maδeu.

***Owein ap Cadwgan... aδoeth nosweith ir castell a niver y gyt ac ef... gwedy gwneuthur *clawδ* dan y *trotheu*... yδ euthant ir castell yδ oeδ Geralt a Nest yn cysgu ynδaw B. 281. *Ow. ap C. came one night to the castle, and a small number with him... they mined under the threshold and got into the castle in which G. and Nest were sleeping.*

10 *trs. into,* Dihyll ni bu hyll na [heu, *antcpn.* :] geu diheu.
  b. *f*einn[yess]it : *h*ein*t*it (*the -nn- are against* sein-iaw).

K 2

BOOK OF ANEIRIN

8·11 e gleδyf : ge(wi)**lyddy**t (**gwyrydd**) [ym penn] mameu.
   b. mu[c]greit oeδ moleit e[f] vab Gwyδneu, *the son of the land of Gwyδneu.* cp. Tal. n. 38·16, and mab Syvno, n. 6·8 ; n. 2·15.
  12 Keredic : car e(i)δig (nis) car[adwy :]ei i glot . . . (i) not.
    *** *This line belongs to the previous canto.*
   b. Lletvegin, *fosterling*=Gr. ap Rhys, *who returned from Ireland in* 1113 *to his paternity in Ystrad Towi.* B. 281.
  13 is tawel, *no c. gloss on* aδwyn. Gr.='aδwynder y Deheu-
  14 y wlad=? i wlad . . . [nef]. ⌊wyr,' B. 310·15.
  15 Keredig, *m.l., c. sug.*, (Hyrwyδ), *spirited.*
  16 ? *read*, ae ysgwyt [eu- :] ev r(y)·grwydr gadlan (ae) waewawr (yn) anghyvan, *or as in am. t.*
  18 diffynnei e vann, *m.l., gloss on* differth i rann. Ys deupo.
      c. *sug* , ys delwy . . . yg Kyman : ? nev lân.
  19 *m.l. ? read as in am. text.*
  20 garadawc, *loved one, gloss on* gadr vab Rhys. B. 297·15-28.
   b. trychwn : tryche1 . . . gomyn-=gyminad (9·1).
  21 ef llithyei wyδgwn : ef llithr[ei]yn waewffyn. ⌈mawr. B. 296-7.
  22 O. vab eulat : ys *vyn*·hyst glyw Owyn, vab e wlat=Cantrev
9·1 o . . o . . . o *scr. stuttering.* Gatraeth . . . Vrynn hydwn. *This refers to the battles at Blaen porth Hoδnant above Traeth Seith, and to Crug mawr in Ll. Goedmor. see am. t.*
  2 gwedy meδ *gloew* ar anghat : gwedy (eu) meδwi y tranghat. *Prisoners were made drunk, and then put to death.* cp. Chware
  3 *no c.* ? *read as in am t.* ⌊pelre a phen Saeson. B.B.C. 48·11.
   b. vyrryon : ? byryan hoedl, meδwon . . . uch (*c.f.*) : am.
  4 *c.f.*, Goscorδ(awg) Mynyδawg [enwawc] en (dyδ) reit.
  5 gwerth eu gwleδ o veδ vu eu heneit, *the cost of their mead feast was their life*=*reptn. of 3b.* ? *read as in am. t.*
  *** *For the list of the fallen heroes (c.f.) see* Bucheδ Gr.
  6 *If* pyll *is right, read,* Madawg a **Chradawg**, Pyll **a** Jeuan.
      gwynua[chy]nnan=gwynvannan.
  7 [peredur=pen : penedur a. d. :] arveu dur benadur [=HeS]
      [gwawrdur] ar a[e]dan=ar·adan.
   b. achubyat eng gawr (*m.l., no c.*) : ? Hyd lawr ysg. (ys) angh-
  8 ac het (y) lleδ[ess]y[n]t [w] y llaδassant.
  9 *no c., paraphrase for,* (Gwych wyr) iw tymhyr nyt ymchwelan.
  10 oδ-uch meδ, *no c., gloss on* ? y llewyn yn llawn [arv- :]
  11 hadrawδ wy. angawr *a paraphrase. see am .t.* ⌊al-aeth.

MISCELLANEOUS NOTES

9·12 gwe*n*w[yn] : gweⲣw=*ch*wcrw. *cp.* guero, 35·15, 37·15.
   b. eu hadlam nyt ma*b* mam *trs. into* [*m*am :]
        *n*am eu hadlam nyt ma*d* ae maeth.
  13 [mor] *no c., a paraphrase for* hir[eu h]etlid a*e* herlid [a*c* . .
      he*t*-[gyll- :] a*r* her(w) aeth. *see* l. 14.
   b. *c.f.* [*en ol*] ? *read* (Oe) tymhyr (sy*r*th) pybyr wy**r** gwinvaeth.
    cp. 20·19, and 'oe dut,' 21·18.
  14 gwlyget gododin *may*=golyget (20·20) *or* goruget gorδin.
In Kulhwch *we read* ' Corn gwlgawt gogodin', *but context is
against construing* ' gwlyget' *as a person. We want a couplet.*
   b. a*n*-cwy*n, no c., metath. for* cwy**ddaw(d)** Myny**ddaw**g en
(ar)**vawc** [e gwn]aeth a phrıt er·byn*it* lleith cy*n*hen traeth.
The *r* in er p*r*yn*u* [: erbyn*it*] *is repln*. [brei]thyell *(read
backwards cp.* n. 4·14)=lleyth, & cat=*a gloss on* cynhen (8·1).
  16 Gwyr a aeth : gwr (δ)aeth (*cp.* 4·1·10, 11·20, 34·11)=Magnus
(yng)·hatraeth ing gât yng·awr, *trouble was got with the war cry,
or* ing (wnaeth) yng·awr.
  17 nerth. *scr. perversion for* Gwrth veirch (serig) seirch . . . ac
ysgwydawr (*n. c.) for* ? gwyr gorwychrawl=*the host of Eiδyn ;
gwrym* seirch is a perversion. The earls wore *bright* mail (*claer*
l. 18), while the Norse mail was *gwrym*, dun or black.
  18 argychwyn *gloss on* a ymdeivl. wae[a]wawr=misprint.
   b. *no c., no sense.* ' Mail' *is not* ' thrown.' ? *read*, A (δ**ug**)
glaer luryg[eu a chleδyvawr :] dorvynyglawr. *see* n. 18·6.
  19 tyllei drwy vyδinawr, *m.f., c.f., paraphrase for*, ev
     dreiddei drwy **vleidd**awr. *note c.*
   b. cwyδei [bym pymwnt, *no c., scr. corruption* :] ? (**sawl** δelei
    draws) i lavnawr. *cp.* 2·7, 5·17.
  20 r*u*-uaw*n*=r*it* uawⲣ hi[r ef] roδa(wr) e ûr (r)ē [al]lawr=i ŵr
[? *a gloss on* lyw] Ren lawr. *see* am. t.
   b. a chet [a] (δı)ch[oel]*w*ein (deg y Kein(t) gerδawr.
  21 Ni : neu*r* wnaethpwyt [neuaδ *no c.*] : or traeth.
  22 mor vawr [mor *repln.*] *or-* : *e c*(y)vawr=y gyvawr.
10·1 *Lit. trans.*='you merited, you possessed Morien's fire, He
would not say that Cynon would not make a corpse.' *c.f., m.f.,
? read*, dy[rl]lyd*it* [mo*t* :] moryt [ta*n* :] tⲣa Moryen (wân)
[ny :]yn·hraeth[ei na] gwnel [e]i (saeth) kelein [Kēnon=]Kynⲣan, (*or* ar traeth gel arvaeth gelein gynran).
  2 son edlydan, *a gloss on what follows.* ? *read*, (oeδ rhwy)van.
   b. sein[nyess]i*t* e gled[-*yf*=*w*=iu=]iⲣ=Sein*ır* i **glod** *ır* [em
penn (*no c.*) garthan, *paraphrase for*] ym **pob** midlan.
  3 n*o*c ac esgyc : ny*t* a*r*·esgy**n** ga*r*rec gy**n**hadvan [vy*r* vawr yng·
hynadvan=*scr. paraphrase*] *see* INTRO, *xxiv.*, & MAP.

BOOK OF ANEIRIN

10·4 *uy*(th) mwy, cysgodwy w**y**s vad porthan. *C. here rescues the sense of the or., and should save us from the apochryphal* ' Wit, son of the Pict.' gysgog**IT** w**IT** *is a scr. stutter, wh. c. doubly rejects.* " *The stone immediately above the high water line* " *had been a shelter to HeS., may it henceforth* " *shelter the good folk of the portlet* " *is a natural friendly wish. see n.* 38·11.

5–6 *These two lines have no c., nor pertinent sense as far as my* ' *seeing* ' *goes. History is the basis of the am. t.*
  b. ny wnaethpwyd neuaδ mor . . . *reptn. of* 9·21, 10·11, 15·2.

6 Moryen eil caradawg, *M., the fosterling of Caradawg. Moryen=Magnus, the son of King Hakon, was never fostered by any Caradawg.* ? *read,* gwaredawg.
  b. [Ny] . . . en trwm *e lwrw* (*no c.*) : en trymysc *y* mynawc.

7 [dywal *antcpn.*] (rhac arth) dywalach no(e) [*mab* ferawc :] *gar* ffwyrawc=*HeS.* Arth=*Magnus.*
  b. ffer y llaw *v*agl-[ei]wys (ffawd) ff(r)owys varchawc. f-*initially*=ff- *but* ffaglu=*to feed the fire with brushwood,* maglu *to ensnare.* ffowys=*he fled ; we want an adj. see am. t.*

8 glew=*brave* ; glyw=*prince* ; llyw=*leader. llu wants llyw.*
  b. [d]*i*as (*antcpn.*) : *l*as (v*u*) d**i**nas [e] llu d**i**·ovnawg.
  c. rac=ranc byδin [*o do*δin :] *e go*(r)δin [bu] wasgarawd ? *if* rac=ranc, *borrowed from O. F.* ranc=*rank, line.*

9 *trs. into,* ygymwy y gylchwy [dan bu aδevawc *no c.* for] a vylchawd. *This line follows varchawg,* ·7.
  b. [en] δyδ gwyth bu adwyth (15) [ne*u* :] ne*p* adveilawc,— ad·weillyawc *does not appear to fit the sense.*

10 bu *y*s-twyth vu *a*twyth. *see* l. 15 *infra.*
  b. dyrllyδyn eillt v., *the villeins deserved the meadhorns* : dy-

11 [Ny] gwnaethpwyd neuaδ . . . *no c.* ? *as in am. t.* [wallyn.

12 [no] Cynon, me**i**n) lary vronn, Cei**n**nion wledig.
  b. [nid :] neud *ef* eisteδei (*no. c.*) ? nid (aeth) eisteδ (wnaeth) en tal lleithic. Cynon, *i.e Owein ap Edwin remained as Castellan at Aber Llëinawg after Lupus had fled. see* 26·2.

13 e neb a wa*n*ei nyt atwe*n*it (*f.c.*), ' *whosoever he thrusted, was not thrust again,*' *wh. is entirely out of harmony with* ' tal lleithig.' *read,* ar neb a va*p*net ni wa*p*edit. *Owein's authority was supreme, and his judgments were without appeal,* i.e. final.
  b. raclym e waewawr *etc. These lines are misplaced they do not refer to Cynon but to HeS. and should come after* 33·9, *q.v.*

14 calch drei (i aesawr), [tyllei vyδinawr :] ryssei liwedawr rhac buan varcha*w*r [rac ry·giawr].

134

MISCELLANEOUS NOTES

10·15 en d. g. (bu) atwyth, [o]cδ [e] lav[n]awr=ev laδawr.
  b. pan gryssei [gynon] : (yn rhyd) ban gryssid gan wyrδ (y) wawr, *or* y wyrδ wawr.
 16 D. en trwm (*no c.*) : ys tryn y discyn ynghysevin.
 17 [cf] *trs. into,* gormes δïosces, ev dorres δin. diodcs ... dodes *both corrupt, influencing each other.*
  b. gwaew ri-eu ryv-[el] : ri yscir [e] uryw=vriw.
 18 chwerthin (*hopelessly inept, no c.*) : cywrenhin=HeS
  b. hut[e*ff*]yt=hudid ... e*l*fin : le*f*in=*l*evin : *r*ewin.
 20 *reptn. of l.* 16 *supra. Omit.* gwerth : gweith.
 21 a gwirawt (*no c.*) : a chyveδ gwin.
  b. heyessit *no c., gloss on* Tavlawr Mwng lavnawr rhwng d. v
 22 arδ. varchawc (*m.f.*) *refers to Magnus who was a King* (ri), *not a* 'marchawc.' = ? (y)*r*hawc arδyrchawt gan erch) orδin, *shortly the one exalted by the terrible gor*δ*ın left, or as in* am. t.
  b. eithin-yn uoleit : eδiu moleit yu = eδyw, m. yw mur : ? mu[c]greit=]mygreit Darw Trin. mur : muc *may*=Mūc i.e. Munc=Mwng. *We should then read*, eδyw ; moleit yw Mwng, greit darw trin, *has gone ; Praiseworthy is Magnus, the fierce bull of battle.* But see 8·11=84.
11·1 *Reptn. of* 10·16·20 Disgyn[sit]en trwm (gyrchyn) ala*r*(chawr), *swans, water lords. cp.* eryron, *eagles, land lords*
  b. oe-d [w]yrein : *oe* δyrein=*wy* δy*l*ein wyr e llu llaes ysgwydawr, *the men of the host with loose shields* (floating on the water), *a gloss on* lu escynawl, *going up* (*out of the water, fleeing*).
 2 [ysgwyt *reptn.*] rac biw *in front of the cattle, herd, motley crowd. cp.* amhad & Tal. n. 39·14. *cp.* 'rayah,' *cattle, by which the Turks call their non-Mahomedan subjects.*
  b. nar *a biform of* ner, *a gloss* : y rhi (=Magnus) vriw B. b.
 3 oδ uch, *no c., gloss for* y·min gwya*l*, *temple, brow*.
  b. a*n* de*l*iit : ? [a*r*] δileit *gloss for* dille(gw)it=dillyngwyd.
 4 gorwyδ gwarëus, *no c., m.l., gloss for* amws, *charger*.
  b. rith*r*i -*n* ych *metath. for* ruthi*r* -*u*-ych=ruthr*w*(s) *w*ych e. d.
 5-6 *no c., m.f., order of words wrong* ? Goruc twrch amot e mlaen ystre gawr, gwrthyat teiling deith ystrywyawr. Twrch : Trwch=HeC., *the Fat*. amot, *scr. corruption for* ovut (*note c*.) e mlaen *gloss for* cyrch (*note c*.). Gwrthyat *gloss for* cam *step, movement* deith, *c. sug.,* (ys) dei*l. see* am. t.
  b.[an] gelwit e nef *gloss for* i wynvyd [bi*t* : bi*r metath. for*] bri. *cp.* A vynn glod bid farw. *Proverb*.

11·7 c myt: en ryt [e[f] krynnit:] y krymid e gat antcpn. for [y gan] waewawr. cat : car (Mon a) Mannan [er] = Magnus, *the friend of* Owein ap *E*dwin, Gr. ap *K*ynan, and of ' Man.'
b. clot, *or. fem. as here, but it appears early as masc.*
8 [na] . . . na bei (*no c.*) : byδit llu iδ[aw] = lluyδ.
9 Amdry*nn*i d*r*y law dry lenn am lwys :
 Amdry*mit* ryd lyw dr(w)y (a)fen an-lwys. *see am. t.*
b. amδiffwys : amδyfrwys d., *beyond the marshland.*
10 [am *reptn. for*] dy·gwyδawδ dellt, "*split*" *arrows, quarrels.*
b. eryr Gwyδien, *the eagle of G. The* ' dellt ' *fall upon* HeS., *around the men of* Gwyδien = ? *Wepre Brook. cp.* Tal. n. 61·14.
11 Gwȳduc : Gwyndu*t* . . . ae waew (*no c.*) : ? i onnen, *or* luiuen (24·17) = lwyven. HeC. *was lord of Llwyvenyδ.*
12 amuc (*reptn.*) : a δuc. gwenwawt : gwyndawt. (*cp.* gwyndawt Gwyndyd werin '). *The first half of this and of the next line should come second.* mir δyn (*no c.*) : wenn = (HeS.) *who is* ' *chief in Gweryd and a joint head* ' *with* HeC. *cp.* Kyvrennin.
13 try(l)wyr yr boδ *metath. for* (y) boδir bun B., *the host of Bradwen* i.e. brad*w* wenn, *broken hero* = HeS. *cp.* A chen bu (h)ir, *but* bet B., *and though it was long (delayed) a grave benefits Bradwen.* B.B.C., 69·3. ac am : a*r* cam hen.
14 deude*c* = deheuec (24·15·21) = dyhewyt [gwenn] abwy(d) am Vadwenn, i.e. mad*w* wen, *the inert hero* = *the dead* HeS. ' mab ' *the scr. turns verb, noun, and adj. into persons !*
15 *Repetition am* dryn-ni [d]ry law = yn dryn yn llaw(r) Ryn dryl(li)enn gweinyδawr, *liegemen, servers.* en : (h)en
17 [en] . . . rac trychant *metath. for* t. . . . rac. *see* n. 24·19.
b. bleiδ heb p[r]enn = Bleiδ*ic* benn, gwn*aeth* gwychrawt, 24·20. 11·20–12·2. *see Variant Versions, & nn.* 34·11–15.
12·3 (*no c.*) Pan (or)vu[ost di] (Rhi lu) [kynniv-yn *metath .for*] y*n*ghynniv clod. *c. and context sug. as in am. t.* [gor di(v)rod.
b. tywyssen : ? cyssyuen = cyssyriyn. *cp.* argyssyrio, *to dread.*
4 re[dyrch] gwy*r* not (*m.'.*) : ri gworuot. *c. and m. disallow* rygyrch gwi*r* not, *he goes straight for the mark.*
5 [di *reptn.*] a cha*r* din drei : ? di*n*drei *or* Mo*r*drei. *Note the mutated* drei. [we*r*in.
b. olut . . . e vedin. *c. and sense sug.,* alltud . . . [e ve*t*in :] y
6 *m.s., c.f. ? a paraphrase for* (Gwyndyd) nid gwynvyd namwyn (pan) vei, *or as in am. t.*
b. men na *metath. for* namen = namyn, nam(w)yn.
12·7–8 *A line is missing and the second line misplaced.*

136

MISCELLANEOUS NOTES

12·7 cann-wr ? *a hundred men, or for* camhwr (campwr), *champion. cp.* camhwr-awg 25·13. en v(y)n ty, *in my hall.*
  b. keny *thou shalt sing*; keniv *I shall sing*; kennyf *with me.*
8 Penn gwyr. *Owein was generalissimo*; *he was also* penn Ceint *wh. c. supports. He was friend & father-in-law of the bard.*
9 nyt wyf mynawc, *a neg. for an affirm. ? read*: neut wyf gwledic. *Gr. was an exiled king,* gwledic. Mynawg *is the epithet of the* Palatine, *but also of* 'a prince,' 21·18. *see* Index.
  b. vy = vi. *The pronoun of the first person never counts as a syllable after verbs.*
  c. gorðin, *push, attack. This is the word perverted by the scribe into* got(o)ðin, *wh. has a syll. too many in 20 or more instances.*
  d. [ny chwarðaſ antcpn. *for*] nȳ gwarthaſ hwerthin, *or* nym gwarth y wherthin. *An allusion to his imprisonment at Chester; or to his retreat to Ireland in* 1098. *cp.* ll. 12–13 *infra.*
10 ronin. *end-rhyme, app. is against* ronyn, *a short while. ?* cunin *or* (b)renin. *cp.* kywrennin.
11 ty deyeryn *an underground prison. cp.* carchar daear, *but see* [*n.* 12·16.
  b. am ben : am ffen, *about the ankle.*
  *** *After* deulin *there is seemingly a lacuna.* [verin.
12 o . . [o] . . o, *scr. stuttering :* am veð-vuelin *yn* ca(e)r traeth-
  b mi na vi aneirin. *m.l., companion line missing. see am. t. and* INTRO., p. *xxxvii.* na *metath. for* an, v : y, i : t = anȳt = anynt, 3 pl. of anu, *minstrel singing. cp.* anant, *minstrels.*
  b. govec : goðec, 3 *sing. pres. Ind. of* goðecu, *chattering. see* INTROD., p. *xxxviii. & xlii.*
13 neu = *now, helps here to draw a distinction between what was sung immediately after the* gorðin *when the facts were fresh, and what was being sung years later by* Taliesin.
  b. dilin *is the prevailing spelling in poetry, but see* 14·13·18.
14–18 *Autobiographic account of the bard's rescue from the underground prison of Hugh Lupus, lord of* Gogleð.
14 Gor. Gog. *metath. for* Gogleð wroleð . . . uy ess-yllut, *no sense, no c., scr. perversion for,* y u(ab) alltud = Gr. ap Kynan.
16 o nerth kleðyf *no. c., & historically false. There was no fighting but a stealthy carrying away of the prisoner.*
17 *f.c.* an- : apwar [daear *f.c.* :] a gwarth . . angheu : anghov.
  b. keneu, *cub*; kenu(ric) vab Llyw-arch. *no c., ? a paraphrase for,* vad devig, *a noble prince. According to* BUCHEDD GR. AP K., *the rescuer was* Kynwric of Edernyon. *If* 'vab' *is right c. sug.,* Meurig (d. 1106), *who had a brother* Llywarch, *wh. c. rejects, and with it goes* 'dihavarch.'

BOOK OF ANEIRIN

12·19–13·2 *The faulty c., context, hist., and fragmentary lines all point to scr. changes. The poet is again autobiographic, and evidently wrote in the first person.*
19 senyllt, *seneschal, a gloss on* menestr.
20 goδolei, *no c., he enriched. Context implies the contrary.*
? *read as in am. t.* ? *in particular* (am llin).
 b. lem- : lëin [ein *reptn.*] *e* ryuel : *o* reuet.
 c. (*no c.*) lynwys[sawr] : (Llych)lyn-wys o[e].
22 gnawt : ? guawr (*wh. belongs to next line*). *c. sug. here,* (oe llaδ) yn neuaδ (bu·m)=bu im.
13·1 *no c.* ymhyrδw-*en sug.,* ym·hyrδwn *en* (p)en(vro) *i.e. at* Mynyδ Carn *in* 1081. *see* INTROD. *xxvi.,* n. 23.
 2 [hyrδ, *reptn.*] ? p(l)eit, *allies, supports for* y nerth. *cp.* B., 269·33. " Gr. ar Yscotteit gyt ac ef yn ganhorthwy iδaw." Lloyd, 380, n. 20. ? *read,* y nerth (ni) di*ff*er*th* ser*th* Artro, 1075.
*** *The bard, Gr. ap K., is here referring to his victory over Trahaearn whose ally was slain at Clynog in 1075. News of the death of Kynwrig app. brought Trahaearn from Arwystli via Drws Ardudwy and the Col valley. Meanwhile Gr. marched to meet him via Harlech, and over the hill along the old road, (seaward of* Tyδyn y velin *and* Dinas Porchellyn), *emerging on the Artro above ' Conical Hill,' and past the steepest and narrowest ravine, a real Glyn Cyvyng, at or near wh. Trahaearn & his men were driven back. So it appears to me, after exploring the possible routes repeatedly. There are ruins of an old mill higher up the Artro. cp. Record of Carn.,* 275, Ll., 381, *and Meilyr's references to* Cadeu Gr. ap Cynan.

> Cad rac (Celynog), mawr enwo(g) δyδ,
> (pan leδit) Kynwric orig lywyδ.
> I gad gynghyweir y·Meirionnyδ
> arglwyδ (Tra) cadarn Haiarn δyvyδ
> Ni noδes mawreδ (rhac cleδ) Merwyδ
> yng·weith Derw, gwae chwerw (ir) chwelidyδ.

The battle before (Clynog), glorious day,
when Kynwrig, a momentary sovereign, was slain.
To the expeditionary encounter in Merioneth
the strong lord Trahaearn " comes."
Rank did not protect (against the sword) of Merwyδ,
In the action among the Oak trees*, bitter was the woe
of him who retreated.

 * The MS. reads ' y ɓaed erw.' *Cp.* ' Bronn yr erw ' on the slope of Bryn *Derw*in. I question the ' erw ' in both cases. ? Bron yr *h*erw, (*cp.* ar ero, 37·13) and Gweith Derw. The oak abounds on the slopes of the Artro, especially on & beyond ' Conical Hill '=? y Vann Ðerw. *see n.* 31·18.

MISCELLANEOUS NOTES

13·3 Gwyr (Llychlyn) nyt [oe-=] ei-δyn [drach] draet ffo, *the Norse, not theirs the [backward] fleeing feet.* BUCH. has " Daenysseit " p. 126 ; B.T. has " yscotteit," but at 12·21 we have [Lych]lynwys. *cp.* n. 34·9.
    b. heilyn achubyat, *no c.* ? ēil*h*yn=enil*l*yn achubyn [bob : ?] y vro, *as the place names testify to this day.* see *Intro.*, n. 23.

13·4-9 = 34·6-10 = 23·15-20. These three versions deserve careful study as they illustrate the way our scribe deals with his original. He adds, omits, changes not only without scruple, but with manifest intent to mislead. See Reprints in parallel columns, p. 102-3.

A. Leech, Llech : Lle*th*, 3 s. *pres. Ind. of* llethu, *to squash.* leudu*d*=leut*u*=llefd*ir* : lleudir(e)δ, *open, or cleared lands.*
    cp. go·leu ; also llewdir, P. 155·39, 166·3, 171·5.

B. leuure=leudvre : lleuδ(y)vre(δ), *clear (shallow) waters. cp.* pylleu goleu, Tal. 77·2. Lleu *might be reptn. for* trei δyvreδ, *ebbing waters.* The reference is to the Lavan Sands=Heleδ. Note that Magnus=dialgur Arvon 34·4, *the avenger of Arvon.*

C. The gododin *fraud required wholesale corruption of the text here as well as the omission of* Heleδ & Iwerδon.
    Nis duc-hwy Duw (rwy) iw dangnev. *cp.* M. 152·5,
    a δuc treis tros (veis) hegr Heleδ   & 206·4.
God may (not) bring to his peace (a ruler) who has brought oppression over the expansive Heleδ *(shallows).* c. accounts for the emendations. erch, *f.c.,* ? *metath. for* hecr, but ' Ar erch Heleδ ' *is prob. the or. of* ARLLECHWEDD. *see* PEM.
    b. Stre=ystre : ystrad. *Note* cynghaneδ.

D. stre=ystre : ys try ; di*t*[h] *tit*h : dic*r*ich=dicirch=dygyrch. ragno *metath. for* ragon : ragom. *cp.* Clytno Eiδın=Cluton Edwin, n. 15·8. *see Intro., xxi., &* n. 17.

E. (wyr Iwerδon). Gr. ap Kynan's *mercenaries went over to his enemies in* 1098. B. 273, Buch. 144, Ll. 409.

F. ancat=ar y anghat=aryf gar : arv yn anghad, *ready armed.*

G. ancat (*reptn.*)=angat : ? an*f*at [cyn : ?] es-gor (vu oe) c.

K.-P. *not in the other two versions. Prob. scr. addition.*

K. Ry. *Its use is doubtful here.* ? *read,* Hu. bebyll, *scr. er. for*

L. b*i*byll, *pl. of* pibell, *pipe* (of wine). diwyll *unclouded, clear.*

M. tymyr *no rhyme nor sense. Context and Hist. sug.,* Saeson.

N. Tec : ? Te*r* (*y*d) ware, *or* (y g)ware.

O. ystre, *the jousting ground, list, field of battle.*

Q-S. *not in the other two versions.* cangen, *a branch* i.e. *a division of the* gens *occupying the fort,* caer wys.

R. keui : kew(r)i, *p!. of* cawr, *champion.*

BOOK OF ANEIRIN

s. tymor (*antcpn.*) dymhestyl. *no rhyme nor sense. ? as in am. t.*

T. temestyl=tymestyl dymor=tymor dymestyl : t*r*a mor d.

U. *e* b*c*ri *r*estyr=t*r*a *m*erin *l*estyr *in the other version.*

V. tra meryn *l*u, *the host beyond the margin.* ? (dy lann δy)ſu.

W. h-eidi*l*yaun : *?* H(u) Eiδinyaun (*l* : r=ṗ : *n* , *not in the other versions.* *cp.* Edernyawn, Keredig-yawn, *etc.*

X-w. [*lu in-* : fuiṗ=] ffwyr (m)eidlyaun, 34·9=meithlyon, 23·18. *? read* ffwyr vaetholion *i.e. Hugh of the Eιδin country violently rushes his retainers.*

x, *b.* kein gadrawt rwyd *peculiar to* 23.18. *scr. addition. Omit.*

Y. let lin lu=rac ri allu : rac [Le*c* :] Llychlyn lu i.e. *the Norsemen* of Magnus=rhi allu, the K*ι*ng's *force. N.B. Here we are told definitely that Hugh of E*ι*δyn rushed h*ι*s retainers against the men of* ' le*c* lin ' =Llychlyn, *we therefore* know *that* cat traeth *was fought between them on the shore of Aber Lleinog in* 1098. cp. BUCH, 146.

z. o dindȳwyt : o diṗdynwyt=o di*r*dynwyd, *if we were racked.* yn dyv*u* wyt *vel en* dynuwyt=eu dy·vi*rv*vyt=ev dy·vyryϭyd (*pret. pass. of* dyvwrw), *he was utterly overthrown.* For *u=ir* cp. Lleut*u* & llefd*ir*, n. A above.

β en dyowu=yn dywovu=dyouu : an dyo*r*vu, *who had crushed us.* dy-*w*o-vu : dy[*ow*= *ou*=] oṗ-vu=dy·orvu.

γ. scuyt grugyn=ysgwyt rugyn : ys cwyδ (yn) grugyn, *he falls all of a heap* ; *ii.* yscwyd grugyn, *he gives those who assembled a shaking* ; *iii.* ysgwyd rug(l)yn, *he gives those who wander a shaking. ii. and iii. pervert history.*

δ. i rac taryf trun=rac tarw trin=rac dole*v* trin. *taryv* : *? ary*-v(aw)*t* tryn. trin, *faulty rhyme.*

ε. HeS. was shot " in the eye," B.B.C., 97, " in the temple," An., 34·30, " on the line made by the helmet," 11·3. see York Powell's *Hist.,* 75 ; Ll., 409. BUCHEDD Griffyδ ap K., 146. INTRODUCTION, *xxxix.*

ζ. dwys, Lat., *dens-us,* wodyn=voδyn.

θ. ge*v*nyn : ge*v*nyn, *they turned their backs. cp.* 20.6, 36·3.

13·10 a*r*af : a*r*yf=arv, *weapon.* e(v) ry·vrwydr[in trin] tra chwar(δ). *cp.* n. 18.3.

11 kwr : cor, kei*r*w : ke*w*ri, *champions,* am gwr : amdwrr (3 s. pres. Ind. of tyrru), *to throng.* vann *c*arw (*due to* keirw) : vancori, *palisading, held fast at the top by plaited strong rods.*

b. bysseδ (y) brych : brych(ion)= ? Bri*t*h(ion) *the Picts. cp.* W. B. Mab. col. 54.

MISCELLANEOUS NOTES

13·12 barr : Barc(odion), *Borderers, Men of the March. cp.* Tal.
b. am *bwyll, m.s., no c., anicpn.* : am ry·gur.   [70·23, P. 2·10·14.
c. dist*ei*r : dystyr ... dis*t*ar : discar, *enemy.*
d. am, *reptn.* yn bwyll(ic) am *r*odic metath. *for* or*d*it.

13 y[s] bro ys brys *metath. for* vrys ys treul[lyawt] rys yn rhyw drec : dres, tres, *labour.*

14 ni hu*n*wy ni [gaffo :] gahwy, 3 s. *pres. Subj. of* cael.
b. [nyt :] ne*b* anghwy, [*he may not* :] *none may escape.*
c. od*ı*wes : ? odawes, *became rather silent,* ' shut up.'

15 ar gynwa*l* c*a*rnwyt : ar gynwa*n* (y) cornwyd

16 n. m δ. vorδwyd ar (gevn) Mein(vuan 1·4) llwyd.   *cp.* amws can*n*, 31·6.* breich hir=*long in the fore-leg* ? *a gloss on* 'Meinvuan.' *cp.* B.B.C. 27·11, POETRY 12·19, 112·3.
b. [gell : cerr=] tyrr i baladr (yn) [gell :] *d*ellt.

17 ge*l*lach : ga*f*lach, ' fork,' *formed by the thighs.* ? *read* (a)e aflach gyll obell, *& his thighs lose grip of the saddle.   Historically true, so would be,* " Tyrr baladr i (lwyven yngorδin rhac Morien). *Note the stutter,* gell ... gell gellach ... gell ... anghell.
b. d*y* wr : dewr ... yn cnoï g(rae)anhell.

18 b*w*ch=boet*ī*=Boet i*n* buδ, (boet) o[e] law, (ac) iδaw boet **13**·19—**14**·1, **30**·12–15.   [yn well.

19 Da i (Von) doeth adon [wy=vy] (aeth) atwen.
****The scribe has changed the remaining verbs from the third to the second person sing. thus confusing the sense.   He has also*
b. ym adawssut : edy.   [*disturbed the order of the lines.*

20 [gwnelut] llaδ- : lluδ-, llosg : llost- [no].

21 wnelut : wnaeth, (*note c.*) ny ... nac ... na *for* neu·r ... ac ... a. *The scr.* has more suo *reversed the sense of the or. to discredit Morien, and save HeS.   c. condemns* ' nac eithaf ' *with what goes before and after.   see am. t.*
b. ysgw*n* : ? yst*u*m (brwysc) drem(yn) [d]¹ p.=Hugh *the Proud.*

22 ny welei[st em]orchwyδ [mawr].   *no c.,* : ? ne(u·r g)wyδei.

14·1 wy leδin (pl.) : ev laδei ny roδei nawδ, *gloss* : ni laesei. 30·14–15 beu*w*el *cp.* beuuef, Tal. 47·12 ; *but* ? *a gloss on* ynys, *or gor*wel. *see am. t. wh. is the best I can suggest.* ? Gwn wys (gron ynys) or mor bwy'r mor *I know the peoples of the round island from sea to its fellow sea.*   [rod=goror.
b. ni weleis marchawc a vei waeth no *odgur* ? *metath. for* gu(o)-

14·2 (*no c.*) Godoδ[in :]an [gomyna*f*—*m* = *r*u, -*f* = *v* = *u* = *n* hence] gor*u*ynan δy·blygid.
b. trumei*n* : -e*u*, & drum : dru*i*n (trwyn), *ness.*

141

BOOK OF ANEIRIN

14.3 essyth (*pl. of* aseth), *dart, headland* as in ' Llan δwyn esyth. (*The* ' esmwyth ' *of Welsh Saints*, ii., 390 *is mistaken*). *Rhyme requires Esyd* [=treissyt 23·12]. *The headland of the Dee Estuary* which was *anciently named* " *Set*-eia aestuar'."

    b. gwas c[h]uant=gwasc(a)rant (d)i·arvant heb [emwyt: emuyc *metath. for*] ermyc, *honour*.

    c. No c., ? read, O gussyl mad Eryr Dwyv Weryd=Cynon *alias* Owein ap Edwin. Dwyw [-ei *dy*=er *ty metath. for*] eryr Dwyv [wrhyt :] W(e)r[h]yt. Dee=' dubr duiu,'=Dyvrdwyv. For the bungle Dwywei see WELSH SAINTS, ii., 387, 392, 341.

    4 *c.f. with insertions, omissions and metath. ? read* [nyt oeδ wael] y rac-ran, gyn[g]hor-wan : cynhorvan (y Gogleδ) *w*(y) eithyn (rhy·lithryn gan liveδ) . . . rac *lan* : rac-ran.

    5 luch bin, *tidal bore. For an account of the bore in the Dee estuary see* Ormerod's *Hist. of Cheshire.* Pin *is the Lleyn word for* pistyll=*water spout or shoot.* March pin=*great* (mill) *race in Bk. of Ll. Dav.* Pynvarch *is the word used for Mill-race in South Cards. Can the* i *of* ' pin ' *become affected by the following a,* as the *i* of ' *dy*-huno ' *by the following u. Cp. March*-ros= Rhos vawr, *march*-liv=*the great pit-saw.*

    b. borfor beryerin, *the Pulford pilgrim.*

    6 llaδ . . . gwan : ? rhuthr. *The* ll *requires an answering spirant*

    b. anysgarat vu y nat ac Aneirin, *m.l., c.f.* : ? (galar), **a**nyscar **a n**ad (gorδ)in, *wh. makes good sense.* cp. INTROD. xxxviii.

14.7 – **15.**1 *The scribe has, app., made a mess here. C., m., and sense are all faulty. I have tried, by omitting reptns., to re-arrange the remaining lines according to sense and context.*

ll. 7·12·17·20, *no c., see am. t.* Ky-vrennin, *co-king, co-ruler, co-regent*=HeS., *the colleague of HeC. If* kywyrein *is correct, c. requires* cy·vreinin=cy·vreint-in, *the older form.*

    8 *If* gwer**i**n *is or., then* fysg**y**olin *is impossible c.* HeS. *ravaged Penmon and beyond, seizing the natives* (gwerin), *and forcing them to fight on his side.* see n. 33·7. *ll.* 8–11=**10** 20·22 *q.v.*

    9 gwirawt, *no c., gloss on* cyveδ.

    b. heyessit e lavnawr, *paraphrase to hide the fall of HeS. who is felled* (cwyδawr) *between his own force and that of the enemy.*

14.10 arδ. varch. *See* n. 10·22.

    b. eithinyn . . . murgreit. *See* n. 10·22.

    *** *Lines* 10–11 *should follow l.* 16 *infra. The scribe transposed and altered the text in order to disguise the fall of HeS.*

MISCELLANEOUS NOTES

14·12 [k. k. k.] *The context shows that the reference is* not *to Kyvrenhin*(=*HeS*.) *but to Magnus and his sudden departure.* Ac yna yδ edewis Magnus vrenhin drwy δeissyvyt kynghor tervyneu y wlat. B., 273·19.
  b. Gwlat atver go·glywer en Dulyn. (Deisyvyd yδ engid o Benrhyn). App. *dilin* is for Dublin=Dulyn *here. Gr. ap Kynan had escaped thither on the advent of the enemy into Anglesey in* 1098. *The end rhyme is -in, wh. is against Dul*YN, *but note the break indicated in the MS. after dilin,* & cp. n. 12·13.
13 dy go glawd *metath. for* dyglogawd=dy·gludawδ, 3 *s. pret. for the pres.* Clud tonn (Iwerδon) bevr bererin. (*note c.*)
14 Men yδ ynt eilyass*af*, 3 *pl. and* 1 *sing. for two* 3*rd singulars.* Pererin (Magnus,) *is the subject of both verbs. see am. t.*
  b. o brei : *mal* beīt=mal beynt *w*rych . . . w[e]yelin.
15 ny *c*hemyδ *n*y haed uδ : nys *k*etuyδ *u*y hae*r* uδ a gorδin. *ch upsets c.* haed=hae*t*=hae*r*.
  b. ny phyrth. *no c., gloss on,* Attal mevl Moryal yn (or)δi(v)lin. Maylor *looks like* Moryal *disguised. See* Lloyd, 389, & n. 15·9.
16 *f.c., and metath. for* ? Parawt (i) δurawt (i grei) gwaedlin. *Magnus had shot HeS. with an arrow a little while before.*
17 [k. k. k. . . . dilin] *reptn. of l.* 12, *q.v.*
18 [ef] llaδawδ [a] cyminawδ (Gynt) a lläin [a] garneδawr tra gygawl (or) gwyr trin. gogyhw*c* (*no c.*) : gyg[o]aw*r* : gygawl o w. t., *scowling.* ? gybawl, *moaning.*
20 [kywyrein] ket-wyr (mor **a**rwyr) gyva*r*vuant.
21 gyrchassant *gloss* : ? ymhyrδassant. (*ch. upsets c.*)
  b. byrr [eu] *h*oedl **h**i**r** vu *h*oed **l'r** ae carant.
22 m.l., *no c.,* gymeint, *gloss for* mwy a [laδ- *gloss for*] lygrassant.
  b. o [gy]*w*ryssεδ (eu) [gw*r*aged :] gwr*t*heδ (ys) gwy*r*th wnant.
15·1 [llawer *gloss on*] aml v**a**m [a]e deigr (**l**am) ar y h**a**mrant.
2 ny : neu·r wnaethpwyd (*reptn. of a stock phrase for*) ? Edryd neuaδ (glyd) yn δi·anav.
3 [l]ew mor hael [ba]ran llew (vael o) llwȳ[byr] vwyhaf *no c. no s.,* [l]ew=ev. llew *may*=llyw *wh. may be a gloss on* glyw *or* rhwyv. llwybyr (*masc.*)=llwyb*r may*=llwy*th* (*masc.*), *tribe. But the adj.* vwyhaf (*like* deccaf, l. 4,) *is fem. ? read,* (o) lwȳ[byr] vwȳhaf=o lwyn vwynhaf, *from the gentlest lineage.* 1. *see am. t.* 2. *? read,* Rhan (vael), ev llyw hael (or) llwy*th* mwyhaf, *he gives* (*boons*) ; *he is a ruler from the biggest tribe* ; 3. (or) llwyδ mwyhaf, *of the greatest success.*
4 vro[nn] adon : adon (y) [vro=]y wlad deccaf. *Possibly a play*
  b. y dias : ȳ=yn dïas=y·nïas ar [llet :] llit. [on Eurgeint.

BOOK OF ANEIRIN

15·5 or [sawl a] wel*ei*s ac [a] welaf y·myt : ac y·myt or wel*i*d (ni) welav [en emδwyn :] δwg arv-gryd, (yn)gwrhyt (i) wriav.

6 *ef lla*δ*ei* oswyδ : oswyδ *a drewy*δ.

9 dy·go·dolyn *an impossible cpd.*, dy *intensifies while* go *modifies the meaning. c. and sense sug.*, dy·gollyn.
 b. ma*m* hwrreith *sug.*, mamhwraeth *but ? sense. ? read*, mau*r* ky*f*reith, *or* hy*r*δieith. *cp.* mevyl Moryal, n. 14·15.

10 eido*l* (*read backward*=) lode*r*= Roger of Montgomery, e. S.
 b. ermyge*i* : -*et* [rac] v(a)re=ware.

11 [b]rein δwyre wybyr ysg[yny]a*l*, (*the crows rise, ascending to the sky*) : rhein vwrye(i yr) wybr ysca*r*.

12 *f*ynn[wyr y- ant*c*pn] *ft*wyr y[*ft rept*n.] temel = *c*evel i.e. *ff*ynn *ff*wyr yn cyvyl, *the attack prospers* ..

13 gwe*b*yl, ?=gwe*v*yl=gwe*u*yl=gwe*ɼ*yl, *quarrels.*
 b. ardemyl *metath. for* arδelui[y]=arδelwy.

14 ma*m r*-eiδun(un) : mau*r* eiδun(wn).
 b. Blaen ancwyn. *The first feast, after seizing* Cynlleith (*before* 1086), *was followed by a peaceful sleepy time, but to-day is a rousing contrast.*

15 aeth*ant* 3 pl. *for* 1 pl. aeth*om.*

16 *Out of two lines only four words survive. The am. t. embodies the history correctly.* lletkynt, '*report,' is prob. a gloss.*

17 *If* lleas *is the key-word, read as in am. t., but ? if* llwydeδ *is not a gloss on* Glas y dyδ. *? read,* kyn llwydeδ llaδwyd δy·δyvu gatraeth. *Before dusk were slain such as come in the battle of the Strand. cp.* dechreu llwydo=*dawn,* or *dusk.*
 b. dy·δaruu *is tautological after* lleas. [rac] *upsets sense.*
 c. [dry]chant. *m.l., historically false. Read,* cant.

19 yt g*r*yssyassant. *no c., m.l.,* : yt veδwant.

20 *c.f., men in stress will praise* (moleint) *the abstemious soul, for "In the day of stress not one is found abstemious." see am. t.* (Ðyδ) reit [en *moleit*=] ev ni cheit [eneit *gloss for*] neb di-.

21 gytvaethant. *no c., gloss on* gynnullant.
 b. amall *upsets c.* Mal(eδ) gwin a meδ a amucsant *satisfies c., but ? read as in am. t*

22 *Text corrupted to hide the fate of* Mynyδawg. *an* dwy*f cannot be for* handwyf, *first person, because the subject is in the third person). ? metath. for* gwyδ *yn* adveil[ly]awc *falls to pieces.* adveillyawc *may be read* atweillyawc=ar-(or)weilliawc, *pierced through and through. cp.* gweillyon, 15·13.

MISCELLANEOUS NOTES

16·1 *no c.* rwyſ : ? rwyδ (weis) *gracious youths.* gwir *upsets c., gloss on* hoff, *or* holl.
  b. o drychan ri·allu. *King's force*=Norse. *The couplet is misplaced here and quite wrong in its facts. see* **6·19–20.**
3 *Metath. for* Hu ynghywyrein vyδei [present].
  b. mal *p*el -a [*r*y :] y*t* [e=]ym- [hu by- *reptn.* :] laδei. *see am. t.*
4 hu*t* amuc ododin *illusion defended* G. (*m. s., no c., no sense*) *Read,* Hu *t*a muc orδin : Hu ra(c gallu) Mūc orδin.
  b. *Metath. for* [en : eu=] ev δy·ad(e)i[*ng antcpn.*] yn : y*ɼ* [ystry*ng* :] ystrin (ar) ystre. [(ed) [emore :] vore.
5 [ac a] dan ga*r* (? ga*w*r, *champion*) Vannan (oeδ) . . . [go] druδ-
  b. *A line is missing at the end. ? as in am. t.*
    16·6–11. *See* **32·2–15,** *and Notes on* **37·10·12.**
6 *If the text here came after* 32·14 *in the or. MS., as context sug., the scr. misread* angou *as* ango*ɼ, wh. is inadmissible as Magnus had already reached the water line,* merin.
8 [en dyδ cadyawr] *scr. addition.* ygclawd : yn claw*r, or* llaw*r.*
9 ei*l n*edic *metath. for* ? eſiced (eſi*u*edic *is m. l., and sense does not*
10–11. *See* VARIANT VERSIONS=p. 106, & 37 M. [*fit context.*
16·12–16 *See* **38·9–14.** *see* VARIANT VERSIONS, p. 101.
16 Arδyledawc=Erδyled canu, *one must sing.*
17 gwrhyt *no c., gloss on* gwychrawc.
18 ruδ-ued-e*l*   ry-*u*-el a eiδu-*n*i   *for*
   ry-ued-ei a *r*u-δ-ei Eiδyn *ɼ*i(v).
19 gwr gwneδ divu*δ*[yawc] *d*imyngyei : [g]or guneδ diveδ im *d*yngyei : gynygei. *See am. t.* & *cp.* gur guneδ 36·5. g*w*neδ=cun-eδ=*the earls of Chester and Shrewsbury.*
  b. or mei*nt* : ? gormei*l* gwlat y dy·glywei
20 [ae] ysgwyt [ysgwyt *reptn.*] a ry·ysgwyd=a·r·ysgwyd.
  b. hu*t* arolli : hyt(r) aroſſ(e)i waew.
21 mal gwin g*l*oew [o wydyr] lestri : gw*r* hoew llest(ei)r(e)i.
  b. aryant [am y] ued, *metath. for* meδ ary(v)ant eu[r d- :] ev [*ɼ* d=] n(i)d (y*l*yi=] yfei. *cp.* n. 19·6.
22 gwinvaeth [oeδ] *w*ae[t ner]th [vab] llyw*r*i : (nid arch)*w*aeth win, ni *v*aeth lywi(e)i. llyw-ri, *the king-leader, i.e.* Magnus. *The scr. misreads in order to mislead. The bard says that the men of Eiδyn drink but Magnus does not ; that love of wine will not nurture one who aspires to lead. The text says the contrary.*
17·1–5·10–12. *A* VARIANT VERSION, (p. 101) *of* 38·1–8 *q.v.*
6 llawen ! [*l*loge*ll* byt :] llocheſſyt, bu di·δichweint *perverts the truth. ? read,* Llanw n(ac aes niw) lloches, bu δichwein.

L

17.7 *Turned to prose*=Hu mynnei ynghylch byd δoli e anant or eur a meirch mawr, a meδ (ae). *Hugh wished on his expedition to give the minstrels some gold and palfreys and mead. see am. t.* e-*idol* : ? doli e, *to give dole to*, or eiδ : ιeδ ol=feδ or(meint).

  b. anant (gy)veδ(ant yn) veδweint [yr eur a meirch mawr a meδ *sug.* dolei *for* ' eidol,' *but c. and sense are wanting.*

  8 namen en [e] delei : namyn ban δelyn o [vyt : vet=] w(l)eδ [hoffeint, *f.c., gloss on*] gercint.

  9 [kyn-di*l*ic : de*f*ic *gloss on*] kynδragon Aeron.

  b. wyr e : e(s) rwy=y(s) cwynoveint.

17.10–12. *See* **38.1–8.** *The first couplet is a reptn. of* **17.1–2.**

17.13–19 *This canto is a later and more corrupt transcript of the original text than that at* 35.12–20, *q.v. The changes all tend to obscure, or gloze over the fall of HeS.*

  22 tywys *f*eis[t] : *f*eis : veis=*w*eis. go*l*ut : go*f*ut.

  b. gweilch *gwrm*δ*e.* cp. *nigri gentes*=*the Norse.*

18.1 meitin : ? mei-δin *field-fort. cp. Maiden Castle,* & Moyδin *in parish of Llanarth, Cards., where* ei=oi (oy,) *in many words,* ei *and* eu *being not always distinguished in sound.*

  b. o gynnu Aber rac fin ? *by raising the Aber at his front door.* ? *read* [o] cynn(i)u=cynniv (17.21) Aber rac f(id)in, *rad. m*idin.

  c. [o] dywys [yn] *antcpn.* : dy·v(r)ys, tywys y[n] δilin.

  2 oeδ garw y gwnae(i)[wch chwi] *It was roughly he shed blood.*

  3 mal yved meδ drwy chwerthin *like drinking mead laughingly. The pouring* (dywall) *of mead might be compared to* ' flowing blood ' *but not the drinking* (yved) *thereof. see am. t., and n.* 8.7-8.

  4 dynin : di*u*in=diwin, *fierce.*

  5 yt laδei *reptn. of l.*4 ? *for* ys trychei, *he cut down.*

  6 ? (yn) dra phenn *over his head, or* benn dra phenn, ' *head over heels.' cp.* pen tra mwnwgyl.

  7 kywyt (*no c.*) : ? kȳ=cynwyd, *destruction.*

  b. kywrennin i.e. ky·vrennin, *no c.*, *gloss* : ? y cynben.

  c. benn *should follow* escyn*n*v : escyn yn benn [ar ystre] l. 8. *When a last word was crowded out of a line it was thrust at the end of some previous line where there was space for it. see* B.B.C. 97.4 golu- *with* dauc *at end of l.* 2 ; 98.4 pel- eidrad (*as above* l. 1).

  d. vu e laδ (*no c., paraphrase for*) trangawl.

  8 kynneδyf *law of priority, natural course, usage. When an officer falls the next in command succeeds by kynne*δv, *as* Owein ap Edwin did *on the battlefield* (ar ystre) *at Aber Llēinawc when Hugh,* earl of Shrewsbury, *the generalissimo fell in the shallows.*

  b. (Nu, Mwng a) ystwng [kyn gorot] oreu [gang *reptn.* :] gynhen.

MISCELLANEOUS NOTES

18·9 diluδ (*no c.*), *without let, a comment on* (a rhein y) dilein.
   b. cathleu, *canticles* : cet bei dilenn.   [oδeu r(y)wy*t*h [ac].
   c. cp. llyw-yδ *with* rhi-yδ, -eδ.   llyvroδeδ (*no c.*) : llueδ llvyr-
10 anglas : gamlas.   a*ff*wyd[eu] : a*fl*wyδ(as).   lov*l*en : lɔy*f*en = lwyven.   *See* am. t.   ' Camlas ' is a grassy wet place, or even a ditch ; also a shore that is wet and weedy.
11 dym̄gwall-*aw* g-[w]ledi-*c* dal : Dyvnwall *r*awg (l)leid δăl, *The one lost in the deep awhile the mud holds.* This is mistakenly wr. Dyvynwa*l* at 20·5, 23·9.   *see* INTRO., *xl*., n. 32.
   b. oebriδ (*m.s.*) : o ebr(u)iδ brennyal.
12 *a*d : *o*(e)δ oergrei g. gwynn(ion vei).
   b. dy[s]giawr : dyc*h*iawr (na) bei—*sense incomplete, l. missing.* ? *read* pan (Bleiδ ae gwel, drei,) d. n. b.
13 bun barn benn : penn bun, *captain of the host* (*a paraphrased perversion* for) Rhi=Magnus *who had no* meirch.   *The unmutated* ba r n *sug.* brau=braw(v) *puts to the test* perchen(awr) meirch [a gwrym seirch] ac ysgwydawr.
14 *y*aen : ? *g*uae l o [gyu] oed disgyn c. esgyn.
   b. [a gwrym seirch] . . .
15 aer [dy-wys *antcpn.*=] lyw=Cynon i.e. Ewein.   garei : ae car.
   b. gwrδ *the violent one*=HeS.   uede*l* : ved(r)e*r*, *is hit.*
16 [gwrδ *reptn.* :] gor-we*l*=gorweδyt.   seirchyawr, *horse trappings*, gloss on *lluryg.* am[*y*]ruδ : am·ruδ.
17 [seingyat *antcpn.*] am *f*eirch (ae) *f*eirch [*s*eingyat :] soniet.
18 dyg-=dyc*h*ïawr, *m.l.*, *gloss on* escawr lluδet.
   b. prose for, en (beis) peleidr eis en [dechreu, *gloss on*] eit en cat.
19 hynt [am] oleu (*trs.*=) goleu hynt [bu] G. (ym)heleidrad.
20 [am *antcpn.*] nat amdi*n*a dy : amδi*u*ad y gell.
   b. [ac] ystavell [*y*t :] *i*t(aw) vyδei. (*trs.*) vyδe¡iδaw ystavell.
21 dyrllyδei, *m.l.* : yvyN veδ melyN maglawr yNgwrys.
   b. aer-gyn-g*l*ys (*trs.*) : cyn aer g*r*ys(syn) gan wawr.
19 1 klyw-[er : eɼ=]*y*n [e ar :] am δerche*δ* (adon).
   b. gwananhon : Gwenn Vannon, *hero of Man*=MAGNUS BARELEG.   by*t* veδ (*m.s., no c.*) : by*r* (gam) veδ.   *See* INTRO. *xxxix*.
2 *Tarw* [bedin . .] *trin*=*the constant epithet of* Magnus Bareleg *and of no other.*   *Cp.* B.B.C. 97·13.
       Tarw trin aɼ vidin blaut, Arbennic llu llid aɼchaut.
       The Bull of Bat!*le aboard his ships stirs up tumult,*
       The captain of the host (=HeS.) *provoked his anger.*
3 kyn kywes*t* dae[a]r . . . by*t* orfun : b*it t*erfyn.
       b. [gododin beδ :] (ar) orδineδ.

L 2

19·4 Bedin=midin *elsewhere, m.l., read,* Mang.
5 lluyδ a [wc] llaw : lly(w)yδ a llaw.
6 go·chwerw, *rather bitter, quarrelsome* ; go[ch]·verw, *rather talkative, noisy* . . *we cannot read* go·vetw, *rather drunk, leading to excess, because* ' ev nɪd yfei,' 16·21, *b*.
   b. mudyn : muner G. [ar y :] yr (Mon) [h]elw.
7 delw, *context sug*., herw . . . mor [a *chyn*-nwr :] gyn=morgun [ym] plymnwyd, *Great lord of Battle*.
8 yn tryvrwyt, *a movement to and fro, ? a ferry*. *cp*. traetheu tryvrwyt *the shores of the Ferry* between Aber Gwyngregyn and
   b. [peleidyr go] gyrrwyt [g]o-glyssur : *a* glasur. [Penmon.
10 *? read,* (cwyδad ir) llawr (h)enafie(i)d. [gwr : gw(o)r].
11 Dy·ffö[rth]es cat veirch [a chat] (yn) greulet (eu) seirch.
12 Mac=Māc=Mang. *cp*. *Fr*. Magne, *Lat*. Magnus. blaenwyδ bedin : vlaen wyr vidin, *leads his marines*.
   b. [dinuſ :] diniſt(ir) [aergi=]a orδi . . . . aer-[ri=]lyw.
13 [an] gelwir [ny :] yn ffaw (o) g. ff.
   b. ech·adaſ, *he did not spare*. ech, *eks, εξ, ex.
14 *no c., no sense*. ? Myn(yδ)awg a orδ(awd) [(ar) traeth] e=en [aɴnor :] aɴuor [hattor.
   b. (gan) Vynawg (ae gatrawd) [am rann, *for his lot*] kwyn-
15 Rac Eiδyn [aryal fflam, *the high spirited one, no c*. :] (y
   b. ef [*d*odes :] godis yn dilis. [catgun) nid atcor.
16 [ef godes rac (armes) tryn [tewδor *no. c.*] : tramor].
   b. disgynnwys. *no c., gloss on* dy·gwyδwys.
17 porthes [mawr bwys :] morbwys, *or ?* gorffwys.
   b. o [osgorδ *m.l., no c*.] : drawd, *journey, expedition*.
18 amδiff-[ry- : ɼy=ny :]yn amδiffwys.
19·19–20·1 *Note the manipulation of the negatives, etc. The c. proves the changes, wh. hide the fall of HeS*.
19 [O gollet :] Collat (y) vorgat [ny bu aeſſawr :] neu'r vu aeth (m)awr [moryet :] morgat & Moryen, l. 20.
   b. [*dy*·fforth-y*n* :] *n*i fforthe*t* ni (chadwet) traeth [y ennyn :]
20 [ry] duc (Moryen)=Magnus, *as context shows*. [(na) llawr.
   b. [peleidyr] *seems to be a scribal expansion*.
21 *p*wys preiglyn *benn p*eriglawr, *a jangle for*
   *g*wys *d*reiglyn beri(glyn) go(d)rigawr. *cp*. " French *f*irms order *f*oods *f*rom Fermany "=goods from Germany. D. *paper*.
   b. [y] ar orvyδ erc[hl]as : as etr(yδ) [penn] (li)wedawr, *peasantry* : ? we(ry)dawr, *lands*.

148

MISCELLANEOUS NOTES

19·22 trin : tryn δygwyδ, Trwch [=*Hugh The Fat*] (deryδ) [trach y l[avn]awr :] tra chyl(ch)awr.
   b. pan [or·*v*yd : or·*f*yd=] orffid [oe] ga*r* (gollid) [ny] bu ffoawr Car gollid=Gwallawg. *see* n. 19·2.
20·1 an dyrlly*f* : o δilin [molet] meδ mely*n*. '*Melyn*' *is the epithet of good honey*, '*melys*' *being tautological*.
20·2-5, & 23·6-9. *See* VARIANT VERSIONS, p. 104.
  A. *This canto, apparently, refers to both the Norse & Saxon invaders. Misled by the interpolated* 'Gweleis' *I have misplaced it. cp.* 38·7=84. *Gr. ap. Cynan is the more likely author.*
  B. [Gwele]is y du-ll : is du l(*i*)l=ys du hil [o ben*n* : bennō=] Ben*m*on dir a δoyn.
  c. [a-]*b*erth am goel : am goel-*v*erth (wy yn) gerth [a].
  D. *variants not easily explicable.*
  E. *I saw who was foremost over the tribe of Redegein. c. and m.f.* [Gweleis *reptn.*] kene*v*in *metath. for* ken*v*ein Redegein. *oed* . . . a*r* dre*f*=r[o]ed a dre(i)*f*(yn)=ryd a dreisyn.
  F. *deu* [oc eu] tre re=*r*ed[-*eu* : *ue*=]*wy* tre(isyn).
  G. [a] gwyr (Mon eil) Nwython [ry·go*ll*- *vel* goδ- :] ry·go(e)thessyn. *The Irish king* Nectan, *in his time, protected the men*
  H. o eir : gwyr.   [*of Mon.*
  I. [gweleis, *reptn.*] gwyr dullyawr gan awr *vel t*yllvawr gan wawr : ? d*r*yllyawr (y) gan awr wyr [a δeuyn *vel* δoyn *gloss on*]
  K. gynhullyn. y gan *w*awr, *with the dawn*=*the time the war-shout* (awr) *was raised. So either reading suits the text.*
  L & M. *See* INTRODUCTION, *xl.*, n. 32.
20·6 [M]at vudic—*perversion* : Advydic ys *g*av[y]n[w]yn : ys *c*evnyn [asgw*r*n=? ys *ch*w(y)rn, *gloss for* ar hyn, *thereupon* aduāon=adva*n*on [ae :] eu llassar tebed[awc :]yn
7 '*Very great the host of the Brave one from over the water*'=*Magnus, or as in am. t. cp.* '*Suddenly King Magnus quitted the country.*' Bruts, 273·19. *no c.* ? *read*, Gwrawl [am] dy·vr[w]ys= dy·vrys [gorv]awr i ly(s iδaw).
8 [gwryt vronn *sense repetn. of* gwrawl :] gw*r*y t*v*ronn=gwy*r* t*r*u[ein], gorwan (lu), wênan arnaw.
9 [nu] rac (δiscyn)naw(δ) *against those who had made a descent* i.e. *the ravagers*. [ri·allu=*King's force, is a perversion,*
  b. yngwyδ gwaed a gwlad *in the presence of kin and country, no c* ? a (orδwy) a gorδrynaw.
10 carav [vy] vuδic (nav) a vu(δ) anaw. lleithic [kynd*il*ic aeron *gloss* :] kynd*ef*ic [ken*h-an* lew : ke*n*hlew an=] ken*ll*iv a*ɼ*(naw).

BOOK OF ANEIRIN

20·11 *Paraphrased couplet. In early Welsh the Subjunctive has no pluperfect tense. see* B.B.C., p. 157, *footnote. The poet being at Castell Aber Ll. had no need to* ' disgyn ' *there—he had only to remain, but he fled to Ireland. see am. t.*

12 carwn neu ch[ab]lwy*f partly reptn. and bungling* :] (gwân)wn a chlwy*f*(wn) ar llä̃in kyn bu y l*l*as (llu) [o*e* las=] o *c*las [u*ff*in :] y ffin, *from the border country.* Eng. *Uffin* = *Ubban,* gen. of *Ubba,* king of Northumberland.

13 car[ass]wn [*eil* :] *ar*·glot (Mwng) [dyfforthes *gloss on*] gorug.

14 ef ... *paraphrase without c. see am. t.*
   b. absence of c. proves the corruption of final couplet. Context, history, & the bard's love of Ow. *sug. as in am. t. But ? read,*
   Nid (hawδ im) adrawδ wrhyd gorδin,
   Nim bei rac Mordrei wyr clodvawr trin.
   '*Tis not easy for me to tell of the bravery of the push,*
   I had not before Mordrei far-famed warriors.
   ma*b k*ei : ma*d*cei : mo(r)*d*rei, -*d*yaw : *t*vaw = *v*aw*r.*

16 (ys) tru[an yw gennyf vy] gwedy lluδiaw (rh)ed (gwys) Goδe*u,* gloes angheu [trwy an*gk* :] amgyffred.

17 [ac] *eil* : a*f* trwm [tru-a[n] gennyf *t*r*s*pn. :] gennyv a thru.
   b. [dy] gwyδaw [an] gwyr (iδaw) [ny] p. o d.

18 ucheneit ac eilywet (*f.c.*). *A paraphrase for ?* Dygn alaeth ac hiraeth vaged, [en ol] gwyr pybyr (oe) tymhyr duδed (*cp.* 9·13, 21·8). *Magnus fell near Downpatrick in August,* 1103, Lloyd, 413–414.

19 Rhuvawn a gwgawn gwiawn *are Welsh names. Magnus and his men were Norse. Text must therefore be corrupt. ? read as in am. t.* gwl- : golyget, *was deemed.*

20 [g]wy[r g]orsav ... [gwrδ] yg caled = wy orsav ynghaled.

21 ys deupo : doδyw (im) e-*u* hen[eit] : e ρhen, [*wy* :] o*e* [gwedy] t.

22 *paraphrase for* a nev vo aδev [a*v* : a*y* =] a*e* neuet.

21·1 *trs.* Ef : ev = eu tres g. tra [gwyar *no c.* :] aches llynn.
   b. [ef] llaδei [val] de[wr] [*dul-l spelled backwards* =] de·lud(e)*i* = di·lydei. *c. sug.,* erlidei ar ny t-echyn.

2 tavl (h)oyw [ac =] as(eth loyw) ysgeth [tavlet] (vr)wydrin.

3 t[e]yrneδ (*m.l., for*) tyrueδ, *commotion.*
   b. mynn[*it* :]*er* [y] cynghor (ner) men [na] leverit.
   *c. l-l*iaws, *reptn.* : ? Y *t*raws vei anwaws nid [ē =]*e*ndewit *i.e.* HeS., *who had been harsh was unattended, being lost.*

4 *no c.* rac [ruthyr :] ffawd bwy(e)llawd [eu] a[chleδyvawr :]

5 handit (y) gwelid [llava*r* =]llawer yn llei*t.*   [llavn lliveid.

MISCELLANEOUS NOTES

21·6 Porth loeδ = Porth lwyδ vyδin, Porth lwyδ laïn. *oe is often written wy. The word is not ' Porthloeδ.'*
  b. rac·yrweδ, *a biform of* rac·orweδ, *lies prone.*
7 gwn-eδ = (*so wr. app. to distinguish*) gwŷn-eδ, *wrath, from* Gwyneδ. bu-ant (*has no subject*) : ? (Hu) vu wy*t*hawc.
8 an *sug.*, an gorvela*ut* enyd ffrwy*ff*aut. *They who had oppressed us attacked us violently for a short while when the news was told. But the bard was not there, hence a*n *is suspect. see am. t.*
21·10–18 *Henry I. invited Owein ap Cadwgan to combine with Llywarch ap Trahaearn, and with the King's own son to attack Gr. ap Rhys, lord of Ystrad Towi.* B., 300-301.
10 pryd-[er = y*t* =] yδ   pryd[er]-[a*f*, older -a*m* =] an*t*.
  b. [*fun* antcpn.] *? read as in am. t.*
11 ? ffun yn or dec, ar[yal :]dal Redec, ar hynt (h)wylaw.
  b. Read 3 s., for 1 pl. as in am. text., but the plpf. is suspect.
  ? read, [ku : kā =] cam y carei, colle(d)ic ffaw. *This refers to the rape of Nest at* 8·10· *see* Bruts, 281.
12 Argoedwys, *men of Argoed.* Owein held Kaereinon, traean Deuδwr, and Aber rhiw. B., 292·10.
13 da*d* : da(r)*b*od[es =]wys, [ar] luyδ P(o)wys ar *ll*es = ar *l*es, or *e*r lles rieu = *Henry I.*
  b. ar δil[yv]yn = ar δilyn goet. *see* B. 301·5–11.
14 dy·[liw = liu : lui = lut =]luδ, *he hinders, stops.* yr, *for the sake of,* (*or* a, *and*) *banquets.*
  b. kyveδ- *wogant* metath. *for* go*vv*ant = co*vy*ant [ef an :] ae dy·δug-[a*r* : āt =]ant dan adlo-[yw =]eu. *see* B. 285·10–15. Tal., n. 39·26.
15 [ac]ar [gr]oen gwyn[n]. *Hist. & rhyme sug.* ar gŵyn O(we)in.
  b. gosgroyw : gos[goryv = gorv =]gorδ.
16 Llwch gwynn (dorret). *This is the battle of* Estrat Brunus (*An. Camb. Ao.* 1116). *Llwch G. is on the Cothi, near its mouth. see Tal.* n. 56·24, B., 302.
  b. [gwynn *reptn.*] dwll : ? (try)doll [ar] ysgwyt [yor, *reptn.*]
17 yspar, ? *adj., speared.* molut myn[ut m]or, *sug.*, molut [*mut*] mynor, *the* [*mute*] *praise of marble.*
  b. [go] gwneif. gwnëiv = *I shall do* ; gwneiff, *he will do. The latter is a monosyllable, and still in constant use on the Teivi.*
18 gw[g]ynei g. *trs.*, = cereint gŵynei hael (a gwyδei).
  b. mynawg oe dut. *cp.* (oe) temyr 9.13, 20·19. Ow. ap Cad. *is styled* ' tywyssawc llu,' ' gwledig ' *and* ' ri,' *king, in Bruts.*
19 e [glut*v*- : glut*u*- : glut*ɼ*- : glu*ɼ*-*t*an =] eglur *d*an(n).
20 eidef : o*r*δeu oeδ . . .

151

21·21 m. *irregular, words deranged.* en trin llet-*veg*-in : *eu veg--trin* lletin : ev *veigryn.* lleδyn (yn)g·wyn [o]ban*t* They ' *start out suddenly* '*i.e. they surprised and slew him in the Gwynn hollow. cp.* Llwch Gwyn, l. 16.

22 kyn glas veδ [a] glas (? gleδ) fu [eu :] i rann . . . [od]

22·1–11 = 23·21 – 24·10, *The variants in these two versions, written almost consecutively, exemplify the careless way in which MSS. were copied, and recklessly altered.* see p. 105.

22·1 Dienhyt=Diheηyδ, 23·21. y bob llawr, *paraphrase no c.,* llanw- *sug.* llyr, *and c.,* bob dyδ. *see am. t.*

   b. e hual=*y* haual 23·21 : hoewal, ' *whirls in eddies.*' Pughe.

  2 twll [tal *read backwards* =]tyll-*fa*(w)*r* . . cas o hi*r* (*no rhyme*)= ? casahe*t. ? read,* g(w)as (vr)athet. *cp.* ' gwedy brathu *H*owel,' B., 304. gwy*t*hawc : gwy*c*hauc 23·22. diffreidyei*t* : diffret, 23·22.

  3 eil g[w]eī*t*[h] :] Geint, *fosterlings of Keint*=Gronw, Ririt, *and* Llywarch *sons of Owein ap Edwin.* B., 303·28. *With* 'eilwith' *of* 24·1, *cp. dialectal* ' lw-eth '=eilweith.

   b. gelwideint : gwelyδeint, 24·1. *trs. to* a seirch (eu) cat veirch (pl.) : a[e] seirch y (sing.) gatveirch, 24·1, (yn)g.

  4 bedin ag kysgo(d)-=bit en an (k)ysgo(d)- 24.2 -*get yt* [*vyd*] *cat* (r.b. =)*rac tyget*=tynged. *cp.* [b]*it* get 24·2=tiget.

   b. voryon, (uoron 24·2) *not a cpd.*=mawrion, *magnates.*

   c. cochro llann : gwychyrolyon, 24·2.

  5 ban ry goδhet [δ+h=*th* : *ll*] : ry gollet.

   b. trwm [en] trin a [llavyn :] lläin 24·3 yt laδei.

   c. garw rybuδ o gat . . . *Howel was wounded and borne home where he died on the fortieth day after his return.* B. 304·14.

  6 cann calan a δarmerthei=gant can yg calan δ., 24·4 *? a paraphrase for,* (an)ant galan gant orugei.

   b. ef gwenit a dan vab ervei ; *antcpn. or paraphrase for* Howel ab Ithel a *orfei i.e.* or*ff*ei. *Historically true. see* Bruts, & Lloyd.

  7 ef gwenit [a] *gan* dwrch, *a juggle for* Wch*dr*(yt). *The sons of Owein with their* ' *Uncle Uchdryt* ' *assembled their men,* B. 304·5.

   b. [vn] rïein [a] mor[wyn] (δilein) a mynawg, i.e. *The sea destroys the Countess of Perche, and William* ' *the Etheling* ' a phan oeδ, *who was the son of a king,* on his travels,=a chan oeδ mab brenhin t., 24·6. *Hist. and c. sug.,* ac a oeδ o dëyrn(eδ) teithawg *and all that there were of lords voyaging. cp.* " And a great company of gentlemen and ladies perished," *Y. P.*

MISCELLANEOUS NOTES

22·9 yng | Gwyndyt [gwaed]glyt gwaredawc = uδ Gwyndyt [gwaet] kilyδ g., 24·7 *for* Kilyδ Gwyndyd uδ waredawd = Owein *whose brother Uchtryt was a* ' *blood colleague*,' ' gwaed gilyδ.'
   b. kyn golo gweryt ar ruδ llary hael *? a paraphrase for* Howel cyn gro δcl ar i ruδ, etvyn, ae cyrchyn ymachluδ. ' vacuo redeunte ' AN. CAM. *cp.* δoeth dygyrchet 24·8. *Both parties retired so that* '' etvyn ae cyrch yn δigythruδ '' *would not meet the case. see* B. pp. 303–304.

10 o glot *a chet* echiawc = y get ae glot echiawg 24·9. *? read,* i ged, (gwych) glod (*red*) echïawg.

11 [*neut*] beδ garthwys [hir o dir] Rywonyawc.
   [*uot*] . . . gorthyn [. . . orthir] Rywynauc 24·10.
? read, (a) thwm (yn-)Garth(m)yn Rhyvoniawc, *or* a beδ yn·hueδ R., *or iii.*, a gorffwys (yng·hwys) R. Gorthir = *the upper part, or highland of* R. = *district around* Garth Garmon, *between wh. and Bettws y coed is* Garthmyn, *? the home and burial place of*

12 dinogat : diuodat, *that was destroyed* = Howel. [Ho. ap Ithel.
   b. ban wreith = banvreith, *highly striped, or spotted ; but a sing. fem. adj. cannot qualify the masc. plurals,* ' crwyn balaod.' Balaod = *wolves* (wh. *are not striped*) ; belaod = *brocks, badgers* ; cathod = *cats* (*then abounding wild*). *? read, i.* Peis δivodad oeδ vreith-vreith O grwyn bela pan (y)w (g)reith, *ii.* P. δ. o. vreith(deg) o grwyn bela ban greithed, *iii. see am. t.*

13 [c]hŵit [c]hŵit. *onomatopaeic* (*without the* ch.), *representing a sort of whistle-call to dogs.*
   b. gochan*wn* gochen*yn* : go·ganei hŵit hŵit hŵitogeith gochenid h. h. wyth g(w)eith.

14 ' dy dat ty ' = *Howel, not his father, Ithel. The scr. is wrong unless Howel's son* (*if he had one*) *was addressed.*
   b. helya : ? heilyaw. llory : llory(f) = llorv.

15 ef [gelwi :] geilw i gwn [gogyhwc : ?] i hely ae dwc. Giff, Gaff, Dïwc = *dog names.*
   b. dhaly dhaly dhwc dhwc : ? dhaly dhwc, dhaly dhwc. *The force of* dh *is uncertain in our MS. If* dh = d *in* daly dwc, *the* dwc *may* = dut : aut *as if borrowed from the Fr.* ' tay aut ' *our* ' tally-ho.' *But if* d *in* dhwc *is reptn. we get* hwc : hoo = hô, *i.e.* daly ho, daly ho. ' Daly' *is a monosyllable ; it is still used by itself to urge on dogs.*

16 *read*, ef (gwanei) bysg yng [corwc : coṉwe =] Conwy.
   b. ban *mal* [llad :] lleδi ll-ew llywywc *if spelled backwards* = ban *lam* llïδell e*n* llyuc*wy* = Llûgwy, *a trib. of the* Conwy. *ll*ïδell : ffithell, *young salmon.*

17 Ban elei [dy dat ty :] Howel [e] vynyδ.

153

BOOK OF ANEIRIN

22·18 penn iwrch, *the head of a buck, but* penniwrch=*the finest buck. I have treated* penn *throughout as an adj.*
  b. [gwythwch *antcpn.* :] gavr, *goat.*
19 *o* venyδ, *from the mountain* : *y* gweunyδ, *the moors.*
  b. rayadyr Derwennyδ. Leland mentions " Llin Thervenid half a mile in length not far from Gerionith." My inquiries about this lake have been fruitless. *The* Derwenyδ *of* 'Celtic Folklore,' p. 34, *is quite another, as pointed out by Mr. E. Phillimore.*
  b. [o :] a gwythwch [a] ll[e]wyn [a] llwyue-[in :]*ni*(t) i.e. *Ll*wyn Llwyvenyδ. *It should follow* Derwennyδ.
21 ni [anghei :] eing [oll] ni vo oradein.
22 Neum doδyw : neu·r δoeth [ang *antcpn.*] kyvwng o anghyvarch (δiscyn) ny[m] δaw [n]yn [dy] vyδ [a uo].
23·1 Ny mag-[wyt :]awδ [yn] neuaδ [a] vei l. [noc ef].
2 [ac ar :] *yn* ryt [benclwyt *looks like* bericlwyd, ? be*ṅr*iwyt : byryit, *cast down, or* briwit *bruised, struck down.*
3 [pennaw*r, chief*=HeS.] oeδ y(ar) varch (gweδig).
  b. pellynnic (=Hu) [e glot] pe[ll *reptn*]ws=pews : pwes=p*w*ys, *weighs down.*
4 golohi*t* [gweir *hir*=gweirhit : gweryt *which* ' tywarch ' *renders tautological here. cp.* gweiryd 5·1.
5 derllyδ[ei :]e*r* [veδ] cyrn (tëyrn) ffyrva[r]ch=HeC.
  23·6–9. *See notes* 20·2–5.
23·10–14 *An abbreviated and garbled second version of* 14·2–7 *q.v. A literal translation of the printed text as it stands, (ignoring c. and lacunae) runs somewhat as follows.* " Gododin *I* grow pale on thy account in the presence of a hundred in vigour (&) in great excitement at (a*m*) the paean of the son of Dwywei of fine manhood. Since he thrusted, amiable (is) the bulwark of battle. Now, (*nu,*) since the earth covered Aneirin *I* cannot (nyt) away with wailing for (a*m*) Gododin." *see notes on* 14·2–7. *I read* gomyn *as* go*r*uyn=gorwynnaf, gno *as* ango, en
23·15–20. *see notes on* 13·4–9 & Reprints. [*as* e*ṅ*=yr, neut *as* nyt.
23·21 *to* 24·10. *see notes on* 22·1–11, & VARIANT VERSIONS, p. 105.
24·11–21. *see notes on* 11·9–19.
24·12 tri hue : hueti*r*=hoetyl=hoedl barvaw*r* dreis(ei) d[i]*l*i plec=d*r*i plyg=driphlyg, *triplica.*
13 a*t* gu*u*c : ar·δûg *emorem* ae *guiau* hem. *The scr. hesitates here between* e·more & Morien, *between* guialen *or* ganghen, *arrow,* and guaiu *spear. Read* (*i.*) *as in am. t., or* (*ii.*) Morien δwg vore ae ganghen.
  b. hancai : *r*hanc (meδ) a [*u*re-ue*t* :] re*u*veδ. [urag :] raug. [denn :] δên(ynt). a*t* gwyr : a*r*wy*r*. *see am. t.*

24·14 a phrydein (*f. rhyme*) : i Bryden = *Wales*.
 b. a*t* gu : argu(δ) kelem (y) rhein ruδ[gu]en = ruδ(en). ⌈wenn.
 15 & 21 deh*euec* = d*yhewyt* [guen *extension*] abwy(d am) mad(w)
 16 Am[gin-yaw : gip : gpi=] gr(e)inyaw(r), d*r*y : r*y*d law(r)
 i.e. Rhyd lawr am greinawr [dry *reptn.* :] da*n* lenn (tonn) [tr*y*m :]
         tran δwys. *see am. t.*
 24·17–19 *The words are in a bewildering disorder. Context sug.*
 (Ku)emp arwr barvau*r* (17) Eiδyn (18) [a breithell] (benn) (ni
 welych) e δrych (18) (na)e lu*i*uen (17) [as *gell* :] ase*th* vreith (17)
 goruch [yd] y [lav] lovlen (18) [ar] (Gwant) Gynt a Gwyδyl
 [a :] *ym*Hryden (19).
 19 *cp.* 11·17–19 a chynyho = cnyy*fi*o = cn*ei*vio, i.e. *he who
 shears the mane of a wolf without a stick in his hand, wonted is a
 brave act in his tent !* There is no alteration too absurd for the
 scr. to make, if it hides the fate of the Deeside Borderers. For
 cynyho 11·17 reads *dalwy.* ? read, (yn vlwng) cnivei Mwng
 Vleiδ(ig) [heb] b[r]enn [en]e : o la*w.* gnawt : g(w)nawt, *was done*
 The literary *gnawd* is obsolete, but *gnawd* as pf. pass. of gwneuthur is constantly used. " Dyna fel y *gnawd* e " = that is how
 it *was done.* Grammarians ignore this form, but here we seem
 to have dialect usage attested. Here read *gwnaeth.*
 20 gwych-*l*aut [= *n*awt 11·18 : gwychpawt] = gwych*r*awd, ? *bravery.* e·ne·lenn = y·ni-lenn *i.e.* yn di-lenn, *in the open.*
 b. pryt-[wyf :]wn [n]y bei varw (drwy) Vor*i*en (l. 13).
 22 see note on l.15.
25·1 Ar*yf, broken letter,* = arv . . . twryf : twrv, *belongs to l.* 3.
 3 me*u* : me*v* = meδweδ . . . ma*wr* : marw-weδ = marweδ
         maty(r)eδ = madreδ.
 4 yst[y]ern gwer(i)n, e am : am e . . . -*gy*rn : d*r*yn = drin.
 b. (o)e uoli = wy volyn ri [a] llu [awr] (marini).
 5 (h)yd y gwele(i)s, or hual-dre(i)s. gall : gap-eδ.
 6 dy·go·[ch*wi* = *chu*i :]lli*tt*-awr = dygollittor. [*ch* = *ll*, *u* = *tt*].
 b. a pheith a pher : ? ar barth Gwyneδ, *or ii.* a phorth a meδ.
 7 Ar uδ uor(d)u(y)a (hyd) y·morva (y ar erch *H*eleδ). *see* n. 13·c.
 b. ac : a*r.* e*i*v-yon- : *h*yn-eiv-, *biform of* hen-ev-yδ.
 8 Trybeδ-[a*w*t, a*u*t :]an*t* raw*t* : rawc. ei*l. cp.* eif (l. 19).
 9 a*m* dal, *about his head :* ae bar [he*n* bann] hep[b *reptn.*]yan.
 10 ed-, *context sug.,* c*y*-wryseδ. Bleiδ : bla(w)δ oeδ [b *reptn.*]
 11 Pubell : *R*uδell pevyr(ant) . . . lwch : l*u*ch.   ⌊leiδiad.
 12 Gweledyδ wy*t* = wyδ = wy*v*, rwy*t* = rwyδ : rwy*v.*
 b. Gwe*l* : Gwe*r*ydon, *the men of* Gweryd = *Dee estuary.*
 c. car[-*ut*] (g)wreiδ *v*yw = *f*yw : *l*yw.

BOOK OF ANEIRIN

25.14 [d]y varw   car*ut* [d]yhe*δ* : car*av* y ve*δ*.
   b. (Hu) var*a*n, *appears,* [mor] yng·hyn-[horyf, *no c.*] : ff̄lam gwy*r* : gwŷt (*note rhyme*).
   15 y am [ga*t* : *car,* r.b. =] *r*ac-bwll (*see map*)... bran *should rhyme with* pwll, ? twll ... kyn*w*yt = kyn*v*(r)yt. *The* pwll *is landward of* Carreg Cynhadvan, *now partly filled up with refuse tipped into it. There is no reference to fighting in this pool.*
   16 go(r)wy*δ*awc ... byt : ? pyt, *pit.*   ar *ll*es : ar*ff* = arves.
   17 pe*t*war : pe*r* : p*a*rwar, *silent.* *cp.* P. 16.21.
   18 [petwar, *reptn.* :] (pan) [*mi* :] *i* (g)*u*elet mi[le]dawr = midawr bi*f*orm *of* midin, *ships* [byt :] (en) *r*yt.
   19 a *ll*avyn eg *w*allt : a *bliv ed bellt*   go·bedr[*or* : *et* =]yt.
   b. gwyll : (dy)wallas *o* :   ē·gyrn = yng·hyrn (hir)las me*δ* y
   20 *o* bli*t*h : *o* barth.   *cp.* 8.8, 33.5.   [mei·*δ*in.
   21 porth loe*δ* vy*δ*in, *cp.* 21.6.   ? *read,* porth lue*δ* [be]din.
   b. Brēeych dud vwlch, *he will breach the land of Brynneich.* 'vwlch' *is a verb when read so, but rhyme rejects it.   ? read,* Breneych dud (bost) (o) var*a*n [res] tost, [be*nn* : be*nit* :] bere*i* waed-[gw- *reptn.* :](l)in.
   22 -*f* = v = w.   cwry*f* : cwr*w*, twry*f* : *t*wr*w* : *l*wr*w*.
26.1 -w = v = f : l.   ha*w* : ha*l*-ffin, kyv*r*- : cyvieith, *men of the same language,* i.e. *natives.*
   2 kynan : can-an : can*av t*eith-[? *r*eith] [fyw :]*l*yw.   *cp.* 2.20.
   b. o von *ar* vreint   *metath. for*   ar Von o vreint.
   3 *t*-ut : (ra)*c* u*δ* [vwlch a*nicpn.*] kyv[*w*lch :]lwch.   CYVLWCH = Keint, wh. borders on Tut Llwch.   This is the region of the LAGOONS *of the Dee estuary.*
   b. gan *a gloss for* (Duc) [gan*δ*o] Vyny*δ*awg.
   c. bu atveillyawc = ? adveilyawc, *or* adweillyawc, *a biform of* arwallawc.   *eu* gwirodeu : ? o*n* gwin ar me*δ*.
   4 *hir*-aeth : ? *bu* aeth [er :] am wyr gatraeth.   [por ? *read,* 6yr.
   5, 6 e*n i* lavn[eu] dur   e*n*·ve*δ*em byr e*n* h[a]ualeu.   bur, ? *pl. of*
   8 *This line has no point, but is a mere truism.* Gr. ap *K*ynan *in exile compares himself to an apple plucked from its tree—the apple cannot thus develop.*   see am. t.
   9 Ni chynny*δ* rhïy*δ* o *δ*y·wall ; *After the Artro fight his fellow countrymen did not support him.* ii. ni chymyd diwyd a dywall,
   b. ni by*δ* doeth [ehov] yn noeth yn yscall.
   10 *m.s., ? read, i.* Pob (dyn) ban rydyngir yt ball.   *ii.* Ban (angel) ry dynger yd ball.   *iii.* Ban y gwir rydyngir yd ball.
   11 *misplaced, should follow line* 15.   As carwn [y ef *c*-a*r*ei :] (ni)*t* a*d*ei anreith (ae) gar ni by*δ* marw yn [*dwyw* : dyww = d*yvv* =] di*ff*-eith.

MISCELLANEOUS NOTES

26·12 [nyt amſud=] neut amluð i vuð i areith.
  b. ni cheri(r) [gyf- antcpn.] ovni(r) (an)ghyvieith.
13 [e mis :] eſnys [emwythw[a]s :] en ſwythus amw(yllt)yn.
14 en [adeſ :] acheſ [tan[g]ðeſ : taɲvcſ (a) gollit.
  b. [adeſ reptn :] ar tev = ar tew led vu[ost] lew [en dyd :] eɲgyt
15 Ruð[w]yt = Ruðit [k. reptn. :] treisiadon.   [(or ergyr) vid.
  b. mein uchel, *High lord* = *Magnus*   medel, 3 s. pres. Ind. of a verb medel-u *as c. proves.*
16 dyven, *sug.*, dy wên, *thy smile, blessing. but ?* dyben ar [warchan *no c., for*] orðen aðevon, *an end of the ' could n't help it ' confession,* (a genid gan wledig Penmon).

26·18–28·6 *Gorchan Cynvelyn consists of three independent parts. Judging by internal evidence 26·18–27·12 belong to Taliesin. HeS. is the Boar who over-ran the country as far as Llandyvrydog, before he encountered Magnus on the Menei ' stream,' avon* (26·20). *see Giraldus's* ITINERARY, *cap.* VII.
18 *The following seems to be the right order of the words* : Pei mi brytwn gwarchan ganwn [pei mi reptn.] tardei gorchegin Gweilging in fwrch trych drwyt (am) torch trych trychethin. *cp.*
  a. Pei mi : perim = peryv (*cp.* 36·12) bryt-wn ...   [18·19 gan-wn : -av . . . -av.
  b. tarðei : a darð gorch[e]cin : gorthrin = gwrthrin *or ?* gorðin.
19 Gweilging *i.e.* gweil·geing, *a rod, placed horizontally on* Y *shaped supports. see* W. B. MAB., 395·10–15.
  b. trych : truch = metath. *for* twrch drwyt (am) dorch.
20 trych (tra) chethin. trych : truch = twrch gyrch[essit] en avon (Menei). *The ' straits ' are locally spoken of as ' avon '.*
21 noe : ? n(awð) oe Geintyon = *Owein and his men who were garrisoning the castle of Aber Llēinawg.*
  b. tyllei garn gaffon : rhyll garn i (w)a(ew)ffon.
  c. [carn-eu ri = taru tren =] tarw trin [wr :] y ar
22 uo-dog-yon : ua(r)-god-yon, esgyrn : ysgyr(yo)n.
  b. vyrr, 3 s. pres. Ind. of bwrw *? a gloss for* vliv [fyrr = vlif].
  c. vyrrvach : ffyrivach (adon) = HeC. (a gwych) v.

27·1 tyl-lei : ? tyr rei i gilvach *some throng into hiding, but context sug.,* gyr rei i gilvach, govurth [gwryt-yach :) gw(y)r hyty(r)ach = hydrach, *the bolder men.*
  b. ryt gwynn : chwyrn ryt, *he rushes to the ford.*   [Flintshire.
  c. Eingylyawn = Einglion, *the men of the Rhuðlan end of*
2 [llað] [yawn reptn.] vriwyn [vriw reptn.] (ar d)al Von), *or* arial Mon, *the active of Mon.*

BOOK OF ANEIRIN

27·3 (ner). cann llwgyr δwg dy·vel (*intensive of* bel), *ravager*.
   b. disgyn n yal a *l*el : anſel. dewr : ? dor, vel cwrr.
4 dy [ſel *reptn.* :] êl. hoel : heol. *h*emin : *k*ernin. gib [e] llawr [a] ge*m*in : ge*r*uin. [ac] e*u*r ar : o oror drein(wyδ).
5 y wynn asseδ *sug*. ' asseth ', ? ' *tusks*,' *but ? read*, Gwynn-eδ as gwelyn, *foaming white they saw him*.
   b. ewyn, *foam*. The hidden were the ' dengyn,' *villeins. cp.* l. 1.
   c. meδ mygyr melyn. *There is a lacuna here. History and other parts of our text suggest as in am. text.*
6 [e greu] : ? a chreu oe g. : *The Boar was shedding the blood of*
7 Ei*l* cre*u* : eiſ gre(i)n oe gylchyn.   [*others rather than his own.*
   b. rac cade*u* k. (*m.l.*) ? rac cady*p* G., *fronting the mighty K.*
   c. [*K*yn*v*elyn *reptn.* :] Ys (y) gelyn, gas nar (a) wna, etc.
8 Go·borth-[yat :]ei adar ar δênyn δ[w]yar. *misplaced.*
9 *g*ra[d] : *c*ra = *t*ra *m*orion ad[an]vordwy[t] haelon.
10 cyvred [ke*r*d :] koed gwyllion (*the witch elms* of Llwyvenyδ) ar we*l*-l*i*[n]*g* : ar we*i*lg*i* dirion, *coast lands*.
11 [eny *v*wyfy dyd taw]. *scribal extension.*
   b. go*m* : go*r*uyniad gelyn, *the great desire of the enemy.*
   ⁎⁎⁎ A fresh poem begins here in other metres.
12 goc*h*awn : go(r)chan[*w* :] o gyrδ keinmyn. *cp.* Tal. 55·8.
13 gwarcha*n* : gwarcha*u*(t), *wardship.*
   b. gorchan (*no c.*) : gorch(en)yn kylch[wy a*ntcpn.*] ŵylad.
14 gwr : gwyr wneδ(yn) G. e*u* gwlad, *i.e. The Norsemen.*
   b. dychi[ann]awr dewr dychi[an]ad : Dewr (Mon lawr) δychïawr δych(il)iad.
15 eiδ*u*n gaer [gl. a*ntcpn.*] *w*eissyon claer cyveithrina*t* (*m.l., c.f.*) *? read*, y rhi gar deithi cyveithrinad.
16 *trs. into*, dy [e]*n* ru*d* kein ynys g[e]wrth ru*d* uo*r*a[w]d *for*, dy·urys gein ynys gwrth ryn vorad *the first rud is antcpn.*, the *second app.* = ryt, *gloss on* ryn.
   b. veδ = (g)*w*yδ-veirch *gloss on* midin, [eithin yn :] yn euthyn neut [ynt :] (leith) [b*l*e*n*nyd :] b*r*einiad.
17 gwarchan (*m.s.*) : gorchenyn G. [ar ododin (*no c.*) :] ryveliad.
18 goruc (no c.) *gloss on* gwnaeth o dyn (aeth δogn gymhwyll-eit : gym-[h*l*lwy =]h*p*wy-at.
19 *trs. into*, (aes) dron (a)e waew(ffon) [oreureit :] lliveit a*m* *r*odes : a*n* *r*odes = an *n*oδes.
20 Etmygit e wrth riv [tec *gloss on*] teleid. a[c] wrth ra*n*n : a wrthry*m*yn wyrt(h) colovn greid. ' Mab Tec vann ' & ' Catvan' *are foundlings both, with no place in the text.*

158

MISCELLANEOUS NOTES

27·21–22 tros, *over* : ar *upon*, . . . buon(t) δeu(r) [en] δyδ rheit.
  22–**28**·6 A variant of 6·19–22. *The confusion of persons is great. Assuming the canto to be the work of* Llwchvarδ, *it must have been written after Cynon had gone over to the men of* Gwyneδ.
  22 no c., trs. into, try wyr athrych[ant :]ir (yn rhych) [athrivgeint :] drigant. *The number* 363 *is pure fiction. The expedition consisted of* 100. see INDEX s.v. cant.
28·1 c.f., ? read, y vreichyell gat (t)raeth(ell) y (d)aethant.
  2 [yt] gryss[assa]yn uc[h] = (a)wr [meδ menestri] : o orlawn (6·20) lestri, *overflowing cups.*
   b. *Three whose names hist. gives* = Owein, Uchtryt, & HeC.
  3 K(u)ynan [a chad] reith a [chat] lle(ith) cat y nant. chad . . . chat . . . gat *are characteristic stutterings. The ground near the entrance to the fort forms a slight ravine,* nant.
  4 dychïorant, m.l., ? (Gynt gym)rant.
   b. Mab Coel. *no c., the bard was not a Coeling. The point here is that he was a ' captive.'* ? read, mal ceith.
  5 m.l., ? read, [ev] niwed nid noδed (Ffreinc) [e] gawsant
  6 [kyrδ]. Kyv : kvy = cwynovant. *The wardship of* Cyn-vel-yn, *the war-leader* (= Magnus) *proved the undoing of the Saxon power.*
  7 *This bit of prose illustrates the wooliness of the scribe's mind. It is doubtful if he had anything to copy for lines* 9–14, *but he wanted support for the corruptions introduced at the top of this page;* (*see also* 6·19). *Hence the rubric to lend authority to the fraud. The following amended version is the best I can suggest.*
    Yman y tervyna gwarchau(t) Kynvelyn.
  Un geinyawc a dal pob canu (yn) odl(eu) y Gorδin herwyδ breint yng·herδ amrysson. (Y mae) tri chanu a thriugeint a thrychant, a thal am bob un. Sev (yr) achaws yw am goffäu yn y canuon rivedi y gwyr a aethant i gatraeth. Ni δyle barδ vyned i amrysson heb y cerδ(eu) hyn, (mwy) noc y dyle gwr vyned ymlaδ heb arveu.
  Yman weithon y dechreu gwarchan Waell (30·6) vael δerw. Taliessin ae cant, ac y rhoδet breint iδi, gymeint ac i (h)oll odleu y gorδin a·r teir gwarchan yng·herδ amrysson.
    Here ends the wardship of Kynvelyn.
  A penny is paid for every canto in the odes to the Push, according to the rules of competitive song. There are three songs, three score, and three hundred, and a payment for every one, because the cantos keep in memory the number of the men who went to Battle strand. A bard should not enter a competition without these odes any more than a man should go to battle without arms.
  Here now begins the paean of the iron-tipped oak Dart. Taliesin sang it, & privileges were granted to it equal to those of all the odes to the Push as well as the three paeans of the competition.

BOOK OF ANEIRIN

28·7 gwarchan, '*super-song*,' *paean. cpd. of* gwor, *vel* gwar *and* cân. *cp.* cae gwar ty, *the field above the house.*
  b. kyn-vel-yn, *war leader*=Magnus.
  c. canu (misplaced)=*canto.* canuawc *reptn.* : ceinyawc.
8 awdl, *an ode,* i.e. *a poem in varied metre. Read* odleu.
  b. goτ[o]δin=gorδin, *the push, great battle of the Strand.*
9 kerδ amrysson, *competitive singing (in verse and minstrelsy).*
  b. 'The cantos number 363.' *As the two books stand there are only* 132, *including repetitions. But both parts lack their endings. If the scr. speaks correctly the greater number of the cantos are lost, which is highly improbable. see n.* 27·22.
  c. [*or* gwarchaneu. *The sentence begins with* 'canu' *therefore* gwarchaneu *should be* canuon].
11 gorchaneu : canuon. rivedi *see* 6·19, 27·22–28·1.
15 *read,* gwarchan Waell vael δerw. *see* 30·6*.
16 *It is not Tal. but the* breint *that* 'confers.' *read,* roδet.
  b. iδaw (*masc.*) *for* iδi (*fem.*)=gwarchan.
  c. odleu, *Odes, pl. of* awdl. *In line* 8 *the* Gorδin *is sung in one Awdl, but here there are* odes, *wh. internal evidence supports, to wit by* Talhaearn, Llwchvarδ, *and* Gr. ap Kynan. *The scr. forgets his perversions, and the truth slips out occasionally. Note that the scr. confuses* canu, gwarchan *and* awdl, *as well as* canuon, gwarchaneu, *and* odleu.
17 oll *qualifies* odleu, *as I understand the text.*
18 Doleυ deμ (r)y·dyr am gaer y[m] di·hun *those awake* (gyrch) am galch [am *reptn.*] claer. *cp.* doleu trin 23·20.
19 aδoeτ adwy-aer, *trsd.*=aer adwy.
20 kys-gut : kys(twy, gwely as edy yn es)gut. *line missing.*
  b. [a*r* reptn. :] a*e* w*r*yt . . . a uebi*r* : a ve*d*it : a vegid.
21 odef-[yn :]wys yas . . . w*r*yt : *v*ryt. [dygw(y)δ e[μ] arv.
22 dy·gwg-[ei] *The scr. seems to hesitate between* dy(s)gog *and*
  b. Huδei onw[l]yδ (yn) elvyδ : (yr) elvyδ huδei onwyδ.
29·1 gw*r* a *r*et : (di) gwa*r*et [pan] dyc[h] : d(r)ic (yng·)[*elwit*, *reptn.* : wely*δ*=] weryδ, sea.
  b. krym, Old Ir. *crum, cruim* : prym=pryf, *a worm.*
2 dykr : dycμ : dygn ymδwyn.
  b. kyveil-[iw : iu=]in na*r* [ei*l*iw=] etryv [et *reptn.*] v*r*wyn . . . emmel=ymhel, Lat. *impellere.*
3 [dywal] Tervyn torres te*r* teithiawl. *read backwards.*
4 uo*l* : vo*r*awt . . . *y* v*r*ascawt : a*m* vras *r*awd.

MISCELLANEOUS NOTES

29·5 mo*r*(dwy)awδ Ryn [*r*y, *reptn.*] *m*id-h*i*n : *uu*δ-h*u*i [*r*yme-, *reptn.*]*n*on : *u*on. dy*ff*y*ll*ei : dy·lys [sei] d*r*e(i)*s*h(yn) [*t*r*a* :] *c*ar Manon=Mannan. *cp.* Cat-Vannan. *ii.* ? tramo*p*ion.
  b. disgleir [yawr ac *antcpn.*] . . . dâl a*et*hon.
7 kyveill *g*awr en-a wel(it).
8 ad[a]wa[v]n=adwân. Treng[syd] : (ni)dre(i)ng a gwyδ[*et*:]*i*t.
  b. yar leithig) ortho*r r*eith t*u*t[h] a the*v*ic. *cp.* 2·20.
9 [e] *g*oscorδ, mawr mur(nid) . . . dheli : δeli(t).
10 *trs. into* : na chyngor na chil gyng[w]yd—*this line lacks its mate.* ? *read*, (ymre*i*chell dim ni ellid).
11 ene*it* : ? *t*eien=*c*ae*p*, *fort.*
  b. ta*l*a*ch* : ta*l*c*ha*(tt)or . . . *uu*δyt : fuδit : *l*uδit.
12 (Bleiδ) [e*f*-gor *reptn.*]=e*l* [g]or E.=el Eiδyn, or racδor.
  b. Kyn*o*n Keint vur, [*rē*=] Rhyn ragor.
13 gossodes [ef] gledy[f=v=u=*p*=]r=gledyr arglawδ (hy vedr rac) mo*r*wyr (dic)   bu*δ*ic *e* ren : *rē*en buδic [e]ny [an] nawδ *v*le(i)δic *ȳ* [*gynn-* :] *a*d-wythic.
15 [dwu-]yn d*i*·*w*yn veis [ky]chwec[h] ny gwyδ(es)
16 [kyc] h[w]erw [ky] chwenyches [kychwenychwy, *mad reptn.*]: (ni δymch)weles, [e*n* : e*u*=]ev lli [*wel-* :]*l*ewes. (Arwyr ymwan).
17 [a] lenwis mi*r* : mi*tl*an [mir *reptn.* :] mor-*eb ed* les.
  b. gode*ml*[es] : godo*pū*=godorun.
18 *te*-i idw- *read backwards*=dwi*r*e i=δ*w*yre i *w*are.
  b. yn[gor-*v*yn*t*=*u*ynn :]*p*yn*n* gwyr gorwynn[af] ry ann(og)et.
19 yn *llwr*w : ? yn *r*huth*r*eu yn [rhwyδ*h*=rhwy*th* :]rhwy*ll*eu.
  b. trs. into (*a*) veδwyd [co*l*lwyd *reptn.* :] cyminwyd *in* enwyt.
20 *r*un : *c*un G., (gan) rên *gloss for* riheδ ry dy*p*uit.
21 Gorthew (bor) [am d]*ȳ*chw*i*l (ffor)δ i chwelid
  The following is the true order of the words after am rwyδ (22) mwy galwant no (21) (*no. c.*) : (ev) alwy o*p* (erlid).
  ysteflit [am ry (22) :]y ar orwyδ (21) melwit, 22=in elvyδ.
22 *a difficult line.* [Ys tofflit *reptn. for*] blivid [llib(ed)=lliv(ed), *gloss on*] llym llain blin blaen-[blen blen]wyδ. ? *read*, ll*ä*in llym (a) **blin** vlaenwyδ **v**livid, *or as in am. t.*
30·1 trybeδ[aut] *y w*-ledic : ev leδ*i*t drybeδ rwng [drem dremrud, *stutterings*] [drem *r.b.*=] mer(y)δ '*marsh, plashes, matweed.*' O.P.
2 ny welet y oδeu dhogyn *r*yd, ny welet y oδeu dhog yn *f*yd
  But for one letter the two lines are word for word the same. Goδeu *is a noun wh.*, (if a true reading), *means* Scrobesburig. dhogyn [*r*]yd *may*=δygyvyd. *c. & context sug., i.* Cigleu (uδ) Goδeu (ban) δygyvyd ; *ii.* Cigleu y go(r)δeu ; *iii.* Clywed i oδeg ; *iv.* Gweled y goδed, *seen was his distress,* but ' fyd '=mud, *mute,* which implies *hearing* rather than *seeing.*

BOOK OF ANEIRIN

30·3 [ny] wel[et] y od*eu* : Gwel*i* y goδiv a δwg yn vud.
   b. mor [er :] var *a* dig δar (ae) di·gar (b)yd
  4 kyn (y)t [-af] digoni*t* (oeδ) welw gynwythic, *or* can wyth (d)ic
  5 kynn lleithig (oeδ) llwyr [*d*elw :] welw   [*with hot anger.*
    kyn y olo (oeδ) go*r*uδ (δ)elw   taf : ta*l*
  6 gwr : gorvawr [y :]o wael*l* vael δerw, *iron-tipped dart of oak*.
   b. *trs.* di*e*iryfad : di*a*rvad (vore) y e*rr*y : re*r*y : re*l*y(w) [par]
  7 arδelw(y) . . . rymyn(nyn) wlad [rymyn *reptn.*] rymd(w)yre.
  8 δisgynn[yawd] *v*lawδ [g*y*mre :] gyn*u*i*r*e, nac : nit.
  9 r*y* : ryn gre *cp.* man-gre. *see* Bruts 284·14.
 10 goδiwe(ss)*y*d [go*t*i*u*es :] go*r*mes odiwe*u*d : *e*diwe*nt* : *de*weint o
    vevl veint gw(a)re.
30·12–15 *is a variant version of* 13·19–14·1 *q.v.* Da (i Von)
   [duyot :] doeth adon [wy=vy] (aeth) ad[on *reptn.* uē=]wen.
   This adon (=Magnus) *is the subject of the verbs so absurdly put in
   the 2nd person singular. see nn.* 13·19–22.
 14 ys gwn dref dy beu*wel* : ? beu*uef* i.e. peues.   There is no c.,
   and m. there is none. The am. t. contains the best sug. I can make
   of this scr. medley. The poet (G. ap K.), speaks the truth in l.* 14.
 15 od gur *trsd.*=gurod : gorot : goro*r*.
 16, 21, 22, 20 Trycan, trychan, Tryca*nt*=trychauc eurdorch*auc*
  (20) a gryssyassant *who rushed* : a gyrchassant *wh. c. sug.*
   b. [en : ue=]wy amwyn [breithell, *no c., nor sense*] : ? y Rhyn
 17 kyt (nat) ry·laδ(at) wy laδasant. [y Rhyd yn bu [e]drywant.
 18 a hyt [orffen *no c., gloss on*] diweδ byt [e*t*myc :]myceδ.
   b. [ac] or [sawl :] *a*mhad **aetha***m* o [gyt *no c.*, :] **vaeth** garant.
   *The Franco-Saxon forces consisted of many races, including the
   native 'dengyn' forced to fight with them. see n.* 33·7.
 19 [tru] namyn [un gwr *no c.* :] y dengyn nid engh*y*ssant.
 20 gw*n* : gw*r* :] gwleδgar [gua*cn* :] gua*n*cawc.   [HeS.
 21 kyu*u*n : kyn*l*i*u*=kynlyw, *a gloss on* dragon. [kyu *reptn.*]=
 22 go druδ : truδ -og *spurred on*, (Lat. *trudere*) *a* grysswys
    ganthuδ : ganthuδ gryss*ant.*
31·1[trychwn *reptn.* :] (Ar **sawl**) athrycha**wr** ni δychwelant.
   [tru nid atcorsant, *scr. paraphrase without c.*]   [gyni(vei).
  2 Dywal *y*gcat (*no c., a paraphrase* :) ys blwng *y*ng·hyuwng (Hu)
  2 as gwnehei (*no c.*) : gyhoeδei, *he would not proclaim peace*.
  3 [yn] dyδ *gwyth nid ef* weith, (*a paraphrase*) : δyδ *lleith y* coch-
    weith ni **oc**hel(e)i
  4 baran (*a gloss*) : dig *i.e.* Baeδ dig oeδ Bleiδic [mab *no c.*] :(i leid)
    el(e)i. E*r* : Eng·(wleδ) gwin (a meδ) [gwydyr] yv[assid] (o) l. ll.

MISCELLANEOUS NOTES

31·5 [ac en] δyδ camhawn [camp *is a perversion*. a wneei :] wnai gam (vri). *HeS. fell and got the wrong kind of fame.*

6 ar [ar*u-*u*l*=] amuſ ca*n*n : ? cauɲ, *the hero.* cp. meinvuan *llwyd* 13·16, 1·4.

31·7–11 *These lines belong to the same ode as* 7·6–9. *They are partly the same, and partly supplementary.*

7 (Vore dwyre), bwys vlaen rhyd·re, ffer[ei] ȳ gadeu.

8 bryt-am gor[l]ew = prydav ore*u* [di·]e. *double neg.*

9 e·chwith la*in* (δ)y·or·wyla*in*. ef gwneei = goruc 7·8.

10 llydw = lleδw, *prostrate* ; gwyδw = gweδw, *widowed*.

  b. kynn oe(t) angheu. Breint mab Bleiδgi = Greit uab hoewgir 7·9. *This variant shows the utter lack of scruple in the scribe. It is not so much that he can't copy correctly as that he wont.* Breint mab Bleiδgi *is a pure myth. see am. t.*

12 kein. *? read,* k*u*n, *or m*ein, *lord. Paleographically we must read,* kein = kaɲ. *cp.* Car Mannan.

  b. Guodeo : Goδeu, *the scrub portions of Schrobes-scire i.e.* Shropshire. *see* Tal., *xiv., & n.* 22.

  c. e cel*y*o : yngele*u* ery : *c*ry : *t*ry·veɲu*t*.

13 [o hanav, *expansion*] ar(tud) a ffyscut as [ei *r*ep*tn*.] ry·angut.

  b. pan esgyn[nei baub ti disgyn, *no c.,* :] (y gelyn rac wnel)hut

14 c(l)euei = clywei gwin(t) gwaed meirw (gy)meint [a] wanut *It would appear that* r (*as in* meirw) *is mute in c.*

15 teir blyneδ ā [phedeir] tu[t]eδ [en : eɲ] vawr-yc-u[ae]*t*.

⁎⁎⁎ *Gr. ap K. returned to Mon in* 1099. *Probably some Norse-Irish friends had interested Magnus in the lot of Gr. whose island home he befriended for* " *three* (*to*) *four years*." *But ? read,* 'pym,' *five,* 1098–1103.

  b. as(tut) cymmyrr hut : cym*in*ut (cyn) [ath :] (ti) voδut.

17 (*no c.*) [pressent, *expansion*] kyvadrauδ *gloss on* Traethad (dy reithad) [oed] (vy) brei*th*-[yaul : au(t)yl :]awdl glut.

31·18–**32**·1 *This canto bears the signature of Griffith ap Kynan. see* INTROD., *xlii., & n.* 36. *cp. n.* 13·2. [*Trahaearn.*

31·18 Pan [gyrcheis *f.c.* :] grysseis (Von rhac treis trahäawg) =

  b. yg *k*y wlat : (yn) yng·wlat yng·hlod oeδ hanvodawg.

19 *the order of the words* = ef roδei(s) [ef dil- :] derllyδei(s o) drull [gwr eur *expansion*] *t*orchawg wi*n* (a meδ) [gloyw glan *f.c.,* :] achlan (d)i·wychïawc. roδeis *is tautological with* derllyδeis *? read* ceveis.

M 2

163

BOOK OF ANEIRIN

31·20 cān wr, *a* 100 *men. no. c., & hist. inaccurate. The number wh. Gr. ap Cynan obtained from Robert of Rhuδlan was* 60 (Ll. 380). *Cp.* Tristan's mission to *I*reland to fetch *I*seult when he was given ' 60 men,' with others of noble rank. *I can only sug.,* can : ca*n*=côr, *a band, corps* ; & wr *r.b.*=rw(y), *excess, extra, that can be spared.*

21 anvonavc eissyllut alltut marchauc, *no c., a paraphrase.*

22 [vn, *only*] mab*o*n i Gy*n*an [*o* dr*a b*annauc :] edr*y*vannawg. The B.B.C. also uses mab*o*n with the sense of mab-*o*n=a scion of royal blood. *see* Tal., *xxvi–vii. -on* is a common *plural* ending, and its use in sing., in words like mab-on, gwr-on, teyrn-on seems to be a ' plural of excellence ' like the Royal ' We.' As far as *c.* is concerned Mab*o*n i Gy*n*a*n* is supported by other examples like gwl*a*t and cl*o*t.

   b. ny : yn sathrau*r* [gododin *no c., m. impossible, and a deliberate forgery*] ar *g*-laur : ar*c*=Ar*t*(ro) lawr.

82·1 neb ffossawd vei lymach no(·m gavlach) ban flifaut. *note disorder of words in text.* nō=nom, llif : flif-aut.

32·2·3·7·8·12·13 *should be compared ; they correct one another.* deo*r*=dewr, sa*r*ff=saif, anysgoc 13=anysgoget 3.

4 cy*nn*i-*v*=cy*m*u-*y*=cymmwy yn rhwy.

4–6 *See Notes on* 37·10,*b.*–12 *where the text is less corrupt.*

5 *a line wanting. see I.* 9 *infra, and am. t. & nn.* 16·10–11

   b. 5, 6, 8–11. *see Notes* 36·10–12.

32·6 kyuyeith=kiwet *l.* 10 *infra.*

8–11 *Another variant version (p.* 106), *the only one with* 4 *ll.*

9 gverit=guereit at 37·11, *bogus forms for* gwaret *as context and rhyme make clear. That* gverit *does not mean* gweithret, *the next line attests.*

10 Meryn=merin 16·11 *for* Mori(e)n. Madyeith=Madyein 16·11.

12 *follows by*δin, ll. 8, 8*b*–11 *are misplaced.*

   b. guol[o]uy : (Hu as) gwelwy Aches (δelwy).

   c. duuy*r* : du*r*uy=du*c*wy. dilin *is the usual spelling in old poetry.*

13 (Hu a saethir) lledruδ lliwir, (y) a(r) v*a*rch [a] cwy(δi)r (y) rac [gododin :] gorδin.

14 rē *c*w=ren *e*w=rhyn ev g. kyw*u*y : ky*n*wy-rein.

15 barδ : bar*th* kēm*r*e : kymm*er* to*t t*-arth : torr arth.

16 *rearranged,* wode*f* s *d*an cwyt *n*y [ysty*n*g *read backward*=] guysty(l)ei *i.e.* Goδe*u* (wy)s *b*an gwyδ(wys) n*w*y gwystlei.

   b. wyn-e*b cpd. of* gwŷn & *b*ē=*d*en=dyn [ca*r* :] ca*l*ed.

17 [e]ry[th]=ryvaccei *i.e.* rac neb dyn caled gwŷn ry·vaccei.

   b. (Rac) diryeit o(eδ) eirch(eit am) veirch (mei) [yg kyndor aur]

MISCELLANEOUS NOTES

32·18 gwryavr hëin waewawr, *f.c. and m. paraphrase for*
Gynt hëyn eis **kelyn** (ae) **creu**δeu.

19 *rearranged*=pan wanet yng·*hyu*(ret) [ef gwanei, *gloss for*)
Mang hyrδei, *ir* eill(t) ne*u*t oeδ *kyu*eillt a mevyl [yt :] ny(w]
dyccei. *Kyu*- is doubly used—in *kyu*(red) and *kyu*-eillt, hence the misplacement.

20 pan dy-*d*-uc=pan δy*d d*ut [k]y*iu*=y*m* ran. The punctum cancels the long half of *h*, leaving *i*.

32·22—33·1–3 *See Notes on the fuller version at* 8·2–7. tutleo= tuδ lew : [t]uδ *t*ew=car tew 8·2=HeC.

33·2–3 *deranged, trsd.*=rwy yar vein *l*lavi erch mygedorth ur ys-geinnyei y onn o bedry holl *i.e.* rhwy(v) yar vein(c) *a* fliv erch [mygedorth :] vollt, [u*r* : u*c*=] *a*c ysgein onn bedryollt. *l*lavj : a fljv=a vliv.

4 *f.c., trsd.*=Ar [dwyn :] dwm [ef] eiδun(wn) aδev [gwa :] *a* gwlad [gwae ni] *trsd.*=galar rac (escar) ac a.g., *see am. t.*

5 *c. and m.f., no rhyme,* Ban [δoethon *gloss on*] Von dreiδ dëon [o Dineiδin barth, *paraphrase for*] Eiδyn ystrat. Din Eiδyn *is the fort at Aldford.* see Tal. *xviii*.

6 de : od(ia)ethol wyf [pob doeth *expansion*] (aeth δiffwys y) wlad. " *When the people heard (of the flight of Gr. and Cadwgan in* 1098 *they turned and fled, concealing themselves by hiding in caves, alder swamps, brackenhursts, steep places, wilderness (' diffwys ') . . . from fear of the Gwerydon i.e. men of the Dee Estuary.* BUCHEDD GR. 144·18-23. *The* Iδewon *of the Buche*δ *is a scr. disguise,*—[id-ew- (*r.b.*) =]we(r)idon=Gwerydon, *the men of Dee Estuary.* Arthur Jones's *note thereon is hopeless,* (p. 178).

7 a Lloegr. *If the fight was with Lloegr how could it take place at ' Dunedin ' in the sixth century? c. sug.*, Yng·HYwrysseδ (Hu) lüeδ amhad, naw *u*gein [am bob un :] (**ceith** δu*g*) o **beith**ynat. *After entering Anglesey in* 1098, *Hugh of ' Ei*δyn *barth' ravaged the country, took prisoners, and marshalled them to fight on his side*)

8 *trsd.* arde*m*yl=Arδel [-*y*m=*y*nt] veirch serig-seirch [d*i*l-lat :] def(ic gw)lat, *the country's prince*.

9 ardwy [ei w]ae[t] nerth(wy) yn gerth *i*r gat.

10 O- : Gosgorδ *no c., gloss on* Gwyr arvawg Mynyδawg ban (vyδant) [e] am drull, gloew y dull, yd gy[n : μ=*r* :]*t*vaethant.

11 o·*r* ancwyn (yn asswyn) [Mynyδawg *reptn*.] cryssasant (10)

12 handit, trist [lawn] vy mryt (rhac y rhyd ant).

b. e(meis) rhwy [ry] golleis [y] om [gwir *no c.*] : (hoff) garant.

13 [o drychan eur dorchawg a gryssyws gatraeth] *expansion by the scr. and repeated from* 30·20–22.

14 [tru] namyn [vn gwr, *no c.,* :] (y dengyn) nyt enghyssant.

83·15 [Gosgorδ *gloss on*] Carant godoδant y·ar [raʋn : ʀaʜn :] (δy)-lann Rhyn (Yng wyδ)veirch eil [iw] eleirch [a seirch gwehin :] ? yδ elbyn.
16 [ac] yng [kynn] or ll*if* (dymhor) lliwed δ*u*gyn.
17 [cn] a mwyn [ca*ll*-eδ : *ll*ac=frac=vrac]=*w*rageδ (twyn) a meδ eiδyn. *cp*. ll*u* : ll*if*, with d*iſ*: d*u*gyn. *In* Eidin & Mynyδawg *we have scr. perversion.* Mynyδawg *was already dead and* Cynon (*i.e.* Owein) *was* pennawr.
18 ? *read* : O gussyl (pennawr) drossei ysgwydawr (a) gwyδei lavnawr ar gronn gaer Rhyn. *The plpf. is suspect and makes the line too long.* grann-aur-g-w̥in : gronn gayr[*u*in : ɼin=]rhyn.
33·19 ce*r*i : ceir=ceiɼ : cein. *gwyl*-[a]-*es* (*both syllables do double duty*)—gwyl : gwyſ & (h)wyl. *trsd.*=cein wys [dis] esgyn-es (i) Gonwy hwyl-es, Gwarth (neb) ni phorthes [san], (g)we*i*(th) ni thechyn. " Hu yarll ar ffreink ereill . . . a δugant ganthunt y Gwyndut ar eiδunt oll hyt yn kantref Ros. *Earl Hugh* (*Lupus*) *and the other Franks took with them the men of* Gwyneδ, *and all that was theirs to the hundred of Rhos* (i.e. across the river Conwy) Bu. Gr., 148, ll. 4–6.
21 Neut eryueis y (*no c., paraphrase*) : ? (yng.wleδ) yvem veδ.
22 yn v*u* gwar(thr)ed. [gwaret pan laδei *perverts the history completely*] : pan laδha(wr vu yscawl) [ac gan lavnawr].
34·1 [*y*n :] ni(w) ysgoget yn [d]aer . . . men y[t welet :] daeret
2 [en emwaret *perverted expansion*] atwythic : ban golled.
3 *trs.* scyn-daut ma*d*auc : Mynawg escyn *r*aud, (awn yn) Elved.
4 de*i* : de*l* [y] (dir) cyuarchant : crymant . . . [h]oed[yl].
5 Eur ceinyo : Eurgeinnyon, *older* Eurgeintion, *the men of Eurgeint, i.e. Northop parish etc., Flintshire.*
b. *trs. and read*, arur*t*hiat Cynon bro(v)wys [meirch :] vreich Brithion, *the opposition of C. tested the power of the Picts.*
34·6–10 see Notes 4–8 and Variant versions, pp. 102–103.
34·11–15=11·19–12·2 *see* Variant versions, p. 106.
A. *E*ur scr. er. : *G*wr [a]*r* vur : v*r*uc=vrys (o).
B. krys g[r]wyd[y]at. *see* A.
C. da [ir *antcpn.*] care*i* [na hair : hair*u*a]=aerva [air, *reptn.*]
D. *a hopeless tangle of corrupt readings.*
E. (ar neb) un [ſſaxa :] Seis sesia*l*at=a(r)leissyat F.
G. a *ry*·ovudwyd ada*t*, *but ?* a *r*g-ovudwyt=a voδwyt [*r*gu= rug gur=] rwng gu(y)c adad.
H. *another hopeless line without rhyme or sense.*
I. pell *read backwards*=lle*p*=lled, *broader*=Hugh the Fat.
K. *still another hopeless line.*

MISCELLANEOUS NOTES

L. *a line missing.   ? read,* (or Rhyd ev acth werydrein).
M. [a vo *byw* o = a vo mwy o, N :] byw.   N, neus : nis, M.
O. *l*ui : fu i [o dam *reptn.*]   [*l*un :] fun.
P. *ll*wy [od am] luch (vun) lyvanad.   *see* O.
Q. [nys :] neus (R) adroδ [a uo byw] *y*n dyδ ple*im*ieīt. *App. the scr.* had *p*reinieint *in mind, on the day they are feasting. Read,* plygat & *note rhyme.*
s. na bei [cin] haval Gin(t) [elweit = :] eilwat.
R., T. *correct by* Q. & S.
16 Di*m* : ? (en) di(c)*in* = Yn δygyn = y·nygn.   *Note the superfluous* ' ci-' *in the line before.*
   b. [o] ā da*m* (*r.b.*) = am δiua uei [ni*mu*[n] :] ruim = rhwyv.
17 huc : hu*t* = huδ.   sd*l*inet : ysdiriet = ysdyriet.
   b. t*r*sd. = llu mawr e*v* laδawδ.   [*the island of Mon.*
18 map : eil Nwython = Nectan, *the Irish King who protected*
19 deyr*n*et (*no c.*), *tyrants, princes* : o dir re(g)et.
   b. g*r*imbuille*r* : g*u* = gy*m*hwylle*t.*
20 gue*ll* : guor *p*rit : drut = gor·δrud.
21 ei*l*th : *l*eith.   ca*ll*-on : *ll*ac-on : *rr*acon : d*r*agon
   b. e*h*el- : e d*a*laeth   [gur : gor] luit : l(y)wyδ.
22 eini*m* : ? cinu(i)*n* = cyn-vin, *the coast.*
   b. tei*n*im : teir : tei*l*in, *enveloping.*
35·1 (Lluryg) ni wisgwys ymyl (Rhi gyrchwys).
   b. imil *reptn.* : u*l*iu = vliv (*see end of next line*) (Llaδ) lwyt (*a*) h.
2 [i] gwaew ac [yscuit :] aseth vliv.
3 no [neim *r.b.* =] Mein ab : eil N.   *cp.* 34·16·18.
2,*b.* (ni weled y·Mon), *h*eb gleδ na chyllell.
   4 [iodeo] *Here the scribe manufactures evidence to support a passage in the* ADDITAMENTA *of the Nennian MS.* §64. " *Nunc facta est strages Gai campi . . . in expeditione usque ad urbem qui vocatus Iudeu.*"   *Now, c. decisively rejects* iodeo, *and so do context and history.   Read,* (Y·nhrin) tra merin trylew ing gahant.   *The* merin *is that of* Mordrei.
   b. tri-*g*-uaid : trîg gwaeδ Ffranc, *the shouting of the Frank, impetuous leader, ceases.   Why ?* (Ev saethwyd ac aseth loew) [bu :] *g*an bor a oreu var(n) Duw. *He was shot with a gleaming dart by a lord who executed the judgment of God.   The third line gave away the* IODEO *fraud hence its omission.*
5 frai : ffra*u*dus lyw.   [bu]bo*n* : bor = bor.
6 [Gnaut . . . gnaut . . . gnaut . . . gnaut . . . =] Guau*r* (*hero i.e.* Magnus) ȳ [ar] fis(c)iolin amdifiyn(ei) (rac) gorδin.

167

35·7 im [blain] *t*rin=i·m*i*tin *in his ships. cp.* Tarw trin a*r* vidin blaut B.B.C. 97·13. ī llwrw (δaeth) a lan(w) buan b*r*(a)thei.
8 rac (? vu) δewr deulu ev δiscynhei.
9 mab(lan) golystan cyn [nei : ni be*i* :] *e*scynnei.
   b. guledic [*i*ta*t* : *i*tta=]ma wledic, *king of the field (of battle).* *e*ndewit a [lauarei *no c., gloss on*] δywedei.
10 scuitaur trei *is manifest nonsense. Rearranged the letters=* is*ct* [uawr]=is*er* : isel drei. *Read*, Mynyδawc arles-[*u*aw*r* :]haw*t* isel drei. *M.'s body was recovered at low ebb.*
11 ? Gwa(e)wruδ Eiδyn uδ rhac (Rhyn) vr(i)wei, or *as in am. t.*

   35·12–20, **17**·13–19. *see* VARIANT VERSIONS, p. 104.
A. ueiri, *if pl. of* maer=*stewards*. ? mei*t*in or (g)uerin ni phorthyn *followed by* [trin :] din orthorret (c.) ' Gwerin ' *alias* dengyn *are the natives He*S. *forced into his service. see n.* 33·7. mo-lut *m*-uet : *m* lut mo-uet=*ni* luδ mo*r*[*ed* :]*e*b.
B. meiwyr, *soldiers. no c.,* ? *read*, dengyn. n*y* : ni. see A.
C. trin *no c., for* ? rhuthr rhi·allu=*King (Magnus's) force.*
D. wanting at 17·13. [drui cinneuct.
E. & F. (*c.f. in both*) ? *read*, baran, tebig tan, deryδ ar led, [*for*
G. & H. Diw Mawrth (wy yn rawth) wisg[assant :]yn duδet. *Omit* cein, *fine*, & gwrym, *dun.*
I. guero : chwerw ... eu c*i*t unet : ev triu(e)*r*et.
K. perideint (*no c.*) *Rearranged, the letters spell* dirperent, *wh. c. changes to* dar*p*erynt [eu] ga*l*ch doet *they got ready their enam-*
M. *Thursday their devastation was unquestionable.* [*elled mail.*
N. '*they counted the dead*' *but no c.* ? cal[a]net : ca*r*net(er)= carneδer [a ciu]ry.(veδ)wet.
O. amdyget : ? amd(r)iget, *lying dead all about. no c.*
P. did*u*rnn : didr*w*m [eu] cit [gueith]ret : cītr(ig)et=cy*n*-driged
Q. divwrn, *without slaughter etc. as in* P. [*pristine inhabitants.*
R. laueneu=llavneu, *blades, f.c. for* arveu dur, *steel mail.* rud *read backward*=dur, *wh. rhymes with* sul.
S. [eu] llavneu rud. *amend as in* R. am-[dyc=]dy*rr*et.
T. & U. clun, *meadow, confused with* glin, *tibia* ; penglin=*knee.* gwaedlu*n influenced by* clun. *The* gwaedl*i*n, *flowing blood, should immediately follow the slaughter of Wednesday.* ? *read* Diw Llun hyd law*r* clun, gwartha*l* weled, i.e. *The survivors are seen going over the field of battle, picking up many things, and then selling or exchanging them. What a finished picture of a completed action this line gives.*
V. & W. n*y*s : ne*u*s adrawδ, *no c. for* adroδyn [gododin :] am or*d*in [gwedy :] am luδed [hir]

x. & y. [rac pebyll madawc *no c.*, *perversion for* ?] am ffawd Mynyδawc ban [atcorhet *no c.*, *gloss on*] δymchweled.
z. *no c. and no companion line.*
35·21–36·2 In order to hide the fate of HeS. the text has been perverted and omissions made.   Line 21 is app. a copy of 11·1. *If* disgyn- *is original ? read*, (Os) trwm disgynn*wn* (ys) dwyre(a)v, *If my fall was heavy I shall rise.* see next note.
 22 e cel-eo *sug.* en-cil-io ne cel(av). -fit : (o) fic.   *C. and hist. sug.*, (Mwy, or treis) encili(eis, ni) gel-av, o sîg cyndevig y ryt mi gav.
  b. cyntebic=cyndevic *the former prince*, or *prince leader* of Castell Aber Ll. = HeS., the ' kynd*ilic* of 17·9, 20·10.
  c. *The order of the words app. should be*, guannannon guic med . . . guirth . . . guryt muiham ac hauc guich fodiauc . . . in ham eithin in uoleit ma*p*-u bod a*t*am *i.e.* Guen Vannon gui*t* (=gwyδ) veδ(won o wlad nav)=HeS., *who feasted his followers.*
36·1 (a deil) Gweryd (eil), Gwrhyt mwyhav *i.e. Magnus captures Gweryd's deputy—Cynon.* *cp.* adlyw gogyvurδ gymrat. 37·4.
  b. The gwych ffodawc=Hugh the Fat, e. of Chester who fled in *summer*, wh. was the height of disgrace.
 2 eithin in . . . ? *read*, *i.* eδyw y·moʀ(dwy) madw boʀ aɾav, *ii.* elei yn **w**yleiδ madw vleiδ aɾav. ma*p* bod-*u* : ma*du* boɾ.
 3 *cen*-nin *may be for* teɾuyn, *boundary, border* [*gloss on* Eiδyn]. But ? [cen- *r.b.* = nec =]*uer*-nin *i.e.* gwernyn, *alder swamp. The swamp is there still.*
  b. (yn ol gwleδ) [g]win [weith a] meδw[eith] oeδyn
 4 o ancwyn (*no c.*, *tautological* : rac ffawd Mynyδawg ant (yn) huim=chwim *m.l.*, *gloss on* ɾuth·*rin.*
 5 o goll gur, *no c.*, *gloss on* o δwyn gw(a)r [guneδ, *lords*] Rhyn.
  b. mal taran nev tar(aw)hei yscwydawr (*a paraphrase to disguise the truth*) ; mal taran (Gynt ae) tar(vyn).
 6 rhac rhynnawd (pawb) e*i*thin-*in* : ɾi=ry edyn.   [y·meiδ*in*.
 7 aruireit[h, 12] : arwy*l*eint [y·meitit = ? meinδyδ *an er. for*
  b. ban cr(y)s [cin[e]rein *belongs to* l. 12, *b.*] (Morien) y·midin.
 8 [o] douis : δovid *ni* dowys [y·ny·fin :] δy·vin.
 9 g=chwanauc i δiuin=δiwin, ' *to act quickly.*'
10 [oeδ mor, *reptn.*] yt wane*i* : gwanet (yn·hrin).
11 esgarwyd [alt, *Ir. for* high] gwanar [gurthyn *f.c.* :] gorδin.
12 m. a. i·more (ban grys cynrein (·7, *b*) (ir gware).
13 ni bu cyvarch rac ystre. *cp.* n. 22·22.
  b. gueir : gueiɾ=gweis gui(t)at yng cin[oror : orro=oere=] wyre cat. gweis, *knights, are the* ca͞t *i.e.* cant) cyveillt ar [g]a*t*at [i *n*it =] in ɾit-re [ge : ce=re, & *n*e : ɾe=re].

169

BOOK OF ANEIRIN

36·16 [e] lau[a]naur=llavnawr. [go] duryf=twrv.
 18 [techin *reptn*.] rac eιδin : (g)*or*διn vre [*uir* u(r)i(u)et=]gwyr
  b. (rac) meint (y meδweint) [a] gaffe*t* [lau]. [vriwed *see* am. t.
 19 *trsd.*=o [hanau-c : ha*ṗ* :] ha*l*-awc nid atcoret.
  b. nyawc (l. 21) : nȳawc=ny*m*- (*read backward*)=Mynawc *i.e.*
  (y) Mynawc (yna weled), cui*r*=cwy*ṗ*=cwyn (22) oeδ arnaw
  [*ac* :] oe [ca*n* : ca*ṗ*=] ga*l*-et.
 20 cyndyn [ca*l*c : ca*ſ*s=]câs [drei] pan *d*rin[i]e*t*.
  b. [grιniei, *reptn*.] ni*t* : neu·r atwanei [ri guanei *antcpn*.]
 ry·gwane*t*.   *Note how the scrιbe is ever falsιfying everythιng
 unfavourable to the Franco-Saxons, by turning the affιrmative
 neur into the negative nyt, and car into escar* (22).
 21 [ocδ menych *extension*] Gwedy cwy*m*(p) [i es] car [i] cym·
  *r*wyn(ed), oeδ gwenwyn[h]ig carei [cet :] *g*ed.
37·1 [a] Cyn i olo [a] dan dydwed [daiar] dyrlys-hei [e *t*ar : [i]
  *c*ar=] gar i [*u*ed(iu *reptn.*)e*t* :] *ṗ*edec (or Reged).   *HeS. was
  buried in Shrewsbury Abbey.   see* n. 5·16.
 2 Hu*i* : Hin-*t*-reuit=Hyn*t* *t*rewid c[l *antcpn*.]ai*r* : ca*n* Gynt
   eilwat.   claer-glaer : ? oeδ glaer *g*lyw.
 3 clae*r* [cleu] na : a*ṗ* c*l*ai*r* air uene*r* : claer oit (y) *d*ae*r* a*ṗ*ueina*t*.
  b. se(it)hi*t* [am] su(δi)t sei*s* [*sic* :] dig sa[*c* : *t*=]d.
 4 [go *reptn*.] gymrat. edi*l*-*i* e-diluui=eδyl *r*y·δylywy.
  b. line wanting.   ? as in am. t.
 5 N*y*s : neus adroδ[gododin]yn δyδ ply[i]ghat na bei [cin *antcpn*]
  haval Gint eilwad (l. 2), *cp.* 34·15.
 7 lau*n* : llaw*ṗ* . . . guo-*rut*=goruδ cuδ y mar(i)an.
 8 la*u*n : llan*u* gur le[i]diat=llanw gor·lediad.
  b. lag*u*-en uδat : *l*aug=*r*hawg en(h)uδat.
 9 fta : as [t] dal Vleiδiad, (nid) Bleiδ cyman.
 10 laur : lla*ṗ*u=lla*n*w. *ni bu* g[w]an : ui d(ia)ngan
37·10–12=32·4·5·8·9·10=16·10·11   *The am. t. is the best amal-
  gamation I can suggest of these.   see* VARIANT VERSIONS, p. 106.
 A. *t*ut vwlch : Bylchit [t. h. c. :]caer treisig [haer=] aer B.
 B. *g*o dileit, o dilei*t*h *no rhyme, no sense.   ?* o *g*ilchet.
 C. en wir i[th] (g)elwir [od-g-*u*ur : *d*og ru*n*=] δ*u*g Ryn wared.
   guereit : gueiret=guaret.
 D. *has* ' gverit,' E. F. G. *read* ' weithret,' *mixing* enwir *and* kywir
   in a hopeless way.   see VARIANT VERSIONS, p. 106.
 H. Rector, H. I. K.=Rac-*taf*, L. *root of tef*-ig & pen-*def*-ig. lywyδ-
 wr=rwyvyadur, I. K. L.=*trans. of* rector. *no c.* ? Rector, (nar
 pob or), mur pob ciwed, *Rector, lord of every land, etc.   For*
 nar, ? *read,* llyw (*upsets c.*), rhwyv, rhi, glyw, nav, ner, &c.

MISCELLANEOUS NOTES

H. & I. kyvjcith, i.e. *native, gloss on* kiwet, K. *the true reading.*
L. catuilet=' Ir. *caithmhilaedh*, battle champion, hero.' Powel.
M. merin a madyen=meryn mab madyeith, N. : Mori(e)n am Hadien mad yt[h] anet. mad-yen, -yeith, *beneficence.*
13 Kyvarvu-āt ar (vuδ h)erw, dyleidiad[lu :] hu (ae bleid veδw).
14 hero : meto=meδw. ac=ae. ac i hepo : ar i [h]enw.
  b. ni bu [h]elw ciwed [guec :] gwyt(h) chwerw.
15 gniffint : cnifynt gwehilion [ar e helo :] avlerw.
17 let [un ero] i.e. (gwys) let(w), *a narrow furrow*.
  b. li-uir *read both ways*=if lluir=ys llwyr.
18 echassav : e gua(e)sav. *cp.* gueu- : guehilon, l.15.
19 [auet :] a ue(le)i [ac] : oe eithav . . . llaryhav.
20 o heit : olieit, *followers* [meirch] yng·aeav.
21 gorthor[e] (gledr) [brein du : bein dur=]bangor.
  b. ar gaer vur (gyrchei) cyn y bei (r)ev orthur, *or* ? ef : en (gw)erthyr, *within the fortification.*
22 cuin uerthig : tuin merthig, *the exhausted hillock.*
  b. difur : ? oeδ difur, *that was defenceless.*
  c. [ig reptn.] kynnor guernoc=*at the entry of the alder swamp, but as the line of defence*, (*the trench is still there*), *ran between* (rug ·21) *the hillock and the swampy ground ? read*, (ae) [gynnor : gyuuor=] gyv·or g., *adjoining swampy or alder-growing ground.*
23 guaurdur : gwant δur.
38·1–8, VARIANT VERSION *of* 17·1–5·11·12, *see p.* 101.
A. (*c.f.*) Erδyled[am] canu (clod) i Gynon.
B. (*m.l., no c.*) [-awc] claer : clod. orchyrδon : ? gorchorδion chiefs. *cp.* gorgorδ, Tal. 55·11. ? gosgorδion.
C. cig *read backwards*=gīt=Gint uereu ni(s) [guant-h *gloss on*] tereu (lyw caer gronn)=Cynon.
D. *second line wanting in variant version.*
E. trs. order. [ac] bu [divant *gloss on*] leith cyn [dileit :] dyrreith (i dir) Aeron. *This line should follow* L.
F. (*no c.*) " And after the ' orchyrδon ' returned, they fill " (Aeron). *But as* "only one returned" *to Aeron, it could not be said to be filled.* Avon=Menei *to which they came to return no more.* ? Dy·leith ni δyrreith, lleinw cyrff avon.
G. *m.l., c.f.* (b)riw[esit i loffen : lovlen :] loyfen=llwyven. [briw *gloss for*] dyrr ar benn eryron llwyd. *This line has no companion to form a couplet.* ? *Interpolation.*
H. [dim :] dyor [cones=torres reptn.] lovl : loyfen=llwyven.

I. e*n* an*u*ıt : e*u* a*u*wyt=eu (h)a*b*wy[d], *their dead bodies. Flanked by vowels* b *often* = v, (u) *and* vice versa.

K. goreu vwyd, *provides food.* c. sug., a vu vwyd ysglyvion.

L. trs. order. Mar*l*hawt Myny*dd*awg, (llyw**ydd**) mâon. *This line should come before E.* 'les' *belongs to* N.

M. For mynawc *read* marthawd *etc. as in L.*

N. e*m d*odes : de*m*-=di*v*odes [itu] : eu harles g. g.

O. no variant version.

P., Q. c.f. in both. text combined in am. t.

R. c.f., m. short, text perverted. guenint lle*δ*int, *active for passive verbs.* ? *read,* gwy*δ*ıd athrig*ı*d llurygogion. *The* eurdorchogion *were the afflicted.* feiu [*looks as if begun as* fei*p*chogion :] fuie=lure(g)ogion.

S. no variant version.

T. oe*δ* ech eu tymhyr, *they were out of their provinces,* (lit. *temporalities*). canaon, *whelps, gloss on* Herwyr. *A paraphrase for* Herwyr oe tymhyr oe*δ* treis(wyr Mon).

U. Lovers of scandal, dressed in fine purple, should luxuriate in this couplet. Though c., Hist., and fact be absent, what of that? The less the truth the greater the sting. Here we see falsehood in the making. The prep. ech, *Lat.* ex *becomes* (m)e(r)ch, *daughter;* eu temhyr, *their provinces, become* Eutem hyr= Eutam=Eudaf hir; treis(wyr) *is clipped into* treis, *and* canaon, *whelps, assume the name of* Gwen Vannan=Magnus *who is thus accused of rape !!* ech *does* **not** *mean* 'merch' *scribes & Dictionaries notwithstanding.*

V. oe*δ* ... *rest of line wanting.*

W. oe*δ* porffor gwisgyad [*ur* d*ir* :] dur amdrychion *purple was the steel mail of the slain. no c., ? read,* a Phorffor oe*δ* gwi[s]g= gw**ych** [-ya-] *δ*or amdrychion.

X. no c., ? read, odid y(porth)id (y)m·harth Vrython. *Note that the mutated* 'Vrython' *is a place-name here.* cp. BRETTON *on the left of the Dee in the Lache country in the hundred of Broxton. Ormerod mentions a* Caer Brithon *under the barons of of Kinderton.* cp. 5·22, 6·2.

Y. c.f., sense not obvious. diw- *may*=diu=dinarth.

Z. c.f., ? read, (ir Rhyn) a *δ*o*δ*yn well no Chynon [g]o-dodin : a *δ*o*δ*yn (o) [*wr*=] *or* bell.

38·9-14=**16**·13-16. *see* VARIANT VERSIONS, p. 101.

A. Er*δ*yled [-am, -awc. [caf-am, caff-at :] cahet *from* cael, *of the same meaning as* caffael.

MISCELLANEOUS NOTES

B. *trsd.*=ri wnaeth [b.] am gatraeth anvad vrithred (ar) gedwyr (Redeg a Mon δengyn). *cp.* 3·5 ; n. 35·12. *About Battle strand terrible the confusion the King wrought upon the warriors of R. and the villeins of Mon.* guanaid ? =' gunai(th) anuad,' telescoped.
C. *Line missing all but the word* cetwyr.
D. Brit *gue* : ueg=uec=wys=Brit(h)wys [a] guiar[ad :](wys) sathar sengyn. sanget. sēgīt, *trsd.*=sengynt. sanget.
E. sanget *v. repeated. Context sug.,* ' Ymlid ' gui[d=t : c=]s=wŷs. *wit, has been taken for a Pictish proper name but the* ' guid ' *of the older text* (38·11) *makes such interpretation impossible.*
F. Dial am [da*l*meδ :] da*r*veδ. (*f*). *b*ual : dial E.
G. o : (gorug) galaneδ [cīuei=]cyn *b*ei (en)·hrigeδ.
I. nis ad[ɲaud=] u*n*awd=ad*wn*awd.
K. *trsd.*=wedy cad gyffro, *after the commotion of war.* cadgyffro *has been mistakenly taken as a proper name.*
L. ceuei : c ɲeī=cynrein. (*b.*) ketbei, *perversion.*
M. au(r)=awr [ci*u*i, ke*u*i=] cyni.
The readings of F. H. L. *expose the scribe's unreliability.*

15 a-dar *m.l. for* a da [am :] onn (bar), [edis :] oδis [mic-as :] mig(n)-a*t* (*note rhyme*), *below the swamp.* ⌈(tal) a rwygat.

16 *e* deuu*n*iat=o δyvwɲiat E-*i*-thu*n*at=Ē ethɲinat a ruhicat : *b.* ef=(Hu) gui*s*gu-f-aur : gui*g*us=gwyδws *l*awr.

17 [e] de[i]uin[ieit] bal-lauc=dewin balawc.

18 tal gellauc cat *This may be read* (*a.*) tat llad cellawg, *a blessed hermit father* (or *friend,* ca*r*) ; *b.* tat ta[l]-gellawg, *a father* (or *friend*) *with a double chin.* (a δarogan), *vaticinates.*
b. tri dyδ eng=ing[iri]awl. e*r*linau*t* gaur . . arwynaul : gawr arwynawl *et er-* =yδ erlyna*n*t.

19 ar[th] *ar* : aɲoc=añoc gui-*g*i-at=gwy-*chr*-at. *This word occurs also at* 11·18, gnawt gwy-*chn*-a[w]t=gwy-*ch*ɲ-*at* ; *and at* 24·20, gnaut guy-*chl*-a[u]t=gwy-*chr*-at. *Here we have* g=*ch* ; i. n. l.=*r.* *The rhyme settles the final syll. as* -at, *not* -awt.

20 ri[allu] er-iglu*n*-at : ergli-*uu*=erglywad.
b. hir [lu *antcpn. of* bu] cent bu gipno *trs. into* hir (o) gipno cyn*n* bu (dan do) ;

21 ma*b* : madw wenn [gāt :] ganad, *was sung—the hero that is still has been praised.*

21–22 *A fragment of two lines which shows that the MS. is 'incomplete. This is most unfortunate as we get the older text more and more in the second part. see* 17·6–9.

CORRECTIONS.

INTRODUCTION, p. *xl*. In continuation of note 28 read :

When Tristan went to the Irish Queen to be healed she "asked his name. Lady, my name is Tantris . . . And as the Queen's daughter thought, suddenly it was as if she saw the name before her, *Tan-tris, Tris-tan*, and she knew the one was but the other *read backwards*." See *Gottfried von Strassburg's Tristan and Iseult*, written circa 1210.

64·3   for 'gwasceryn' read 'gwesceryn.'

note 2·15 Mab botgat, (m.l., no. c.) : ? *i*. Mab Bargat=Bargod, *a son of the Border*. cp. Bargat, Bargod-varδ, *a border bard*, wh. Tal. was.   *ii.* [mab *r.b.*=] Ban bor cad *when the war lord*. If 'Bargat,' or 'Bor cat' *be right c.* shows that 'gwnaeth gwynnieith' *is a paraphrase for* δiffeith wlad [gwreith e *l*aw :] wr(th d)eith*i*aw.   *iii.* Mab *Roger* gwynnieith wnel w. d.   *iv.* Vu leith wnaeth wynnieith w. d.   Mab Bargod, Mab Roger, Por cad, & 'Vu leith,' all=HeS.

note 2·16. ke*t el*-wyn*t* e lanneu : ky*r*ch e(u) gwyn*n* lanneu e [benydyaw, *perversion* :] anreithaw. See Gir. Camb. ITINERARY cap. vii., Ll., 409.

note 4·17 *add*—? if 'diedyrn' is not for 'di·dëyrn ?

GENERAL INDEX

Ab', ab, ap=Aber, aper, *xxxix*.
Aber, kynnif 17·21, gynnu 18·1=94; aer : aber a dan (y gaer) 5·12 =48; ebyr 1·17=4.
Aber Gwyngregyn, *xxiv*. [*xxxix*.
Aber Lleinog, *v*., *xxii*., *xxiv*., *xxvii*.,
abwy, abwyd. see gwenabwy.
Additamenta in *Harl.* MS. 3859, *vii–viii.*, *xli.*
adebon 26·8·16·17=aδevon 80.
adon 15·4=84, (26·22=98).
adon [*wy*=*vy*] 13·19, 30·12=68.
aduaon 20·6=28 ; *cp*. canaon.
ad- see at- [38·7*
aedan, ac, 9·7=ar adan 34.
aergi 19·12=aerlyw 66 ; aergwn 3·5=70.
aer *dywys* 18·15=aer*lyw* 36.
cp. 19·12. *Cynon*.
Aeron, *xvi*., *xxii*., *xxiv*., 6·2=[16]; 6·21=30 ; 17·9=28 ; 20·10= [28] ; 38·2=82 ; 6·1=Ceintyon 16 ; 2=marro *i.e.* in aeron 1·9* ; 84=urython 17·5, 38·8.*
aervre 7·11=6.
aes 17·6=28.
affrei 6·10=abret 32.
alarch, deu, 6=dan eleirch 7·16 ; eleirch 33·15=10. [35·21*=80.
alauoeδ 11·1 = alarchawr 20 ;
Aled *xvi*., 22·3, 24·1=90.
alltud 74=olut 12·5.
alltut marchauc 31·21*=52.
amhat 33·7=16 ; 10=sawl 30·18. *cp*. 16·13, 38·10, 33·7.
amot 1·17=aruot 4 ; amodet 35·16
amrysson 28·7·13·17. [=38.
amws 20=gorwyδ gwareus 11·4.
Amwythig (5·16)=48, [*cp*. aruul.

anant 17·7=28 ; 22·6, 24·4=90.
anaw 20·10=28.
ancwyn 33·11=10 ; a. Mynyδawg
anδyledawr 4·15=72. [36·4=80.
Aneirin, *xi*., 1·1, 12·12*=aneir im 78, *xxxviii*., *xliii*. [δin 64.
Aneirin 14·7=Godoδin 23·14 : gor-(ang)hyvieith 26·12=80.
angor 32·2·7·11=56.
Anhon 23·16=gwen Vannon 54.
(ar erch *Heleδ*) 25·7*=Arllech-weδ 24. *cp*. 13·4=54 c.
arbennawr 4·14=72.
arδerchawg varchawg 14·10=64 16·18=74.
Argoedwys 21·12=86.
Arllechweδ, 13,c =54 ; 25·7=24.
Arth (10·6)=36 ; 16·7=56 ; 38·19 =gawr 18.
arthur 37·21=? garth(v)ur, 82.
Artro, *xvi*,. *xxvi*., 13·2=52 ; 32·1*
arveu dur 9·7=34. [=52.
Arvon, *xvi*., 34·5=36 ? *read*, ar
ar*u*ul 31·6=? am*u*l 96. [Von.
arwr y dwy ysgwyd 7·10*=6.
aseth 82=cleδyf 20·14. [28.
asgwrn=ys chwyrn 20·6 : ar hynn
athryc-hant 5·18=athricant 16.
athrychan*t* 31·1=athrychau*r* 10.
athrychant 6·19=30. see Try-chant. [*standing of* 28·1.
athrychant 28·10*. *scr*. *misunder-*
atre 16·4=20.
atveillyawc 10·10=36 ; 15·22=
atvydic 28=20·6*. [14 ; 26·4=24.
aval . . . avall 26·8=80.
avon 17·2=aeron 38·2=82.
avon (Menei) 26·20=98.
axa 11·21,* Saxa 34·15=62.

baeδ coed (i.e. Gr. ap Rys) 8·20=
baeδ dig oeδ Bleiδig 31·4=96. [88.
baläod 22·12=? cathod 90.
bann. *see* Vann.
bangori 58=vanncarw 13·11.
barδ 28·13*; 32·15 = bar*th* 58.
  pl. beirδ 7·14=6.
Barδ Llycheu 30=28·4*
Bargodıon 58=barr 13·12; 98=
  uodogion 26·22.
Barvawr 24·12·17=40. *HeS.*
Basingwerk Abbey, *xi.*
bedyδ 3·21=70.
*be*din : *mi*din 1·18=4; 2·19=68;
  16·7=56; 19·4*=66; 32·3·8·13
  =56; gwyδ-midin 19·12=66;
  g.-meirch: midin 27·16=42.
bedin 22·4=bid in 90; 3·22=
  blin 72; 25·21=din 22; ve*d*in
  21·6=? we*r*in 60, *cp.* 12·6.
beδin 10·8=36, 10·21*=20; 12·21
  =52; 15·5=84; 21·3·6=58, 60;
  12·6=*werin 74; rwng dwy
  veδin 14·9=64; rwg dwy vyδin
  10·21=20.
being, 12·8=82; 33·3=8.
beis 29·15=dy·wyn veis yghynnor
  46; (v)eis 7·8=32; e·*m*eis 18·18
  =36; (33·12)=10.
bela 16·3=20.
Beli bloeδvawr 11·2=20. *HeS.*
Bernicia, *xix-xx., xxxvii.*
bin, Llwch, 14·5*=64.
biw 11·2*=20.
Blaen claer eching gaer 5·1=72.
Blaen Porphor 5·4=72. *HeS.*
Blaen (llueδ=Owein) 5·2=72.
Blaen Gwyneδ 6·12=32. *Penmon.*
(Blaen) Lloegir wehelyth deithawg, *xl.* [cangen, wialen.
blaenwyδ 30·1 = 46. *cp.* asen,
Bleiδ caeawg 1·22=Noble Lupus,
  4; 37·9=100; (18·12)=94;
  (29·12)=44; 24=uδ 25·7.
bleiδ : blawδ 25·10=22; *visage*,
  32·12=56.

bleiδ . . . prenn 11·17, 24·19=
  Bleiδ*ic* benn 40. *HeS.*
Bleiδic *mab eli* 31·4=*i leid elei*
  96. *HeS.*
Bleiδiat 37·9=100; 25·10=? lcıδ-
  iat 22. *HeS.*
Bleiδyan 7·17=6. *HeS.*
(Bleiδieit 32)=6·10; cat vleiδyeu
  27·22=42.
Bleiδgi 31·11 = hoewgir 7·9*=
  hoew Ri 32. *Magnus.*
Blwchbard *viii.*, note *n. see*
  Llwchvarδ. [*HeC.*
bod-u, map 36·2*=madw bo*r* 80.
Botgat, mab, 2·15*=mab Bargod
  68, 174. *HeS.* [*xviii.*
Bradley, Dr. *Henry,* on *Otadinoi,*
Bratwen 11·14·19=40; 13·20,
  30·13=68. *Broken hero*=HeS.
Bre, gweis 17·22=94; gwarth-
  19·12=66; rhwyv 30·7=68;
  gwlat 30·10=68, racvre 15·10=
  12; rac eiδin vre 36·18*=62;
  see vre, gweryt.
breichir 13·16=20.
breichyawr 6·16, breichyaul 31·17
  =breithawdl 18, 76.
breint gorllin 26·2=24.
breint mab Bleiδgi 31·11=greit
  uab hoewgir 7·9*=32.
breithell 1·19=draethell 4; 24·18*
  =40; 30·16=Rhyn 10.
breithyell 9·15*=lleyth 34; 4·16*
  = Gwraeth *veif* 12; 28·1 =
  ? brei*c*hyell, *armlet,* 30.
Brenneych 3·6=70; Brennych
  2·8=4; Brēych 20·5 & Vrych
  23·9 = 28; *xvi.* Brēeych dut
  bost 25·21=52, *xix-xx.*
breych 12·21=52.
Brych [23·9], 13·11=Brithion 58.
Bryn Edwin, *xliii.*
Brynn hydwn, *xvi.,* 9·1=88; b.
  cyngrwn 70 = maen gwynngwn
  3·9, (cp. ca*er* gyngrwn 5·22=
  16); brin butucre 36·14*=60.

GENERAL INDEX

Brython 34·5 = Brithion 36.
Brython, o, 6·1·2* = 16 ; o barth urython 17·5, 38·8 = 84.
Bual lled 34·13 = 62.   HeC.
bual 5·9 = 48 ; buelin 12·11 = 78, 26·13 = 80.
bubon 35·5 = bu bor 38.
buδvan 7·17 = kuδ van 6.
buδugre 15·10 = 12 ; butulee 36·14* = 60.
bun benn 18·13 = Rhi 96.
bur 26·6* = 26.
bwyllyat 4·1 = bwyat 72.
byδin, dwy, 10·21, 14·9. see beδin.
byδinawr 2·6 = δywanawr 4 ; 4·16 = a gyrch lawr 72 ; 9·19 = vleiδ-awr 34 ; 10·14 = liwedawr 18.
byrn 8·4 = 8.
byrr vlyneδ 2·14 = 68.
bysseδ 13·11 = 58.
byt 19·2* = byrr (gam) 28,

cad gyffro = cyffro cad 16·15, 38·13
cadreith 28·3 = reith 30.   [= 74.
cadveirch 19·11 = 66.
Cadwgan = Tevic 8·8 = gwanar 84 ; son of Gwyδneu 8·11 = 84.
Caeawg Vleiδ 1·22 = 4.   HeC.
Caeawg Vynyδawg 1·10 = 2, 1·16, 2·5 = 4.   HeS.
caer 5·1 = 72 ; 28·18 = 44 ; 11·20, 34·11 = 62 ; c. gyngrwn, xvi., xxv., 5·22* = 16 ; (caer gronn 38·1) = 82 ; c. vur 37·21 = 82 ; c. wys 13·5 = 54 Q ; ar vann caereu 26·3 = 26. cp. 27·15, 32·7.
Caer lleon, xxiii.   [90.
calan, diw 7·20 = 6 ; 22·6, 24·4 = calaneδ 17·16, 31·6 = carneδer 38.
calc drei 36·20* = 62.
calch 23·4 = 8 ; 28·18 = calch claer 44 ; calch doet 17·15*
callon ehelaeth 34·21 = dragon y dalaeth 78.
camp. camhawn 31·5 = 96 ; camhwrawg darw 25·13 = 24.

canaon 38·7 = 84.
cangen 13·5 = 54 ; 18·7 = 94.
cann (adj.) 31·6.
cann calan 22·6 = calan gant (verb)
cann llucyr 27·3 = 96.   [90.
cȧn wr 31·20* = ? coρ rw(y) 52.
cann wr 12·7 = 82.
cant. aeth canwyr i gatraeth 34·20 = 78 ; cant o deyrneδ 34·19 = 76 ; rac cant ev gwant 18·2 = 94 ; 36·8 = 60 ; yngwyδ cant 23·10 (cp. 14·2 = 64) ; cant en divant 2·8 = 4 ; can(t) llewes 19·17 = 66 ; namen un gwr o gant 1·15 = 2 ; 17·20 = 94.
cant 24·4.
canthuδ 30·22 = 10.
caradawc (adj.) 8·20 = cadr 88 ; 10·6* = waredawc 36 ;
Caradawc 9·5 = Cradawc 34.
caradwy 8·12·15 = 84, 88.
carchar 12·16 = 52 ; cp. ty deyerin 12·10 = 52.   [98.
carn gaffon 26·21 = c. gwaewffon
carrec vyr vawr yng·hynhadvan 10·3 = Carreg Cynhadvan, xvi., xxv., 36.
casnar 27·7 = 98 ; kysnar 5·20 = 16. cp. xxvii., n. 23. Magnus
caṯki, deu, 6·21 = deu gaŗ ŗhi 30. Ow. and Uchtryd.
caṯlew 8·2 = caŗ ṯew = 8. cp. tut leo.   Hugh the Fat.
catlew 28·3 = 30.
catnant 28·3* = 30.
caṯpwll 25·15* = ŗacpwll 24.
catraeth, aeth 2·21 = 70, 4·2·10 = 72, 3·3·10·14·19 = 70 ; 6·17 = 30, 9·16 = 34, 17·3, 38·5 = 84, 34·20 = 76 ; aethant 28·1 = 30 ; δaeth 4·10 = 72 ; crysswys 4·4 = 42 ; cynhen 8·1 = 6 ; breithyell 4·16 = 12, 9·16 = 34, 28·1 = 30 ; rac 15·17 = 14, 33·22 = 12 ; e 14·8 = 64, 28·12 ; am 16·13 = 74, 38·10 = 74 ; o, 9·1 = 88, 12·12 =

78 ; yg 20·11=82 ; gwyr 26·5= 26 ; c. gochre 19·11=66 ; gwr (δ)aeth i gatraeth . . y·Mordrei 4·10·15=72 ; cynhen xvii., xix., xxv.
Catterick, xvii., xix.
catvan 27·20.
cat Vannan 1·21*=c(or) advan 4 ; car 16·5 = 20, 11·7 = (Mon a) mannan 20 ; tra : car Manon 29·6=44. see Guannannon & Mannan.
catuilet 16·11.
catvleiδyeu 27·22=42.   [=90.
catvoryon 22·4=gwychrolion 24·2
cavall 35·1=78.
kedyr(n) cat 31·8=30.   [82.
Keid-yaw, mab, 20·15=Mordrei
Kein guodeo 31·12*=76.
Keint, xvi., xxiv. Kein mur 29·12 =44; penn (K.) 12·8=82; Kein-(u)as 32·20=76; Ceinnyon wledic 10·12=36.   Ow. ap Edwin.
Kein(t) gerδawr 9·21=34 ; K. (etmygyδ) 4·8=42. Llwchvarδ.
Ceinnyon 19·6=66 ; 26·21=98; (6·1=16); C. wledig 10·12=36; Eurgeinyon 34·5=36.
keirw, van- 13·11=Vann kewri 58.
keisyadon 26·15=treisadon 80.
(ceith=) amhad, xc., 33·7=16.
kelein 10·2=34 ; 24·14=40 ; k. wenn 13·19=68.
kelin, gwaewawr, 32·18=74.
(Kelynawg 31·20=52).
kemre 32·15=kymmer 58.
ken(drag)on 6·21=30.
keneu vab Llywarch 12·17=Kenwrig vad devig 52.   [28.
kenevin : kenvein Redegein 20·3=
kennin 5·11=cevnyn 48 ; 36·3= ? wernyn 80. cp. 16·9.
Kenan, Kenon. see Cynon.
kenh-an lew 29·12=kenlliv ap-(naw) 44.
kenon 10·1=kynran 34 ? 6·21=30.

kerδ 84=cein 8·9; 28·14; k. amrysson 28·9·17; 27·10*=coed 98. pl. kyrδ 8·13=88 ; 27·12=42.
kerδawr 2·12=4; 3·16=70; 9·21= 34. pl. kerδoryon 7·20=cerδor-(cerδenhin 12·12=78).   [iaeth 6.
kerδet 33·21=12.
keredic 8·12=car eiδic 84. O. ap Cadwgan.   [88.
Keredic 8·15=Griffyδ (ap Rys)
ketwyr 14·7·12·17·20=64 ; 16·13, cetwir 38·10=74.   [13·11.
cewri 54=keui 13·6; 58=keirw
Chester, earldom & See of, xx. see Hu Vras.
chwegrwn maban i Gynan 3·9= 70.   O. ap Edwin.
chwerthin 10·18=Cyvrenhin 20.
ki. aergi 19·12*=66; aergwn 3·5= 70; catki 6·21=30; erthgi 4·15 =erchei 72.   [xliii.
Kian=Kinan 3·9=70, 31·22=52, kilyδ 4·9=42 ; 24·7=90.
cinim 36·12=60. see cynniv.
Cinon 38·1=82. see Cynon.
Cint, cin, cit, cig, kynt, kynh. see Gynt.
cintebic 35·21=cyndevic 80. see kyndilic.
cipno 16·15, 38·13=74 ; 38·20=
ciwet 7·7=cleu 30.   [18.
clas uffin 20·13=clas y ffin 82.
clawδ gwernin 16·9=clawr g. 56.
clawδ Offa, xix.
clawr clas 5·15=48.
cleδ, cam 25·4=cam goleδ 26.
cledyf 8·11=88; 10·3=36; 12·16= 52; 20·14=82 ; 12·20=cleδ 52, 35·2=cleδ 78; 29·13=cledyr 46.
(cledr) 37·20=82.
clotuan 32·21=74.
Clut, xxi–xxii.
Clynog, xxii., xxv.
Klytno, 15·8=Klyton 84; Clytno Eiδin xxi–xxii = Cluton Eiδin xxiii. Cleton-us in Geoff.

GENERAL INDEX

coed gwyllion 27·10*=98
? *witch-elms*, Llwyvenyδ.
coel, ma*b* 28·4=? mal ceith 30.
coel verth 20·2, 23·6=28.
Coleselt, *xvi.*, *xliii*. [22·16.
Conwy *xvi.*, 33·19=10; 92=Corwg
cordirot 12·3=cor di*v*rot 72.
corn kuhelyn 26·13=cyrn buelyn
kuhelyn 26·13=buelyn 80. [80
cun Gogleδ 46=Gogleδ *r*un 29·20.
c*u*n Goδeu 76=*K*ein Guodeo
   31·12*   HeS.
cunet 38·12, 16·19=cuneδ 74 ;
   36·5=80.   HeC. and HeS.
cunin 78=? ronin 12·10.   HeC.
kunyn 30·21*=dragon 10   HeS.
Cwnlleith, *xxiii.*, 15·9·16=Cyn-
   lleith 12, 14.   [5·16=48.
kwr 13·11=côr 58 ; ? gwr : côr
Cynan, *xxv–xxvi.*, 52, 70=*K*ian
kynan 26·2=canav 24. [31·22, 3·9.
cydywal 6·5=gydvaeth 32,
Kynδelw, *xxiii.*
Kyn-dilic 20·10 = Cyn-defic 28 ;
   17·9=cynδragon 28 ; cintebic
   35·21=cyndevic 80.   see tebic.
*** *As proper name, see the
   Extent of Denbigh.*   [74.
kyndor, yng, 32·17=dyrreith drei
cynghaneδ=*consonance*, *xiv.*, n. 7.
cynhen [cat] traeth 8·1=6 ; 34=
   catraeth 9·16; 94=gangen 18·9;
   (82=12·7).
cynhorawc 1·22=4 ; 1·10, 2·5=
   Mynyδawg 2, 4.
ky[h]uran 32·21=im rann 76.
kynlas 29·14=cyn llas 46.
Cynlleit*h*, *xxiii.*   [72.
kynniv-yn 12·3=yn kynniv clod
cyngrwn 5·22=16. *see* Caer G.
Cynon, *nom de guerre* of Owein
   ap Edwin who with Uchtryd,
   his brother, led the expedition
   of 1098 against Gr. ap Kynan.
   Cinon 38·1=82 ; Kenon 38·9=
   84 ; 6·1=16 ; 6·21=30 ; 26·2=
   24 ; Cynon 6·3=16 ; (10·6)=36;
   10·12=36 ; 10·15=18 ; 15·3=
   84; 34·6=36; *K*enan 29·12=44
   taken, deil 36·1=80, cymrat
   37·4=62; reverses his arms.
   see Ow. ap *E*dwin & *xxi–xxii*.
kynon : kuynan 28·3=30.
cynran 2·6, 8·15 ; cynrein 6·1,
   7·15, 15·11.
Kynri 6·1*=*U*chtryd 16.
cynvan 9·6=cwynvanan 34.
Kynvelyn, gorchan, 27·13=42 ;
   gwarchan 27·13·17=42, 28·6=
   30 ; K. gasnar 27·7=98; cadeu
   K., 27·7 = *b*adeu gelyn = 98 ;
   K., gwr wneδyw Gwyneδ i wlad
   27·14=42   =*Magnus.*
cynwa*l* 13·15=cynwa*n* 20.
cynweis 29·14=46 ; -was 31·16=
Kynwric, *xxv.*   [76.
kynwyt 25·15 = ? cyn*b*ryd 24 ;
   kywyt 18·7=cynwyd 94.
cyrδ Kynvelyn 28·6=30.
cyrn (hir)las 25·19=22 ; *see* corn.
cyrn, cam 25·4=cam drin 26.
kysnar 5·20 ; *biform of* casnar, *q.v.*
cyvarch, ni bu, 36·13=60.
cyveδ mawr 7·6=30.
Kyveili*n* na*r* 29·2=44.   HeC.
   see cyvrenhin.
kyueillt 1·7=2 ; 3·7=70.
kyueill*y*aur 29·7=k. gawr 44. HeC.
Cyvlwch 26=26·3, *xliii*.   Keint.
kyv*r*eith 26·1=kyvieith 24 ; kyu-
   yeith 37·12=58.
cyvlavan 9·22=34.
cyuoedyon 5·14=48.
cyvran benn 11·12=38.   HeS.
ky*w*reint 17·6=cyvreint 28 ; kyw-
   renhin 12·13=78 ; 14·12=64
   ky*w*rennin 14·7=64, *xxii.*; kywrennin 18·7=cynben 94. *see*
   10·18=20.   HeS.
Kyvwlch 26·3 = Cyvlwch 26.
Cyvwlch hir 4·21*
kywlat 1·16=2 ; 31·18=52.

dhaly dhaly 22·15* = 90.
dar 30·4 = 46 ; 38·15 = 18 ; *cp*.
  gwäell vael derw 30·6 = 46.
David ap Owein Gwyneδ, *xix*.
Deheu 21·15 = 86 ; o barth D.
  8·8 = 84.
Deivr dır, *xix–xx*.   *Deira*.
Deivyr diuerogyon 6·2* = 16 ;
  gwyr Deivyr a Brynneich 2·7
  = 4. *see xvi., xix*.
dengyn 3·5 = 70 ; (4·2) = 72 ; (30·19)
  = 10 ; (33·14) = 10 ; (38·11) = 74.
deon 33·5 = 16.   [58, 38.
deor 32·2·7–12, 35·8 = dewr 56,
Derwennyδ, rayadyr, *xvi*., 22·19*
  = 92.   ? *Ter- q.v.*
eu deyrn vaon 5·22 = 16 ; deu
  gatki 6·21* = 30 ; deu ebyr
  28·18* = 44. [dyhewyd 38, 40.
deudec 11·14 ; deheuec 24·15·21 =
dewin balawc 38·17 = 18.
di·eδyrn 4·17 = ? di·dëyrn 12.
Dievyl duon, *xxvi*., n. 23.
Dilin 14·13 = *Du*lyn 64. *cp*. d*u*w,
  diw 17·14·15.
dilin, dyδ 12·13 = 78.
dilin 14·16 = ? diflin 64.
dilyw 3·6 = 70.
dillat 33·8 = defic gwlat 16.
din drei 12·5 = ? din (Mor)drei 72.
din Eiδin barth 33·5 = Eiδyn ystrad 16.
dindywyt 13·7, 23·19, 34·9 = di*n*-
  dynwyt 54.
di*n*ogat 22·12* = di*uo*dat 90.
din*ul* 19·12 = din*ift*(ir) 66.
diryeit 32·17 = 74.
diu, diwMerchyr, Gwener, Sadwrn,
  Sul, Llun, divyeu 17·14–15, diu
  & d*u*wMawrth 17·14 & 35·14–18
Diwg 22· 16 = 90.   [= 38.
dragon 7·2·22 = 6, 78 = callon ehelaeth 34·21.   *HeS*.
dhreic, ruδ 29·7 = 44.
Domesday Survey *xxi–ii*., *xliii*.
drwch 22·7? = Wchdr(yt) 90.

du tigirn, vii–viii., n. *u*., & *xli*.
dwy vyδin 10·21 = 20 ; 14·9 = 64.
dwy ysgwyd 7·10* = 6.
Dwyw -e*ı* yd 14·3*, 23·11* =
  Dwyv Eryr 64.
drych 24·18 = 40 ; (20·5) = 28. *cp*.
  dyrch : drych 12·4 = 72 ; drych
  draed ffo 13·2 = 52.
dyvel 27·3 = 96 (cpd. of *dy* & *bel*).
Dyvrdwy, *xix*. see Dyvyr.
Dyvynwal 20·5,* 23·9 = 28 ; Dyv*n*-
  wall 18·11* = 94 ; *xl*., n. 32.

ebyr 28·18 = e(v) *d*yr 44.
Edernion, *xxiii*.
eδil 37·4 = eδyl 62.
eδystrawr 5·4 = 72.
*E*dwin, mab 20·14 = 82 ; meib
  Godebog 4·18* = 12.
eidef 21·2 = orδeu 88.
Eiδi*l*yaun 34·8 = Eiδy*n*ion 54.
Eiδin, uδ 35·11 = 38 ; or 29·12 =
  44 ; vre 36·18* = 62 ; meδ *E*.,
  33·17 = meδ ei*δ*yn 10 ; *E*ı*δ*yn,
  rac 19·15 = 66 ; drych E., 24·18 =
  E. benn 40 ; *E*. eurwychawg
  5·18 = 16 ; gwyr E., 62 = (37·5) ;
  E. gaer 27·15 = [42] ; E. ysgor
  4·5 = 42 ; cynted eiδyn 5·9 = 48 ;
  din Eidin barth 33·5 = ystrad
  16 ; *xvi*., *xxi–xxiii*.
Eidol 15·10* = ? Roger 12 ; 17·7* =
eiδol 18·12 = 94.   [[28].
eil gweith 22·3, eil with 24·1 =
  eil *K*eint 90 ; eil 25·8 = ? Cynon
  26 ; eil Nwython 20·4, eir N.
  23·7 = 28.
ei*l* 27·7 = ei*ſ* 98 ; ei*l* nedig 16·9 =
  e*ſi*ged 58 ; 20·17 = a*ſ* 76 ; *eil* clot
  20·13 = a*r*glod 82 ; eil 10·6 = fu
  36.
eillt 32·19* = 74 ; eillt . . . Gwyneδ
  19·1 = 28.
Eingylyaun, *xvi*., *xxv*., 27·1 = 96.
eissyllut alltut marchawc 31·21 =
  52. *cp*. essyllut 12·14 = 52.

GENERAL INDEX

eithinin 36·2=eðyw yn 80 ; 36·6
=ry·edyn 80 ; eithın-yn 27·17
=yn eithyn 42 ; 10·18·22, 14·10
=eðyw 20, 64.
Eivyonyð 25·7=henevyð 26.
eleırch 33·15=10. see alarch.
elfin 10·18=leſın, levin, rewin 20.
eli 31·4=i leid eleı 96   cp. mab bleiðgi.
Elidyr Sais, *xix*.
Eluet, *xvi.*, *xix.*, 34·3=Elvet 12.
emis 26·13=eſnis=evnys=80.
enaffed 19·9*=henaſieid 66.
enouant wyr 17·9=wy c(w)ynoveint 28.
enys (Mannan) 27·16=42.
(erch Heleð 25·7)=24 ; 54.
erthgi 4·15=erchei 72.
ervei, vab, 22·7=(Howel) vab (Ithel a) orffei 90. [*HeS.*
Eryr 1·16=4 ; 6·5=32 ; 7·13=6.
Eryr 2·3=4 ; eryr Gwyðyen 11·10 =38. *HeC.*
Eryr Dwyv Weryd 14·4*=64. *O. ap Edwin.*
Eryr, diechyr, 21·20=88. *O. ap Cadwgan.*
erirhon 38·3, eryron 17·2=84.
esgyrn 26·22=ysgyr(io)n 98.
Esyd, Trwyn, *xvı.*, *xxv.*
Etwin, *homo liber*, *xliv.*, n. 37.
Eudaf hir, merch, 17·11*=ech eu temyr 38·7=84.
essyllut 12·14=i vab alltud 52.
Essyth 14·3=Esyd 64. *Seteia.*
eulat, vab, 8·22=vab e ulat 88.
eurdeyrn dorchawg, tri, 5·19=16.
eurdorchauc, 30·20=10 ; 31·19= 52 ; 33·13=[10].
eurdorchogyon 17·3, 38·6=84 ; 34·18=76.
Eurceinyo 34·5=Eurgeintion 36.
Eurgeint, *xvi.*   *see Keint.*
euruchawc 5·19=eurwychawg 16.
Eva, verch Vadog ap Mred., *xxii.*

Ewein. *see* Oweın.
ferawc, mab, 10·7=Ffer y llaw 36.
ſyrrvach 26·22=98 ; mab feruarch 23·5=t. ffyrvach 8. *HeC.*
ffin 5·18*=16 ; clas y ffin 20·13= (ffithell) 92=22·17.* [82.
foawr 20·1=68 ; ffoawd (6·21)= fodiawc 36·2=80.   [30.
Franc 35·4=38 ; Freinc (6·20)= 30 ; (28·6)=30.

gaffon 26·21=gwaewffon 98.
garth, rac, 32·15=58.
garthwys 22·11*=gorthyn 24·10= ? Garthmyn 90.
(gavyr) 22·18*=92.
Gaff 22·15=90.
geiluuat 37·2=62 ; geluat 37·6= 62 ; geilweit 34·15=62
genealogies, old Welsh, *xxxix.*
gentiles nigri, *.viii.*, *xlii.*
Geoffrey of Monmouth, *xv.*
Giff 22·15=90.
glas heid 15·12=12 ; glas veð 2·21 =70.
Glyn Cyvyng *xxvi.*, n. 22.
Godebawg, meibyon, 4·18*=12.
Godeu, *xvi.*, 18·19=36 ; Godef 20·16=76 ; Guodeo 31·12=76 ; Wodef 32·16=74. *Shropshire.*
godoðin *xvi–xix.*,=
i. *gorðin*, *xxv.*, 1·14=2 ; 2·13·18 =68 ; 4·1=72 ; 9·14=34 ; 10·8=36 ; 10·22=20 ; 12·13 =78 ; 12·21=52 ; 17·18= 35·19=38 ; 23·14*=64 ; 32·14 =56 ; 35·6·19=38 ; *gorðineð* 19·3=28 ; (gloss for) *ryveliad* 27·18=42 ; (gloss for) *sathrawr* 32·1=52.
ii. =verbs, *godoðan* 14·2, 23·10 =64 ; 33·15=10 ; *a δoδyn* 17·5, 38·8=84 ; a orðawd 19·14=66 ; orðin 16·4=20.
iii. =place, godoðin ystre 13·4, 23·15, 34·7=Heleð Ystrad

54; [14·10]; 20·14 = Mordrei 82; 1·18 = Llychlyn 4.
iv. = An Ode, *awdl y g.*, 28·8. *odleu* 28·17, 1·1 = 2, *adrawδ y g.*, [1·14, 7·4]; 17·18 = 35·19 = adroδyn am orδin 38; 37·5 = adroδyn 62.
Gogleδ, i rann 2·3* = 4; gwroleδ yng·Ogleδ 12·14 = 52; cynhorvan (y G.) 14·4 = 64; cun Gogleδ 29·20 = 46; *see xvi., xx., xxi., xxiv.–xxvii.* [ystan 38.
golistan, mab, 35·9 = mablan gol- 'gor' guneδ 16·18 = 74, 36·5 = 80.
gorchan 25·1; 26·17; 27·13 *see* gwarchan
gorδin 12·9, 14·15, *xvii., xxiv. see* godoδin, gurthyn.
gorllin 26·2 = 24.
gormant, guir, 36·3 = 80.
gormes 10·17 = 20.
gorseδ 12·19 = 52.
Gorthew 29·20 = 46. *cp.* e gar Tew 8·2. *Hugh the Fat.*
gorthir Rywynauc, yn, 24·10 = 90.
Gorthyn 24·10 = 90. *see* Garthmyn [11·4 = amws 20.
gorwyδ 29·21 = 46; g. gwareus grann 2·1 = 4. [gayr ꝑin 10.
grann-aur g-uin 33·19 = gronn grad voryon 27·9 = Tramorion 98.
greit uab hoewgir 7·9* = breint mab bleiδgi 31·11 = 32. *see* mur greit.
(Griffyδ) ap Cynan, *xviii–xxviii.*, hurries to Anglesey 31·18 = 52 maban i Ginan edryvanawg 31·22 = 52; maban i Ginan o vryn cyngrwn 3·9* = 70, an exile's son (12·14 = 52), who had lived in exile (31·21 = 52); led knights of the Palatine (31·19), fought at Artro (31·22) and in Penvro 13·2 = 52; in prison (12·10–12 = 78) & delivered 12·16 = 52; In 1098 'lost by force what he had made secure' in 1094, and "quitted the Rhyn" *i.e.* Anglesey 3·7·8 = 70. Fruitful the conflict he did not promote 3·4 = 70. The Norse supported him against the army and attack of Brynneich (12·21 = 52), who coveted the country that will lift him up (30·8 = 68). News of the Norse victory is whispered in Dublin (14·12 = 64), & forthwith Gr. celebrates it in song 12·13 = 78. A weary prince, he will not avenge the *gorδin*, 12·9 = 78; Magnus understands his strait (13·19 = 68) and gave him the land of the dispossessed earls (16·19 = 74) even the country of highfamed Mordrei 32·21 = 74; his father-in-law 3·9 = 70, *xxxii.*, statute of, *xxxvii.*
Griffyδ ap Rhys = Lletvegin 8·12—9·2 = 88.
groen gwynn, ar, 21·15 = ar gŵyn Owein 86. *O. ap Cadw.*
grugyar vreith 22·18 = 92. [*nus.*
Guaur, hero (J.D.) 35·6 = 38. *Mag-*
Guodeo 31·12 = 76. *see* Godeu.
guacnauc 30·21 = guancawg 10.
gurthyn 36·11 = gorδin 60. *cp.* gorthyn.
gwaed gilyδ 22·9 = 90. *Uchtryd.*
gwael *m*ael derw 30·6 = gwael*l u*ael δerw 68.
gwaetnerth 16·22 = 74; 33·9 = 16.
gwaewffon 42 = 27·18; 98 = 26·21.
Gwallawg, *xxxix* (Blaen) Lloegr, *xl. see* Dyvnwall.
Gwananhon 19·1 = Gwenn Vannan 28; 23·16 = 54; Guannannon 35·22 = G.V. 80; treis Gwananhon 17·11 = treis canaon 38·7* = 84. *see* cat Vannan and Mannan

GENERAL INDEX

(gwanar) 8·8=84. *Cadwgan.*
gwanar gurthyn 36·11=g. gorδın 60. *HeS.*
gwanargwcilgi 36·15=60. *Magnus.*
gwanar 5·2 ; *adj.* 2·18=68.
gwarchan=gorchan 26·8·17·19= 80, 96 ; 28·6·7·15·17 ; -eu 28·11 *see* gorchan
gwarcha*n* 27·13=gwarcha*ut* 42 ; 23·11=cyssul 14·3=64
gwaro 24·3=garw 22·5=90. [*HeS.*
gwas 1·2 = 2; mygrwas 1·3 = 2 *Kein uas* 32·20, 31·16=76. *Ow.*
gweis 6·13 = 18 ; gueir 23·4, 36·13=gweir̯ [8], 60 ; (32·18) =74 ; cynweis 29·14,(30·1)=46.
gwawrdur 9·7=[34].
gweilging (yn) fforch 26·19=96.
gueilgi-*ng* 36·15 = 60 ; gwe*ll*ing 27·10=gweilgi 98.
gweir 23·4=gweir̯ [8] ; 36·13=60.
(g)ueiri 35·12*=? gwerin 38.
Gweiryd 5·1*=Gweryd 72.
Gwelydon 25·12=Gwerydon 26. *see* Gweryt.
gwenn, mab, 8·1=mad*w* wenn 6, 11·14=40; 24·15·21 = 40; 38·21 =18.
gwen-abwy(d) 11·14, 24·15·21= 40; 38·3=84; 8·1=celein wen 6.
Gwener, diw, 17·16, 35·16=38.
guengat, mab, 38·21=madw wenn ga(na)t 18.
gwennwawt 6·22=30 ; 11·12= gwyndawt 38.
gwerin 14·8=64; g. enwir 4·18= pleid *E*dwin veib 12 ; 35·12= 38, gwern 25·4=26. *cp.* 35·12. *see* amhad.
gwern 25·4=gwerin 26 ; clawr gwernin 16·9=56, ? 36·3=80.
gwernol 37·22=82.
Gweryt, *xvi.*, 11·13=38 ; 5·1*= 72; vre : wer-yt 7·16*=6; wr-hyt 14·4, 23·11 = Weryt 64; Gwelydon 25·12=Gwer- 26.

gwe*un*yδ 92=venyδ 22·19.
gwevrawr 1·22=4.
Gwgawn 9·6=34 ; 20·19=[76].
Gwiawn 9·6=34 ; 20·20=[76].
gwin o bann 21·21=Gwynn bant
gwinwit 12·6=gwynvydig 74. [88.
Gwledıc 5·8=glyw 48, [18·11*= ? Mynyδawg 94 ; 30·1=Mynyδ- awg 46]; 29·14=Vleiδig 46. *HeS.*
Gwledic Ceinnyon 10·12=36. *Owein ap Edwin.*
Gwledic, ma, 35·9=38. *Magnus.*
gwlyget 9·14=gol- 34 ; 20·20=76.
gwr gwneδ 16·18=74, 36·5=80 ; gwyr gwneδ*yn* 27·14=42.
Gwrawl 3·5=70 ; G. amδyvrwys 20·7=28. *Magnus.*
gwrduedel 18·15=gwrδ vedrer 36.
gvreith 4·16=12 ; 8·6=8
gwrmwn 3·5=garm gwn 70.
gwrvan 20·8=28.
gwr-uelling 5·16=gor..wellig 48.
Gwryat 9·1=88.
Gwryen 8·22=88.
gwrym-seirch 9·17=serig seirch 34 ; 12·22 = gwawr wyarawl yar y seirch 52 ; 18·13=[96].
gwrym duδet 17·14=cein duhet 35·14=duδet 38.
gwrym gaen 16·7 : claer gaen 56.
gwrym·δe, gweilch, 17·23=94. *Norse.*
gwrym·δe, gweilgi, 36·15=62.
gwyalvan 8·17 = 88 ; 26·1 = 24 ; 4·9=gwyal 42.
gwya*l*fin (pen)festinyaw*l* 11·3=20.
gwyδ bedin 19·12=g. midin 66.
(gwyδ)veirch 48=aer feirch 5·12 ; 10=meirch 33·15 ; veδ=gwyδ- meirch 27·16=midin 42.
Gwyδneu, mab, *xvi.*, 8·11=84. *O. ap Cadwgan.*
Gwyδyen 11·10=38.
Gwyδel 48=ueδel 5·11·12
Gwyδyl 24·14·19=40 ; *xxvi.*
gwyndawt 38=gwenwawt 11·12

Gwyndyt 22·9, 24·7=90 and 70= Gwynnodynt 3·12; 6=Gwyn 7·2; G. e, 52=(Gwyndyt) eıssyllut 31·21; 38=Gwȳducıı·ıı.
Gwynn 9·1·6=88, 34.
Gwynn bant 21·21=88; =Llwch Gwynn 21·16=86. [ant 34.
wynn a chynvan 9·6=gwynovwynnassed 27·5=96. *cp.* B.B.C. 67·3.
Gwyneδ 2·3=4, 27·14=42; blaen G.6·12=32; *xvi., xx.*, y·Mordrei (G.) 6·4=32, 6·13=18; parth (G.) 25·6=24; eillt G., 19·1·2=28.
gwynngwn, o vaen, 3·9=o vryn *or* vann cyngrwn 70; *cp.* cyngrwn 5·16=16.
Gwynnodynt 3·12=Gwyndyt 70.
gwyr gormant 36·3=80. [evyδ.
gwyr gorwyn 29·18=46. *see* hengwys odiaethol 16=deethol-wys gwythwch 22·18·20=92. [36·6.
Gynt 24·18=40; Cınt eiluuat 37·2, cit eluat 37·6, Cin elueit 34·15 = Kynh-eilweing 12·2 = 62; kynt 15·16=14; cig 38·1* =82; (Gynt) 1·12=2, 7·11=6, 20·5, 23·9=28, 24·13=40; 32·18 =74; 36·6=80.

Haelon 27·9=98.
(*H*akon, mab, 19·2)=28.
ha*l*awc 36·19*=62.
*H*alkin, *xxiv.*, Halkeyn, n. 20
Harley MS. 3859, Facs.*vi.-viii., xli.*
hawfin 26·1=hâl ffin 22. [54.
Heidi*l*yaun 34·8=H(u) Eiδy*n*ion (*H*eleδ) ystrat 54=godoδin ystre 13·4, g. stre 34·7; y ar erch heleδ (=Arllechweδ) (25·7)=24; 13, c. *xxiv., xxviii.*
henevyδ 26=Eivionyδ 25·7; gwyr gorwyn 29·19=46.
heli 13·19=68.
heyernin, cadwyn, 12·11=78.

herw 37·13=82; 29·15=46; herwyr 84=(38·7). *cp.* 9·8=34.
hir 4·17·21=12; 2·11=[4], tut vwlch hir 4·6=tut vylchir 42; gelorawr hir 4·19=olochir 12; 4·21=[12]; hi*r* ef *r*oδei 9·20= hi *r*oδawr 34.
Hoδnant 88=(9·1).
hoew *gir* ac 7·9=hoew *ri gar* 32.
Hope, *xxii.*
(*H*owel ap Ithel) 22·6·17=90, 92.
*H*owel ap O. Gwyneδ, *xix.*
hwegrwn mab Cynan 3·9=70. *xxxii.* Owein ap Edwin
Hu 16·3·4=20; 17·7=28; 28·22= huδ 44; 29·18=46; *H*u 54=lu 34·8; 37·13=82; *H*u2=athi 1·5 (Hu) 70 = 3·6; 6 = 7·4·10·18; 64=14·9; 94=17·22; 60=21·7; 54=23·16; 24=25·14; 96= 31·2; 56=32·12; 82=37·13; 18=38·16; *v., xxii., xxiv., xxxiii.* The above references identify Hu with Hugh *the Proud* earl of Shrewsbury. As lord of *Mont*-gomery he figures as *Myny*δ-awg, and is called the 'son of Syvno' (6·8*) because his father was lord of Cwm Syvno. In 1098 the Fat earl of Chester, Hugh Lupus, set out to conquer Gwyneδ. HeS. shares in the expedition (5·17-22=16), joining his forces, and assuming the lead (B. 272-3). He is, therefore, called twinruler, cyvreint 17·6 = 28, cyvrenhin 12·13=78; 14·7·12=64; k. benn 18·7 = 94; cyveilin nar 29·2=44, and cyvran benn 11·12=38. He was chief in the Dee Estuary 11·12, lord of Eiδyn 35·11=38, 34·8=54, 24·17=40, & of Pulford 5·4=72, 25·20 = 22; dragon 7·2 = 6, of Aeron 6·21 = 30, cyn·devig

GENERAL INDEX

20·10=28 ; llywyδ maon 17·4, 38·4=82; steel-mailed generalissimo 9·7 = 34 ; ravages Mon, capturing xc. villeins, 2·16 = 68 ; 33·5-8 = 16, then follows high revelry at the Castle of Aber Lleinog 5·9= 48, 7·2·7=6, 30 ; 10·20 = 20 ; a strange fleet arrives unannounced 22·22=8 ; 36·13=60 ; *H*ugh rushes to meet it 1·17= 4 ; 16·4=20, 32·12=56 ; as he advances into the shallows (beis), he is marked out & shot by Magnus 25·14 = 24 ; 13·21=68 ; 14·9=64 ; 18·6= 94; 9·18=34 ; 11·18=40; 23·3 =8 ; 7·13=6 ; his body is left in the sea 29·18-30·6 = 46 ; 24·16=40; 7·4-22=6; 34·12= 62; 37·8-10=100; bed-fellow of worms 29·1 = 44 ; recovered at low tide 5·6=72, taken to Redeg 37·2=62 ; (buried after 17 days at Shrewsbury) 5·16 =48 ; Mab Botgat 2·15=Bargod 68, 174*. *see* Mynyδawg, Bradwen and Madw-wenn.

Hu (Vras). The first Palatine (Mynawg) of the earldom of Chester (Gogleδ) was *H*ugh *the Fat*=Tew 8·2=8, 26·14= 80, Gorthew 29·20=46, Trwch 11·5=20, 19·22=68 ; Ffyrvach 26·22=98, 23·5=8 ; Bual lled 34·13=62, alias *Lupus*=Bleiδ 1·22=4, 37·9=100 ; uδ 25·7= Bleiδ 24. *cp*. Bleiδiat, Bleiδig, and Bleiδian). Noble *L*upus leads in the conflict 1·22=4 ; attacks the ship 26·14=80; checks the violence of those disembarking (2·2=4) by an enveloping movement 11·5= 20 ; the *F*at one hies beyond bounds *i.e.* fled 19·21=68, 6·21=30, in summer departing by sea 36·2=80 ; *cp*. 7·1=6. Mynawg 10·6=36, 19·4·14=66, 31·20 = 52 ; madw bor arav 36·2=80, cwyn oeδ arnaw oe galed, neu'r adwanei rywaned 36·19=62, adwan ni dreing a gwyδid 29·7=44. Though he comes to Gwyneδ's (war), Gogleδ is his country 2·3=4, *xx.*, Hydwn, Brynn 9·1=88. [*xxvi.*
hyveiδ 2·11=hyder 4
hyδ, penn-, 22·18=92.
hualeu 26=26·6.

Iodeo 35·4*
*Y*euan 9·6=34.
ylvach 27·1=gilvach 96.
Yonawr 7·20=6.
Yor 21·17=86.
Iffac 8·8=ys tanc 84.
(Iwerδon 54=13·4, 23·15, 34·7 ; ywrch 22·18=92. ⌊64=14·13)

Jones, Sir Evan D., Bart., n. on Mynyδ Carn *xxvi.*

*L*ache, *xxiv*. cp. Tut Llwch.
Laenauc, *xxxix-xl.*
*L*upus. see Hu Vras.
llaïn 2·14, 3·17 ; 14·18, 20·12, 21·6, 24·3, 39·22, 32·4, lleïn 14·14=64.
*L*lan-llaw-harne, *xxvi*,. n. 23.
llassawr 20·6=28.
Llech 13·14, 23·15, Lleech 34·6= Llêth 54.
Llechweδ, ar- *see Heleδ.*
lleid 2·9=4, lleir 21·5=lleit 58, lled 4·14=llei 72 ; 31·4*=96; du leidiat 37·13=82.
lleithic 10·13=*bench* 36.
llestyr, trameryn, 34·8=54.
llestri, llawn 12·19=52, 31·5=96; gwydyr l. 16·21=74.
Le*t* lin 34·9=Lle*ch*lyn 54.
Lletvegin 8·12=Gr. ap Rhys 88.

BOOK OF ANEIRIN

lleudud 34·6, lleutut 13·14, llefdir 23·15 = lleudireδ 54. [δyvrcδ 54.
leudvre 13·14, leuvre 34·6 = leu-
*L*lewelyn ap Gr., *xix*.
*L*lewelyn Varδ *xxi*., *xxii*.
lliveiriant 70 = beiryant 2·22.
lliwet 25·17 = 22, 33·16 = 10, (verb 36·16), -awr 3·21 = 70.
lliuidur 37·11. *see* Rector.
Lloegyr 11·16 = 40, 33·7 = 16.
Lloegrwys 7·7 = 30, 14·22 = 64; 18·22 = Lloegr 28.
llovlen 19·20 = 68, 24·18 = 40.
llo*y*fen = llwyven 17·2, 38·2; 18·10 = 94; lluiuen 24·17 = 40.
Llwch, tut, *xliii*.
lluch bin 14·5* = 64; ll. δor, 14·5 = Llwch Gwyn 21·16 = 86. [64.
Llugwy, *xvi*., 92 = Llywywc 22·17*
llumen 24·17 = lluiuen 40.
Llu*n*, diw, 17·18, 35·18 = 38.
lluric 18·11 = 94; llurygogyon 15·16 = 14, 38·7 = 84.
Llwch fun liuanat 34·14 = 62.
Llwchvarδ was the bard, *i*. of *H*ugh the *P*roud; *ii.* of Cynon, and *K*ing Magnus = Morien, *xxxii.*, &c. *xlii*. At Mordrei Gwyneδ I drank mead and wine 6·4 = 32, 6·14 = 18, in the company of the Knights 6·13 = 18, & sate late with HeS. 4·21 = 12. We rushed against Morien 6·15 = 18, the hateful lord, 5·20 = 16, 27·7 = 98, whom we met on a plundering expedition 37·13 = 82; I heard the King's loud shouting 38·20 = 18, and the dirge of lances 31·9 = 32; darts were showered at the edge of the shallows 7·7 = 32, I prophesied that HeS. would die through Morien 24·20 = 40; Dead my former prince, the flood covers him 20·10 = 28; Minheu (Varδ Llycheu) gymrant 28·3 = 30, ceint wacdffreu wawt 6·22 = 30; I have sung a lament 18·19 = 26, 17·6 = 28. For a year there was grief for the men of Catraeth whose cherishing is mine 26·4 = 26. Ewein succeeds to the command, ys cynneδv escyn Ewein yn benn 18·8 = 94; trouble followed from repressive acts of oppression 25·5, I saw the wantonness of the men of Gweryd 25·12 = 26; The Villeins of Gwyneδ ask Gwenn Vannan (= Morien) for protection, for a stay of the lust of war, for an end of the oppression 29·2 = 28; I will sing of Magnus's doings 31·8 = 30, 27·13 = 42; I love the victorious *K*ing who benefits minstrels 20·10 = 28: his life story his Keint admirer will sing 4·8 = 42. The *F*erry was given to the ruler of the Rhyn country, and a meed of fair fortune to Keint's minstrel, 9·20 = 34, *vii. n., xlii.-iii. see* Blwchbard. [92.
Llwyn Llwyvenyδ, *xvi*., 22·21* =
Llychlyn 54 = let lin 34·9*; 4 = (1·18); 52 = (13·3).
Llynwyssawr 12·21 = Llychlynwys 52; 4·19 = 12.
llychwr 14·5 = 64.
(llynghes 1·16 = 4).
llynn 21·1 = 58.
Llywarch, keneu vab 12·18 = ? Kenwrig vad devig 52.
Llywarch of Arwystli, *xxiii*.
llyw*r*i 16·22 = llywi(e)i 74.
Llywywc 22·17 = Llyucwy 92.

ma*b* = ma*d* 1·9 = 2; 2·3 = 4; 4·9 = 42; [7·17]; 9·12 = 34, 10·4 = 36; 14·3 = 64;
mab bleiδgi rac 31·11 = hoewgir ac 7·9 = 32.

GENERAL INDEX

[mab] bleiδvan 7·17 = Bleiδyan 6.
map bod-u 36·2 = mapu bol = madw bor 80.
mab Botgat 2·15* = Bargot 68, 174.
mab brenhin 24·7 = mab teyrn 22·8 = 90. *Wm., the Etheling*
mab keid-yaw 20·15 = Mordrei 82.
mab kilyδ 4·9 = m. Gilyδ 42. *HeS.*
mab klytno 15·8 = mabon Clyton
mab Coel 28·4 = mal ceith 30. [84.
mab Dwyw-*eidy* 14·3 = mad *eryr* Dwyv 64.
mab eli 31·4* = i leid elei 96.
mab ervei 22·6, uruei 24·5 = a orvei 90.
mab eulat 8·22 = glyw y wlat 88.
mab ferawc 10·7 = car ffwyrawg 36. [vach 8.
mab feruarch 23·5 = teyrn ffyr-
mab gwenn 8·1 = madw wenn 6 ; 11·14, 24·15·22 = 40.
mab guen gat 38·20 = madw wenn ganat 18. [ystan 38.
mab golistan 35·9 = mablan gol-
mab Gwyδneu 8·11 = 84. *Ōw.* [*ap Cadwgan.*
mab hoewgir ac 7·9*. *see* mab bleiδgi.
mab Llywarch 12·18* = 52.
mab llywri 16·22* = 74.
mab madyeith 32·11, madyen 16·11 = 58.
map Nuithon 34·18 = eil Nwython 76 ; 35·3 = 78 [36.
mab peithan 10·4* = mad porthan
[mab] tec vann 27·20 = teleid 42.
Maban y Gian 3·9 = 70 ; 31·22 =
mab(lan) golistan 35·9 = 38. [52.
Mac 19·12 = Mang 66 ; Muc 16·4 = Mwng 20 ; Mwng 11·17, 24·19 = 40, *vi–ix*.
mad. *see* mab. [12.
Madawg 9·5 = 34 ; 34·3 = Mynawg
Madawg, pebyll 1·14 = Redeg 2.
Madawg 35·20 ; pebyll M. 17·19 = Mynyδawg 38.

madw. 8·1 = 6 ; 11·14, 24·15·22 = 40 ; 38·20 = 18.
Madyen 16·11, Madyeith 32·11 = 58. *Magnus.*
mael derw, 28·15,* 30·6* = 46.
maen gwynngwn 3·9* = 70. *cp.* Caer Gyngrwn.
maen anysgoc (*anchor*) 32 = 56.
Manau Guotodin, *xviii.*
MAGNUS, *King of Norway, xxxiv., bareleg, xxxix.*, Māc 19·12 = Manc 66, (4·14 = 72, 19·4 = 66, 20·20 = 76, 32·19 = 74) ; Mūc 16·4 = Munc 20 ; Mwng 11·17, 24·19 = 40; Mein 8·5 = 8, 35·3 = 78 ; Mein uchel 26·15 = 80 ; Teithawl Ri 25·5 = 26 ; adon 13·19, 30·12 = 68, archawr 29·6 = 44 ; marthlew 8·7, 33·1 = 8 ; erch drewyδ 4·6 = 42 ; arth arwynawl 16·7 = 56 ; Tarw Trin 10·19·23 = 20, 37·17 = 82; Buδig Nav 20·10 = 28 ; Reen Buδig 29·13 = 46; Morgun Plymnwyd 19·7 = 66 ; Rector, rhwyv pob or, mur pob ciwed 32·10 = 58 ; *Madyen* 16·11, 32·11 = 58 ; *Mwynvawr* 3·13·18 = 70 ; *Dewr* 32·3·7·12 = 56 ; *Gwrawl* 3·8 = 70, *Gwrawl* amδyvrwys 20·7 = 28 ; Guaur 35·6·7·8 = 38 ; Llyw (marini) 26 = 25·5 ; Gwanar gweilgi 36·15 = 60 ; Pevr bererin 14·13 = 64 ; *Moryen* 18 = (6·14) ; 6 = (7·3) ; 10·1 = 34 ; 10·5 = 36 ; 11·12 = 38 ; 13·20 = 68 = (19·20). Rhi grysswys gatraeth tra mor ehelaeth 4·4 = 42 ; 25·5 = 26, 35·1 = 78 ; 32 = 56–58 ; 20·6·10 = 28 ; car Vannan 1·21 = 4 ; 16·5, 11·7 = 20, 29·6 = 44 ; Gwen Vannan, 19·1 = 28, 23·16 = 54 ; 35·22 = 80, 17·11, 38·7 = 84. *see* Du tigirn, cat-Vannan, Gwananhon, Mannan. *see* Morem ; Tal., 17·18*

187

BOOK OF ANEIRIN

mam 12·15=52 ; 9·12=nam 34 ; 15·14 = maur 12 ; deigr mam 15·1=64 ; mameu 8·11 = 84.
Mannan, cat 11·7, 16·5=car 20, Manon 29·6*=44 ; guannannon 35·22=gwen Vannan 80 ; 19·1 =28, 23·16=54 ; 17·11 (=38·7) =84., xviii. see *Magnus*.
manawyt 1·19=4.
maon 4·17=12, 5·22=16 ; 17·4, 38·4=82 ; 17·11.
map. see mab.
*m*ap=*in* ap=yn Aper, *xl*.
marchawc 5·20=16 ; 10·7=36 ; 10·22* = [20] ; 14·10* = [64] ; 16·5=20 ; 30·15=[68] ; 16·18= gwychrawg 74 ; alltut m., 31·21 =alltudawg 52 ; 38·4 = llywyδ 82 ; -ogyon 13·22=68 ; 26·22=98.
Marchia, *xxiii*.
marchlew 8·2, 33·1 = marchawg glew 8 ; 8·7=Mar*t*hlew 8.
Margam Abbey, *ix*.
(marini 26=25·5).
ma*r*ro 1·9*=*in* aeron 2.
Masgiuc clop, *xxxix-xl*. *Magnus*
Mawrth, diu, 17·14, 35·14=38.
meδgyrn 10·10=36, 22·5=8.
meδ gwyn 4·2=72. see glasveδ.
meibyon Godebawg 4·18=Edwin veib 12.
Meilyr, *xxvii*., n. 23.
Mein 8·5 = 8 ; ab N. 35·3 = 78 M. uchel 26·15=80. *Magnus*.
Mein 10·11=*Cy*non.
Meinvuan 1·4=2 ; 3·6=20.
meitin 18·1 = 94, 25·20 = 22 ; i meitit 36·7= ? meiδin 60. *cp. Maiden* Castle.
meiwyr 17·13=[38] ; ? : morwyr 29·13=46.
melwit 29·22=*in* elvyδ 46.
menavc. see Mynawg.
Menei, *xxv*., avon 26·20=98
menwyt 29·20=? *in* enwŷd 46.

merch eu-daf hir 17·11*= ech eu tymhyr 38·7=82.
Merchyr, diu, 17·15, 35·15=38.
Merin aMadyen 16·11=Meryn mab Madyeith 32·10=Moryen am·Hadyen 58.
Mer-sete, *xxiii*.
mit 26·14=80 ; midin 36·7=60 ; im . . . *t*rin 35·6=i·mitin 38 ; bedin : midin 1·18=4 ; 16·7= 56 ; 32·3·8·13=56 ; 19·12=66 & 42=veδ=gwyδ-meirch 27·16.
miledawr 25·18=midawr 22.
midlan 46=mi*r*an 29·17.
milcant 3·11=milaur 70.
minauc, Minidauc. see Myn.
mir δyn=wenn 11·12=38. *HeS*.
moethyδ 4·3=72.
Mon 26·2=24 ; 29·5=44 ; (3·7= 70 ; 4·7=42 ; 4·17=12 ; 7·22= 6 ; 11·7=20 ; 13·19, 30·12=68 ; 19·6=66 ; 20·4=28 ; 27·14= 42 ; 31·18=52 ; 33·5=16 ; 38·11
mor ehelaeth 4·4=42. [=74).
Mordei 1·14=Mordrei 2 ; 4·15, 5·3 =72 ; 32·21=76 ; (17·7=28) ; 20·15*=82 ; M. (Gwyneδ) 6·4= 32 ; 6·13=18. Note that the "thrusting was done" ymlaen Gwyneδ *i.e.* Penmon 6·12=32 ; ar lawr Mordrei 1·14=2 ; *xvii., xix. Aber Lleinog strand*.
moreb 29·17=46.
M*o*rem 24·13·21=Morien 40. see Magnus.
mor a chyn- 19·7=Morgun 66.
mordwy 20·7=28.
morva 25·7=26.
morwyn 22·7, 24·6=[90].
Moryal, *xvi., xxi.*, 14·16*=64.
Moryd 10·1=34.
Moryen 10·1=34 ; 10·5=36 ; 11·12 =38 ; 13·20=68 ; (6·14 = 18 ; 19·20 = 68) ; 6=peithing 7·3.
Morem 24.13·21=40. *Magnus*.

GENERAL INDEX

Mūc = Munc 16·4 = 20 ; Mwng 11·17, 24·19 = 40 ; (4·4 = 42 ; 4·14=72 ; 5·21=16; 9·19=34; 10·21=20; 12·5=72; 18·8=94; 19·4=66 ; 20·13 = 82 ; 20·20= 76 ; 32·19=74 ; 35·1 =78), vi.-x., xlii. see Magnus

Munghu. see note *u*, p. *ix*.

*m*uet 35·12* 38=nyuet 17·13.

Mwynvawr 3·13·18=70. *Magnus*.

Mygrcid 8·11=84. *Nest*.

Mynawg 10·6=36 ; 19·4·14=66 ; 31·20=52 ; 36·20*=62 ; (6·21 =30). *Hugh Lupus.*

Mynawg mab teyrn teithawg 22·8 =menavc 24·6=90 ; =(son of Henry I.) lost in White Ship.

Mynawg 21·18=86. *O. ap Cad.*

Mynawg blin 12·9=78 ; 6·13*= 18. *Gr. ap Cynan*

Mynawg Godoδin 19·14=Mynyδ-awg a orδawd 66; mynawg maon 17·4·10=m. marchawg maon 82, 38·4=llywyδ maon 82.

*Myny*δawg=Hugh of *Mont*gomery, earl of Shrewsbury. 26·4= 24 ; 35·10=38 ; 17·4, 38·4=82 ; gosgorδ V., 15·18·22=14; 3·13·18 =trawd V. 70, 19·17=66 ; 9·4 = Gosgorδawg M. 34 ; 33·10= gwyr arvawg M. 10 ; *ancwyn* 33·11=10 ; 36·4=80 ; 9·14= cwyδawd M., 34 ; neges M.,17·4 ·10=82 ; *cussyl* M. 33·17=c. pennawr (Cynon) 10 ; *me*δ*gyrn* M., 10·10=36 ; Caeawg V., 2= c. kynhorawg 1·10; arvawg V. 4 =caeawg k., 2·5 ; *M.*, 4=Hyveiδ 2·11 ; 46=gwledic 30·1 ; 66 = Mynawg godoδin 19·14 ; 38=Madawc 17·19, 35·20 ; 82 =mynawg maon 17·4·10. *see* Hu *i.e.* HeS.

Mynyδ Carn, *xxvi.*, *n*. 23.

Nanhyver *xxvi.*, n. 23.

Namyn un gwr o gant 1·15=n. y dengyn 2, 30·19, 33·14=10.

namyn tri 6·20, 28·2=30.

nar 16·9*=58 ; 44=nac 29·2 ; *see* casnar.

naw ugein (ceith δug) 33·7=16.

neb : nev : neu=nep 29·8=44.

*n*edig, ei*l* : eifuedig 16·9*=eficedig 58.

neim ab : mein eil N. 35·3=78.

Neirin, *vii.*, *xliii*.

(Nest 8·11*=84).

neuaδ 9·21 = 34 ; 10·5·11 = 36 ; 12·22=52 ; 15·2=84 ; 23·1=8 ;

Northumbria, *xx*.

Nuithon, map 34·18=eil N. 76 ; 35·3=78 ; ei*r* N., 23·7 = gwyr N., 20·4=eil N. 28.

nyuet 17·13=*m*ue*t* 35·12=38.

od gur : goro*t*=goror 30·15=68.

od guur=δog ru*n* 37·11=δug Ryn 58.

onn 18=am 38·15 ; onn bedryollt 8·5, 33·2=8 ; onwyδ 29·9=44 ; onnen 38=gwayw 11·11.

orthoret 35·13=38. (verb).

Oswestry, *xxiii.*

oswyδ 4·6=42 ; 15·6=84.

Owein ap Cadwgan 21·10-22= 86 ; =eryr 21·20 = 88 ; mab Gwyδneu 8·11 = 84 ; mynawc 21·18=86; yor 21·17=86, *xxiii*.

Owein (ap Cradawc ap Rhyδerch ap Tewdwr) 8·22=Owyn vab y wlat 88.

OWEIN (dewr vab Edwin, *xxviii.*, *xxxvi.*,*xliii.*,20·14*=82; kyveillt (HeS) 1·7=2 ; escyn yn benn 18·8=94 ; ad·lyw gogyvurδ 37·4 =62 ; Penn (Ceint) tal beinc a δyly 12·8=82; eur drysor blaen Porffor δosparthei 5·4 = 72 ; blaen llueδ 5·2=72; aergi 19·12 =aerlyw 66 ; as Commandant

of Aber Lleinog Castle he bears the *nom de guerre* of Cinon 38·1 =82 ; Kenon 38·9=84 ; 6·1= Cynran o Aeron 16 ; Cynon 6·3 =16 ; (10·6)=36 ; 10·15=18 ; Kein *u*as 32·20* = 76 ; adon y wlad deccav 15·3=84; Ceinnyon wledig 10·12=36 ; uδ Cyvlwch *i.e.* Keint 26·3 = 26 ; Kenan, Keint vur, (Rhyn) ragor 29·12 = 44 ; teithlyw ar Von 26·2 =24 ; eisteδ ar dal lleithig, ar neb a varned ni waredid 10·12 =36 ; father in law of Gr. ap K., *xxxii.*, 3·9=70, 31·22=52.
Owein ap Edwin *xxxvi.* see Cynon.

pabir, leu, 4·21=12.
paleography, *xliv.*
pasc 5·5=pasc(awl) 72.
pebyll Madawc 1·14*=p. Redeg 2 ; 17·19, 35·20=Mynyδawg 38.
peby*r* 9·13=34 ; 20·19=76.
peδyt 25·17=22.
Peis dinogat 22·12=p. δivodat 90.
peith 25·6=? parth (Gwyneδ) 24.
peithan 10·4=? porthan 36.
Peithliw : peith-awr 25·5*=? *t*eithawl ri, llyw 26.   *Magnus.*
Peithing [peith] yng 7·3*=? Morpeithynat 33·8=16. [yen boen 6.
pel a : bela 16·3=20.
pellynnic 23·3=8.   *HeS.*
(pen)ffestinawl 11·3=20.
(Penmon) 2=pē vro 1·8* ; (5·14) =48 ; 16=pymwnt 5·17 and o vrython 6·2*; *xvi.*
Penn tir 20·2, 23·6=Penmon 28.
pennaw*r* 23·3*=8 ; pennor 13·22 =68.   *HeS.*
pennawr 10=[Mynyδawg 33·17]
Penvro 52=[13·2].   [*Cynon.*
Peredur 9·6=Penadur 34. *HeS.*
periglawr 19·21=66.
Perim 96=pei mi 26·18 ; Perym 36·12=60   *HeS.*

pharǎon, mûd, 29·7=44. *HeS.*
pin 14·5*=64.
plygeint awr, 12·2=dyδ pleimieit 34·15=plygad 62.
plymnwyt 5·14=48 ; 19·8=66.
po vro 1·8*=Penmon 2.
por 25·6 = 26 (HeS.) ; gorthew (bor) 29·20=46 ; madw bo*r* 36·2=80.   *HeC.*
pur 26·6*=26.
Porfor 17·12=84; 25·20=22 ; Porphor 5·4=72.   *Pulford.*
Porfor beryerin 14·5=64.
(Porth Hoδnant 9·1=88).
Powys 21·13=86.
prit 34·20=drut 76.
pryd*e*in 7·20=prydan 6.
Prydein 24·14=Pryden 24·19= 40 ; enys P. 5·8=evnys P. 48.
pryder 21·10=prydyδ 56.
pryv 44=krym 29·1.
Pyll 9·6=34.
pym pymwnt 2·7*=ym plymnwyt 4 ; 9·19=sawl δelei 34.
pymwnt a phymcant 5·17*=Penpysc 22·16·19=92. [mon p. d. 16.

Ractaf 16·11. *see* Rector
*r*ac- traeth, 28·1=30.
ragno 13·4=ragon 23·15=54.
Ranulf, *ii.*, *xi.*
Rayadyr derwenyδ 22·19=92.
*r*awd 29·4=44.   [16·11=58.
Rector 32·5·10, 37·11, Ractaf
Redec, 21·11 = 86 ; 30·9 = 68, 37·2*=62 ; *r*et 38·11 = Retec 74 ; gw*n*ed 6·11 = *r*edeg 32 ; 2=(1·14) ; hearth of R., *xxiii.*, border of R., *xxiii.*
Redegein, *xxiv.*, 20·3=28.
Rëon ryt, *xxi.*
Ri, 31·11, 7·9*=32 ; 20=(11·2) ; 25·5=26 ; 26·21=98 ; 38·10= 74 ; rieu 10·17=ri 20 ; ren 29·13 =riheδ 29·20=46 ; 18·13=96, (4·4=42, 12·3=72, 35·1=78).
      Magnus.

GENERAL INDEX

ri allu 13·7, 38·20=54 ; 16·1 ; 20·9=28.　*Magnus's force.*
rihyδ 5·10=48 ; (26·9)=80.
Rïein 22·7,* 24·6=90.　*Countess*
rïein gareδ 25·12=26. [*of Perche.*
Rïeu 21·13=86.　*Henry I.*
Rin, Ren. *see* Rynn
Risserdyn, *xxii.*
Robert of Ruδlan, *xxv.*
rodawr 22·2, 23·22=90.
Rodri ap O. G., *xix.*
Roger, e. of S., *xxi.*
run 29·20=cun 46.　*HeC.*
R*u*-uawn 9·20*=R*it* vawṗ 34.
Ruvawn 20·19=[76].
rwyf bre 30·7=68.　*HeS.*
rwyv 33·2=8 ; 34·16*=76. Magrwyfyadur 32·5·10, 16·11=56.[*nus see* Liuidwr 37·11.
Ryd, ? 7·10=6 ; 24·11·16*=40 ; 30·3=46 ; (10·15=18 ; 34·13=62) ; Ryt 1·13*=2 ; 5·8=48 ; 6·15*=18 ; 11·7*=20 ; 23·2=8 ; 25·10·18=22 ; 27·1=98 ; 32·20=76 ; (33·12)=10 ; (11·9)=38 ; Rit 35·22=80 ; rit vawr* 9·20 = 34 ; ritre 36·14* = 60 ; Rydre 31·7=30.
Rynn 3·8=70 ; 5·9 = 48 ; 6·7 = 32 ; 29·18*=46 ; (11·15=40 ; 12·3=72 ; 20·21=76 ; 37·10 =58 ; 35·11=38 ; 38·8=84) ; rȳ gre 30·9=68 ; rē 29·12= 44 ; 32·14 = 58 ; rhen 76=e ṗhen 20·20 ; Rin 29·5 = 44 ; 33·15·19*=10 ; 36·5=80 ; 10= breithell 30·17 ; rū=ryn 27·16 =42 ; *v., xvi., xviii., xxi., xxiii.*
(Rys, Gr. ap, 8·20=88). [ion 98.
r*y*vel uo*d*ogyon 26·22=*Vargod-Rywonyawc, *xvi.*, 22·2·11 = 90, Rywynauc 23·22, 24·10=90.

Sadwrn, diu, 17·16, 35·17=38.
Saesson 4·7=42, 14·1=68.
Saxa 34·15=axa 11·21=Seis 62.
Seis 62=Seic 37·3 ; (30·15)=68.
secisiar 34·12 = leissyar 11·21= sisialat 62.
scithuet dyd 4·7=seithnyδ 42.
senyllt 12·19=52.　*see* menestri.
Seteia Aestuaria, xxv.
Shrewsbury Abbey, *xxiii.*
sic sac 37·4=62.
Sul, diu 17·17, 35·18=38.
Syvno 6·8*

Tal briw vu 13·9, 34·10=54 ; tal a rwyged 38·16=18.
tal being 12·8=tal lleithig 82.
Talhaearn,*viii.,xx.,xlii.*, pp. 2-15.
talvrith 7·10=taleith 6.
Talyessin 12·12=78 ; 28·15* ; *xliv.*
Tarw beδin 8·21=88.　*Gr. ap Rys.*
Tarw camhwrawg 25·14=24. *HeS.*
Tarw Trin 10·19·23=20 ; 13·9= 54 ; 14·11=64 ; Taro Trin 37·17 =82.　*Magnus.*
tebic=tevig 8·8=gwanar 84. *see* kyndilic, kyntebic. [27·20*=42.
Tecvann, mab, . . . wyr catvan *t*eith 29·9=*r*eith 44, *cp.* 2·22 reith- teithawl ri 26= -awr peith- 25·5* ; gwr teithiaw*l* 25·20=22 ; teith- yawl ter 29·3=44　*Magnus.*
Teithieid 5·17=16,　*Borderers*
Teith*l*yw 26·2*=24　*Kynon cp.* reithuyw 2·20*=68, & peith- liw 25·5=26.
teithawg, teyrneδ, 22·8=90.
tevig 8·8=gwanar 84.　*see* kyn- dilic.　[*HeC.*
Tew 26·14=80 ; uδ Tew 32·22=8.
Teyrn oeδ deithawg 22·8*=90.
torr arth 32·15=58.
Trahaearn, *xxvi.-xxvii., xxxi.*
tra Manon 29·6=car Mannan 44.
Tramorawr 5·3=72.
Tramorion 98=grad vorion 27·9.
Treb, *xxiii.*, n. 19.
Trei 4·11,* 5·6=72 ; (7·2)=6 ; isel d. 35·10*=38 ; Din d. 12·5*=72.

treuyδ, e(r)ch, 4·6=42. *Magnus.*
Trev-red, *xxiii.*
tri, namyn, 28·2=30.
Tri char . . tri ffin gatvarchawg . . . tri theyrn . . . tri Eurdorchawg &c. 5·17–22=16.
trothwy 84=8·9* ⌈64.
Trum Essyth 14·2=Truin Esyd
Trwch 19·22=68; 11·5=20. *HeC.*
Trycant 30·20, trychan 30·21·22, 33·13, athrychant 31·1=trychauc, athrychaur 10.
trychant, o, 15·18=o gant 14,
trych 26·21=Twrch 96. [[16·1*].
try wyr a thrivgeint a thrychant 6·19, 27·22=30. *see* 28·9.*
Tryvrwyd 19·8=66. *Ferry.*
tut anaw 27·10=98.
tut leo 32·22=uδ tew 8. *HeC.*
Tut *Llwch, xvi., xxiv.,* 42=tut vwlch 4·8; 25·2.
tut vwlch 25·21=tud bost 22.
tut vwlch hi*r* 4·6=tud vylchit 42.
tut *vwl*ch 4·8=tud Llwch, 25·2*
tut vwlch 26·3=rac uδ 26.
tutvwlch 32·6, 37·12 = Bylchid caer treisig 58.
twm 33·4=26 ; (20·11)=82.
Twrch 17·21=94; drwyt 26·19·20 =96, 98.
Twrch 11·5=Trwch 20.
Twrch 22·7, 24·5=Wchtryt 90.
Twyn (33·17)=10 ; 37·22*=82 ; 33·4=twm 26.

unben 11·17=40=*HeC*. after the fall of HeS.
urython. *see* Brithion.
u*f*fin, o*e* las 20·13*=o *c*las *y* ffin
ugein, naw, 33·7=16. ⌊82.
vgein cant 2·8=4.
Vann 2·2 ; 20·8=28 ; v. keiru 13·11=V. gewri 58 ; v. caereu 26·3=26 ; v. karw 13·10=vangori 58
Villeins, nine score, *xxvii.,* 16.
Votadini, *xviii.*

Wchtr(yd), *xxvii.,* 22·7 = 90; gwaed gilyδ O. ap Edw. 24·7,
weilgi(ng) 27·10=98. ⌊22·9=90.
wit 16·14=guid 38·11=guis 74 ; wit vab peithan 10·3=wys vad porthan 36.
wledic 29·14=vle(i)δig 46.
w-ledic 30·1=leδit 46.
wyt, dindy, 34·9=dindywyt 13·7, 23·19=di*r*dynwyt 54.

Yal, *xxi.,* 15·10=12.
yor 21·17=86.
Ystrat 54=stre 34·7 ystre 13·4, 23·16.
ystre 11·5=20 ; 16·5=20 ; 17·21= 94 ; 18·8 ; 29·17=46 ; 36·12= 60 ; godoδin ystre 13·4, g. stre 34·7=*Hele*δ ystrad 54 ; ystre ragno, 13·4, ragon 23·15=ys try ragom 54.

SD - #0044 - 280824 - C0 - 229/152/16 - PB - 9781332998425 - Gloss Lamination